APA Handbook of
Interpersonal
Communication

APA Handbook of
Interpersonal
Communication

Edited by
David Matsumoto

American Psychological Association • Washington, DC
Walter de Gruyter, Inc. • New York, NY

Published by
American Psychological Association
750 First Street, NE
Washington, DC 20002
www.apa.org

APA Handbook of Interpersonal Communication; David Matsumoto, Editor
Derived from original work edited by Gerd Antos and Eija Ventola, Eds., in cooperation with Tilo Weber, and Gert Rickheit and Hans Strohner, Eds., and published by Mouton de Gruyter, an imprint of Walter de Gruyter GmbH & Co. KG.

Chapters 1–11 were originally published in *Handbook of Interpersonal Communication*, Gerd Antos and Eija Ventola, Eds., in cooperation with Tilo Weber, 2007, Berlin, copyright © 2007 by Walter de Gruyter GmbH & Co. KG. Chapters 12–13 were originally published in *Handbook of Communication Competence*, Gert Rickheit and Hans Strohner, Eds., 2008, Berlin, copyright © 2008 by Walter de Gruyter GmbH & Co. KG. All rights reserved.

To order
APA Order Department
P.O. Box 92984
Washington, DC 20090-2984
Tel: (800) 374-2721; Direct: (202) 336-5510
Fax: (202) 336-5502; TDD/TTY: (202) 336-6123
Online: www.apa.org/books/
E-mail: order@apa.org

Typeset in ITC New Century Schoolbook by IBT Global, Troy, NY

Printer: IBT Global, Troy, NY
Cover Designer: Naylor Design, Washington, DC

The opinions and statements published are the responsibility of the authors, and such opinions and statements do not necessarily represent the policies of the American Psychological Association.

Library of Congress Cataloging-in-Publication Data

APA handbook of interpersonal communication / edited by David Matsumoto. — 1st ed.
    p. cm.
  Includes bibliographical references and index.
  ISBN-13: 978-1-4338-0780-0
  ISBN-10: 1-4338-0780-7
  ISBN-13: 978-1-4338-0781-7 (e-book)
  ISBN-10: 1-4338-0781-5 (e-book)
 1. Interpersonal communication. I. Matsumoto, David Ricky. II. American Psychological Association. III. Title: Handbook of interpersonal communication.
  HM1166.A65 2010
   302—dc22   2009052507

British Library Cataloguing-in-Publication Data

A CIP record is available from the British Library.

Printed in the United States of America
First Edition

Contents

Contributors

Jannis Androutsopoulos, PhD, King's College London, England

Alexander Brock, Halle University, Germany

Maureen Ehrensberger-Dow, PhD, Zürich University of Applied Sciences, Switzerland

Alexandra Georgakopoulou, PhD, King's College London, England

Howard Giles, PhD, University of California, Santa Barbara

Anu Klippi, PhD, University of Helsinki, Finland

Anna-Maija Korpijaakko-Huuhka, University of Tampere, Finland

Miriam A. Locher, PhD, University of Basel, Switzerland

David Matsumoto, PhD, San Francisco State University, San Francisco, CA

Peter Muntigl, University of Salzburg, Austria, and Simon Fraser University, Canada

Daniel Perrin, PhD, Zürich University of Applied Sciences, Winterthur, Switzerland

Margaret J. Pitts, PhD, Old Dominion University, Norfolk, Virginia

Nancy M. Puccinelli, PhD, Northeastern University, Boston, Massachusetts

Louise J. Ravelli, PhD, University of New South Wales, Sydney, Australia

Paul J. Thibault, PhD, University of Agder, Kristiansand, Norway

Caja Thimm, PhD, University of Bonn, Germany

Maree Stenglin, PhD, University of Sydney, Australia

Tilo Weber, PhD, University of Nairobi, Kenya

Peter R. R. White, University of Adelaide, South Australia

Introduction

What can be more important in today's world than communication? Communication is the fundamental process by which humans live as social animals. Because of communication we can come together to build families, social networks, and professional associations. Because of communication we can work with very different others toward a common goal. Because of communication we can organize sports, leisure, and recreational activities. And unfortunately, because of (mis)communication we can argue, fight, and wage war.

Thus, it is fitting that the study of communication is a field of active scientific and scholarly endeavor, and equally fitting that much of the state-of-the-art knowledge in this area be brought together in handbooks such as this one and its companion handbook, the *APA Handbook of Intercultural Communication*. Communication has been studied from many different perspectives (e.g., basic and applied sciences) and disciplines (e.g., sociology, linguistics, psychology), and indeed today these efforts have amassed a wealth of information about communication. The purpose of these two handbooks is to compile, organize, and synthesize much of this knowledge.

It's important to have a working definition of *communication*, and as the reader will readily see, each of the chapters present a common yet unique perspective on what such a definition may entail, either explicitly or implicitly. It may be impossible to arrive at a definition of communication with which all will agree. At the same time, I strongly believe that it is important for authors to make explicit their working definitions, and for readers to be able to know what those working definitions are (and of course to have their own working definitions).

For me, a common thread among all definitions of communication involves some degree of message or information exchange between two or more interactants. Indeed, the encoding and decoding of such messages forms the foundation of any communication episode. And because this information exchange occurs through multiple channels and multiple signals, and through both verbal and nonverbal behaviors, communication is a rich, complex process.

I believe that one very important function of communication is the conveyance of intent (and, indeed, this is a perspective that is echoed by most of the authors in these volumes). One of the reasons why humans can produce and live very successfully in highly complex, layered social networks is because we can communicate intent and share intentions with others. Some scholars believe, in fact, that shared intentionality is an ability unique to humans (Tomasello, Carpenter, Call, Behne and Moll 2005).

In my view, shared intentionality is one of the major reasons why human cultures have survived and thrived. While there are many definitions of *culture* (as there are of communication), I define culture as a meaning and information system that is transmitted across generations (Matsumoto and Juang 2007). Shared intentionality allows for human cultures to evolve and have three characteristics that nonhuman cultures do not: social complexity, differentiation, and institutionalization. And because communication is at the heart of the conveyance of intent and the production of shared intentionality, it is therefore at the heart of human cultural life. Without communication as we know it today, we would not have human cultures as we know it today. And the survival success story of humans, which has occurred because of the evolution of human cultures, would not have been possible without communication. For this reason alone, communication is an incredibly important topic not only for people today and tomorrow but also for humankind throughout the millennia.

An Evolving Understanding of Interpersonal and Intercultural Communication

Of the many potential ways of divvying up the field, one major method is the distinction between *interpersonal* and *intercultural* communication, the former referring to communication among individuals of the same cultural background using the same cultural framework, and the latter referring to communication among individuals who are agents of different cultures, and who use different cultural frameworks. This distinction is important because of the implicit association of the communication process to cultural frames. Different cultures promote different procedures and meaning systems in the encoding and decoding of messages, and even when the same language is used, underlying cultural differences in frameworks can produce differences in meaning of the language (e.g., American vs. British vs. Australian English, or different meanings of the same terminology among branches of the military).

Sometimes, however, the distinction between interpersonal and intercultural communication can be blurred. After all, intercultural communication has traditionally been considered essentially interpersonal communication among people from different cultures. And given that no two people are exactly alike, even when from the same linguistic culture, almost any interpersonal communication can be considered (to some degree) intercultural (just ask any married couple whose members come from two different familial cultures).

I believe that, interestingly, much of the blurring of the distinction between interpersonal and intercultural communication has come about because of our increased understanding of *person* and *culture* and the intricate relationship between the two. Indeed, it is clear today that it is almost impossible to consider one without the other, and they both co-evolved to have the capacities, abilities, competences, and dispositions that allow for communication to occur. Much of what you will read in the remaining chapters in both handbooks, therefore, reflects this fuzziness, which is inevitable given the nature of the topic area and the rather artificial distinction we scientists have placed in use.

Thus, although the distinction between interpersonal and intercultural communication has proven to be a very useful one in the field, it is not without pitfalls and limitations. Regardless, this distinction has been the major way in which research and theorizing has been organized in the field, and for that reason these handbooks maintain that distinction.

The Influence of Changing Technologies on Communication

Transportation and communication technologies have transformed our world in ways previously unimaginable, and they promise to continue to do so in the future. Communication no longer occurs just within the domain of face-to-face encounters. E-mail, Facebook, Twitter, Skype, and video teleconferencing have all changed the ways in which communication occurs. Moreover, transportation technologies bring people from disparate cultures together more easily today than ever, and it is not uncommon to communicate with people with very different cultural frameworks in our everyday lives, where it would have been unthinkable even 50 years ago. Fifty years from now we will likely be communicating with technologies we cannot even imagine today.

The dynamic nature of our ever-changing world brought about by technologies has produced new challenges in our ability to communicate effectively and efficiently. Understanding intent correctly is a major concern for businesses, governments, and individuals. Fittingly, a great deal of contemporary research has been directed toward understanding the ways in which communication has changed (or not) as a function of these evolving technologies, and this is reflected in many of the chapters in both handbooks. As technologies continue to evolve, so will the challenges they bring to bear on effective communication; future research efforts will undoubtedly keep up with these changes, resulting in a very dynamically fluid field of scientific endeavor.

The chapters in this handbook are the state of the art at this slice of time given the evolving nature of communication and our understanding of both communication and culture. This handbook is divided into two major sections, reflecting two broad ways in which work in each area has evolved. The first section deals with theoretical perspectives; chapters in this section provide different conceptual frameworks with which to understand the state-of-the-art knowledge in both fields. The second section deals with applications, describing how research findings have been instrumental to the development of intervention programs to improve communication, to the identification of key factors (competencies) that appear to be the key ingredients of effective communication, and to the examination of the efficacy of such programs.

Overview of the *APA Handbook of Interpersonal Communication*

Theoretical Perspectives

In Chapter 1, Pitts and Giles take what they call the "linguistics for problem solving approach" and argue that communication cannot be understood outside of the interpersonal relationships and the contexts in which they occur. These relationships and contexts, in turn, are dynamic and complex, and the authors suggest that researchers pay greater attention to the dynamic interplay between communication and cognition that occurs within these contexts. They strongly suggest that the perspectives, tools, and methodologies involved in understanding and examining the social psychology of interpersonal relations have much to offer the field and study of communication.

In Chapter 2, Thibault integrates not only verbal communication but also nonverbal behaviors in understanding face-to-face interaction. He argues for the interaction between individuals—the interindividual—as an important unit of analysis in understanding communication, rather than individuals per se. Thibault correctly suggests that much of interaction, and thus communication, emerges as a result of interactions between the affordances of individuals, with their biological constitutions as well as their social and cognitive skills, and that the social and cultural world is embedded. Interestingly, Thibault cites Darwin's work on emotion and nonverbal behavior in much of his analysis and questions the function of communication, whether merely for information exchange or for behavior management. These questions are related to the issues of intent communication raised earlier in this Introduction.

In Chapter 3, Thimm takes up the issues we discussed earlier concerning how technological improvements have influenced communication, arguing for the importance of interpersonal contact in computer-mediated human communications. Thimm describes many of the latest technological tools, such as YouTube, e-mail, Facebook, and the like, and suggests that scholars should analyze technology and human communication not only on the level of the words but also on the level of the user's influence (I would include intent). By examining communication in terms of content, participation, and sociability, communication is understood from a different perspective.

In Chapter 4, Ravelli and Stenglin describe the importance of spatial semiotics in communication—how the signs and symbols associated with spaces influence communication. In particular, these authors argue for the importance of social semiotics, which study how spaces allow humans to feel. Power, dominance, conscientiousness, security, and other personality and social characteristics of individuals and groups can be communicated via space, and Ravelli and Stenglin argue effectively that this communicative aspect of the environments within which individuals live, work, and play should not be forgotten in theorizing and studying communication.

In Chapter 5, Locher reminds us that much of communication is related to concepts of face work, identity work, relational work, and rapport management, and the "social positioning of self and other." Indeed, language helps construct identity, and Locher leverages research on politeness and gender to exemplify the close, symbiotic relationship among these concepts. Other than being mere information exchange, communication fulfills important functions of constructing and modifying the identity of all interactants in any communication episode.

In Chapter 6, Brock offers the interesting hypothesis that humor, in its many forms, is a problem-solving activity. Brock correctly points out that the field of humor research, at least from a communications standpoint, still lacks precise theoretical frameworks and even definitions of terms and types of humor. Brock argues that observable functions of humor are a communicative response to the needs or problems that naturally arise in normal daily human interactions. Much humor may be a way of treating communicative problems arising from insufficient communicative competencies.

In Chapter 7, White presents appraisal theory as a theoretical framework and an evaluative method for investigating the nature of attitudinal meanings and the mechanisms by which these attitudes are activated linguistically. An understanding of how positive and negative attitudes are conveyed and negotiated is extremely important for students of communication, particularly those interested in the functionality of language. White argues that the evaluative methods of appraisal theory can identify patterns of co-occurrence and interaction in texts between different appraisal systems, which affords conclusions concerning communicative outcomes that are most likely associated with the text.

Applied Perspectives

The applied section begins with Chapter 8, in which Weber focuses on the concept of everyday communication. He argues convincingly that although this type of communication is often ignored by those who study language and communication, it is a vital and important aspect of communication. As do other authors, Weber argues that everyday communication plays an important function in everyday social interaction and is an important prototype category that originates in folk or ethno categorization. Thus, everyday communication becomes a relevant yet problematic category in interpersonal communication research. Of particular importance are Weber's six dimensions of everyday communication, which characterize and define the construct as well as distinguish it from others. Such contributions can be especially useful for future theorizing and empirical work.

In Chapter 9, Muntigl discusses the role of communication in counseling and psychotherapy. He notes that while interest in discourse structures during psychotherapy and counseling has increased over the years, interest has usually been in using discourse to uncover more important aspects of the psychotherapeutic process, rather than in focusing on discourse as an important unit of analysis in and of itself. Muntigl argues that discourse-based analyses in these areas can indeed shed much more light on therapy and counseling, and that examining the details of social interaction based in discourse can tell us important things about how "clients and therapists come to shared our divergent understandings of experience." Muntigl argues for the continued bridging of the gap between the linguistic descriptions of interactions and the psychological processes associated with therapy and counseling.

In Chapter 10, Androutsopoulos and Georgakopoulou focus on how discourse among youth provides important clues concerning interpersonal management. They structure their discussion around the discursive processes of alignment and convergence on the one hand and the setting of boundaries and misalignment on the other hand. They examine language choices that are mobilized when youth interact and that contribute to interpersonal relationships of alignment or misalignment. They also include an interesting discussion of how emerging media technologies influence these processes among the youth within youth cultures.

In Chapter 11, Korpijaakko-Huuhka and Klippi examine the language use and discourse skills of elderly people. In contrast to the typical deficit paradigm of communicative abilities in older people, these authors argue convincingly for a more positive conception of communication in this group, noting that older people should be considered competent communicators with active and satisfying lives. They suggest that it is important to understand changes in communicative abilities and functions, but equally important to find ways for older people to maintain and enhance their active communicator role and autonomy in various life situations. These authors' outlook is bright, upbeat, and very important for the increasingly aging populations of many countries and cultures of the world.

In Chapter 12, Puccinelli examines the "other" world of communication, nonverbal behavior, arguing that nonverbal behavior is a key component to communicating needs and desires. Puccinelli cites much evidence to suggest that the majority of information exchanged in communication episodes, especially sensitive information, is communicated nonverbally. She reviews evidence for the skills associated with effective encoding and decoding of nonverbal behavior skills, all of which supports her contention that nonverbal behavior clearly plays a critical role in being a competent communicator.

Finally, in Chapter 13, Perrin and Ehrensberger-Dow address the important topic of media competence. As described previously, evolving and emerging communication technologies are demanding changes in the ways in which human communication occurs. Media can facilitate, impede, or hinder certain types of communication and language use, and how people communicate depends very much on the medium in which they choose to do so. Within that range of possibility, people can use different media more or less skillfully, appropriately, and effectively. Perrin and Ehrensberger-Dow highlight this in illustrations of medially transmitted communications, explain the research methodologies in this area, and present an overview of research into appropriate and successful language use via media. Of particular importance are the gaps they identify in the research literature, providing an important platform for future work.

Conclusion

The chapters bring together much of the state-of-the-art literature on interpersonal communication. They represent well the emerging and evolving nature of communication and its highly interconnected relationship with culture. They leverage research on new technologies and culture, and they highlight the pitfalls and challenges in understanding and studying communication today. Regardless of the approach, technology, and time period, human communication will continue to be one of the most important aspects of our lives and behaviors and will form a bedrock for our families, communities, and society at large. The chapters in this volume will form the foundation for much theorizing and empirical work today and for the next generation of work in this area.

References

Matsumoto, David and Linda Juang. 2007. *Culture and Psychology* (4th ed.). Belmont, CA: Wadsworth.

Tomasello, Michael, Malinda Carpenter, Josep Call, Tanya Behne and Henrike Moll. 2005. Understanding and sharing intentions: The origins of cultural cognition. *Behavioral & Brain Sciences* 28: 675–735.

Part I

Theoretical Perspectives

1

Social Psychology and Personal Relationships: Accommodation and Relational Influence Across Time and Contexts

Margaret J. Pitts and Howard Giles

1. Introduction

Everyday communication can be problematic, but we are relatively good at managing it. How is this accomplished through interaction? As scholars across disciplines move forward in the pursuit of understanding, explaining, and even predicting outcomes and processes related to human interactions, we also become increasingly aware of the intricacies involved in such interpersonal encounters. Relational processing is at the root of most of our daily encounters whether with a long-term relational partner, a stranger with whom we share a brief encounter, or the cashier you greet everyday purchasing your morning coffee. The complexities of interpersonal connections are situated in an array of dynamic human features and personal attributes such as experience, developmental process, and social and personal identity orientations.

The question is: What tools can scholars of human interaction use to make sense of these seemingly kaleidoscopic encounters? Scholars tend to investigate encounters grounded in the scholarship and epistemological and ontological positionings of their primary field. Perhaps this is rightfully so. However with this chapter, we urge scholars to move beyond disciplinary borders and into specific sites of human interaction and meaning-making. Along with Knapp and Antos (2008), this necessitates that we start by looking at some of the challenges we have with current theories, tools, and methods for understanding interpersonal relationships across contexts and across interactions. Such an approach highlights the imperfection of language and communication behaviors among individuals and between groups (see Coupland, Giles, and Wiemann 1991; Giles, Gallois, and Petronio 1998). And, when applied to the social psychology of interpersonal relationships, it helps to identify locations of disconnect between cognition, language, and communication in everyday encounters and work toward applied manners for mending problems therein.

Berger (2005) argues that research that *does not* seek to problematize the fundamental processes underlying social interaction and goal achievement might be interesting, but does little to promote theories of interpersonal interactions. Our goal with this chapter is to highlight social psychological approaches toward theory, method, and tools for investigating and problematizing interpersonal encounters. We do so first by problematizing traditional approaches to the study of interpersonal relationships.

Without careful attention to tools and methods of conducting relationship research, theory development can become constrained. Theories of interpersonal interactions can move forward to help us make sense out of everyday interactions—theories that are relevant to real world, real time encounters. However, they need to account for more specialized communication *contexts* (e.g., service, health, and family) and *relationships* (e.g., strangers, acquaintances, lovers, family members, intergroup relationships) in everyday settings across the lifespan (Nussbaum and Coupland 2004; Pecchioni, Wright, and Nussbaum 2005). From this perspective, we echo Knapp and Antos' (2008) call for investigators to actively engage in the problematics of blurring applied and basic research and the problematics of engaging in everyday interpersonal encounters—an approach they refer to as "linguistics for problem-solving." In doing so, we argue that it is time to put interpersonal theories into action and into context. Moreover, we agree with Fiedler (2006) that language is not without social cognition *and* social cognition is not without language. Understanding language as a problem-solving and problem-evoking instrument heightens the necessity of applied theories of interactional competence. We emphasize the importance of investigating these everyday encounters from a longitudinal, developmental perspective. This can be accomplished by entering and investigating real life encounters where dynamic communication is happening and where we can "see" talk in action.

2. Interdependent Theorizing About Personal Relationships

The shift of focus, at least in the area of interpersonal communication, from theories of persuasion and social influence to theories of disclosure, development, and dissolution marks the trend over the last four decades toward a more relational focus on interpersonal interactions (Berger 2005). Unfortunately, and perhaps ironically, despite the social and interdependent nature of interpersonal relationships, scholars have systematically explored them from a single-participant, rather than dyadic, research paradigm with a primary focus on self-reported data that situates the participant in a space devoid of any social, environmental, political, and emotional context (Acitelli, Duck, and West 2000; Ickes and Duck 2000). Instead, it is the dynamic interplay between people in relationships that should be explored, as this is where the primary relational functions are being managed and negotiated (e.g., Friesen, Fletcher, and Overall 2005).

Surprisingly little attention has been oriented toward how relational partners creatively and communicatively develop "couple" or "family" identities. These identities are often distinctive and positive images of themselves *as a unit* that relational partners can chose to act out in the presence of particular others (Giles and Fitzpatrick 1984). Couple-focused social comparisons necessarily become active and salient for all relational units involved in such conversations. Relatedly, it is fairly uncommon to explore personal and relational contradictions as witnessed in multi-leveled discourse, or discourse with multiple goals, such as marital conflict co-occurring with supportive relational talk (Verhofstadt et al. 2005) or "selfishly" initiating rapport-building while maintaining an other-orientation (Pitts and Miller-Day 2007). Investigations that take such a perspective emphasize the inherent dialectics and dualities in relationships and relating—such as developing a public and private couple identity while maintaining public and private individuality. Relational contradictions are "emergent in the communicative choices of the moment, but those choices reflect, in part, the constraints of socialization and what transpired in the prior history of the relationship" (Baxter and Montgomery 1996: 59). Thus, relationships should be viewed as part of a dialectic system, not just as individuals and dyads, but also as couples and individuals within a larger societal context (Brown, Altman, and Werner 1992). Couples experience dialectical tensions within their relationship as well as between their socio-cultural relationships, including kinship, friendship, and other social relationships (see Rawlins 2004). What we should strive to find are answers to the questions about the dynamic interplay of human interactions across time and context that provide us with a better understanding of the ways in which such subjective and intersubjective interactions influence everyday living (Ickes and Duck 2000). Although theorists are no longer woeful about the lack of theories relating to interpersonal interactions (Ickes and Duck 2000), there is still a need for current and new theories to draw from a more interactional, dynamic theoretic paradigm.

3. Accommodating to Relational Partners

Interaction has been described as "a multi-event process that involves the connections between each partner's observable behaviors and the others' subjective responses (i.e., thoughts and feelings)" (Surra and Bohman 1991: 282). New and developing theories can gain much from this approach while being pushed to examine the dynamic interaction between communication and cognition shifting, thus providing a link between cognition, communication processes, and intersubjective interpretations across time and across interactions. Here we argue for a shift of attention from intrapersonal processes to interpersonal processes with a focus on language and cognition. Such an approach fosters an understanding that language and behaviors have a cognitive counterpart, and that cognition is structured through language and context. Historically, Kelley and Thibaut's (1978; Kelley 1979) interdependence theory, and later Rusbults' investment models (Rusbult, Drigotas, and Verette 1994), have maintained a focus on interpersonal *processes* (Rusbult and Arriaga 2000) from a primarily social psychological perspective, while Giles and colleagues' (Giles 2008; Giles, Coupland, and Coupland 1991) communication accommodation theory takes a language-focused approach toward understanding interpersonal encounters and mutual influence.

Both theories take into account fundamental influences that shape interactions by addressing the self, the cognition/goal, and the actual interaction. However, the triangle of influence is not equilateral in that these two theories do not put the same attention on each of the three influences (i.e., interdependence theory focuses more on the cognitive processes while communication accommodation theory focuses more on the communication and resulting outcome). Moreover, *accommodation* is at the nexus of each theory determining relational satisfaction, relational closeness, interactional competence, and so forth. However, the core meaning of accommodation in each theory differs. An interdependence perspective on accommodation regards it as a pattern of interaction involving the suppressed desire to match a partner's destructive interaction in order to respond in a more constructive manner (Rusbult and Arriaga 2000; Rusbult, Yovetich, and Verette 1996). In this way, accommodating to a partner who is behaving negatively by responding in a constructive rather than destructive manner will serve to preserve the relationship, but might come at a significant cost to the accommodating party (Rusbult, Yovetich, and Verette 1996). In a way, by *accommodating* to the partner (in this sense by responding constructively) a person actively demonstrates her/his affiliation with her/his partner.

Communication accommodation theory is primarily concerned with the motivation and social consequences underlying a person's change in communication styles (verbal and nonverbal features such as accent, volume, tone, language choice) to either accommodate or not accommodate their interactional partners (Giles et al. 2007). In both theories, motivation plays the driving role for accommodating (or nonaccommodating) behaviors. Interactants may take into account such variables as long-term goals, social norms, and/or a desire to preserve the other's well-being. Kelley (1979) and Rusbult, Yovitch, and Verette (1996) describe this as a transformation of motivation wherein interactants strive to maximize the partner's outcomes, a joint outcome, to achieve equity, or to defeat the partner. Motivation to accommodate (or not) in communication accommodation theory is derived from similar relational features, but contextual features as well; social power and status are a prerogative of it (Gallois, Ogay, and Giles 2005).

Communication accommodation serves both cognitive and affective purposes in interpersonal settings. Cognitive purposes are met when accommodation facilitates comprehension, prevents misattributions, or stimulates a shift in communication that is more suitable to a particular context or mode of relational development. Affective needs can be met through convergence so as to appear more likeable, or diverging to reinforce distinctiveness and a sense of positive personal identity. Convergence is typically associated with seeking affiliation, social approval, compliance, and communication effectiveness. Divergence is typically associated with seeking distinctiveness and/or expressing social disapproval (Harwood, Soliz, and Lin 2006). There are exceptions, however, such as when too much convergence, or overaccommodation, results in negative outcomes. For example, when patronizing speech (e.g., simplified grammar and slow enunciations) directed at older people is seen by cognitively-active members of this social group as utterly demeaning and condescending (Williams and Nussbaum 2001).

A final feature of communication accommodation theory, for our purposes here, is its capacity to account for compelling intergroup processes not usually accountable under the rubric of "interpersonal communication", yet are fundamental to it (see Gallois and Giles 1998). Some years ago, Tajfel and Turner (1979) proffered the distinction between encounters—even dyadic ones—that were either "interindividual" or "intergroup". The former were interactions that are based solely on the personal characteristics of the parties involved (e.g., their personalities and moods) and not at all dependent on their respective social category memberships. Hence, accommodation-nonaccommodation in these cases would be toward or away from the idiosyncratic communication attributes of the other. Intergroup encounters were the converse, and so accommodation-nonaccommodation was pitched vis-à-vis the other's and one's own social category memberships (sexual orientation, gang, sorority, religious, political, etc.). This class of interactions was regarded by these authors as constituting and actually defining a very large proportion of all the interpersonal situations we encounter. Even the most intimate communication—such as between spouses who have been married for decades—can, at times, be usefully understood and analyzed in intergroup terms (e.g., talk about who does the cleaning, caring for the children, and shopping und cooking).

Rather than construing these dual entities as polar opposites of a single interactional continuum, scholars (e.g., Giles and Hewstone 1982) have felt it prudent to represent conversational possibilities as being located along two orthogonal continua, namely interindividual (high-low) and intergroup (high-low). This lends the possibility of encounters being construed as high on *both* dimensions, either in sequences within any conversation or between them, as in the case whereby a son first discloses to his mother that he is gay. The history of their relationship dictates that interpersonal salience would be high, with the mother dealing with her son as the unique person she has known since birth. Simultaneously, her son's homosexuality should be pertinent, potentially shaping the encounter in so many ways.

4. Message Production in Relationships

Other psychological perspectives on interactions, albeit from communication science, such as message production, skill, and design (Greene 1997; Greene and Lindsey 1989; Greene et al. 1997; O'Keefe 1997), interaction goals, and message organization (O'Keefe and Shepherd 1987; Ryan et al. 1996), and conversation planning (Waldron 1997), help us understand the development, output, and adaptation of messages in interaction, but rarely do they take a dyadic perspective. Action assembly theory, for example, attempts to "specify the mechanisms by which output, so conceived, is produced, moment-by-moment, during ongoing interactions" (Greene 1997: 152), but focuses on the behavior of an individual at any moment of time. Moreover, a message-production focus inherently misses perhaps the most important factor when determining message effectiveness (i.e., how it is received and interpreted). Because of the dynamic nature of conversation and cognitive processing, social psychological theories of relationships must move toward a better understanding of the cognitive and language shifts in an interaction. Although message design models, for example, state a focus on message adaptation (O'Keefe 1997), adaptation in this sense refers to developing a message that meets situational and goal needs, but not necessarily message adaptation across an interaction.[1] A second criticism of planning approaches to message production is that the focus rests too much on the cognitive processing and not enough on the larger social forces (context, relationship, conversational direction) that influence the interaction (Waldron 1997). Conversational and relational goals change in interaction (Greene 1997; Ryan et al. 1996), plans get thwarted (Berger 1995, 1997; Berger and diBattista 1993), and people may simply become distracted or too cognitively overloaded to communicate effectively. Any of which could occur to one person, one time, in one action. Or, more likely, all of which might occur several times, across several interactions, for several interactants.

5. Methods for Investigating Interpersonal Relationships

The study of the social psychology of interpersonal relationships has been stifled by a persistence to look only narrowly at the act of *relating*. Methods have myopically focused on single-participant relationship reflections, staged laboratory investigations, and/or solitary case studies in a singular point of time. Yet, relationships develop in context, many in the workplace and others outside of it. In order to appreciate the unique ways in which relationships are socially constructed and maintained, they must be studied from within their larger contexts including the broader socio-cultural history, developmental and relational status, emotional, health, family, and social network, as well as economic influences in which they are embedded (Acitelli, Duck, and West 2000).

Taking relational and developmental status into account can lend significant insight into the influences interpersonal communication can have on future interpersonal encounters and relationships across the lifespan (Alberts et al. 2005; Nussbaum 2006). We know, for example, that an interaction between long-term partners is influenced by their relational history, the present context, and can have implications for their future interactions as well as a significant influence over each other's lives (Rusbult and Arriaga 2000). Much of this can be studied through the process of encoding and storing messages across time. For example, partners encode and store past experiences as knowledge structures (Fletcher and Thomas 1996) that later help serve to interpret or guide future interactions. Overtime, interpersonal interactions can work in a self-fulfilling or expectancy-confirming manner, thereby shaping not only the individual, but the relationship as well (e.g., Murray and Holmes 1996). Moreover, interpersonal relationships, even between the same partners, change across the lifespan as partners and individuals shift their life-task focus from, say, becoming good parents to managing a retirement lifestyle (Cantor and Malley 1991). Similarly, Carstensen's (e.g., 1995) socioemotional selectivity theory suggests that people are searching for different meanings in

---

[1] This is in comparison with *communication accommodation theory* which does take into account shifts in accommodative strategies within a single interaction (Gallois, Ogay, and Giles 2005).

their relationships with others as they move into the second half of their lives. Socioemotional selectivity theory predicts that when time boundaries (i.e., end of life) are perceived, people prioritize present-oriented and emotionally meaningful goals over future and knowledge-oriented ones. Such shifts in priority influence social preferences, social network composition, emotion regulation, and cognitive processing (Löckenhoff and Carstensen 2004). Accordingly, as people age, they are motivated to reach emotionally meaningful goals and seek out interpersonal relationships and social messages that fulfill that need (Cantor and Malley 1991; Fung and Carstensen 2003). Interpersonal relationships among elder adults or between people in inter-generational relationships are necessarily different than those among younger adults or children, especially in terms of relational maintenance, motivation, and communicative work. Thus, a look at messages across time with a focus on lifespan development gives us insight into quality and expectations of relationships in later life (Pecchioni, Wright, and Nussbaum 2005).

In addition to actual interactions, people frequently generate and manage relationships cognitively through series of imagined interactions. Such interactions are often the source of relational expectations, but are also practice realms in which individuals are able to rehearse or replay various relational encounters (Honeycutt and Cantrill 2001). The knowledge structures developed over the course of (real and imagined) relating help interactants to predict, explain, and control interpersonal interactions, while at the same time can serve as relationship-enhancing tools (Fletcher and Thomas 1996). As such, pro-relational modes for relating and partner accommodation may become routine after time (Rusbult et al. 1996). This is especially salient among close interpersonal relationships marked by positive illusions and idealization of a romantic partner early in a relationship that not only positively influences relational satisfaction (Murray, Holmes, and Griffin 1996a), but through interaction over time also aids in the social construction of the ideal romantic partner (Murray, Holmes, and Griffin 1996b). Therefore, methods that focus on *relating* across time and encounters rather than on individuals or relationships are paramount.

A lifespan perspective takes into account the consequences and benefits of communicating across time. Moreover, longitudinal studies such as the *Marital Instability over the Life Course* (Booth, Amato, and Johnson 1998; Kamp Dush, and Amato 2005) help to charter relational change and relational satisfaction across time in close romantic relationships. Using paradigms of interdependence and accommodation might allow scholars the ability to map personal and relational transformations across time. For example, partners or interactants who behave, communicate, and interpret in a relationship-enhancing manner and in ways that maximize individual and relational outcomes positively affect present and future interactions. This type of communication promotes long-term well-being, establishes a sense of trustworthiness, and lays the groundwork for future reciprocal interactions (Rusbult and Arriaga 2000).

Methods for developing a more comprehensive view of relationships must center on looking within *and* outside of personal relationships. A social psychological perspective "implies a focus on the relation between structures and processes at the individual level, with those operative at the dyadic level", but in doing so, does not deny the importance of investigating interpersonal interactions in their wider social contexts (Fletcher and Fitness 1996: xii). Longitudinal and lifespan approaches toward the study of interpersonal relationships are not the only directions that will advance knowledge. Interpersonal scholars could spend more time developing knowledge surrounding the mundane side of relating and everyday conversations (Alberts et al. 2005). Duck (1992: 69) suggests:

> In everyday life, we make many snap judgements about people and form instant likes and dislikes. We all know that we can create 'irrational' first impressions, sudden lusts and likings, and intense hatreds for strangers. We can like the manner of a person who has not even uttered a word to us. So, paradoxically, the study of initial responses to strangers makes sense as a starting point for understanding long-term human relationships; it is at this point when relationships most often start or fail to start.

A "problem-solving" approach also necessitates a focus on interpersonal relationships as they naturally occur in a variety of everyday contexts (i.e., relationships in action). While there has been a strong focus on investigating romantic and other close interpersonal relationships, less attention has been paid to other types of interpersonal encounters such as those between strangers, acquaintances, service personnel, and others with whom we interact on a frequent basis but have not developed a particularly close relationship (for an exception see Ventola 1979).

Even within the domain of close interpersonal relationships, romantic relationships among primarily young adults have received the majority of attention while relationships among older adults, some family relationships, and friendships have received less attention (Pecchioni, Wright, and Nussbaum 2005). Research that neglects to account for changes across the lifespan is missing most of the *relating* that is happening. To remedy this requires a focus on stability *and* change in personal relationships and a look at life transitions beyond just ageing, adolescence, or college transitions, and into other life course changes such as parenting, relocating, changes in career or health status, or personal milestones.

6. Research Tools for Investigating Relationships in Action

Relationships are dynamic entities, on-going processes that are influenced by everything that is around them (Planalp and Rivers 1996). Acitelli, Duck, and West (2000) argue that when investigating *the social* there are three quintessential relational elements that must be attended to: the psychological congruence and empathic understanding between two people, the interdependence of their behaviors, and the larger social contexts in which the interactions are embedded. Because social relationships are experienced subjectively and change across time, the tools we use to explore those relationships must be sensitive to capture relational nuances as they occur. In addition to investigating communication across relational or lifespan transitions Nussbaum (2006), Acitelli, Duck, and West (2000) and others (e.g., Alberts et al. 2005) suggest researchers should attend to even those relational enactments that appear to be trivial or routine in nature, paying more attention to the subjective and intersubjective nature of relationships and relating. Routine ways of relating has received very little attention from scholars across disciplines (Berger 2005), but are rich areas to explore in an effort to uncover how relationships are accomplished. Indeed, how often have we heard responses like "same old, same old" to the question, "how are things going?"—a response that is often verbalized by other parties as being a healthy state of affairs given the presumed and valued stability together with a lack of stress and uncertainty.

7. Relating in Real Time: Charting Interpersonal Goals and Emotions

Contributions from the field of cognitive psychology have provided evidence that people's on-line processing is inextricably related to knowledge structures developed through relating in interpersonal encounters (Fletcher and Thomas 1996). The availability and accessibility of knowledge structures and relational elements, such as commitment and accommodation, can have an incredible influence on present and future thoughts and communicative behaviors (Etcheverry and Le 2005). Language in action develops, modifies, enhances, and perhaps even dissolves the knowledge structures we can access. For example, rewriting negative scripts for self- or other-talk into positive ones can serve to generate new knowledge structures of self and other and over time if negative scripts are not accessed they can weaken. Knowledge structures that develop over the course of relating and relationships help us to create scripts and schema that guide both verbal and nonverbal interactions. These relationally constructed scripts also provide information about the nature and course of various emotions in their relationships (Fitness 1996). Unfortunately, ascertaining some of the cognitive influences on the message output in an interaction poses the most difficult challenge.

This challenge has been met in present times through convenient digital media methods such as digital recording and replay (e.g., Verhofstadt et al. 2005), unobtrusive audio recordings of daily conversations (e.g., Alberts et al. 2005), and through more traditional methods such as maintaining a diary across interactions (Duck et al. 1991; Goldsmith and Baxter 1996), or at the very least comparing self-report data with observations (e.g., Qualter and Munn 2005). These research tools provide the researcher with the important ability to capture talk in action, and in the case of diary studies offer longitudinal insight. Researchers (and participants) can take a discursive psychological approach to charting shifts in cognition and language outcomes by looking closely and reflecting on interactional goals in a moment-by-moment manner (see Wetherell, Taylor, and Yates 2001). Warner (2002) suggests a microanalytic approach (e.g., detailed information about the behavior, affect, and/or physiology of social interaction among participants) to capture the moment-to-moment exchange of behaviors that occur as partners are relating in everyday contexts. The widespread availability of the internet and computer-mediated interfacing offers yet another tool for the examination of on-line processing.

"Lurking" in a chat room or instant-messaging forum where the researcher provides participants with changing goals in an interaction could be a useful way of charting language shifts as they relate to new interpersonal goals.

In addition to investigating dynamic interaction goals, Berger (2005) suggests social interaction researchers should take more interest in the role of emotions in both close relationships and more impersonal relationships to glean a better understanding of how emotions shape our communication and how context and rules for communicating shape our display of emotions. A recent special issue on emotions in personal relationships (Fitness and Planalp 2005) points to the inextricable, yet complicated ways that emotions influence relationships and vice-versa. Moreover, a lifespan focus on emotions and relationships provides evidence that older and younger adults experience and process emotions differently (Carstensen et al. 2000). Fitness (1996) argues that an emotion-script analysis provides insight into the on-line processing of relational interactions and would be useful in providing an additional link between relational cognition and communication. This could be particularly insightful across age cohorts and across relationship types. Research that does take an interaction-focus moves a step closer to understanding the dynamic as well as dialectical nature of language and behavior, but often does so in ways that are limited in terms of time and task (Rusbult, Yovetich, and Verette 1996).

8. Conclusion

With this chapter, ways in which we can better investigate, better understand and, as a result, better *relate* across interpersonal contexts are highlighted. By taking a "linguistics for problem-solving" approach, we first argued that interpersonal relationships and the contexts in which they flourish (or falter) are dynamic and complicated. Linguistics for problem-solving involves socially accountable applied research (Knapp and Antos, 2008) designed to bring the research focus out of laboratory and to the actual sites of linguistic and cognitive behavior. People *relate* through various forms of talk (self-talk, relational talk, computer-mediated talk, public discourse, etc.) simultaneously forging and auditioning different personal, relational, and social identities. Thus, we must strive to capture relating where the vast majority of relating is occurring. That is, we should focus our attentions toward everyday contexts across a variety of relationships from impersonal encounters to our most intimate ones. Moreover, the changing social psychology of individuals, relational partners, and even social groups over time warrants a life-span approach. For example, investigating the long-term influence of communication and accommodation across time and across relational context is an important next step in understanding the social psychology of personal and intergroup relationships as they develop over time.

More and more, scholars are investigating the interdependence between communication and cognition. However, as we argue earlier, researchers tend to approach social interaction primarily from either a communication or a cognition perspective, rather than emphasizing their powerful mutual influence. We hope to have successfully argued for a shift in focus that includes the dynamic interplay of communication and cognition. We further hope that the perspectives, methods, and tools for investigating the social psychology of interpersonal relationships offered herein provide a fertile ground for future research and theory development.

References

Acitelli, Linda K., Steve W. Duck and Lee West. 2000. Embracing the *social* in social psychology and personal relationships. In: William Ickes and Steve Duck (eds.), *The Social Psychology of Personal Relationships,* 215–227. Chichester: Wiley.

Alberts, Jess K., Christina G. Yoshimura, Michael Rabby and Rose Loschiavo. 2005. Mapping the topography of couples' daily conversation. *Journal of Social and Personal Relationships* 22: 299–322.

Baxter, Leslie A. and Barbara M. Montgomery. 1996. *Relating Dialogues and Dialectics.* New York: Guilford Press.

Berger, Charles R. 1995. A plan-based approach to strategic communication. In: Dean E. Hewes (ed.), *The Cognitive Bases of Interpersonal Communication*, 141–179. Hillsdale, NJ: Lawrence Erlbaum.

Berger, Charles R. 1997. *Planning Strategic Interaction.* Mahwah, NJ: Lawrence Erlbaum. Berger, Charles R. 2005. Interpersonal communication: Theoretical perspectives, future prospects. *Journal of Communication* 55: 415–447.

Berger, Charles R. and Patrick di Battista. 1993. Communication failure and plan adaptation: If at first you don't succeed, say it louder and slower. *Communication Monographs* 60: 220–236.

Booth, Alan, Paul R. Amato and David R. Johnson. 1998. *Marital Instability over the Life Course: Methodology Report for Fifth Wave.* Lincoln: University of Nebraska Bureau of Sociological Research.

Brown, Barbara, Irwin Altman and Carol Warner. 1992. Close relationships in the physical and social world: Dialectical and transactional analysis. *Communication Yearbook* 15: 508–521.

Cantor, Nancy and Janet Malley. 1991. Life tasks, personal needs, and close relationships. In: Garth J.O. Fletcher and Frank D. Fincham (eds.), *Cognition in Close Relationships,* 101–125. Hillsdale, NJ: Lawrence Erlbaum.

Carstensen, Laura L. 1995. Evidence for a life-span theory of socioemotional selectivity. *Current Directions in Psychological Science* 4: 151–156.

Carstensen, Laura L., Monisha Pasupathi, Ulrich Mayr and John R. Nesselroade. 2000. Emotional experience in everyday life across the adult life span. *Journal of Personality and Social Psychology* 79: 644–655.

Coupland, Nikolas, Howard Giles and John Wiemann (eds.). 1991. *"Miscommunication" and Problematic Talk.* Newbury Park, CA: Sage.

Duck, Steve. 1992. *Human Relationships.* 2nd edition. Newbury Park: Sage.

Duck, Steve, Deborah J. Rutt, Margaret H. Hurst and Heather Strejc. 1991. Some evident truths about conversations in everyday relationships: All communications are not created equal. *Human Communication Research* 18: 228–267.

Etcheverry, Paul E. and Benjamin Le. 2005. Thinking about commitment: Accessibility of commitment and prediction of relationship persistence, accommodation, and willingness to sacrifice. *Personal Relationships* 12: 103–123.

Fiedler, Klaus. 2006. *The art of exerting verbal influence: being informative but subtle.* Keynote speech presented at the International Conference on Language and Social Psychology, Bonn, Germany.

Fitness, Julie. 1996. Emotion knowledge structures in close relationships. In: Julie Fitness and Garth J.O. Fletcher (eds.), *Knowledge Structures in Close Relationships: A Social Psychological Approach*, xi–xv. Mahwah, NJ: Lawrence Erlbaum.

Fitness, Julie and Sally Planalp (eds.). 2005. Special issue on emotions. *Personal Relationships* 12.

Fletcher, Garth J.O. and Julie Fitness. 1996. Introduction. In: Julie Fitness and Garth J.O. Fletcher (eds.), *Knowledge Structures in Close Relationships: A Social Psychological Approach*, xi–xv. Mahwah, NJ: Lawrence Erlbaum.

Fletcher, Garth J.O. and Geoff Thomas. 1996. Close relationships lay theories: Their structure and function. In: Julie Fitness and Garth J.O. Fletcher (eds.), *Knowledge Structures in Close Relationships: A Social Psychological Approach,* 3–24. Mahwah, NJ: Lawrence Erlbaum.

Friesen, Myron D., Garth J.O. Fletcher and Nickola C. Overall. 2005. A dyadic assessment of forgiveness in intimate relationships. *Personal Relationships* 12: 61–77.

Fung, Helene and Laura L. Carstensen. 2003. Sending memorable messages to the old: Age differences in preferences and memory for advertisements. *Journal of Personality and Social Psychology* 85: 163–178.

Gallois, Cindy and Howard Giles. 1998. Accommodating mutual influence in intergroup encounters. In: Mark. T. Palmer and George A. Barnett (eds.), *Progress in Communication Sciences* 14: 135–162. Stanford: Ablex.

Gallois, Cindy, Tania Ogay and Howard Giles. 2005. Communication accommodation theory: A look back and a look ahead. In: William B. Gudykunst (ed.) *Theorizing about Intercultural Communication,* 121–148. Thousand Oaks, CA: Sage.

Giles, Howard. 2008. "When in Rome . . . or not!": An accommodating theory. In: Leslie A. Baxter and Dawn O. Braithwaite (eds.), *Engaging Theories in Interpersonal Communication,* 161–173. Thousand Oaks, CA: Sage.

Giles, Howard, Nikolas Coupland and Justine Coupland (eds.). 1991. *The Contexts of Accommodation.* New York: Cambridge University Press.

Giles, Howard and Mary Anne Fitzpatrick. 1984. Personal, group and couple identities: Towards a relational context for the study of language attitudes and linguistic forms. In: Deborah Schiffrin (ed.), *Meaning, Form, and Use in Context: Linguistic Applications,* 253–277. Washington D.C., Georgetown University Press.

Giles, Howard, Cindy Gallois and Sandra Petronio (eds.). 1998. (Mis)communicating across boundaries. *Communication Research* 25(6): 571–720.

Giles, Howard and Miles Hewstone. 1982. Cognitive structures, speech, and social situations. *Language Sciences* 4: 187–219.

Giles, Howard, Michael Willemyns, Cindy Gallois and Michelle Chernikoff Anderson. 2007. Accommodating a new frontier: The context of law enforcement. In: Klaus Fiedler (ed.), *Social Communication,* 129–162. New York: Psychology Press.

Goldsmith, Deanna J. and Leslie A. Baxter. 1996. Constituting relationships in talk: A taxonomy of speech events in social and personal relationships. *Human Communication Research* 23: 87–114.

Greene, John O. 1997. A second generation of action assembly theory. In: John O. Greene (ed.), *Message Production: Advances in Communication Theory,* 151–170. Mahwah, NJ: Lawrence Erlbaum.

Greene, John O. and A. E. Lindsey. 1989. Encoding processes in the production of multiple-goal messages. *Human Communication Research* 16: 120–140.

Greene, John O., Marianne S. Sassi, Terri L. Malek-Madani and Christopher N. Edwards. 1997. Adult acquisition of message-production skill. *Communication Monographs* 64: 181–200.

Harwood, Jake, Jordan Soliz and Mei-Chin Lin. 2006. Communication accommodation theory: An intergroup approach to family relationships. In: Dawn O. Braithwaite and Leslie A. Baxter (eds.), *Engaging Theories in Family Communication: Multiple Perspectives,* 19–34. Thousand Oaks, CA: Sage.

Honeycutt, James M. and J. James G. Cantrill. 2001. *Cognition, Communication, and Romantic Relationships.* Mahwah, NJ: Lawrence Erlbaum.

Ickes, William and Steve Duck. 2000. Personal relationships and social psychology. In: William Ickes and Steve Duck (eds.), *The Social Psychology of Personal Relationships,* 1–8. New York: Wiley.

Kamp Dush, Claire M. and Paul R. Amato. 2005. Consequences of relationship status and quality for subjective well-being. *Journal of Social and Personal Relationships* 22: 607–627.

Kelley, Harold H. 1979. *Personal Relationships: Their Structures and Processes.* Hillsdale, NJ: Lawrence Erlbaum. Kelley, Harold H. and John W. Thibaut. 1978. *Interpersonal Relations: A Theory of Interdependence.* New York: Wiley.

Knapp, Karlfried and Gerd Antos. 2008. Introduction to the handbook series. Linguistics for problem solving. In: Gerd Antos and Eija Ventola in cooperation with Tilo Weber (eds.), *Interpersonal Communication,* v–xv. (Handbooks of Applied Linguistics 2.) Berlin/New York: Mouton de Gruyter.

Löckenhoff, Corinna and Laura L. Carstensen. 2004. Socioemotional selectivity theory, aging, and health: The increasingly delicate balance between regulating emotions and making tough choices. *Journal of Personality* 72: 1395–1424.

Murray, Sandra L. and John G. Holmes. 1996. The construction of relationship realities. In: Julie Fitness and Garth J.O. Fletcher (eds.), *Knowledge Structures in Close Relationships: A Social Psychological Approach*, 195–217. Mahwah, NJ: Lawrence Erlbaum.

Murray, Sandra L., John G. Holmes and Dale W. Griffin. 1996a. The benefits of positive illusions: Idealization and the construction of satisfaction in close relationships. *Journal of Personality and Social Psychology* 70: 79–98.

Murray, Sandra, John G. Holmes and Dale W. Griffin. 1996b. The self-fulfilling nature of positive illusions in romantic relationships: Love is not blind, but prescient. *Journal of Personality and Social Psychology* 71: 1155–1180.

Nussbaum, Jon F. 2006. Lifespan communication and quality of life. Presidential speech presented at the International Communication Association, Dresden, Germany. Nussbaum, Jon F. and Justine Coupland (eds.). 2004. *Handbook of Communication and Aging Research*. Mahwah, NJ: Lawrence Erlbaum.

O'Keefe, Barbara J. 1997. Variation, adaptation and functional explanation in the study of message design. In: Gerry Philipsen and Terrance L. Albrecht (eds.), *Developing Communication Theories*, 85–118. New York: State University of New York Press.

O'Keefe, Barbara J. and Gregory J. Shepherd. 1987. The pursuit of multiple objectives in face-to-face persuasive interactions: Effects of construct differentiation on message organization. *Communication Monographs* 54: 396–419.

Pecchioni, Loretta L., Kevin B. Wright and Jon F. Nussbaum. 2005. *Life-Span Communication*. Mahwah, NJ: Lawrence Erlbaum.

Pitts, Margaret J. and Michelle Miller-Day. 2007. Upward turning points and positive rapport development across time in researcher-participant relationships. *Qualitative Research* 7: 177–201.

Planalp, Sally and Mary Rivers. 1996. Changes in knowledge of personal relationships. In: Julie Fitness and Garth J.O. Fletcher (eds.), *Knowledge Structures in Close Relationships: A Social Psychological Approach*, 299–324. Mahwah, NJ: Lawrence Erlbaum.

Qualter, Pamela and Penny Munn. 2005. The friendships and play partners of lonely children. *Journal of Social and Personal Relationships* 22: 379–397.

Rawlins, William K. 2004. Friendships in later life. In: Jon F. Nussbaum and Justine Coupland (eds.), *Handbook of Communication and Aging Research*, 273–299. Mahwah, NJ: Lawrence Erlbaum.

Rusbult, Caryl E. and Ximena Arriaga. 2000. Interdependence in personal relationships. In: William Ickes and Steve Duck (eds.), *The Social Psychology of Personal Relationships*, 79–108. New York: Wiley.

Rusbult, Caryl E., Steve M. Drigotas and Julie Verette. 1994. The investment model: An interdependence analysis of commitment processes and relationship maintenance phenomena. In: Daniel J. Canary and Laura Stafford (eds.), *Communication and Relational Maintenance*, 115–139. San Diego: Academic Press.

Rusbult, Caryl E., Nancy A. Yovetich and Julie Verette. 1996. An interdependence analysis of accommodation process. In: Julie Fitness and Garth J.O. Fletcher (eds.), *Knowledge Structures in Close Relationships: A Social Psychological Approach*, 63–90. Mahwah, NJ: Lawrence Erlbaum.

Ryan, Richard M., Kennon M. Sheldon, Tim Kasser and Edward L. Deci. 1996. All goals are not created equal: An organismic perspective on the nature of goals and their regulation. In: Peter M. Gollwitzer and John A. Bargh (eds.), *The Psychology of Action: Linking Cognition and Motivation to Behavior*, 7–26. New York: The Guilford Press.

Surra, Catherine A. and Thomas Bohman. 1991. The development of close relationships: A cognitive perspective. In: Garth J.O. Fletcher and Frank D. Fincham (eds.), *Cognition in Close Relationships*, 281–305. Hillsdale, NJ: Lawrence Erlbaum.

Tajfel, H and John C. Turner. 1979. An integrative theory of intergroup conflict. In: William G. Austin and Stephen Worchel (eds.), *The Social Psychology of Intergroup Relations*, 33–53. Monterey: Brooks/Cole.

Ventola, Eija. 1979. The structure of casual conversations in English. *Journal of Pragmatics* 3: 267–298.

Verhofstadt, Lesley L., Ann Buysse, William Ickes, Armand De Clercq and Olivier J. Penne. 2005. Conflict and support interactions in marriage: An analysis of couples' interactive behavior and on-line cognition. *Personal Relationships* 12: 23–42.

Waldron, Vincent R. 1997. Toward a theory of interactive conversational planning. In: John O. Greene (ed.), *Message Production: Advances in Communication Theory,* 195–220. Mahwah, NJ: Lawrence Erlbaum.

Warner, Rebecca M. 2002. What microanalysis of behavior in social situations can reveal about relationships across the life span. In: Anita L. Vangelisti, Harry T. Reis and Mary Anne Fitzpatrick (eds.), *Stability and Change in Relationships,* 207–227. Cambridge: Cambridge University Press.

Wetherell, Margaret, Stephanie Taylor and Simeon J. Yates (eds.). 2001. *Discourse as Data: A Guide for Analysis.* London: Sage.

Williams, Angie and Jon F. Nussbaum. 2001. *Intergenerational Communication across the Lifespan.* Mahwah, NJ: Lawrence Erlbaum.

2

Face-to-Face Communication and Body Language

Paul J. Thibault

1. Introduction

Face-to-face communication is a form of action system which is specialized for interaction with others of the same species, as well as between species (e.g., languaged bonobos such as Kanzi and humans). Many other animals also engage in forms of intra-species face-to-face communication. In both the human and nonhuman cases, other members of one's species constitute fundamental resources in the animal's environment. The notion of face-to-face communication brings together in the one term three different through related organizations of doing. These are: (1) the neuroanatomical capacities of the individual participant organisms; (2) the individual *qua* social-agent-in-interaction; and (3) the networks of communicative practices and conventions in which individual agents participate and in which specific occasions of face-to-face communication are embedded. This chapter will explore the need to re-frame face-to-face communication beyond purely proximate and local processes in the here-and-now (Sections 1–2, 10–14.). The concept of face-to-face communication will then (Sections 3–5.) be examined in terms of a number of evolutionary and developmental layers which exert mutual influences on each other. The separation of *language* and *paralanguage* will also be re-examined (Sections 7–9). With the aid of a brief analysis, I shall propose a re-exploration and further development of Scheflen's concept of the *face formation* (Sections 10–11.). I shall conclude with some reflections based in part on the work of Latour which suggest that a point-to-point network ontology is a more useful theoretical perspective for exploring the intersection of local and nonlocal factors in occasions of face-toface interaction (Section 12).

2. Process and Structure in Face-to-Face Communication

Since the early work of pioneering figures such as Birdwhistell (1952, 1961, 1970), McQuown (1957), Trager (1958), Pittenger, Hockett, and Danehy (1960), and Scheflen (1973, 1976), the study of face-to-face communication has always been concerned with understanding both communicative processes and structures. *Process* refers to the various behaviors in real time that enact and contribute to the embodied performance of face-to-face interactive or communicative encounters between individuals. *Structure* refers to the underlying mechanisms which make face-to-face communication possible. Face-to-face communication is a very complex and intricate phenomenon, involving (1) neural connections between motor and sensory systems; (2) a range of somatic resources such as vocalizations, head movements, eye gaze, posture, body movement, gestures, facial expressions, and the integration of these with external affordances in the environment; and (3) social coordination between individuals, and cultural forms of learning and conventions of interaction.

The very term *face-to-face communication* puts the focus on the most proximate effects of the here-now communicative event on the participating individuals. This is the time scale which we inhabit and relate to in our everyday interactions with others. In actual fact, a particular communicative event always involves a complex and simultaneous folding together of many different time scales, ranging from very fast short scales of neural activity to the very long and slow time scales of cultural and biological evolution (Lemke 2000a; Reed 1996: 30–31; Thibault 2000).

We can use the idea of the *three-level scalar hierarchy* developed by Salthe (1993: 36–52) to aid us in keeping straight the levels of relations involved. The term *face-to-face communication* puts the emphasis on the proximate and local processes on the time scale of human action that we associate with real-time and with processes in the here-and-now. However, face-to-face communicative interaction is an emergent level of organization which does not come from just anywhere and cannot be explained only in terms of real-time processes. Instead, it emerges *between* and is a result of the interactions among previously existing levels in a more complex system of relations. Communicative behavior or interaction is distributed in a number of different, yet closely related, ways across a hierarchy of interconnected levels on different time scales. For our present entirely heuristic purposes, these can be roughly approximated in terms of three-level hierarchy analysis as follows:

1. semiotic-informational constraints distributed over the higher-scalar level of the ecosocial semiotic system in historical-cultural time (level L+1)
2. the real-time of co-constructed inter-individual activity of social agents-ininteraction on some occasion (level L)
3. the neuroanatomical processes, capacities, and affordances of the human brain and body as biological initiating conditions in the micro-time scale of bodily dynamics and the pico-scale of neural dynamics (level L-1).

Three-level hierarchy analysis always requires a focal level that is inserted between the highest and the lowest levels. In the present case, the focal level, L, is that of face-to-face communicative activities, which are (1) initiated and made possible by the neuroanatomical capacities of individual organisms (L-1) and (2) regulated and entrained by a social-cultural system (L+1). The hierarchy of three levels proposed above is not an exhaustive picture of all the (very many more) levels of relations involved. Instead, it is a heuristics for showing the necessity of thinking minimally in terms of three levels in order to construct a conceptual framework that can help us to better grasp the real complexity of the relations involved and to avoid the temptation to resort to simplicity and reductionism. Human interaction cannot be explanatorily or causally reduced to processes at the level of the individual organism (L-1) just as it cannot be wholly explained in terms of cultural dynamics (L+1). The communicative capacities of humans depend on the biological initiating conditions and cognitive abilities of individuals (L-1) without which the individual would be unable to participate in interaction with others. These capacities include the neuro-social capacity for intersubjective attunement that is manifested in the earliest stage of caretaker-infant dyads, intrinsic motivations and value-settings that induce individuals to seek and explore the interactive potentialities of others. Level L specifies the emergent inter-individual patterns and properties that results from the coordinated activities of two or more individuals in interaction. Face-to-face communication has emergent properties that cannot be reduced to the actions of the individual participants. Instead, it has properties which depend on the real-time synchronization of the behavior of each individual participant. Finally, there are the higher-scalar boundary conditions of the given social-cultural system (L+1). These regulate and constrain the lower level behaviors and body-brain dynamics of individual organisms on the basis of cultural conventions and norms of patterns of learning. Norms and conventions enable individuals to come to a mutual understanding of the nature of the given social situation and hence to provide solutions to the problem of coordinating their behavior on the basis of such understandings. Norms and conventions of this kind enable agents to account for institutional and social realities and to participate in social and cultural life on the basis of stabilized norms of interaction which have evolved in historical time.

3. The Developmental Significance of the Face as an Affordance for Interpersonal Attunement With Others

That infants are strongly attracted to faces is evident from the very earliest stages after birth. Johnson and Morton (1991) argue that newborns orient to faces as a preferred source of interpersonal contact with mothers and other caregivers on the basis of an initial intrinsic bias or value-setting that sets the parameters for further development to occur. The prone posture of newborns also works to facilitate this emphasis on the face as a source of interpersonal contact. On the basis of this initial value-bias, infants become progressively more attuned to stimuli—visual, auditory, kinetic—that originate from faces on the basis of their close up encounters with others in ways that set off a developmental cascade (Thelen and Smith 1994: 315). Initially, the newborn orients to an overall topology based on the low dimensional differentiation of the face into regions corresponding to the eyes and mouth. Gradually, as the process of attunement increases in the first few months, infants become more attuned to the face as a source of multimodal sensory information which affords interaction with others. Furthermore, the behavioral evidence suggests that infants are adaptively biased to attend to the array of stimulus information provided by faces as an affordance for interpersonal contact and social interaction in ways that is reinforced by the association of the face with values such as affect, nurturing, and care. From the outset, the infant actively orients to and explores the array of multimodal stimulus information afforded by others' faces. The visual, auditory, kinetic, and haptic information that originates from the other's face is correlated in real-time with the infant's own exploratory movements of his or her head, neck, eyes, mouth, and so on, as he or she actively explores and samples the stimulus array. In this way, infants quickly learn, for example, that facial movements and voices are correlated as sources of information about the interactive possibilities of another person.

Experimental evidence shows that infants are able to correctly match, for example, seeing a moving mouth with hearing a spoken voice. Moreover, they are aware when the two modalities do not match (Kuhl and Meltzoff 1982, 1984). This research suggests that infants relate what they see, hear, feel, and so on, in the faces of others to their experience of their own living, moving, and feeling bodies. The infant's capacity for inter-body attunement to and resonance with the articulatory gestures of a caregiver's face shows that our innate capacity for attuning to others is the very ground on which all forms of interpersonally coordinated face-to-face communication are established. Infants are able from the outset to match their experiences of movement perceived in others to their own experiences of their own kinetic bodies in ways that promote further exploration of and interaction with others. Trevarthen (1978: 130) has pointed out the kinetic basis of the infant's experience of the world and how, in particular, sensitivity to animate movements hones the infant's capacity "to accurately distinguish self-made change in sensory signals from effects caused from outside" (Trevarthen 1978: 130; see Thibault 2004a: 57–59 for discussion).

The strong attraction of newborns to the faces of caregivers is grounded in a mirror neuron system which provides the neurosocial basis for the development of intersubjective awareness and dialogic engagement between persons (Rizzolati and Arbib 1998). Infants are active participants in a dialogic matrix of animated inter-individual activity in the infant-caregiver dyad from the time of birth. The mirror neuron system provides the neurobiological basis for the developmental emergence of all forms of face-to-face interactive encounters and will be discussed in the following section.

4. The Mirror Neuron System and the Dialogical Matrix of Communicative Behavior: The Development of Intersubjectivity in Early Infant Semiosis

The dialogic matrix of face-to-face communication is grounded in a mirror neuron system which supports intersubjectivity and other-centered participation (Bråten 1992, 2007a, 2007b; Halliday 1975). The mirror neuron system fires when the participant perceives another's other-centered action or experience, leading to the pre-enacting or the co-enacting of what the observed participant is about to do such that the observer co-authors or co-participates in the observed action of the other. The mirror neuron system is therefore foundational for the emergence of dialogical capacities in humans. The human capacity for interpersonally coordinated dialogic exchange is naturalistically grounded. In their seminal paper *Language within our grasp*, Rizzolati and Arbib (1998) provided indirect evidence of a mirror neuron system in the human brain. The mirror neuron system provides the neurosocial support for intersubjective attunement, including alter-centric participant perception, and interpersonally coordinated interaction. The mirror neuron system is a direct and unreflective means of modeling others' actions from one's own perspective and of co-participating in a virtual way in the construction of the other's action. This provides new perspectives on infants' capacities for "interpersonal communion and altercentricity" (Bråten 2007a: 3). The existence of mirror neurons shows that the capacity for intersubjective awareness and communion—e.g., self-with-other resonance and altercentric mirroring of the observed other's actions—are founded on intrinsic biological capacities which are further shaped and specified in the course of development. Bråten provides a range of examples of how both infants and adults show overt manifestations, entailing pre-enacting or co-enacting movements, anticipant or concurrent mirroring or simulation of what the perceived patient or performer or partner is about to do or say, as if being a co-author of the newborn's attempt to imitate, or of the other's intake of the afforded food, or of the crossing of the obstacle, or of the conversation partner's statement (Bråten 2007b: 112).

Stein Bråten (2007a: 3) has linked the discovery of mirror neurons to the three layers of intersubjectivity that Bråten and Trevarthen have argued as emerging in the development of infants. *Table* 1 presents the three layers of intersubjectivity that are evidenced as a developmental emergence in the first two years or so of the infant's interactions with caregivers.

Table 1. Bråten's three layers of intersubjectivity (2007a: 3)

Layers of intersubjectivity	Age of infant	Characteristic semiotic, developmental achievements
Primary Intersubjectivity	First nine months	Movement based affective attunement with others, especially caregivers; negotiation of affect and feelings in reciprocal proto-dialogical contact based on inter-individual body dynamics, including smiles, touching, body movements, gaze, voice prosodics
Secondary Intersubjectivity	From around nine months to about two years	Members of dyad (caregiver—infant) jointly focus on objects of attention and emotion referencing; relationship building based on trust and companionship; object-oriented learning through other-centered participation
Tertiary Intersubjectivity	Around two to six years	Symbolic conversations with actual and virtual others, concomitant development of skills for naming objects and events, and leading to 2nd order mental simulation of the minds of others in dialogue; tracking of selves through narrative and autobiographical skills

Much of the neurobiological research on mirror neurons nevertheless continues to emphasize the brain at the expense of the living, moving, feeling body as the ground for all forms of communicative behavior. This emphasis therefore often fails to fully appreciate the body-centered basis of our moving as the means for moving others and being moved by others.

5. Communication as a Bridge Between Solipsistic Brains and Dynamic Bodies: Sex, Lies, and Semantics in the Layers of Face-to-Face Communicative Behavior

Freeman (1995: 89) defines communication as the "priming and enaction of cooperation between solipsistic brains". This gets at the essential point though it can be refined to include both cooperation and competition as forms of coevolution between organisms and their environments, including most significantly others of the same species. Thus, cognition evolves from the management of the organism's engagements with the physical world to the management of the organism's interactions—cooperative and competitive—with other organisms. The development of a central nervous system is a specialized internal subsystem that (1) links effector and sensory surfaces in rapid, energy efficient ways; and (2) the stimulus information from the external environment gets linked to internal patterns of nervous system activity in a circular self-modifying loop. The emergence of such capacities permits the animal to go beyond the self-regulation of the metabolic processes essential to life such that adaptation to the world, including others of the same species, takes place through cognitive and semiotic meta-control of the body's exploratory and performatory capacities (cf. Section 10.). In complex organisms, the nervous system on this basis develops capacities for the off-line exploration and simulation of virtual mental worlds based on digital semantic categories that are decoupled from immediate environmental stimuli and cues so as to facilitate anticipatory thinking and silent mental rehearsal of future actions that are contemplated, yet may not necessarily be undertaken.

Brains are solipsistic, as Freeman (1995: 3–4) puts it, in the sense that their self-organizing dynamics create networks of relations based on unique individual experiences. However, brains also need to communicate with other brains in order to calibrate their own dynamics with those of other brains in the interests of interpersonal coordination of behavior. In doing so, communicative behavior arises. Communicative behavior can involve stimulus information from all the sensory systems—audio, visual, olfactory, gustatory, haptic, kinesic. It also recruits intentionality in the form of the distance receptor systems for sights, sounds, and odors, the hippocampal system for localizing targets in space and sequencing events in time, the limbic system for generating actions and expectances by reafference, and the intentional structure of cortical neurophil that provide attractor basins for generalization and classification during multimodal convergence into the limbic system (Freeman 1995: 89).

Face-to-face communicative behavior can be seen as a complex layering of different kinds of interaction systems that have evolved to bring about different kinds of cooperation and calibration between solipsistic brains and dynamic bodies. A number of different interaction systems will be referred to below as being characteristic of the diverse ways to engage in various forms of face-toface communicative behavior (see also Freeman 1995: 89–92; Reed 1996: 92 for further discussion). The following interaction systems can therefore be differentiated:

1. *The sexual reproduction system*: this is the most basic form of interactive cooperation and, in vertebrates, including humans, often involves complex and intricate interactive-communicative displays and skills associated with courtship and copulation.

2. *The inter-individual coordination of behavior system*: animals that live in herds and packs (e.g., wolves) have developed elaborate systems of signals to indicate the intentions of individual members of the herd or pack in the interests of coordinating the behavior of the group. This means that the group can respond collectively and in a coordinated fashion to a specific situation, e.g., when seeking sexual partners involving competition between males, when responding to threats, or when coordinating an attack on prey.

3. *The nurture, caring, and grooming system*: many animals care for their young and behavioral suites have evolved to bring others into cooperative relations based on forms of mutually caring and nurturing activity (e.g., feeding, grooming, preening).

4. *The empathy and inter-individual affect-based attunement system*: the behavior and associated emotion states of one animal are capable of inducing a corresponding emotional state in another animal in ways that lead to direct interaction between them (De Waal 2007: 52). Such behavior is typically intentionally directed or addressed to a potential interactional partner. This layer of face-to-face communicative behavior perhaps most closely corresponds to the expressive systems identified by Darwin that have evolved for the expression of affect and "inner" emotional states (see below Section 9.).

5. *The Machiavellian interaction and social intelligence system*: primate social lives require that individuals keep track of the thinking and behavior of the individuals with whom the primate engages in social transactions. This explains why primate social life is characterized by the formation of political alliances, kinship relations, hierarchical relations of dominance, friendship, and so on. These transactions tend to be spread over diverse individuals, times, and places and call for the use of strategic thinking and intelligence that may involve calculation, deception, lies, guile, cunning, and the ability to imagine possible future outcomes of strategic behaviors. Thus, the drive for social power and the competition for mates fostered the development of so-called "Machiavellian" social intelligence and forms of interaction in social primates (Whiten and Byrne 1997; Gavrilets and Vose 2006).

6. *The intersubjective awareness system*: this is a further layer of cognitive-affective development that is probably confined to humans and some other primate species. This layer involves the emergence of selfhood and

a corresponding capacity of selves to differentiate the perspectives, feelings, and intentions of others from their own. Unlike system (4) above, this interaction is not symmetrical, but is based on the self's capacity for other-centered altruistic sympathy with and understanding of the distress of another. In the human case, this system undergoes a number of developmental stages that have been the focus of pioneering work by Trevarthen and Bråten (cf. Section 4., *table* 1).

7. *The semantic-representational system*: the semantic system of human language functions to digitally compress semantic classes of representations that are decoupled from specific perceptual, actional, and environmental cues (Ross 2007: 714). These representations allow the individual organism to express meanings about its environment, rather than its own internal states (Reed 1996: 92). The categories of the semantic system are then (relatively) decoupled from environmental stimulus information of the kind that is picked up by the organism's perceptual systems though it can also be used to represent specific perceptual and environmental cues. Such digital forms of representation are virtual systems of second order cultural constructs which afford inter-generational cultural accumulation and learning (Ross 2007: 715). They enable the robust tracking over space, time, and individuals of features that do not pertain to the domain of first-order experience, but to a virtual second-order cultural one affording off-line reasoning, planning, and mental simulation. As distinct from Darwin's expressive system, which serves to signal the animal's emotion states and intentions to others, the semantic system—sometimes called the content of symbolic communication—is buffered from changes in the organism's internal states and is therefore robust to such changes due to the fact that the patterns of neural activity associated with semantic classes of representations are not directly coupled to stimulus information. It is this fact of the robustness of the semantic class of representation which *incorrectly* leads to the idea of a fixed and transmissible information content that is attached to a signal form with an invariant structure. This in turn leads to the notion that something called "language" is constitutively separable from "paralanguage" and kinesics *qua* non-verbal behavior (cf. Section 6. below).

In all of the cases mentioned above, communication *qua* inter-organism cognition and interaction is based on the fact that the perception-action cycles of organisms that interact in the ways described above as various forms of faceto-face interaction are mediated by semiotic-informational processes that lift the organism "above" the requirements of metabolic regulation and adaptation.

Information in this sense is intentionally directed to the world (referentiality), but it is also closely tied to self-referentiality. The informational coupling between central nervous system activity and the world is interpreted in the self-referential perspective of the organism, based in the first instance on the *felt* (not cognized) self-coherence of the proto-self and the separation of the internal milieu of the proto-self from the external world beyond the skin (Damasio 1999: 133–167).

6. What is Communicated in Face-to-Face Communication?— Information Transfer vs. Management of Behavior

The idea of face-to-face communication also implies that something is communicated between the participating individuals. According to the dominant paradigm over the past few decades, communication involves the transfer of information from one participant to another. Moreover, the concept of information is itself fraught with difficulties which have nontrivial implications for the ways in which we theorize communicative processes. One problem with the idea of information is that it is seen as a stable commodity which is transferred from one participant to another in sequences of purely local dyads, e.g., A–B, C–D, E–F, etc. In their important study of animal communication, Owings and Morton (1998: 228) point out that this view fails to explain the effects of communication processes on larger time scales beyond the proximate here-now one, with its concomitant focus on the immediate effects on the participating individuals. Owings and Morton propose the alternative concept of *accomplishment* as a way of focusing on the effects of communicative processes on different time scales. They point out that whereas it is difficult to establish what is conveyed over time scales longer than the proximate one, it is on the other hand more feasible to ask what is accomplished over different time scales. As Owings and Morton (1998: 228) point out, some interval of time must pass before something is accomplished.

Owings and Morton show in their studies of animal communication that physical signal form itself is enormously variable at the same time that there are clearly identifiable types of signals that can be modulated in a wide variety of ways depending on the kinds of management effects that the signaling agent seeks to accomplish. Rather than communication involving a sender transferring information to a receiver, Owings and Morton show that communicative acts seek to change or manage the behavior of others in ways that are in the interests of the manager. These researchers therefore postulate the concept of *management* to refer to this function of communicative acts. *Management* refers to the ways in which the forms of signals are adjusted or modulated. Owings and Morton (1998: 83) report that adjustments or modulations of a particular signal or display are a means of "varying managerial effort independently of switching among categories of vocalizations". Adjustments to signal form vary independently of which signal form-types are used and can be deployed across multiple performances of the same signal form. The capacity to adjust signal forms in this way is a managerial strategy for adjusting behavior "to bring current circumstances into line with the manager's interests" (Owings and Morton 1998: 49). Management is therefore focused on what is accomplished. It is interactive and transformative of the situation.

The concept of management puts the explanatory focus on *behavior* rather than information transfer and accordingly helps to explain the remarkable variability of signal forms in both animal and human communication on this basis, *viz.*, natural selection favors those signal-forms which are most effective in changing the behavior of others in ways that benefit the manager (the signaler) (Owings and Morton 1998: 40). If they were not successful or effective in bringing about the effects desired by the signaler, then they would be de-selected and fall out of use. Importantly, motivational and emotional factors, rather than information-processing, lie at the core of this shift in emphasis. It is often assumed that information is contained ready-made in the signal form without taking into account that the signal form must be converted by processes in the central nervous system into meanings which are cognitively and semiotically salient for organisms (Freeman 1995: 105–106; Thibault 2004b: 109–118).

Assessment does not refer to the speaker's assessment of the informational content of a proposition (cf. Halliday [1985] 1994: 68–71 on *clause as exchange*), but to the adaptive behavioral adjustments that animals, including humans, make by selecting and directing their attention to those cues, including those provided by signal forms, for appraising individuals and situations (Owings and Morton 1998: 49). In the human case, assessment requires and is based upon a high degree of inherent reflexivity: the coordination of agents in face-to-face communicative activities is inherently reflexive, depending on the resolution of my understanding of your understanding of my understanding etc. of the situation.

It is widely assumed by many theorists (e.g., Trager 1958; Hauser, Chomsky, and Fitch 2002) who distinguish between *language* and *paralanguage* or *body language* and assign them to separate channels or codes that language in particular is a stable encoder of information which is transferred from sender to receiver. In this view, the sender encodes information in the linguistic signal and sends or transmits this information to the receiver. It is assumed that the information so transferred impacts on and affects the behavior of the receiver. However, this view fails to account for the active and enactive character of assessment (Owings and Morton 1998: 55). Assessment is an active process of adjusting behavior to fit present circumstances. The assessor is actively engaged in a self-interested process of hunting for and extracting information that will aid in this process of assessment. Managers accordingly seek to influence the behavior of assessors by "affecting the conclusions they reach in assessment" (Owing and Morton 1998: 55). Changes or adjustments in the form of the signal can therefore be used by managers to regulate or change the assessor's behavior in order to bring it into line with the manager's interests. Pragmatically, modulations of the signal form can be used to achieve the interactive goals or purposes that serve the interests of the manager. Assessors are rewarded for responding as expected just as managers are rewarded for getting what they were seeking. The rewards for attending to signaling behavior are therefore mutual and serve to bring about value oriented courses of action (e.g., protection, finding food, fleeing a predator, finding a mate).

Now, in the literature on the separation of language and paralanguage (e.g., Trager 1958; Austin 1965; Poyatos 1993) it is often assumed that language forms are logically invariant and segmental whereas paralanguage is variable and suprasegmental. Paralanguage may indicate the speaker's internal emotional or physiological states. Paralanguage and kinesic elements may also "color" segmental linguistic units such as phonemes and combinations of phonemes (Poyatos 1993: 129). In this view, language is established as a synchronic system of stable or (relatively) invariant forms that realize or express their meanings. The term *paralanguage* refers to a range of phenomena which are seen to combine with or accompany language. These include the many ways in which something is said (*how it is said*) as distinct from the linguistic content (*what is said*) and how people move their bodies in conjunction with the linguistic messages they utter. Paralanguage thus serves to qualify and modify the linguistic message in ways that may support or contrast with the overt linguistic message. Paralanguage is variable and unstable and is extrinsic to the definition of language, according to this definition. Thus, paralinguistic behaviors such as "drawl", "sing song", and so on, are variables that may accompany and contextualize an invariant and stable core linguistic form in various ways. This view rests on the fatally flawed assumption that paralanguage "accompanies" or "combines with" language to qualify it (cf. Section 7. below). Moreover, the language component serves to convey or transmit a stable quantum of information from a sender to a receiver. At this point, the alternative view that "languaging" behavior *qua* process—not language *qua* determinate thing—is inseparable from body dynamics comes into clear view. In the alternative view, it is an intrinsic feature of language behavior that signal forms are adjusted or modulated in ways that serve managerial ends in the way defined by Owings and Morton. Moreover, there is an entire repertoire of ways in which signal forms may be modulated. Owings and Morton (1998: 83) propose the following examples of adjustments to vocal signals: adjustments in sound frequency, in sound clarity or other tonal qualities, inflection patterns, amplitude, duration, and in complexly patterned combinations of these.

Owings and Morton cite many instances of animal signaling, e.g., the prairie dog switching from *barking* to *yipping* and the *zit* calls of eastern kingbirds to show that signaling can vary according to the type of signal and that different signal types can also be modified by the phenomena referred to above. Thus, eastern king birds modulate the frequency of their quavering across different kinds of vocal calls—e.g., *zits* and *t-zee* calls—in ways that suggest this pervasive variation is due to "managerial activity" across diverse time frames and serve to regulate accomplishments such as feeding and reproduction (Owings and Morton 1998: 84–85). The observations of these authors are also supported by the research of Slagsvold (1977) on the song activity of twenty species of birds in forested areas of southern Norway. Slagsvold showed that bird calls are varied and modulated in relation to accomplishments and factors on various time frames, including breeding and egg-laying and environmental conditions such as temperature, snow-melt, and environmental phenophases.

Analogously, Halliday ([1998] 2003: 21) shows how infants learn after the first year to separate the articulatory and prosodic aspects of phonation such that different articulations—typically rapid postures and movements of tongue, lips, soft palate, larynx—can be combined with different prosodies (e.g., timbre, voice quality, melody, rhythm) so that the same articulatory segment can take on different tones or voice qualities. In Halliday's theory, interpersonal meanings tend to be enacted by prosodies which operate on the segment as a whole, e.g., a particular pitch contour or voice quality spreads across and modifies an entire segment rather than being confined to its individual constituents. Interpersonal meaning in this account is enacted when one unit modifies or deforms the shape of a particular unit for interactive-evaluative purposes (McGregor 1997: 210).

Darwin has described exactly the same phenomenon in his classic study, *The Expression of the Emotions in Man and Animals* (1872). For example, he describes in great detail two antithetical body postures deployed by dogs to display anger and affection, respectively (Darwin [1872] 1998: 55–56). Darwin's description of these two antithetical modes whereby the dog modulates the shape of its whole body is clearly interactional, rather than serving in a purely individual-centered way as the outward expression of an inner emotional state of the organism. There is a clear perception of the other—dog or master—as an addressee to whom the display is directed. The principle of antithesis refers to the ways in which contrasting deformations or modulations of the animal's body display opposite feelings such as anger and affection *qua* interactive stances that are adopted with respect to the dog's addressee. The meaning of the two poles suggests a vague analogue to the distinction between negative and positive polarity in the mood component of the clause (Halliday 1994: 88–89). The negative pole (anger) proscribes amicable contact and readies the animal for fight and/or flight from possible threat or danger. The positive pole (affection) prescribes close contact and the active seeking of a relationship of care and nurture with the addressee.

Pfaff (2006: 77–78) reformulates the traditional division of the arousal systems into the sympathetic and parasympathetic systems. Alternatively, he argues that arousal states, as in emotionally laden behaviors such as those described by Darwin, are based on two key factors: (1) teamwork or coordination between autonomic, cortical, and behavioral systems (e.g., cardiovascular and respiratory systems); and (2) a high degree of sensitivity on the part of the organism and hence a high information content on account of the enhanced sensitivity to environmental states (e.g., the appearance of threat) that the arousal of the systems mentioned in (1) entails in the face of uncertainty and unpredictability. Uncertainty and unpredictability cause autonomic arousal and place the animal in a state of readiness to deal with the new situation. Dogs, as Darwin's description illustrates, have a high degree of informational sensitivity to others and to the possible responses they require from them.

Canine display of anger and affection, as described by Darwin, is the enactment of an interactive stance. It depends at least implicitly on the ways in which the dog perceives others, rather than on the basis of explicit representations. Specifically, it depends on an inter-individual principle of affective linkage which is based on the addresser's implicit understanding of the addressee's capacity to respond to the dynamical movements of the addresser in ways which activate in the addressee corresponding dynamical body states and feelings that are connected to the subjective experience of the feeling body by the proto-self (Damasio 1999: 133–167; cf. Section 9. below). It is a capacity which is much more basic than the abstract and cerebral notion that the addressee must map the addresser's behavioral state onto the addressee's own representations. This capacity for affective linkage as described here lays the foundation for more developed layers of empathy to develop in social animals such as primates. The other is thus recognized as the source of body feelings and related emotion displays that support and give rise to empathy-based co-affiliation and co-action. At still higher levels approximating the human capacity for dialogue, these prior capacities of empathy pave the way for the capacity to view things from the perspective of the other.

At any rate, dogs, in interaction with both other dogs and humans, demonstrate a capacity for mimicry and emotion transfer which in some respects resembles the earliest form of intersubjective communion between mother and human infant (see de Waal 2007: 52–54, on the notion of *animal empathy*). As de Waal shows, interactive displays of the kind discussed by Darwin are based on the need to coordinate action and movement in inter-individual ways which require that the animal has the capacity to be attuned to and responsive to the behavioral and affective states of others of the same species. De Waal uses the term *emotional contagion* (2007: 52) to refer to the ways in which one animal's emotional state can affect that of another. However, de Waal also recognizes that more is involved than one animal causally influencing another through such displays. Modulations of body shape and movement are directly interactive and show features of addressivity—the behavior is actively directed at another, it seeks and anticipates a response, and very often it gets it.

In the accounts cited above, the modulation or reshaping of a given unit by another unit (e.g., prosodic units modifying articulatory ones) shows the principle of management/assessment at work. Halliday (2003: 219) observes that interpersonal prosodies occur on a more extended time frame with respect to the constituents that express the separate parts of a referential structure. They extend over and modify entire units of variable duration. Essentially, the time frame of prosodies, which are spread over an entire unit—e.g., the interrogative mood of the clause *what's the time?* to signal its interactive status as a question—, serves to maintain, over that time frame, a behavioral state of the individual with respect to some aspect of the environment with which the individual is interacting. Prosodies are dynamic responses to and adjustments to the environment of the speaker. They are a mode of regulation which is based on a controlled or modulated transformation from one bodily state to another over a given time frame. Articulation, on the other hand, is a mode of regulation based on the dynamical control of the vocal tract postures required to produce different sounds. Reed (1996: 85) observes that "movements are nested within postures in the sense that a movement involves not only a change of state from one posture to another but always the maintenance of some postural orientation as well" (1996: 85).

Language behavior is the result of the global order produced by many diverse local interacting components that are spread across brain, body, and environment. The observable bodily dynamics of articulation and prosodies in vocal tract gestures, along with the neural processes that coordinate vocal tract activity, and relevant environmental factors (e.g., addressing someone in an angry tone to show disapproval of his/her behavior) constitute a coupled system in the sense that some parameters of each system involved are functions of state variables of the other systems involved. The observed vocal tract behavior is not, then, under the control of a central processor in the central nervous system which sends commands or issues instructions to the body to behave in a certain way. Instead, vocal tract behavior is the result of the mutual influence and modulation of neural, bodily, and environmental/situational factors that interact on and are distributed over diverse time scales.

The separation of language and paralanguage takes it as axiomatic that language is a system that realizes well-defined input-output functions by processes of encoding and decoding meanings. Such a view is especially suited to a focus on the referential-representational function of language as being encoded in well-defined constituents. Absent in such an account is a richly temporal and dynamical focus on the many non-representational dimensions of language which are not readily describable in terms of code-like input-output devices. Moreover, once we shift the focus to the ways in which *languaging activity* is distributed in complex ways between brain, body, and world, then the temporal aspects of the languaging activity will be seen to be more central. In the perspective of dynamic systems theory (Thelen and Smith 1994), brain, body, and world are coupled systems. Coupled systems mutually perturb each other's dynamics on many different time scales of the processes involved. Systems so coupled mutually constrain and influence each other and give rise to the semiotic developmental trajectories of agents. An individual's developmental trajectory is a form of historical emergence because it entails the accumulation of meanings along the entire trajectory, rather than "in" the agent per se at any given moment in time.

Rather than the transference of coded information, which amounts to an externalist perspective on the relevant system of relations (minimally, the interactants, their viewpoints, the "thing" they interact about, the system of interpretance that mediates and makes possible the interaction), management reflects the agent's efforts to acquire information about the assessor (the addressee) by evoking a behavioral response on the part of the assessor. The amount of uncertainty that the manager has to deal with tends to increase as the manager attempts to get more information about the environment, including most importantly information about the assessor. This is so because the search for information is an active and exploratory one (Gibson 1966; Gibson and Pick 2000). In seeking information through their own exploratory and performatory activity, agents impact on their worlds in novel ways that generate more uncertainty. Permutations, modulations, or variations of signal form over sequences of behavior mean that the degrees of freedom available to the signaling agent are not fixed, but revisable over time. How will the assessor react? There can be no total certainty about this. The modulation and variation of signal form therefore amounts to a kind of irregularity which gives rise to uncertainty for any agent needing to relate to the signal form as meaningful or environmentally salient. Modulation and variation of signal form are a kind of behavioral plasticity. If language really did consist of sequences of regular, invariant forms, there would be no uncertainty, no change, no dynamism, and no unpredictability. Communication would not surprise us, and we would quickly fail to be aroused. Indeed, communication would be decidedly dull and ineffective.

According to one of the central tenets of Shannon's (1948) theory of information, a high level of information is associated with these factors of uncertainty, change, dynamism, and unpredictability. The dynamic modulation of signal form is high on information and therefore has more potential of arousing stimulating behavioral responses. Thus, affect charged modulation of signal form and interpersonal prosodies, as described by Owings and Morton,

Halliday, and Darwin, produces irregular, unpredictable, and surprising patterns, rather than code-like regularities. The modulation of signal form can arouse enthusiasm, fear, joy, surprise, anxiety, and so on, depending on the combinations of stimuli involved in concert with situational and other factors. They are still patterns, but they are not totally predictable or regular ones. Modulations of signal form are deformations of an array of stimulus information that serve to respond to salient environmental changes and to move others—assessors, addressees—to act. For this reason alone, it is important to stress that modulation of signal forms is intrinsic to the dynamics of languaging behavior and cannot be separated from language as a separate, yet combinable paralanguage (see Section 7.).

7. Some Contrasting Ways of Talking About Language and Body Language

The term *body language* perhaps paradoxically is associated with the separation of *language* from what has been called *paralanguage* (Hill 1955: 257–258, 1958: 408–409; Trager 1958; Poyatos 1993) and *kinesics* (Birdwhistell 1952, 1961). Hill is credited by Trager as the one who first coined the term *paralanguage*. Hill has summarized this position as follows:

> A part of communicative activity which is outside the area of microlinguistics, but is not on the straight line which leads from sentence to style, is what can be called para-linguistics. The chief investigator here has been Henry Lee Smith and, for a second part of the field, Ray Birdwhistell. Neither has carried his work as far as might be wished, but each has at least demonstrated that there is an intimate relationship between the expressive features, which accompany speech, and speech itself, and that these expressive features pattern in a way similar to linguistic patterns and are learned, rather than innate (Hill 1958: 408; see also Hill 1955: 257).

Expressive features and linguistic patterns are opposed to each other along the same lines that Hill, in the paragraphs preceding the passage cited above, opposes stylistics and linguistics. Stylistics, Hill writes, seeks to explain "as much as possible of linguistic variation" (1958: 403) above or beyond the levels covered by microlinguistics (phoneme to sentence). In this view, variation is extrinsic to the definition of microlinguistic patterns and is the province of stylistics, rather than linguistics proper. Expressive paralinguistic features are likewise opposed to core speech patterns in the above quotation. In both cases, the opposition illustrates a divide between stable invariant or core properties of language, defined as a three-level system based on sound, form, and sense (Trager 1958), and extending from phoneme to sentence. Stylistics and paralinguistics, on this definition, pertain to language-as-interaction and the different forms of organization that are not captured by microlinguistic categories.

This separation is based on the notion that *language* is separable from *para-language* and *kinesics* and that it is therefore definable on the basis of intrinsic criteria which distinguish it from the latter. One consequence of this separation is that language itself was seen in terms of abstracta which were detached from bodies, brains, and the world. This separation often went hand-in-hand with the idea that language was a symbolic system for the encoding/decoding and transmission of mental contents from one mind to another whereas body language was primarily seen as expressive and emotional. The dominant traditions in 20th century linguistics, under the influence of Saussure's methodological separation of *langue* and *parole*, have focused their attention on form-based abstractions and their regularities. Language was cognitive and referential; body language was expressive and interpersonal in this view. This contrast is summarized in *table* 2:

Table 2.   Some contrasting ways of thinking about body language and language

Body language	Language
body	mind
expressive	communicative
behavior	cognition
feeling, affect	concepts, cognition
natural	conventional, normative
ephemeral	stable
analogue	digital
style	code
freedom	constraint

The contrasting ways of thinking about body language and language proposed in *table* 2 suggest, in actual fact, the inherent vagueness of the many degrees of freedom of the body's interactive possibilities. Terms such as *body language* and *language* seek to isolate specific phenomena and to treat them as sharply defined classes even though they may be said to interact with and overlap each other. Developmentally, biological systems move from a relatively vague embodiment to an increasingly more specified and definite one (Salthe 1993; Thibault 2004a, b). The problem faced by analysts of embodied face-to-face interaction is that bodies and their interactive potential are always to some degree inherently vague. The problem arises when analysts, guided by the notion that language is a well-defined code, seek to specify well-defined linguistic units such as phonemes in contrast, for example, to the vague or ill-defined paralinguistic *vocal qualifiers* first described by Trager (1958); see also Austin (1965). Here is Austin on this distinction:

> A dilemma arises when features paralinguistic in origin result in permissible phonetic and phonemic strings. *Yes* said with drawl is *yeah* /ỹ é ħ/ and with clipping *yep* /ỹ é p̌/. There is also *nope* /n ó w p/. These forms may as often end in [ʔ] as in [p⁺] but the final stop is *never aspirated*. The whole problem of "free variation" must thus be considered in the light of paralinguistic communication. *Help!* with [p‘] is clipped or shortened (*The situation is desperate!*).
>
>   Vocal qualifiers are employed either to reinforce the linguistic message or to contradict it. For the affect of drawl Smith has the example of

"Yĕah, he's a real nice gŭy" where the paralinguistic signal contradicts the linguistic one. ♪ *Good-bye, now* ♪, with sing-song, obviously tries to mitigate the farewell, a signal to have it cancelled or one for future meetings. *I really should be getting ŏn* with over-slow tempo asks for an invitation to stay. *And now that that's settled, let's get on tŏ . . .* with over-fasttempo says *let's forget it* (Austin 1965: 33).

Austin sees paralinguistic vocal qualifiers as either reinforcing or contradicting a coded linguistic message. Meaning is thus created by combining two distinct systems, e.g., the paralinguistic "affect of drawl" combines with the linguistic message *Yeah, he's a real nice guy* to contradict it. There is, then, equivocation or ambiguity of meaning depending on the way in which paralinguistic and linguistic elements are combined. The presumed fact of their separation into two distinct paralinguistic and linguistic systems and their combination and recombination is based on the notion that the analyst can definitely describe real entities such as phonemes that are separable from paralinguistic features such as drawl, sing-song, and jerky. What is correspondingly lost sight of is that the physical form of the signal is not invariant, but can be varied and modulated in very many ways which enable signalers to achieve particular behavioral effects. Moreover, these variations and modulations are not extrinsic to the form of the signal as some external force that impinges on it, but are constitutive of its micro-temporal dynamics.

The separation of linguistic and paralinguistic items is based on the view that language consists of strings of formal properties which we equate with verbal patterns that can be described and annotated on the basis of script-like notations (e.g., phonetic or alphabetic script) (see Linell 2005; Harris 2001). Para-linguistic elements are aspects of body dynamics from which verbal patterns are abstracted and which elude their reduction to script-like regularities. In this view, *language* is taken to be strings of physical invariants—e.g., phonemes—to which meanings are attached in a process of encoding. Paralanguage, in this view refers, to more primitive body dynamics which are not the same as the words actually spoken. In the process, our definition of language itself is reduced and impoverished. First, an ungrounded linguistic utterance such as Austin's example *Yeah, he's a real nice guy* (see above) is combined with a paralinguistic item so that the meaning of the utterance can be interpreted by agents. This view fails to see that language is always already grounded by the ways in which it is integrated to cognitive, affective, and bodily dynamics of real-time interaction. Language is not reducible to formal strings and text-like entities that are separable from bodies. Instead, language is fully integrated with body activity and cannot be separated from it except by an artificial process of abstraction. This, then, poses the problem as to how formal strings are linked to meanings or are made meaningful for an agent, i.e., the symbol grounding problem (Harnad 1990) posited by computationalists in trying to discover how formal strings of symbols connect to the world. Usually, this is solved by postulating a central processing unit in the brain-mind of the individual which treats sequences of forms as inputs to which meanings are assigned by an encoding/ decoding process.

It is therefore problematic, to say the least, to postulate an a priori distinction between the verbal and non-verbal aspects of face-to-face communicative behavior. Linguistics has tried to isolate the verbal part of human behavior from the rest of communicative behavior and then attempt to construct a science of language—*viz.*, linguistics—on the basis of this artificial separation. One of the earliest theorists of paralanguage, George L. Trager (1958: 2), argued that language was "accompanied by other communication systems, one of motion—kinesics, and one of extra-linguistic noises—vocalizations" (1958: 2). On this basis, Trager argued that communication "was divided into language, vocalization, and kinesics".

However, there is compelling neurobiological and developmental evidence which suggests that a more integrative approach is required. Take, for instance, the relationship between speech and gesture. Semiotic systems such as gesture, which is integrated with speaking and therefore not dissociated from it, is controlled by meanings in Broca's area that also control the activity of speaking (McNeill 2005: chapter 8). Iverson and Thelen (1999) also produce developmental evidence for a coupled speech-gesture system. They describe the ontogeny of coupled oral and limb movements in terms of four stages:

> (1) *initial linkages*: hand and mouth movements are loosely coupled from birth; (2) *emerging control*: increasing adaptive use of hands and mouth, especially marked by rhythmical, sometimes coordinated, activities in both manual and vocal modalities; (3) *flexible couplings*: emergence of coupled, but not synchronous gesture and speech; (4) *synchronous coupling*: more adult-like, precisely-timed coupling of gesture and speech (Iverson and Thelen 1999: 29).

This developmental trajectory typically unfolds as follows. *Initial linkages* are seen in newborns in the form of mutual spontaneous hand-mouth coordination. *Emerging control* is characterized by rhythmical vocal and manual babbling in which babbling and rhythmical hand-arm movements are mutually entrained. *Flexible coupling* is seen in the use of gestures prior to words to indicate or anticipate phenomena. The use of gesture at this stage is predictive of but only weakly entrained by words. An 11 month old infant observed by the author since birth manifested the first appearance of this stage when the father was pointing out ducks to her during a walk by a lake in their neighborhood. The infant then began systematically using pointing to indicate a wide variety of phenomena (ducks, aeroplanes, and so on) which would sometimes co-occur with vocalizations but were not tightly synchronized with them. *Synchronous coupling* starts to occur from 14 to 18 months and is characterized by meaningful synchronous couplings of word and gesture in ways that indicate that gesture and language are under the control of the same brain area (see above).

In the same infant mentioned above, I have observed during the developmental period in question—14 to 18 months—the spontaneous emergence of synchronized speech-gesture complexes such as the following:

- Infant looks at father + says "hat" + lightly taps her head with right hand to indicate where her hat should go. This gesture + speech complex typically occurs when the infant wants to put her hat on prior to going outdoors.

- Infant approaches father, saying "hand" and raising and extending her hand to take father's hand in hers. This gesture + speech complex typically occurs when she wants to hold hands with her father and go for a walk together outside.

In both these cases, which are regular occurrences in the interactions between father and child in the period in question, along with others, hand-arm gesture and speech are tightly synchronized components of a single whole-body sense-making activity. The higher control level in this case is probably at this stage semantic in a rudimentary way: synchronized hand-arm gestures and vocal tract gestures are both under the control of the same higher-order constraint in the brain. It therefore makes little sense to say they are two separate modalities that are "combined". Rather, as MacNeill (2005) has shown, they are functioning components of the same overall phenomenon, which also provides compelling evidence for the sensorimotor basis of thought (Iverson and Thelen 1999: 36). Iverson and Thelen use dynamics to explain that gestures and speech are controlled by a common semantics, are tightly synchronized by temporal coupling, and have a common integrative basis in cognition and perception. It makes little or no sense to talk of "combining" gesture and speech, because this kind of explanation is externalist and based on linear causality. Thus, one kind of action is "combined" with another, as seen from the point of view of an external observer who is independent of the perspectives of those for whom the synchronized body movements in question are signs of something.

The internalist view, in contrast, requires that we take into account the viewpoints of the agents involved (i.e., infant, father) for whom the body movement is meaningful. Something can only be a sign from the internalist viewpoint of someone. The concept of *circular causality*, on the other hand, is a better prospect for developing an integrated explanation which involves hierarchical interactions of very large numbers of semi-autonomous components, including neurons, intentions, body parts, and environmental features, which give rise to the emergence of macroscopic populations of dynamical patterns on many scalar levels (e.g., neural, bodily, environmental) that shape and modulate the whole-body sense-making of individuals-in-interaction.

To separate *gesture* from *speech* as two distinct "modalities" or "channels" of communication fails to show that the self-organizing dynamics of the whole system of components in interaction cannot be causally/explanatorily broken down into isolated constituents. A new kind of explanation based on complex nonlinear interactions across different levels and timescales is required (cf. Section 2. above). In the examples above from my own observations of an infant, we could say that her actions are shaped by the circular relationships on many levels and timescales of the self, current awareness, past states, the body, intentions, the cultural world, and the physical environment. The brain, as Freeman (1995) points out, anticipates future possibilities, which the infant's whole-body sense-making (see examples above) seeks to bring into actuality in ways that support the efforts of the self to shape its own future. Self-organizing brain and behavioral dynamics are globally orchestrated as a globally internal state variable of neuronal dynamics that modulates an action trajectory of the entire whole body towards the achievement of a particular value. The resulting action trajectory is in the perspective of the self, which Freeman describes as emerging in the dynamics of the limbic system. The global organization of brain and body dynamics occurs on the basis of the infant's knowledge of her current environment organized in terms of how a desired value (e.g., *put her hat on* or *go for a walk outside with daddy*) can be achieved by harnessing the interactive potential of her body *qua* dialogically intermediary interaction with her father.

Bonobos such as Kanzi at the Great Ape Trust, Iowa also show the co-articulation of vocalization and gesture (Segerdahl, Fields, and Savage-Rumbaugh 2005: 131, 186–187; see Tomasello 2006 for a contrasting view). In the example shown in *figure* 1 below, Kanzi holds a point gesture to show that he wants to go to the room on the other side of the window that he points to. During the act of pointing, he also vocalizes at one stage. The pointing gesture + vocalization, along with gaze vector, seem to have a clear function of inducing the human researcher/interactional partner to open the door. They are interrelated and synthesized as components of a single overall meaning complex which signals something like "open the door; I want to go there". It is Kanzi's whole body which is making meaning here, not his finger *per se*.

Seen from the perspective of Kanzi's use of vocalization + gesture, we see evidence for the synthesis of vocal and manual gestures under the control of meaning in hominid evolution. The meaning effect which is obtained is not the result of simply "adding" one resource to the other. The relationship between the two resources is not an additive one. Rather, they are functional components in a single overall meaning system. The meaning potential resulting from the integration of gesture, gaze, body orientation, and vocalization in the interaction between Kanzi and the human researcher cannot be explained in terms of the meaning of the separate components *qua* semiotic modalities. Each of these resources multiplies the meaning potential of the others so as to create a very large multi-dimensional space of semiotic possibilities (Lemke 1998: 91–96). A given episode, such as the one shown in *figure* 1, is a narrowing down, a honing of the possibilities of that space in ways that fit the purposes and understandings of the participants in the particular situation from their respective points of view. The basic principle at work is the co-contextualization of somatic and extra-somatic resources so that the meaning of any given resource (e.g., pointing) is made more definite or specified by the contextual redundancies it shares with other resources (e.g., vocalization + gaze vector + point + window on other side of room, etc.) in this particular *dialogical array*— see Hodges (2007) for this term—consisting of a fluctuating behavioral flow that is fundamentally based on degrees of irregularity and unpredictability instead of the regularity and predictability of the code model of communication. The coupling of point, vocalization, gaze, and so on, is based on timing. Timing in living systems means irregularity and uncertainty in ways which increase the level of information in the system.

In this way, a local consistency obtains relative to the viewpoints of the agents enmeshed in this world of potential signs such that the meanings

	JUN 24 1999 3:08:05 PM	JUN 24 1999 3:08:07 PM	JUN 24 1999 3:08:11 PM
J	 *Think we can do some more work? Do you want to do some more work on your keyboard?*	 Jared tracks K's arm movement and begins to lean towards lexigram indicated by K.	 *Go where?* Looks at lexigram *Where do you want to go, Kanzi?*
K	Facing Jared, begins to avert gaze on "work"	Points to lexigram	

	JUN 24 1999 3:08:12 PM	JUN 24 1999 3:08:13 PM	JUN 24 1999 3:08:16 PM
J	 Maintains same posture	 *You want to go in there?*	 *I can't let you in there right now. We can ask Liz when she comes back*
K	Points to window	Retracts point and begins to turn towards J	Shifts to new posture on "back"; vocalizes: V

Figure 1. Kanzi's point gesture + vocalization

made with one resource from one sign system are seen to support or be consistent with other resources from other sign systems. By the same token, different semiotic resource systems do not necessarily make the same meaning in different ways. For example, the lexicogrammar and semantics of natural languages are especially good at organizing the phenomena of our experience into discrete classes or categories. The semantics of natural languages typologizes the world into digital categories. It has evolved above all to perform this function. Gesture, on the other hand, is a topological-continuous (analogic) mode that operates in a visual-spatial dimension, unlike spoken language, which depends on the pick up of acoustic information about the speaker's vocal tract activity.

The emphasis on first-order languaging as micro-temporal behavioral dynamics allows us to re-focus attention on language activity ("languaging") as being an integrated, co-orchestrated, and co-constructed whole bodily movement of individuals-in-interaction, rather than the products of single individuals or their minds. The micro-temporal bodily dynamics of first-order languaging is the missing link in accounts of language which focus on second-order language patterns (e.g., regularities and rules of grammar, semantics, and discourse). This level is itself informational and cognitive (Bottineau 2003). Typically, it is seen as the coding of the second-order units referred to above (e.g., Halliday 1994; Langacker 1987). Micro-temporal bodily dynamics is information on smaller, faster timescales that may escape normal levels of awareness. First-order languaging is less amenable to being analytically segmented into text-like units (verbal patterns) and their relations in text-like entities. Rather, it is integrated behavior of the organism that is selected for by the affordances of the other embodied agents with whom one interacts.

First-order languaging is both contextually constrained by grammar and contextually integrated to it. It is *not* the encoding of grammar by bodily expression. Individuals lock into and interact in micro-time with the embodied resources of others as cognitive resources for getting things done in concert with other aspects of their shared cultural environments. Moreover, this is not achievable by a single mode (e.g., vocal tract gestural activity) in isolation, but is constituted by the co-orchestration in micro-time of constellations of bodily and neural resources that are distributed across all of the individuals-in-interaction. This is always achieved in concert with other features of their jointly constituted environment (e.g., relevant tools, artifacts, technologies, physical settings, and so on). The individual does not therefore "acquire" language as something pre-packaged which is already "out there" and which is extracted from the environment (e.g., others). Individuals interact with other individuals in ways that harness and synchronize the micro-temporal dynamics of their jointly enacted neural-bodily activity in ways that change perception, cognition, affect, and action.

8. Reinstating the Behavioral Dimension

An earlier generation of students of body language squarely put the emphasis on *behavior* in contrast to the processing of text-like symbolic forms that has characterized most of the work in both language processing and the cognitive sciences until the more recent rise since the early 1990s of theories of embodied-embedded cognition, which have developed alternatives to the computational model of symbolic processing (Wheeler 2005). The pioneering work of Birdwhistell, Scheflen, and others in the 1950s and 1960s developed sophisticated analyses of the minutiae of real-time face-to-face interaction. For example, Scheflen claimed that

> [. . .] changes in the position, orientation and relations of persons are called behaviors. These behaviors define and are defined by territories. *The study of human territoriality is the study of human behavior* (Scheflen and Ashcraft 1976: 4; authors' emphasis).

Scheflen located the study of behavior in an ecological context in which living persons move around, take up positions, and orient to each other in the forms of bounded space which he defined as a territory. Persons establish, define, move in, and use territories by virtue of the kinds of bodily interactions that they engage in. Furthermore, for Scheflen, a territory is not a pre-given entity, but a dynamic and time-bound field of relations that is embedded in and defined by larger-scale territorial fields. A territorial field, Scheflen argues, is "a more extensive and often more lasting field of relations of movement and other behavior" (1976: 5).

Scheflen was interested in what people actually do in small-group interactions such as psychotherapy transactions (Scheflen 1973). To analyze psychotherapy transactions, Scheflen, who was trained as a medical doctor, was influenced by the first attempts in the mid 1950s to produce film recordings of such transactions. He gradually came to see, under the influence of general systems theory, the necessity of dispensing with encoding-decoding and stimulus-response models that focused on individual aspects of behavior. This led to an approach that took the interpersonal and inter-individual dimensions of behavior to be fundamental. Scheflen (1973: 6) referred to this approach as the *behavioral systems approach*. According to this approach, behavior is not defined on the basis of individual organisms but instead on the basis of the patterned relations of inter-individual behavior that takes place between people and which constitutes communication. With remarkable foresight, Scheflen argued:

> If we were to study communication, then, we had to retrace our steps from the high-level inferences of the psychological and social sciences and get back to the study of behavior itself. We had to examine action, describe it, analyze its form, and try to define meaning behaviourally (Scheflen 1973: 7).

Moreover, this attention to behavior and its fine-grained analysis on the basis of filmed episodes of real-time interaction was not a return to the behaviorist and neobehaviorist tenets which sought to reveal neurophysiological and cognitive processes. Scheflen was interested in the study of behavior and its structure "in its own right" as a technique for revealing how communicative behavior becomes meaningful (Scheflen 1973: 7).

To this end, Scheflen, Birdwhistell, Bateson, and others also drew on the methods developed by Sapir, Bloomfield, Pike, and Harris in structural linguistics. They pioneered techniques of behavioral analysis that sought to synthesize behavioral episodes in order to reveal behavioral integrations at levels larger than the sentence. In this way, they attempted to understand how different behaviors were integrated in the overall stream of communicative activity. Scheflen also highlighted the significance of technology for the recording and transcribing of the complex, time-bound communicative events in the behavioral systems view:

> To study such complexity, we needed a technology. We cannot examine multiple modalities of behavior in detail at a single observation. Armed with eyes, ears, and a notebook, the observer has his hands full merely to hear the speech and to note the gross actions of one participant. The sound motion picture and, more recently, the video tape provided the needed technological means for thorough observations. Given a film record we can go over again and again the events of a transaction, systematically observing one, then another, behavioral modality and testing their various relations until we have described the synthesis of elements in the over-all picture (Scheflen 1973: 8).

In many respects, the study of *body language* and *language* have gone their separate ways since the pioneering work of Birdwhistell, Scheflen, and others in the 1950s and 1960s. Body language early came to be seen as the domain of inquiry of a separate and parallel study of paralanguage (e.g., Birdwhistell). Consequently, the study of language was linked more and more to the study of mind and cognition at the same time that the bodily dimensions of interaction were not seen as intrinsic to the definition of human intelligence. Language was modeled in terms of disembodied symbol strings that could be defined and explained independently of human agents, their perspectives and their bodily activity. Moreover, the symbolic aspect of language in this perspective was seen and analyzed largely in terms of a hierarchy of constituents, seen by many as the defining characteristic of the grammar of natural languages. The interpersonal and prosodic aspects of language *qua* bodily activity were ignored or down-played in favor of a partial view of language as essentially consisting of abstract lexicogrammatical forms.

9. Interpersonal Communicative Behavior, Norms, and Affect

Norms are everywhere in human interaction. People must signal that they understand and orient to norms concerning how to create and maintain relationships with each other and how to create and maintain a self. Co-constructed micro-temporal body dynamics (first order languaging) is more fundamental than words in signaling and organizing the moral order of a social group. These body-based events are emergent patterns of bottom-up activity that nevertheless enable individuals to engage with recurrent patterns and to connect their activity to higher-scalar forms of social organization beyond the body.

It is in this sense that people execute skillful performance in order to display how they fit in with the moral order (Goffman 1963).

Norms are tied up with values and the social judgments and accounts agents make about themselves and others. Heterarchies of fluctuating and sometimes competing value-systems come to the fore even in the same situation and regulate the actions of individuals. Co-constructed body dynamics of first-order languaging, as we saw above, is not reducible to body movements *qua* events, but is constrained and interpretable in many different ways under different normative and contextual descriptions of intentional actions. It is on this basis that affect-charged interactional routines arise. For instance, the examples of vocalizations coupled to gestures in the episodes of infant-father interaction mentioned above are based on timing and agent-environmental couplings in time that give rise to responses that "feel right" in the given situation and which appear to interactants as natural and transparent. Father and infant draw on their experiences of their interactional history to anticipate each others' responses and in so doing they respond in ways that seem motivated and intelligible. They therefore construe each others' actions as purposeful and intentional according to the norm-based standards of some moral order.

Cowley (in press) has pointed out that we *feel* words just as we hear them. We feel and hear an auditory pattern with which we actively engage and explore as a patterned auditory event. A vocalization or other form of body movement can function as an "inducer of emotion" (Damasio 1999: 68). The micro-temporal dynamics of a "loud" or "aggressive" voice, for instance, is such an inducer of emotion and concomitant body feeling. The feeling of the other's voice—not just the hearing—provides a basis for affective linkage between interactants. This capacity reaches right back to the earliest forms of intersubjectivity that characterize the infant-caregiver dyad (cf. Section 4 above). Vocalizations, gestures, and other forms of body movement are emotion inducers in the sense that they provide a means of directly mapping the other's feeling state onto the self in ways that alter one's own body state and consequent ways of responding in value-weighted ways at the same time that they enable the addressee to feel the bodily feeling-state of another. This, in turn, provides a basis for the later development of higher levels of empathic identification in ways which increase the capacity for caring, sympathy, and support.

At a still higher level of intersubjective perspective taking, one is able to take the other's perspective, to anticipate their intentions and to understand their feelings. Typically, language is associated with higher cognitive and conceptual abilities and body language with feeling and expression where it is assumed that the "ascent" to language is a progression from the one to the other. This view misses the far more fundamental point that whole-body-face-to-face interaction systems have evolved precisely as a means of coordinating feeling and affect between persons no less than higher-order thinking or reasoning of the kind we associate with conceptual and representational semantics (Sarles 1977; Bouissac 1999). The connection between the two perspectives is bodily movement. For instance, Abercrombie (1967: 97) has written of the "phonetic empathy" that is reciprocally felt by participants in spoken dialogue on the basis of their entrainment to and mutual attunement to the rhythms of their speech and the ways this enables speakers to tune into the body dynamics of the other. Moreover, organisms respond to very many levels of constraints—neural, bodily, social, cultural—in developing ways of acting and meaning that benefit themselves and the social groups they belong to. The view of language as codelike input/output machine for processing symbolic forms has been massively biased towards the idea that language is an instrument of cognition and rational thought. Damasio's neurobiological theory of the centrality of body feelings and emotions to consciousness, cognition, and higher-order rational thinking offers a new perspective for demonstrating the centrality of affect and body feelings to languaging activities and hence to signal form and function.

The invariant character of linguistic forms that is presupposed by the linguistic approach described above is based on the idea that recurrent regularities that are collected over time provide the basis for postulating an abstract system of types. However, face-to-face communications such as conversations make use of meaningful patterns that depend on very small-scale micro-temporal dynamics of the kind that cannot be captured on the basis of a pre-existing system of regular form-meaning correlations. Paralinguistic and kinesic features of speech are ill suited to their description in terms of recurrent types. Rather, their patterning occurs on very small, fast micro-temporal scales of fine-grained bodily dynamics. Cowley (1994) shows, for example, how rhythmic means are used by interactants in conversation to achieve specific, usually interpersonal ends, such as "sharing enthusiasm", which are interactional achievements whereby the behavior of others is managed and regulated. Moreover, rhythmical patterning *qua* form of body movement, is patterned, but not regular so that its analysis can never be captured in terms of *a priori* regularities of linguistic form (Cowley 1994: 354; cf. Section 6. above). Cowley shows that it is intrinsically irregular rhythmic patterning that gives rise to an experience of rhythm by the individual participants in the conversational event. Rhythm is therefore grounded in the first-person experiences of individuals engaged in conversation in ways that enable them to assess, manage, and resonate with each other in real time. It is a primordial form of inter-body attunement that takes as its "deictic" centre the tactile-kinaesthetic body as the very basis for organizing self-experience, but also for experiencing others. Bühler's ([1934] 1990: 117–131) notion of the *here-now-I system of subjective orientation* precisely renders the way in which the material, not just conceptual, basis of these deictic words *qua* "gesture-like clues" (Bühler 1990: 121) serves to orient intersubjective perception and cognition of the situations in which they are uttered.

Accounts of language which are founded on form-based regularities and their invariant character either miss the point of or marginalize such phenomena as mere paralinguistic "accompaniments" to language (Trager 1958: 2; cf. Section 7. above). In doing so, these approaches fail to see that micro-temporal forms of movement patterning such as rhythm are fundamental to verbal behavior on time scales that simply do not register on the radar screen of those linguistic theories based on form-based regularities of recurrent types. We experience vocalizations, gestures, facial expressions, and other body movements as "sad", "frightening", "joyful", and so on. Whole body movement dynamics are directly geared to and communicative of affect in ways that cut across all the expressive modalities and show that the common denominator is their shared basis in movement. This fact alone should induce researchers to rethink the division of *language* and *body language*. The division is misleading for two reasons. First, it is underpinned by the assumption that language is a stable code-like system of invariants that is separable from body dynamics. Secondly, the term *body language* directs attention away from movement as the common factor in all modes of sense-making by virtue of the way in which the topological-quantitative variation that is characteristic of movement under some normative construal, including gesture, facial expressions, eye gaze, and so on, cannot be assimilated to a view of these as language-like or code-like "channels" of communication.

The central lesson to be drawn from this discussion for our present purposes is that the presumed invariance of linguistic forms *qua* types is an artifact of a metalinguistic approach which focuses on and equates language with virtual second-order cultural constructs of the kind we typically associate with verbal patterns such as lexicogrammatical and semantic regularities (Section 7.). Lexicogrammatical forms are naturalistically grounded as patterns of neural activation that are sensitive to and interact with other neuronal patterns rather than interacting directly with environmental stimulus perception that is picked up by perceptual activity. Such systems of neural patterns implement networks of decoupled representations that increasingly cue further associations of such representations in a "symbolic" system that is more and more buffered from environmental perturbations (Deacon 1998: 79–92). They are therefore able to track virtual cultural constructs over diverse persons, places, and times beyond the here-and-now in ways that are decoupled from and not directly under the control of perceptual stimulus information. Instead, they are under the control of other symbolic items in networks of symbolic associations between thematically linked items forming networks of representations that can be modified, updated, changed, and so on, through the modification, addition, or subtraction of specific items (Thibault 2005a).

10. Scheflen's Concept of *Face Formation*

Face-to-face interaction takes place "in" and constitutes what Scheflen and Ashcraft (1976: 5) refer to as "a more extensive and often a more lasting field of relations of movement and other behavior". Minimally, face-to-face interactions consist of dyads of two persons who "tend to co-orient and use parallel or congruent postures" (Scheflen and Ashcroft 1976: 97). A number of people may physically cluster together, but do not co-orient interactively speaking. In the latter case, people are not engaged in face-to-face communication even if the fact of their clustering may be communicative to an outside observer (e.g., a number of non-affiliated individuals standing in a queue or a crowd of unrelated individuals all attending to the same phenomenon (Scheflen and Ashcraft 1976: 102). The members of a dyad co-act, are mutually involved and in some kind of relationship of affiliation or involvement (Scheflen and Ashcraft 1976: 103). Whenever people come together and face each other in this sense, they form what Scheflen and Ashcraft call a *face formation* (1976: 107). A face formation is constituted when people come together and take up locations in the space that is so constituted.

A face formation is, then, the higher-scalar organization within which face-to- face communication is embedded. A face formation is constituted when two or more persons: (1) co-orient; (2) take up congruent postures; (3) take up locations or positions in the space of the formation; (4) use the space so constituted to form relations of co-action and co-affiliation of various kinds and to varying degrees; and (5) they and the elements of the face formation are coupled to interactionally significant environmental affordances such as relevant objects, artifacts, physical settings, designed spaces, and so on. Face-to-face communication is embedded in this higher-scalar arrangement as a dialogic matrix in which the whole body posture-movement system of each individual participant is deployed to accomplish the co-enacted exploratory and performatory activities—the terms are Gibson's (1966: 45–46)—whereby the dialogical matrix is established and maintained. In turn, the dialogic matrix is grounded in the capacities of each individual for self-initiated movement and other forms of exploratory and performatory activity so that they can couple with each other in interactively and cognitively salient ways. The whole body posture-movement system makes use of postures and movements of the body and can itself be divided into a number of different regions. These are: (1) the head-face system; (2) the torso and upper limbs system; and (3) the lower limbs-torso-head system.

We can once again put scalar hierarchy thinking to good use to show that face-to-face communication can be seen in terms of the three interrelated scalar levels of hierarchical organization discussed in Section 2., as follows:

> L+1: the face formation
> L: the dialogic matrix
> L-1: the individual whole-body-posture-movement system of nested levels of performatory activity.

11. A Brief Analysis of a Face Formation

The following example is transcribed from a television reality show concerning the life of a family in Sydney (Australia). The two interactants, Laurie and Noeleen (hereafter, L. and N.), who are husband and wife, argue about Laurie's inability to make any of the pens that he is trying to write with work. The exchange takes place around a bar in the kitchen-dining room area of their Sydney home.

The analysis will focus on the performatory activities of N.'s movements and postures as a nested system of a number of action systems in relation to L. For the purposes of the present discussion, I shall refer to the following body units: (1) the head, including gaze and vocal tract activity; (2) the torso; and (3) the upper limbs. The analysis below is divided into three postural units with associated movement transformations, identified as *Bodily States* 1, 2, and 3, respectively, in the transcription and discussion below.

The Transcription: From *Sylvania Waters*, Episode 1 of a six part series about a Sydney family, ABC Television, Sydney, July 1992

Bodily State 1	

N: no language	
L: no language	

Figure 2a.   Bodily State 1

Observations on Bodily State 1:

N.'s head and upper body posture is oriented to the pen rack on the table as she moves towards and takes a pen from the rack with her right arm-hand. Head, gaze, upper body, upper limbs, and lower limbs (locomotion) are all oriented to and adjusted in relation to the pen L. is seeking to take from the rack.

Bodily State 2	
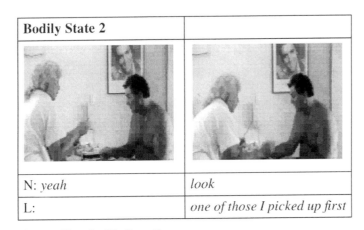	
N: *yeah*	*look*
L:	*one of those I picked up first*

Figure 2b.   Bodily State 2

Observations on Bodily State 2:

N.'s head and upper body posture reorient to face her husband, L. She holds the pen in her right hand ("yeah") to show him as she leans across the table to write with the pen ("look") she has taken on a sheet of paper located between

N. and L. on the table. Vocal activity: L. says "yeah" as she holds the head-upper body posture indicated here and holds the pen in front of L. to show him. She then lowers her right upper arm-hand to begin writing. She utters "look" as she begins writing. The controlled transformation of the right upper arm-hand from the raised position to the lowered position in order to write is synchronous with the uttering of "yeah" (arm-hand-pen raised) and "look" (arm-hand-pen lowered to writing position). The linguistic units are synchronized with the body movements in ways that are directed to constraining and directing L.'s perception and understanding of the pens.

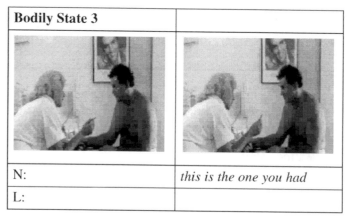

Bodily State 3	
N:	*this is the one you had*
L:	

Figure 2c.   Bodily State 3

Observations on Bodily State 3:

N. reorients by engaging L.'s gaze and raising her right fore arm-hand which is holding the pen in front of L. to show him. On performing this upper limb action, she says "this is the one you had".

As Reed (1996: 85) points out, there are various levels of postures and nestings of these as well as controlled transformations from one posture to another (movement). A movement is both a change of state from one posture to another at the same time that it is the maintenance of some postural orientation. For example, in Bodily State 2, the overall postural orientation of the head and torso is maintained whereas the right upper arm-hand-pen undergoes a controlled transformation as it is lowered from the showing position to the writing position. Furthermore, the movement from one state to another is synchronized with the two vocalizations. The first of these ("yeah") serves to call L.'s attention to the overall shift in attention which she is asking L. to undertake (i.e., "attend to what I am showing you"). The second ("look") directs L.'s attention to N.'s writing with the pen on the paper.

However, all of the action systems referred to here (head, gaze, torso, upper arm-hand(-pen), and vocalizations) are fully interactive. Thus, they are otherdirected, other-sensitive, and other-calibrated. They therefore play their role in creating or sustaining a relationship between N. and L. that is based on many levels of reflexivity in addition to the observables of the situation. At the same time, all of these action systems act on and transform the situation, its representations, and its conventions through the cognitive and semiotic work done by the mutual management and assessment of each others' behavior in order to bring about perception-action transformations in the other. In this last sense, each action system is oriented to the seeking of values. Thus, the action of moving the arm-hand(-pen) from the raised to the lowered position, as described above, seeks to move L. to a new perception and understanding of the status of the pens.

12. The Face Formation is Embedded in and Coupled to a Local Micro-Ecology

Face-to-face interaction does not only occur between the human agents who participate in the face formation. Interaction also takes place between agents and aspects of their physical-material environments, including artifacts, texts, tools, objects, physical settings, the built environment, etc. When an agent participates in face-to-face interaction with others, the physical world beyond the body is coordinated with the actions of interacting agents. This coordination gives rise to ways of thinking and reasoning that extend beyond the body. Such distributed forms of cognition emerge as a result of the interactions in real-time of the neural and non-neural bodily resources of agents, on the one hand, and selected features of the physical-material environment in which the interaction is embedded, on the other hand. In this view, features of the physical environment are cognitive artifacts that serve to transform thinking processes in a larger, more distributed system in which cognitive resources are not confined to biological individuals, but are distributed over an extended system involving brains, bodies, and aspects of the external world (Hutchins 1995; Clark 2001). In the interaction between L. and N. that is analyzed in Section 11. above, this involves aspects of the physical world that function as cognitive-semiotic resources and which play their own role in the process of finding a solution to the problem of the recalcitrant pens. The most salient of these material resources are summarized below.

Physical Setting:

Face-to-face interaction is always embedded in, coupled to, and co-constructs a local micro-ecology comprising socially meaningful configurations of objects, surfaces, media, architectural spaces, and what these afford the inhabitants or participants. In the present example, the bar table is one item that plays a mediating role in the cognitive ecology that is mediated by the interaction between L. and N. The bar table participates in activities of the following kinds:

- activities concerned with the preparation, serving, and consuming of food and drink
- supporting objects, both functional and aesthetic (pen racks, bar tables, etc.)
- other activities such as writing a letter, scribbling with pens, as here

- a focal point for interaction or conversation in that bar brings participants together and enhances face-to-face orientation and mutual gaze
- divides and defines boundary between kitchen and living space as two
parts of a larger whole; a kind of permeable buffer between these two
areas
- bar is spatially contiguous with the kitchen to which it is attached and
which it extends.

The Physical Setting:

The physical setting is itself a mediator and enabler of interaction rather than
a neutral and inert setting *per se.* In the present example, the following observations are relevant:

- The relations between embodied participants-in-activity and physical
setting are mutually constitutive.
- The situational specificity of the argument about the pens is generated
by the relations between the acts of trying out different pens and the
physical setting of the kitchen-bar.
- Interactionally familiar activities tend to take place in settings that are
culturally fashioned to be an integral part of the activity (e.g., the surfaces, objects, furnishings, division of space, etc. in relation to the intentional acts of participants); cf. L.'s writing at the bar; N's moving back
and forth in the kitchen.
- Particular arrangements of these physical settings are inscribed with
metafunctionally describable semantic values: (1) what experiential
meaning is stored in objects and configurations of these; (2) what interactive procedures are entailed between participants and objects; (3) how
are objects arranged in particular coherent spatio-temporal configurations, relations of dependency, and so on.
- Objects (e.g., pens) are not simply tools that participants manipulate to
produce a cognitive result; rather, participants place themselves in specific embodied and interactive (hence semiotic) relations with selected
aspects of the physical setting; it is this which produces meaning, knowledge, "cognition".
- Person-acting-in setting: knowledge and cognition are organized not as
decontextualized, abstract ways of thinking and knowing, but in interactively structured relations between participants and physical-material environments.
- Language is not a universal calculus for abstract rational thinking
and reasoning but a semiotic resource co-deployed with other semiotic
resources whereby solutions to problems co-emerge with selected aspects
of the situation in the course of participants' interaction with these;
in interacting with the physical environment, participants use this to
organize and reorganize it until a coherent and meaningful result semiotically and materially emerges from it.
- Semiotic interaction with the material environment imposes value on
it; the fact that L. and N. are in the kitchen-bar area paradigmatically

defines where they are in relation to where they are not, and hence the value of the activity they participate in along some of its dimensions.

- Semiotic values are embodied in room- and other-sized configurations of participants, objects, surfaces, etc.

13. Re-Framing Face-to-Face Communication: Towards a Network Ontology of Distributed Actors and Mediators on Diverse Scales of Time and Place

The lesson to be drawn from the above analysis is that there is more to face-to-face interaction than the complexities of the many modes of embodied signaling that interactants must attend to and interpret. This is something that we have shared for a very long time with our primate ancestors and extant sibling species, such as bonobos and chimpanzees. It is the oft made point of many popular accounts of how to both deploy and decipher the subtle cues of "body language" that we constantly attend to in order to enhance our chances of social success, to bypass cognition to make snap judgments without knowing why, and so on (see, for example, Malcolm Gladwell's (2005) bestselling *Blink*). The collective patterns that emerge from myriad interactions that make use of subtle cues of voices, facial movements, eye movements, body posture, and so on, are things we share with our primate cousins and siblings. Face-to-face interaction thus brings to the fore the ways in which the humanization of our bodily affordances for interaction has been shaped by a long natural and cultural history. As Latour (1996: 230) points out, we have been immersed in a primate social life that long preceded humanity.

Theories of interaction are confronted with the question: what is the starting point of the explanation, the social structure or the specific occasion of interaction? It is an analogous problem to that faced by sociologists who must contemplate two possible points of departure—social structure or action—for the study of society. Latour (1996) points out that the two points of departure entail, respectively, the "globalization of structure" and the "localization of interaction". The very term *face-to-face interaction* presupposes a reduction or a partitioning so that, as Latour (1994: 230) puts it, the whole of social life is not mobilized by a particular local interaction. The notion of *social structure*, on the other hand, presupposes that any given interaction is an instantiation or a manifestation of an all pervasive global social structure. Latour comments on this predicament as follows:

> [. . . O]ne must have seen a troop of some 100 baboons living in the midst of the savannah, looking incessantly at each other so as to know where the troop is going, who is with whom, who is grooming whom, who is attacking or defending whom. Then you must carry yourself away in your imagination to those scenes beloved of interactionists where a few people, most often just two, are interacting in cloistered spots hidden from the view of others. If "hell is other people," as Sartre said, then baboon hell differs from human hell, since the continuous presence of all creates a pressure quite other than that of closed-doors of interactionism—to such a degree that a distinction must be drawn between two entirely different meanings

of the word interaction. The first, as given above (pp. 229, paragraph 2) applies to all primates, including humans, whereas the second applies to humans alone. In order to retain the usual term, it is necessary to talk of *framed interactions*. The only difference between the two derives from the existence of a wall, a partition, an operator of reduction, a "je ne sais quoi" whose origin remains, for the time being, obscure (Latour 1996: 231).

Face-to-face communicative behavior has been studied for the most part with a focus on real time—the here-and-now—of the fractions of seconds, seconds, and minutes of the behavioral acts produced by individuals as these unfold in time. Individuals mobilize somatic and extra-somatic resources to achieve their goals and realize their intentions. Each act is a behavioral form that displays some features which are stable and predictable whereas others are flexible, variable and adaptive to the moment. Transcriptions freeze the time-locked character of realtime behavior and consequently encourage the coding of the resultant static "data" on the basis of stable and predictable regularities. These stabilities have in turn been attributed to global social structures or language or language-like systems. However, these approaches fail to capture the dynamically emergent character of behavior as it is soft-assembled in real-time in response to particular tasks and emerging values.

Face-to-face interaction cannot be explained by program-like regularities deriving from global systems. Instead, it strategically mobilizes and harnesses the available bodily and environmental resources which themselves have their histories and individual characteristics on their respective time scales. Communicative behavior is directed towards the obtaining of certain results; it is anticipatory, rather than being a backwards looking response to prior stimuli (Bickhard 2005: 207–208; Thibault 2005a, 2005b). Participants in interaction do not sit around waiting to respond to particular stimuli; rather, their actions lock into and make use of available somatic and extra-somatic affordances to achieve future-oriented results—meaning. Gibson's concept of affordance puts the emphasis on the *specificity* of the relations between organism and environment (Bril 2002: 122). The morphology of the human body is a primary affordance in face-to-face interaction and the properties of the human body are accordingly central to the control of dialogically coordinated inter-individual interaction. When L. and N. interact in the episode discussed above, their co-produced communicative behavior is a dynamic result of their neuromuscular status, their intentions, the physical setting, the bar around which they are aligned, the pen rack, the pens they hold and write with, and the way their bodies move. Their actions make use of all of these factors in real time at the same time that each of these components has its own history on its own time scale. For instance, the room, the bar table, and so on were designed by architects and built by craftsmen in other times and places, yet the agency of their work makes itself felt in the here-and-now of the particular occasion of interaction. They organize and "frame", as Latour puts it, the face-to-face interaction that takes place in the here-and-now. The two participants each have a life history—a biography—as well as a history of a shared relationship as husband and wife extending over years in ways that also contribute to the shaping of this particular interaction.

The same can be said of the semiotic resources that are deployed. These have a history of individual patterns of use in the two individuals and also a cultural history that goes well beyond the time scale of the here-and-now interaction that is briefly analyzed in Section 11. Thus, we see that diverse dynamical histories ranging across fractions of seconds, minutes, weeks, months, years, and centuries are all seamlessly interwoven into the real-time localized occasion of interaction. The agents and agencies—the actants in Latour's Greimasian turn of phrase—that frame and hold the interaction together are in actual fact not necessarily human at all. They include the objects, the physical settings, the tools and implements, the furnishings of the room. Their effects are not all proximate and local, not all in the here-and-now, but are distributed across diverse times and places. Nevertheless, they continue to participate in and to shape the interaction that takes place in the here-and-now (see also Lemke 2000a; Thibault 2000). Scheflen and Ashcraft similarly point out how objects, furnishings, and what they call "set ups" comprising preexisting arrangements of furnishings and so on in, for example, a room, structure the possibilities of interaction: "A set-up provides a prearranged site and defines what is to occur there" (Scheflen and Ashcraft: 1976: 135). A set up thus anticipates types of interaction and types of interactional roles that are embodied on specific occasions by particular persons.

By the same token, the set up is itself the result of the activities of other actors and agencies in other times and places. The actions of L. and N. in the example are shared with the actions of other agents and agencies which are "dispersed in other spatio-temporal frameworks and who exhibit other kinds of ontology" (Latour 1996: 239). They too are embedded in and participate in the interaction in real-time such that all of the diverse times and places are interwoven in the real-time interaction. This has nothing to do with the instantiation of a global social structure in a local instance of interaction. We do not go from the hub of macro-level social structure to some point of localized micro-level interaction. Instead, we go from point to point in a network of many potentially interconnected points. There is no hub; just many point-to-point connections.

In the proximate and localized view of face-to-face interaction, individuals are said to "use" words, gestures, pens, and bar tables. Aside from the spin of the externalist discourse, the idea of "use" here, in turn, entails the existence of a meaning-making subject with certain skills and capacities and an object (e.g., signs, pens) which the subject acts upon, uses. The point of origin of the resulting action is therefore located in the subject (Latour 1996: 237). Latour suggests an alternative view in which words, body movements, pens, and bar tables are events which provide opportunities for and prompt other actors to act. Importantly, Latour also extends our understanding of the term *actor* to include the non-human world of objects and their potential for agency and transformation. They too act in their own way. In this view, signs are not vehicles or carriers of meanings that are attached to them by an encoding process. In Latour's terms, signs are not "intermediaries" which "represent" or "express" untransformed meanings, but *mediators* (Latour 2005: 39–40) which provide opportunities for meanings to be transformed. Mediators provide and mediate possibilities for action which other actors can take up and transform in the service of their own projects. Mediators are distributed between different actors and agencies (human and nonhuman) as networks of interconnected actors that are spread across a diversity of time-scales, rather than being confined to a particular local moment of "sign-use" or "interaction".

Interaction on a particular occasion is then the result of the cross-linkages over many scales of space and time of interconnected networks of actors and mediators, both human and nonhuman, semiotic practices, material processes, human artifacts and technologies. None of these constitutes a higher-order or more global level of social structure or a social semiotic that is encoded in signs. Instead, the network connects distant times, places, and persons to locally present and proximate ones on a point-to-point basis. Face-to-face interactions are emergent and distributed outcomes of the ways in which material processes are contextualized by cognitive and cultural dynamics in and through contextualization processes that are created in human activity. Furthermore, individuals and their first-person experiences both constitute this system through their activities at the same time that individuals are constituted by their participation in the networks of interconnected actors that stretch out in many different directions across space and time. Moreover, the interpersonal coordination of individuals is itself not something which is confined to the localized scale of the here-and-now interaction, but is spread across diverse times and places beyond the here-now.

How, then, can the actor hold together in this diversity and spread of factors over space and time? Latour's answer, which is a familiar one, is through the narrative creation of an "I" for which we construct an autobiographical continuity over time (1996: 239). This process is itself made possible by the skillful use of our body as the ground of this "I". The "singularity" of this "I" is grounded in our unique embodiment (Harré 2001: 60–61). The self is at the centre of a perceptual field and the points of view that are attributable to the self by virtue of its bodily positioning at the centre of the perceptual field. The self has a unique embodiment which situates it in and connects it to its external milieu (esteroception) as well as to its internal one (proprioception) through the dynamical capacities of the living, feeling animate body to attune to and resonate with other similar bodies. That is the ground and the starting point of all forms of face-toface interaction.

14. Conclusion

The concept of face-to-face interaction puts the emphasis on an inter-individual unit of analysis, rather than individuals *per se*. Many properties of interaction are emergent results of the interactions between affordances of the biological individual, the social and cognitive skills and knowledges of individuals, and the social and cultural worlds in which the interaction is embedded. The fine-grained analysis of face-to-face interaction reveals the ways in which multi-agent, multimodal interaction co-deploys somatic and extra-somatic resources and affordances in the co-construction and mutual development of the meanings and activities that serve to create and enhance their perception and understanding of their worlds. It is therefore possible to reconceptualize cognition and thinking as distributed processes that are spread across persons, times, and places, rather than being confined within the brains of individuals. This has important future implications for the ways in which we theorize language and other semiotic resources and their role in human cognition and development. A related task for future research is to understand on the basis of sustained empirically grounded research how different timescales of semiosis are implicated in and play a determining role in the shaping of any given occasion of face-to-face interaction.

References

Abercrombie, David. 1967. *Elements of General Phonetics*. Edinburgh/Chicago: Edinburgh University Press.

Austin, William. 1965. Some social aspects of paralanguage. *The Canadian Journal of Linguistics* 11(1): 31–35.

Bickhard, Mark H. 2005. Consciousness and reflective consciousness. *Philosophical Psychology* 18(2): 205–218.

Birdwhistell, Ray L. 1952. *Introduction to Kinesics: An Annotated System for Analysts of Body Motion and Gesture*. Washington, DC: Dept. of State, Foreign Service Institute.

Birdwhistell, Ray L. 1961. Paralanguage 25 years after Sapir. In: Henry W. Brosin (ed.), *Lectures on Experimental Psychiatry*, 43–63. Pittsburgh: University of Pittsburg Press.

Birdwhistell, Ray L. 1970. *Kinesics and Context: Essays on Body Motion Communication*. Philadelphia: University of Pennsylvania Press.

Bouissac, Paul. 1999. The semiotics of facial transformations and the construction of performing identities. *Journal of Comparative Cultures* 3: 1–17.

Bråten, Stein. 1992. The virtual other in infants' minds and social feelings. In: Astri Heen Wold (ed.), *The Dialogical Alternative: Towards a Theory of Language and Mind*, 77–97. Oslo: Scandinavian University Press.

Bråten, Stein. 2007a. Introduction. In: Stein Bråten (ed.), *On Being Moved: From Mirror Neurons to Empathy*, 1–15. Amsterdam/Philadelphia: John Benjamins.

Bråten, Stein. 2007b. Altercentric infants and adults: On the origins and manifestations of participant perception in others' acts and utterances. In: Stein Bråten (ed.), *On Being Moved: From Mirror Neurons to Empathy*, 111–135. Amsterdam/ Philadelphia: John Benjamins.

Bril, Blandine. 2002. L'apprentissage de gestes techniques: Ordre de contraintes et variations culturelles. In: Blandine Bril and Valentine Roux (eds.), *Le Geste Technique: Réflexions Méthodologiques et Anthropologiques*, 113–149. Ramonville Saint-Agne: Éditions érès.

Clark, Andy. 2001. *Mindware: An Introduction to the Philosophy of Cognitive Ccience*. Oxford: Oxford University Press.

Cowley, Stephen J. 1994. Conversational functions of rhythmical patterning: A behavioral perspective. *Language & Communication* 14(4): 353–376.

Cowley, Stephen J. In press. The codes of language: Turtles all the way up? In: Marcello Barbieri (ed.), *The Codes of Life*. London: Springer.

Damasio, Antonio. 1999. *The Feeling of What Happens: Body, Emotion and the Making of Consciousness*. London: William Heinemann.

Darwin, Charles. 1998. *The Expression of the Emotions in Man and Animals*. Third edition. (With introduction, afterword, and commentaries by Paul Ekman). London: HarperCollins. First published London: Murray [1872].

Deacon, Terrence. 1997. *The Symbolic Species: The Co-Evolution of Language and the Human Brain*. London/New York: Penguin.

De Waal, Frans B. M. 2007. The 'Russian doll' model of empathy and imitation. In: Stein Bråten (ed.), *On Being Moved: From Mirror Neurons to Empathy*, 49–69. Amsterdam/ Philadelphia: John Benjamins.

Freeman, Walter J. 1995. *Societies of Brains: A Study in the Neuroscience of Love and Hate* (The Spinoza Lectures, Amsterdam, The Netherlands). Hillsdale, NJ/Hove: Lawrence Erlbaum.

Gavrilets, Sergey and Aaron Vose. 2006. The dynamics of Machiavellian intelligence. *Proceedings of the National Academy of Sciences* (PNAS) 103(45): 16823–16828.

Gibson, Eleanor J. and Anne D. Pick. 2000. *An Ecological Approach to Perceptual Learning and Development*. Oxford: Oxford University Press.

Gibson, James J. 1966. *The Senses Considered as Perceptual Systems*. Westport, CT: Greenwood Press.

Gladwell, Malcolm. 2005. *Blink: The Power of Thinking without Thinking*. New York/London: Back Bay Books, Little, Brown and Company.

Goffman, Erving. 1963. *Behavior in Public Places: Notes on the Social Organization of Gatherings*. London: The Free Press.

Halliday, Michael A.K. 1975. *Learning How to Mean: Explorations in the Development of Language*. London: Arnold.

Halliday, Michael A.K. 1994. *Introduction to Functional Grammar*. 2nd ed. London/Melbourne: Arnold.

Halliday, Michael A.K. 2003. Representing the child as a semiotic being (one who means). In: Jonathan J. Webster (ed.), *The Language of Early Childhood: Volume 4 in the Collected Works of M. A. K. Halliday*, 6–27. London/New York: Continuum.

Harnad, Stevan. 1990. The symbol grounding problem. *Physica D* 42: 335–346.

Harré, Rom. 2001. Metaphysics and narrative: singularities and multiplicities of self. In: Jens Brockmeier and Donal Carbaugh (eds.), *Narrative and Identity: Studies in Autobiography, Self and Culture*, 59–73. Amsterdam/Philadelphia: John Benjamins.

Harris, Roy. 2001. *Rethinking Writing*. London/New York: Continuum.

Hauser, Marc, Chomsky, Noam, and Fitch, W. Tecumseh. 2002. The faculty of language: What is it, who has it, and how did it evolve? *Science* 298, 22 November, 2002: 1569–1578.

Hill, Archibald A. 1955. Linguistics since Bloomfield. *Quarterly Journal of Speech* 41: 253–260.

Hill, Archibald A. 1958. *Introduction to Linguistic Structures: From Sound to Sentence in English*. New York: Harcourt, Brace and Company.

Hodges, Bert H. 2007. Good prospects: Ecological and social perspectives on conforming, creating, and caring in conversation. *Language Sciences* 29: 584–604.

Hutchins, Edwin 1995. *Cognition in the Wild*. Cambridge, MA: The MIT Press.

Iverson, Jana M. and Esther Thelen. 1999. Hand, mouth and brain: The dynamic emergence of speech and gesture. In: Rafael Núñez and Walter J. Freeman (eds.), *Reclaiming Cognition: The Primacy of Action, Intention and Emotion*, 19–40. Thorverton/Bowling Green, OH: Imprint Academic.

Johnson, Mark H. and John Morton. 1991. *Biology and Cognitive Development: The Case of Face Recognition*. Oxford: Blackwell.

Kuhl, Patricia K. and Andrew N. Meltzoff. 1982. The bimodal perception of speech in infancy. *Science* 218: 1138–1141.

Kuhl, Patricia K. and Andrew N. Meltzoff. 1984. The intermodal representation of speech in infants. *Infant Behavior and Development* 7: 361–381.

Langacker, Ronald W. 1987. *Foundations of Cognitive Grammar. Vol. I. Theoretical Prerequisites*. Stanford, CA: Stanford University Press.

Latour, Bruno. 1996. On interobjectivity. *Mind, Culture, and Activity* 3(4): 228–245.

Latour, Bruno. 2005. *Reassembling the Social: An Introduction to Actor-Network-Theory*. Oxford/New York: Oxford University Press.

Lemke, Jay L. 1998. Multiplying meaning: Visual and verbal semiotics in scientific text. In: James R. Martin and Robert Veel (eds.), *Reading Science: Critical and functional perspectives on discourses of science*, 87–113. London/New York: Routledge.

Lemke, Jay L. 2000a. Across the scales of time: Artefacts, activities, and meanings in ecosocial systems. *Mind, Culture, and Activity* 7(4): 273–290.

Lemke, Jay L. 2000b. Opening up closure: Semiotics across scales. In: Jerry L.R. Chandler and Gertrudis van der Vijver (eds.), *Closure: Emergent Organizations and their Dynamics*, 100–111. (Annals of the New York Academy of Sciences 901.) New York: New York Academy of Sciences.

Linell, Per. 2005. *The Written Language Bias in Linguistics*. Oxford: Routledge.

McGregor, William B. 1997. *Semiotic Grammar*. Oxford: Clarendon Press.

McNeill, David. 2005. *Gesture and Thought*. Chicago: University of Chicago Press.

McQuown, Norman. 1957. Linguistic transcription and specification of psychiatric interview materials. *Psychiatry* 20: 79–86.

Owings, Donald H. and Eugene S. Morton. 1998. *Animal Vocal Communication: A New Approach*. Cambridge/New York: Cambridge University Press.

Pittenger, Robert E., Charles F. Hockett and John J. Danehy. 1960. *The First Five Minutes: A Sample of Microscopic Interview Analysis*. Ithaca, NY: Paul Martineau.

Pfaff, Donald. 2006. *Brain Arousal and Information Theory: Neural and Genetic Mechanisms*. Cambridge, MA/London: Harvard University Press.

Poyatos, Fernando. 1993. *Paralanguage: A Linguistic and Interdisciplinary Approach to Interactive Speech and Sound*. Amsterdam/Philadelphia: John Benjamins.

Reed, Edward S. 1996. *Encountering the World: Toward an Ecological Psychology*. New York/Oxford: Oxford University Press.

Rizzolatti, Giacomo and Michael A. Arbib. 1998. Language within our grasp. *Trends in Neuroscience* 21(5): 188–194.

Ross, Don. 2007. *H. sapiens* as ecologically special: What does language contribute? *Language Sciences* 29: 710–731.

Salthe, Stanley N. 1993. *Development and Evolution: Complexity and Change in Biology*. Cambridge, MA/London: MIT Press.

Sarles, Harvey. 1977. *After Metaphysics: Towards a Grammar of Interaction and Discourse*. Lisse: The Peter de Ridder Press.

Scheflen, Albert E. 1973. *Communicational Structure: Analysis of a Psychotherapy Session*. Bloomington/London: Indiana University Press.

Scheflen, Albert E. (with Ashcraft, Norman). 1976. *Human Territories: How we Behave in Space-time*. Englewood Cliffs, NJ: Prentice-Hall, Inc.

Segerdahl, Pär, William Fields and E. Sue Savage-Rumbaugh. 2005. *Kanzi's Primal Language. The Cultural Initiation of Primates into Language*. Basingstoke: Palgrave Macmillian.

Shannon, Claude E. 1948. A mathematical theory of communication. *Bell System Technical Journal* 27: 379–423, 623–656. [Currently *Bell Lab Technical Journal*]. Downloadable version: http://cm.bell-labs.com/cm/ms/what/shannonday/shannon 1948.pdf.

Slagsvold, Tore. 1977. Bird song activity in relation to breeding cycle, spring weather, and environmental phenology. *Ornis Scandinavica* 8(2): 197–222.

Thelen, Esther and Linda B. Smith. 1994. *A Dynamic Systems Approach to the Development of Cognition and Action*. Cambridge, MA/London: Massachusetts Institute of Technology Press.

Thibault, Paul J. 1994. Text and/or context? An open question. State-of-the-Art article. In: *The Semiotic Review of Books* (Toronto) 5(2). Downloadable version: http://www.chass.utoronto.ca/epc/srb/srb/textcontext.html.

Thibault, Paul J. 2000. The dialogical integration of the brain in social semiosis: Edelman and the case for downward causation. *Mind, Culture, and Activity* 7(4): 291–311.

Thibault, Paul J. 2004a. *Agency and Consciousness in Discourse: Self-other Dynamics as a Complex System*. London/New York: Continuum.

Thibault, Paul J. 2004b. *Brain, Mind and the Signifying Body: An Ecosocial Semiotic Theory*. Foreword by Michael A.K. Halliday. London/New York: Continuum.

Thibault, Paul J. 2005a. What kind of minded being has language: Anticipatory dynamics, arguability, and agency in a normatively and recursively self-transforming learning system, Part 1. *Linguistics and the Human Sciences* 1(2): 261–335.

Thibault, Paul J. 2005b. What kind of minded being has language: Anticipatory dynamics, arguability, and agency in a normatively and recursively self-transforming learning system, Part 2. *Linguistics and the Human Sciences* 1(3), 355–401.

Tomasello, Michael. 2006. Why don't apes point? In: Nicholas J. Enfield and Stephen C. Levinson (eds.), *Roots of Human Sociality: Culture, Cognition and Interaction*, 506–524. Oxford/New York: Berg.

Trager, George L. 1958. Paralanguage: A first approximation. *Studies in Linguistics* 13(1): 1–12.

Trevarthen, Colwyn. 1978. Modes of perceiving and modes of acting. In: Herbert L. Pick and Elliot Saltzman (eds.), *Modes of Perceiving and Processing Information*, 99–136. Hillsdale, NJ: Lawrence Erlbaum.

Wheeler, Michael. 2005. *Reconstructing the Cognitive World: The Next Step*. Cambridge, MA/ London: Massachusetts Institute of Technology Press.

Whiten, Andrew and Richard W. Byrne (eds.). 1997. *Machiavellian Intelligence II: Extensions and Evaluations*. Cambridge: Cambridge University Press.

3

Technically-Mediated Interpersonal Communication

Caja Thimm

1. Introduction

Online media have influenced global communication like no other media technology in the last decades. But it is not the degree of media exposition of individuals all over the world or the possibility of presenting oneself on a website or ordering a book online, rather, it is the interpersonal contact function of computermediated communication that has shaped and still is shaping human communication. As early as 1993, Howard Rheingold commented on the communicative force of computer-mediated interaction:

> The idea of a community accessible only via my computer screen sounded cold to me at first, but I learned quickly that people can feel passionately about e-mail and computer conferences. I've become one of them. I care about these people I met through my computer (Rheingold 1993: 1).

Technically-mediated communication is now a part of daily interaction. It helps us maintain existing relationships and fosters the creation of new contacts (Thurlow, Lengel, and Tomic 2004).

In the early 1990s, the idea of having a look-alike avatar in a virtual "metaverse" like *Second Life* wearing digital copies of one's own clothes or sporting a copy of one's real haircut was probably far-fetched. Today, however, computer-mediated communication has taken over many communicative functions, and is everywhere to be found. Whether in organizational communication (Thimm 2002) or in interpersonal exchange in learning contexts (Mazer, Murphy, and Simonds 2007; Thimm 2005); whether in dyadic or group interaction—technology has already influenced many settings of interpersonal contact. And there will be even more ways to meet in "cyberspace" as another technological trend brings additional change: the "social web", or—as Tim O'Reilly named it in 2001—the *web2.0*, has started to turn the internet into one big meeting place for people all over the world (Haas et al. 2007). Social websites on which millions of mostly young users have created a gigantic universe of interpersonal networks may be regarded as the start of a new age of technically-mediated relations.

Language occupies a privileged position in the co-production of inter-subjective experiences, whether online or offline. When people speak, their proximity to one another in physical terms also translates into relational terms (cf. chapter 2, this volume). This is because speech serves not only as a means of expression; rather, it is used to construct reality and shape relationships. It is by means of linguistic exchange that people reproduce the normative basis of society. There are many implications to technically-mediated communication, some of which are pertinent to a communication-oriented view of society. For one, in technically-mediated communication there is a lack of physical co-presence, which means that visual and physical cues are eliminated. Mediation also eliminates the physicality of interaction and thus the countless paralinguistic cues provided through facework, such as body language or intonation. The integration of space and time also changes. Consequently, mediated communication involves phenomena on several different levels simultaneously: the facework of interaction, the speech contexts, and the intrinsic relationship of action to time and place.

Many technical applications reflect these changes, some of which will be introduced briefly in this chapter. Tools such as e-mail (4.1.), chats (4.2.), instant messaging (4.3.), blogs (4.4.), multi-user dungeons (4.5.) and social websites (4.6.) such as Facebook, Youtube, StudiVZ, or Flickr, have influenced interpersonal communication on a large scale. With the introduction of *Second Life* (4.7.)[1], interpersonal communication once again takes a new dimension.

Another important factor which has changed interpersonal communication is mobile communications (4.8.). With more than 30 billion e-mail messages and 5 billion text messages exchanged over mobile phones every day, technically-mediated interpersonal communication is available to everyone in most parts of the world.

Due to these developments, we have to analyze technology and human communication not only on the level of text or talk: today, it is the user's influence, in terms of user-generated content, participation, and online sociability, which forces us to look at interpersonal communication from a very different perspective.

2. A Framework for the Analysis of Technically-Mediated Interpersonal Communication

Digitalization and liberalization as well as economic growth and modernization of information and infrastructure have encouraged the innovation and diffusion of a wide range of technical (phone- or web-based) media dedicated to interaction and communication among smaller, more targeted groups. A number of significant changes in interface and transmission, such as the development of user-friendly software, and decreased production costs have made these media available for millions of people in both private and professional

---

[1] Facebook (http://facebook.com), YouTube (http://www.YouTube.com), Second Life (http://secondlife.com), studiVZ (http://www.studivz.net), flickr (http://www.flickr. com); all sites accessed December 10, 2007.

situations. Subsequently, these media forms have given rise to a wide range of new types of text, such as personal web pages, blogs, networking sites, and online journalism.

These phenomena have been dealt with traditionally within the fields of corpus linguistics and conversation analysis (Runkehl, Schlobinski, and Siever 1998; Thimm 2000; Baron 1998; Beißwenger 2001). But technology has been developing at such a fast pace in the last 20 years, that the resulting media usage was not hitherto foreseeable. For example, SMS was initially designed for internal use but it is now used by millions of people, with billions of text messages being sent around the globe daily. Since around 1998, a new generation of the websites began to flourish which not only integrate user-produced content, but are based upon it. These innovative sites or media are called *social software, network media,* or simply, *web 2.0.* To keep pace with such technical innovations, applied linguistics needs to modify its treatment of these developments in the personalization of media usage.

When looking at personal media usage, two forms or modes of communication are distinguishable: *presentational* and *interactive.* The presentational mode is used to attract and direct attention to one's own ideas, thoughts, opinions, and information of other sorts, as for example on personal homepages on the web. The interactive mode refers to such media as tools and channels for ongoing contacts with specific others, and as a means for coordinating activities in professional and family life, the mobile phone being the typical case. Up until the 1990s, these modes could be linked to distinct technological platforms. One could distinguish between *presentational web-based media* (personal web-sites and web-diaries, blogs), and *interactive phone-based media.* The two modes belonged to two different media and technical platforms—the computer and the mobile phone. However, this technical distinction has become obsolete as a consequence of digital convergence. Now, the two platforms are used interchangeably for both presentational and interactive purposes. Firstly, mobile phones are increasingly used for web services, bridging on-line television and on-line newspapers and combining interpersonal communication (telephone, text messages) with public media (TV, radio, newspapers). Secondly, a number of web-sites, such as blogs with RSS and track-back functions, or podcasts, employ both the presentational and interactive modes. Lastly, social networking sites such as Facebook or StudiVZ and many blogs have emerged which also apply both the presentational and interactive functions in the construction and reproduction of relevant social networks for various purposes. Consequently, within the field of applied linguistics, there is a need for a broader theoretical and methodological framework when studying these increasingly complex types of interaction in changing technical environments.

3. Theoretical Approaches to Technology, Media, and Communication

Looking at ways to categorize and describe technically-mediated interpersonal communication requires a variety of approaches (Höflich 2003). As categories like *anonymity, privacy, space, time,* and *distance* have gained importance in the overall description of interpersonal interaction, so the levels of analysis have changed (Döring 2003). The internet provides asynchronous communication via e-mail, bulletin boards, and computer conferencing, and it provides synchronous communication via chatting or real-time conferencing, instant messaging, or chats in multi-user dungeons. In addition, virtual simulation activities, such as online seminars, virtual field trips, and virtual experiments are also possible on the web.

In general, the focus of studies on communication and the use of new media has shifted over the past 20 years from a more technologically-oriented approach to one that puts emphasis on social context. The media richness model as put forth by Daft and Lengel (1984) proposed that the use of a certain medium in a communicative activity is influenced by the way medium capacity (*richness*—presented as objective characteristics of the medium) and the nature of the task (*uncertainty/equivocality*) fit together. The authors claim that media vary in their capability of reducing equivocality and ambiguity. A medium is regarded as "rich" if it facilitates feedback, communicates multiple cues, presents individually-tailored messages, and uses natural language. Trevino, Daft, and Len-gel (1990) concluded that media can be ranked according to their "richness", with face-to-face (FTF) communication ranked highest, formal numeric text lowest, and e-mail somewhere in between.

With computer-mediated communication (CMC) media becoming widely available and more people using e-mail, voice mail, and the internet, the focus shifted to researching the social influences, network contexts, and processes of media uses and perceptions (Walther 1992). Others (Turkle 1984, 1996; Thimm 2000; Thurlow 2004; Döring 2003) proposed that the characteristics of a medium are defined and appropriated through the social activities for which the medium is used.

How does technically-mediated communication differ from more traditional face-to-face relationships, and which kinds of participant contexts might influence these differences? New media may complement current interpersonal and telephone communication or may lead to additional and specialized uses (Höflich and Gebhardt 2005; Kim et al. 2007). Furthermore, mediated communication can foster connected presence or communicative readiness, whereby people manage multiple encounters at the same time and across time, signal ongoing awareness of relationships with specific others, indicate their availability, and maintain a social context (Herring 1996).

All experience is situated in time and space, but communication technologies decontextualize communication and interaction from the *here and now*, and change the grounds on which face-to-face interaction is based. This *dislocation of temporality* from contextualized experience in the world is one of the fundamental operations of mediation. Communication technologies are as much about time and temporality as they are about distance and space. Synchronous media permit direct communication in real time. Asynchronous media permit communication only through use of a recording medium (e.g., text) and not in real-time. Both intervene in *the temporality of interactions*. Online media construct virtual immediacy with respect to our access and presence to each other, we become virtually equidistant to one another. We are also increasingly available to others for communicative purposes due to the new technologies that permit this. Technology becomes a means of production for interpersonal interaction because it makes communication possible regardless of spatial (and temporal) distances. Connective technologies radically transform our presence and availability to others in relational and temporal terms.

People bring their real-life problems and personalities with them into their "virtual" lives. Computer-mediated communication must therefore include, inherently, all kinds of interactive content. Theoretical frameworks that are capable of accounting for this major shift in mediated communication are therefore *multidisciplinary*, and often only focus on one specific perspective of communication in "cyberspace" (Thiedecke 2003). It is necessary, for linguistic approaches as well as for others, to integrate theories from various related fields such as media research, social sociology, or psychology.

3.1. The Neurophysiological Approach to Technically-Mediated Communication

Media theorist Marshall McLuhan based his theories of media-human relations on assumptions about the physiological makings of humankind and the impact of technology thereon (McLuhan 1964). He construed media to be an "extension of man" and thus laid the foundations for the *neurophysiological paradigm* of media theory (McLuhan 1962: 72).

In *The Medium is the Massage* (1967), McLuhan insisted that we cannot understand the technological experience from the outside. We can only comprehend how the electronic age "works us over" if we "recreate the experience". For McLuhan, "the new media [. . .] are nature" since technology refers to the social and psychic "extensions" or "outerings" of the human body or senses (McLuhan 1967: 62). McLuhan considered his description of communication media to be universal because he viewed all technology as a force pushing "archetypal forms of the unconscious out into social consciousness." In this understanding, technology is an *extension* of biology: the expansion of the electronic media as *a metaphor for* or *the environment of* twentieth century experience implies that, for the first time, the central nervous system itself has been exteriorized. Humankind is becoming a part of the technological network by participating intensively and integrally in a *technostructure*, which is nothing but a vast simulation and "amplification" of the bodily senses. McLuhan proposed that technologies are no mere add-ons to whom and what we are, but rather, they alter us as though the technologies *really were* extensions of us. Living in a world where humans turn into machines may sound like the work of science fiction, but for McLuhan, it was the reality of our mediated, technologized world. Consequently, he described humans as *modified by* technology. This very controversial approach (cf., e.g., Bolz 1993) to the relationship between humankind and technology has influenced the debate on media, technology, and human interaction to a large extent (Thimm 2003). McLuhan's *neurophysiological paradigm* offers a framework for understanding and conceptualizing the self in an increasingly medialized environment.

3.2. Social Capital and Mediated Communication

A second approach to media and communication which has received wide international attention is based on the works of Pierre Bourdieu (1991) and his concept of *social capital*. This term broadly refers to the resources accumulated through relationships between people. Bourdieu and Wacquant define social capital as

> [. . .] the sum of the resources, actual or virtual, that accrue to an individual or a group by virtue of possessing a durable network of more or less institutionalized relationships of mutual acquaintance and recognition (Bourdieu and Wacquant 1992: 14).

Resources from these relationships can differ in form and function based on the relationships themselves. For individuals, social capital allows a person to draw on resources from other members of the network(s) to which he or she belongs. These resources can take the form of useful information, personal relationships, or the capacity to organize groups. Access to individuals outside one's intermediate social circle provides access to non-redundant information, resulting in beneficial ties such as ones that would lead to getting a job or a promotion.

The internet has been linked both to increases and decreases in social capital (Adler and Kwon 2002; Huysman and Wolf 2004; Quan-Haase and Wellman 2004; Williams 2006). It can be argued that internet use detracts from face-toface time with others, which might consequently diminish an individual's social capital. Other research suggests that online interactions may supplement or replace FTF-interactions, thus mitigating any loss of time spent online (Wellman et al. 2001). Recently, researchers have emphasized the importance of internet-based linkages for the formation of weak ties, which serve as the foundation of building social capital. Because online relationships may be supported by technologies like distribution lists, photo directories, and search capabilities, it is possible that new forms of social capital and relationship building will occur in online social network sites (Lin 2001). Accumulation of social capital might be augmented by sites that support loose social ties, allowing users to create and maintain larger, diffuse networks of relationships from which they could potentially draw resources (Wellman et al. 2001).

For the analysis of technically-mediated communication, this theoretical framework can be regarded as one of the most promising approaches that are able to account for the interrelationships of social values, communicational exchange, and technology.

3.3. Virtual Sociability

The concept of *virtual sociability* is associated with the opportunity for individuals to form aggregations across space and time via computer-mediated communication systems, such as internet chat rooms, bulletin board systems, and other multi-user contexts (Jones 1995; Höflich 2003; Bigge 2006). If it is assumed that communication in virtual environments involves the participatory engagement of various individuals, a virtual community can be understood by examining the activities of its participants (Williams 2006). Both individually and collectively, users maintain and change the prevailing notions of the online community. These electronic gatherings require negotiations of rules, norms, and technical procedures (Walther 1992, 1996). Thus, computer-mediated groups fit the description of an interpretive community actively constructing meaning for themselves.

Although it has been stated that technologically-mediated modes of communication are necessarily impoverished and antisocial (Walther, Anderson, and Park 1994), recent findings show that there is potential for online social communications to sustain and even enhance human communication (Bell and Kennedy 2007). But by the same token, it cannot be denied that generalizations about computer-mediated communication are inherently problematic, conflating important differences in the specific affordances and communicative practices of different technologies. As Herring (2004) notes, computer-mediated communication is clearly affected by technological variables such as synchronicity, granularity, and multimodality. There is also a range of social variables, for example the amount of time participants spend online, the nature of their relationship, and their levels of motivation, which empirical research proved to be an influential part of the nature of such communication (Döring 2003). In this regard, mediated and unmediated communication is both equally situated and context-dependent; and mediated practices are intricately embedded in the daily lives of users.

Mediated proximity, however, is explained by its lack of physical reality and context (e.g., Herring 2004). Communication and events are removed from objects, bodies, and faces. Messages are delivered without the context of speech and gesture that might help to decipher their original intent. Interactions unfold in an often disordered progression, lack coherence and clear reference (Storrer 2001), and are removed from the physical experience of being present with another. The importance of knowing what is going on in an interaction shifts to issues created by the introduction of technology; for example, who is on, who is referring to whom, etc. Participants—often unwittingly—attend to matters of production rather than to each other.

One of the major claims of the sociability approach is based on the observation that in online communication there is a general tendency for individuals to engage in greater self-disclosure and more intimate exchanges. Online communication tends to become "more than just skin deep" and to do so quite quickly (Walther 1996). There are a number of unique qualities of the internet that facilitate self-disclosure and intimacy online. Among the motivational forces of this kind of interactive behavior is a greater sense of anonymity or non-identifiability that leads to a reduced feeling of vulnerability and risk on the part of the individuals. This is complemented by the absence of traditional gating features such as physical appearance, mannerisms, apparent social stigmas such as stuttering, or visible shyness or anxiety which may prevent the establishment of any close relationship. Online communications make it easier for users to find others who share our specialized interests and values, particularly when there is a lack of "real world" counterparts. Furthermore, users have more control over one's side of the interaction and how one presents oneself.

Some authors claim that the internet has an enormous potential for providing tools to create effective inter-group contact (Floyd 1996; Thiedecke 2003). Its unique characteristics provide a basis for such a contact, for example, by creating a secure environment, reducing anxiety, cutting geographical distances, significantly lowering costs, and by creating equal status, intimate contact, and cooperation (Walther, Anderson, and Park 1994; Bell and Kennedy 2007). In addition, it offers the chance to receive approval from authorities. The internet is also a major source of information, and its ability to answer questions and provide knowledge in real time makes it a uniquely useful tool in promoting inter-group information exchange, such as in online forums. The internet may be said to provide opportunities for successful contacts which are superior to those provided in a traditional face-to-face meeting. There clearly are, however, potential obstacles to establishing a contact in cyberspace: uncertainty about the gender and age of the contact, and the possibility of becoming a victim of cybercrimes such as cybermobbing. Some means of making contacts on the internet, however, prove to be exceptionally effective tools which improve interpersonal and inter-group relations.

Interactive learning systems are just such a platform where the technology interacts with each user individually (Thimm 2005). In addition, *social websites* show new ways of taking over social contact functions for millions of users.

4. Technically-Mediated Communication: Forms of Text and Talk

As recent research shows, people increasingly use all kinds of media in combination for interpersonal contact purposes. Boase et al.'s (2006) nationally-representative survey for the United States found that people who kept in contact with those closest to them via e-mail also had more frequent and intense exchanges on the telephone with them, and more face-to-face contact with those less important to them. Internet users had more of such less important relationships. Further, e-mail users received more support from their contacts, and even more so if they used multiple new media (such as instant messaging, mobile phone, PDA, text messaging, or wireless internet connections). These findings point to the complexity of combining various means of relaying messages and organizing interpersonal relationships through media.

Of the many ways to make use of technical infrastructures for communicative purposes, the following will be introduced briefly: e-mail (4.1.), chat (4.2.), instant messaging (4.3.), blogs (4.4.), social network sites (4.5.), multi user dungeons (4.6.), and *Second Life* (4.7.). Mobile phone communication (4.8) will also be briefly discussed.

4.1. E-mail Communication

The final years of the 20th century saw the introduction and widespread adoption of e-mail as a means of interpersonal interaction. Whether in the private or the professional sphere (Waldvogel 2007), e-mail is the most common of all methods for developing and maintaining technically-mediated interpersonal contact today. It may also be regarded as the most important single tool for communicating and developing relationships since the telephone. As a means of communication, it has received wide attention in applied linguistics (Baron 1998, 2000; Kleinberger Günther and Thimm 2000; Ziegler and Dürscheid 2002). E-mail is not just electronic mail sent via the internet; e-mail communication creates a psychological space in which pairs of people—or groups of people—interact.

E-mail can be characterized as "text talk"; users type words to communicate via e-mail. More technologically-sophisticated methods enable the incorporation of pictures and sounds into the message. The typing/writing barrier filters some people out of the e-mail world. The benefits and drawbacks of e-mail communication have been widely discussed and can be summarized as follows:

In the typed text of e-mail which goes by situated rule of conduct (Ziegler and Dürscheid 2002), other people's faces or voices are lost. But creative means were developed to make up for this limitation, such as *secondary orality* style of writing (Koch and Österreicher 1985). One graphically-realized strategy is the use of so called *emoticons*. As the term *emoticon* suggests, these keyboard faces are used in texts to enhance emotional expression. E-mails show a wide variety of style features and modes of communication. We find creative text and sign combinations in different languages (*donde trouve io the wörterbuch*; 'where's the dictionary?') or various forms of conveying emotionality—from the simple smiley to complex graphematics (*aber klAAr spendIEr ich dIr ein BII-IER*; 'Of course I'll buy you a glass of beer!'; Kleinberger-Günther and Thimm 2000). Despite the lack of face-to-face cues, conversing via e-mail has evolved into a sophisticated, expressive form of interpersonal exchange, whether in private or in business communication.

E-mail exchanges do not occur in *real time*. Unlike face-to-face encounters which are synchronous, e-mail interactions do not require participants to respond on-the-spot. Because e-mail communication is asynchronous, the rate at which interaction takes place is flexible. A dialog may occur over the course of minutes, days, weeks, or months. Most e-mail programs allow for a "carbon copy" ("cc") to be sent to people or allow users to create a mailing list. These features help expand a dyadic conversation into a group. Often enough, they are the cause of e-mail based interpersonal conflicts. Forwarded mails or especially including the previous mails as automatic attachments can be the source of interpersonal conflicts.

Although e-mail certainly is a major part of modern interpersonal communication, it has shortcomings which have to be taken into account. For one, there is the notion of social and information overload: people can be stressed by the fast pace of incoming messages which are sent by different types of people with many different agendas, and are filled with all sorts of information, some valuable, some useless. Also, missing face-to-face cues makes e-mails potentially ambiguous. Even sophisticated e-mail users might experience miscommunication. Unwanted and uninvited mail, *spam*, has started to be a severe problem.

Some authors claim that due to the distance caused by mediated communication, individuals quickly open up and reveal a great deal about themselves in e-mail (Siegetsleitener 2001). An excessively rapid and even "false" intimacy may develop which might turn into undesirable reactions. One highly underestimated risk is the public character of seemingly private communications. Privacy in e-mail communication is tenuous, although people often perceive it as private. An e-mail message is a record of an exchange that can be accessed by, forwarded to, or unintentionally sent to a third party or an entire group of recipients. E-mails now count as legal documents and can be treated as evidence in a court of law. This threat to privacy has become one of the central issues concerning most technically-mediated types of communication.

4.2. Chat Communication

One of the most frequent online activities of internet users is the use of chat rooms. Chat rooms are forms of text-based communication that allow individuals to interact with each other over the internet. This type of communication has been likened to other forms of communication, such as casual face-to-face interactions and telephone conversations, because it allows the exchange of short synchronous messages in real time (Beißwenger 2001; Herring 2006).

In chat rooms, two or more people are allowed to post messages in real time and see the messages on their screens as they are posted. When they enter chat rooms, they are required to create a nickname which participants use to identify who messages come from. However, since the nickname does not necessarily reveal the participants' identity or their gender, they can remain anonymous if they wish. When comparing chat rooms with face-to-face communication, the lack of communicative directness becomes obvious; problems of cohesion and reference determine the communication. Participants in chat rooms can only communicate with others through "typing" their messages. Although chat room communication is often very personal, it is lacking certain types of information, including physical appearances and nonverbal cues. Both visual anonymity and text-only communication characterize chat communication and determine its content.

Chats can be used for various purposes. Beißwenger (2001) and Beißwenger and Storrer (2005) show a variety of chat types, from tutoring in e-learning, to chats as tools in intercultural exchanges and recruitment, to chat in therapeutic discourse. Below, a short excerpt (with the psychologist John Suler) demonstrates the confusing referentiality of the exchange. To avoid addressing the wrong participants, these experienced users use the nicknames as points of reference:

1. Andrea: Is anyone here currently involved with someone they first met online?
2. Butterfly: I don't quite agree Andrea. I like the physical a whole lot too.
3. M-W: That collaborates my theory Kimberley.
4. Storm: People that are susceptible to projections get involved in online romance a lot

5.	Peg:	yes andrea
6.	JohnSuler:	that's an interesting collection of people, Kimberly.
7.	Butterfly:	bingo MW, it's 95 % projection
8.	Linux:	I was involved for a year and a half with someone I met online
9.	LullySing:	What do you mean by currently involved . . . R/t or C/t
10.	Diane:	I was married to the man I met online just last week.
11.	Kevin:	I separated from a women I met online after 3 months
12.	Peg:	congrats dianne!

In general, internet chat is classified as a hybrid medium between written text and spoken language. This leads to some theoretical and structural consequences for an account of the textual mode of this sort of dialog (Beißwenger 2003). The text-based character of internet chat has lead to the assumption that chats are "written conversations", applying verbal strategies which can be characterized as *secondary orality* (Koch and Österreicher 1985). Looking at the functional side of chatting, one can conclude that chats have taken over many functions of interpersonal exchanges (Herring 2006). Internet chat has proven to be a productive and creative form of technically-mediated interpersonal exchange.

4.3. Instant Messaging

Instant messaging (IM) offers two functions unique to computer-mediated communication: the ability to identify who is connected to the shared space between or among friends, and the ability to conduct a text-based conversation in real time (Schneider et al. 2005). Not only in contexts of private interaction but also for the work-place, instant messaging has proven to be a practical means of interaction (Quan-Haase, Cothrel, and Wellman 2005). Increasingly, IM software features audio and video components as well. Instant messaging has proven to be one of the most popular online applications, resulting in dramatically increased internet connection time. This phenomenon fosters a sense of (online) community that perhaps no other application has achieved (Kim et al. 2007). Some reasons for the popularity of instant messaging may be that this form of communication is inexpensive compared to other forms of media such as the telephone. Beyond economic factors, some other attributes also contribute to its acceptance. Near-synchronous and text-based, instant messaging may be administered in one-on-one or in group communication, virtually combining features of the telephone, e-mail, and chat rooms into one (Lewis and Fabos 2005). Instant messaging is particularly popular with teens who keep in touch with their classmates and friends via instant messaging in selected groups.

History has shown that communication technologies are not replacing faceto-face interactions (e.g., Walther 1992), but they are definitely influencing the way in which people communicate. Instant messaging is an important tool for local people to stay connected. The feeling of closeness enforced by simultaneous online presence and the limited amount of people participating in a given IM interaction makes it a very effective mode of targeted interaction.

4.4. Blogs

Within the last few years, a new genre of computer-mediated communication has emerged (Bruns and Jacobs 2006; Burg 2004; Schmidt 2006, 2007; Ingenhoff, Schneider, and Tanner 2008). Web logs, or *blogs*, are frequently updated websites where content (text, pictures, sound files, etc.) is posted on a regular basis and displayed in reverse chronological order. Readers often have the option to comment on any individual posting, which is identified by a unique URL. With comments and references to other online sources in the postings as well as with links to favorite blogs in the sidebar (the *blogroll*), blogs form a clustered network of interconnected texts: the *blogosphere*. Schmidt (2007) states that even though the majority of blogs are of the personal journal type which deals with the blogger's personal experiences and reflections, there is a certain part of interpersonal communication necessary.

There are two structural relationship types in blogs: hypertextual relationships (hyperlinks) and social relationships (social ties). While hypertextual relationships result from blogging episodes, social relationships can be maintained additionally by other means of communication and interaction outside of blogging (e.g., face-to-face interaction or the exchange of personal e-mails). Hypertextual relationships are established through different mechanisms built into the blogging software, the most important being *permalinks*, which make it possible to point directly to microcontent rather than linking whole blogs (see Schmidt 2007). The basic relationship is between two blog postings, where one posting refers to another by including a hyperlink to the permalink of the cited posting. *Trackbacks* make these links reciprocal by adding a backlink from the cited to the citing post, turning it into "distributed conversations". Another way to establish relationships between blogs is through the use of comments.

Hypertextual relationships can also convey different aspects of social relationships, such as in expressing consent or dissent with the cited source, signaling a friendly or professional affiliation, or just adding to the context to the original posting by providing links to additional information. The blogosphere can therefore be regarded as a focused and specified network in which communication takes place via applying text and links.

Especially in journalism or corporate communication (Ingenhoff, Schneider, and Tanner 2008), blogs have come to have significant influence upon public opinion. Some researchers even see bloggers as the new "whistleblowers" in cases where personal knowledge becomes an important factor in issues management (Thimm and Berlinecke 2007).

4.5. Social Networking Sites

Social networking sites (SNSs) such as such as Facebook, Friendster, MySpace, and the German StudiVZ, allow individuals to present themselves, articulate their social networks, and establish or maintain contact to others (Lenhart and Madden 2007). Social network sites enable individuals to articulate their social connections visibly on the site, a practice that supports individuals' interest in pursuing self-presentational and social goals. *Friends*-links offer users a variety of social contacts, allowing them to explore and interact with a larger network via profiles and the communication tools they offer. Together, individual profiles, *friends*-links, and communication tools make up the backbone of social network sites.

As Lenhard and Madden (2007) point out, these sites can be oriented towards work-related matters (e.g., LinkedIn.com), initiating romantic relationships (the original goal of Friendster.com), connecting those with shared interests in music or politics (e.g., MySpace.com), or the college student population (the original incarnation of Facebook.com and StudiVZ.com). Participants may use the sites to interact with people they already know offline, or to meet new people. Face-book, for example, enables users to present themselves in an online profile, accumulate *friends* who can post comments on each other's pages, and view each other's profiles. Facebook, StudiVZ, and SchülerVZ members can also join virtual groups based on common interests, see what classes they are in together, and find out about each other's hobbies, interests, musical tastes, and romantic relationship status by reading through the information on members' profile pages. Previous research suggests that Facebook users engage more in "searching" for people with whom they have an offline connection already than in "browsing" for complete strangers to meet (Bigge 2006; boyd 2006). But Facebook has also been used for coordinating purposes by teachers in classrooms as well as for self-presentation and trust building (Mazer, Murphy, and Simonds 2007). Its applications for communicational purposes are therefore very broad indeed.

In brief, it can be summarized that online social network sites support both the maintenance of existing social ties and the formation of new connections. Online identities tend to raise individual consciousness insofar as they enforce additional self-reflection. When putting up a profile, one has to consider who should have access to their information, what their favorite music styles are, and perhaps even describe personal hopes and dreams on a matching platform. The various risks, however, which users often take unknowingly by uploading private photos (boyd 2006), personal information and stories about intimate life details, have been highly underestimated.

4.6. Multi-User Dungeons

Multi-user dungeons (MUDs) are text-based virtual realities, adventure role-playing on the internet (Curtis 1997). In contrast to new commercial and graphical virtual worlds, they have existed in one form or another for over 20 years (Keegan 1997). MUDs are more socially-oriented than newsgroups, yet more centered around a common interest (role-playing) than chats, combining characteristics of different forms of virtual communities. Although most MUDs are simply text-based, they feature a highly-developed social system. While computer-mediated communication can take place synchronously or asynchronously, multi-user dungeons are synchronous. They often involve competitive role-playing games. They are typically set in fantasy worlds in which players create their own "characters", choosing a name, a gender, and a race (e.g., demon, elf, gnome). To join these virtual worlds with virtual rooms, shops, pubs, towns, streets, forests, seas, ships, etc.—each described by text only—players log on to a server hosting the MUD. In most cases, no graphical elements are provided. These virtual worlds change continuously; they are dynamic worlds developed by their "inhabitants" (players) and thus form universes of their own.

4.7. Communication in Virtual Worlds—Second Life, a Case Study

Introduced in 2002 by Linden Lab, *Second Life*, often regarded as the first "metaverse", hosts a virtual world in which its users (also known as *residents*) take on a so-called *avatar* persona with which one can interact with other avatars and the virtual environment. Second Life provides a few rules and structures as well as a simple interface for customizing one's avatar and for building objects within the world. The idea of being able to purchase digital goods with *Linden Dollars* has started up a veritable economic metaverse along side the fantasy environment. This has resulted in a massive burst of creativity leading to the development of a complex and engaging multifaceted society with its own economy, value systems, and socio-political structures.

The open-ended design of Second Life means that it lacks most elements that would classify it as a game. It has neither a set of goals, nor rank values, nor rules, nor contestants. All of these elements have to be quantified subjectively by the individual him-/herself. Second Life allows its users to construct a complete alternate reality with social groups, pastimes, and possessions.

Each member of Second Life adopts and adapts the form of an avatar that can be customized to a very high degree, creating what he or she looks (or would preferably look) like (Schroeder 2002). The avatar forms can be human or non-human, but the vast majority of avatars appear to take on a humanoid form. The avatar is the locus of identity in Second Life. When signing up for an account, new residents must choose a first name and a last name with which they can be identified. Second Life provides a number of mechanisms for communication and coordination. Users may chat if they are "physically" in each others' proximity in the game world, or instant message each other if they are not.

Participation in virtual *metaverses* like Second Life is particularly cumbersome "because the reach of fully-intentional communication has been expanded from purely verbal to nonverbal levels" (Geser 2007). Thus, users/avatars are not only made responsible for the things they say, but also for the precise way they look and behave. While physical bodies are shaped by exogenous biological factors, the avatar is completely the product of one's own fantasy. Second Life's open-ended and social nature appeals to a broad range of users, from teenaged action gamers to middle-aged women. Such diversity leads to the creation of an environment that is quite like a neighborhood. Second Life appeals to people eager for experiences that are difficult for them to find in the physical world. Some of the purchases or attires, like a special hair-do or outfit, lead to differences in status between avatars. In their analysis of social differences in Second Life, McKeon and Welch (2007) found four axes of social status along which residents may occupy different positions: citizenship, wealth, reputation, and level of education.

When looking at the role of interpersonal interaction in Second Life, some new phenomena need to be considered. In telephone conferences as well as in internet relay chats and e-mail exchanges, social interactions are completely reduced to a focused interaction centering on explicit formal issues; in Second Life, such exchanges are embedded in a wider setting that encompasses preceding stages in which members notice and greet each other, engage in small talk, joking, and personal exchanges. Also there are subsequent phases where participants may continue talking in smaller groups and on more informal levels. Such casual informal talk serves the purpose of social exchange and helps to establish interpersonal bonds and multilateral networks.

There is a considerable amount of evidence suggesting that such "virtual encounters" are considered substantially rewarding to all participants. As they take place in a situated social environment, they have much more similarity to face-to-face contacts than simple chats or e-mail exchanges. Studies which assessed the rate of user acceptance of virtual worlds and, specifically, Second Life, show that about 70 % of online users agree that Second Life improves collaboration and communication; more than 60 % feel that it improves cooperation between people (Gscheidle and Fisch 2007). Other results indicate that people are using Second Life not to change their identity, but rather to explore and visit new places and meet new people (Haas et al. 2007).

If users accept *virtual worlds* as a new way and channel to communicate, collaborate, and co-operate, and if institutions emerge that offer a valuable service for their users, virtual worlds might become the next generation of platforms for internet users. However, in order to become mainstream, virtual worlds like Second Life have many challenges to overcome, particularly in the case of user.

4.8. Mobile Phone Communication

Mobile phone communication has introduced new parameters for interpersonal interaction. For one, it offers ubiquity and accessibility (Thimm 2003) as well as increased immediacy and intensity of interaction. In the "third wave of mobile communication" (Steuerer and Bang-Jensen 2002), we are not only seeing text message and mobile phone usage on the rise, but also specific services such as geographic orientation with GPS devices, visual communication by digital photos, and e-mail communication via internet mobile phones.

Of the various functions besides verbal telephone interactions, it is especially the short message service (SMS) that has had the most profound impact on interpersonal interaction. SMS is seen as a "specific constellation of structural and semiotic features which provides the basis for the emergence of particular speech genres as determined by the communicative purposes of specific users" (Androutsopoulos and Schmidt 2002). On a situational level, SMS is primarily used for emotional, phatic, and action-oriented purposes (e.g., arranging meetings). With regard to interactive structures, SMS is mainly used in dialogs which follow highly-standardized sequence patterns. From a microlinguistic point of view, the prevailing tendencies of SMS messages are: (a) reduction, which is attributed to both the technical restrictions of the medium and the conceptually spoken character of its use, and (b) creative language use, which draws on and playfully combining a wide range of linguistic resources (Döring 2002).

5. Potentials, Limits, and Deficits of Technically-Mediated Communication

In many studies, two conflicting attitudes towards technically-mediated interpersonal communication—particularly online communication—can be found. Accordingly, technically-mediated communication is seen as either being characterized primarily by major deficits, or as generally enhancing interpersonal communication.

The fact remains, however, that the very nature of communication changes when it is mediated by communication technologies. Critics see mediated communication as impersonal, artificial, or even hostile. It has been said that computer-mediated communication lacks many aspects of traditional communication such as physical presence, social, nonverbal, and contextual cues. From this point of view, computer-mediated communication is utilitarian and not relational; and as it lacks many face-to-face cues, it is more prone to misunderstandings and interpersonal conflicts. Text-only computer-mediated communication has been claimed to be interactively incoherent due to limitations imposed by messaging systems on turn-taking and reference (e.g., Döring 2007).

New technologies and new modes of communication are constantly coming into use. It can be argued that computer-mediated communication can, to a large degree, liberate relationships from the confines of physical locality, thus creating opportunities for new—and genuine—interpersonal relationships and communities (Rheingold 1993; Turkle 1996). Technically-mediated interaction is generally assumed to fall short on many factors underlined in conventional theories of relationship development. Traditional personal relationship theory suggests that the relative lack of social cues and the potential for feedback delays lead to uncertainty as to how users should and are expected to behave, and how behavior can be explained. Media richness theorists (Daft and Lengel 1984) suggest that computer-mediated communication has a narrower bandwidth and less information richness than face-to-face communication. They argue that different communication channels have different ways of processing information: rich media is more suitable than lean media for conveying socially-sensitive or intellectually-difficult information, and for persuading, bargaining, or getting to know someone.

Walther's (1992) social information-processing theory is representative of many previous studies supporting the enhancement approach. Walther emphasizes that because people need to manage uncertainty and develop relationships, they will adapt the textual cues to meet their needs when faced with a channel that does not carry visual and auditory cues. Using e-mail as an example, Walther illustrates that it provides no less opportunities for positive personal relationships than face-to-face communication over time. In conclusion, he suggests that computer-mediated communication is suitable to convey relational messages, but that that requires more time.

6. Where Do We Go From Here? Future Developments

The transformations resulting from our use of technology as a production format ultimately become embedded in new social practices. Our dependence on the possibility of communicating anytime anywhere is going to increase even further. The impact of communication technology on our experience and pursuit of interpersonal relations, as well as on the ability to contribute to reproducing society, trust, and social commitments, is enormous. Even if on an interpersonal level we find it difficult to achieve a sense of being in the same "space", our proximity to one another is different when technically-mediated than when we communicate face-to-face. Many people now feel closer to their communicative partners when they interact via mediated channels. And as we spend greater amounts of time in technically-mediated communication and experience, these attributes of technical proximity will increasingly become a matter of day-today life.

The popularity of technically-mediated communication will continue to grow independently of developments in the social and communication sciences. Just as the telephone has altered the notion of conversation by enabling a form of live talk between people in different geographical locations, the web, similarly, is now broadening the concepts of immediacy, presence, and intimacy. And with the onset of social websites and user-generated content, we have moved one step closer towards the "digital self".

References

Adler, Paul S. and Seok-Woo Kwon. 2002. Social capital: Prospects for a new concept. *Academy of Management Review* 27 (1): 17–40.

Androutsopoulos, Jannis K. and Gurly Schmidt. 2002. SMS-Kommunikation: Ethnografische Gattungsanalyse am Beispiel einer Kleingruppe. *Zeitschrift für Angewandte Linguistik* 36: 49–80. http://www. ids-mannheim.de/prag/sprachvariation/tp/tp7/SMS-Kommunikation. pdf (last access: September 27, 2007).

Baron, Naomi S. 1998. Letters by phone or speech by other means: The linguistics of email. *Language & Communication* 18: 133–170.

Baron, Naomi S. 2000. *Alphabet to Email: How Written English Evolved and Where It's Heading.* New York: Routledge.

Beißwenger, Michael. 2003. Sprachhandlungskoordination im Chat. *Zeitschrift für germanistische Linguistik* 31 (2): 198–231.

Beißwenger, Michael (ed.). 2001. Chat-Kommunikation. Sprache, Interaktion, Sozialität & Identität in synchroner computervermittelter Kommunikation. Perspektiven auf ein interdisziplinäres Forschungsfeld. Stuttgart: ibidem.

Beißwenger, Michael and Angelika Storrer (eds.). 2005. *Chat-Kommunikation in Beruf, Bildung und Medien. Konzepte, Werkzeuge, Anwendungsfelder.* Stuttgart: ibidem.

Bell, David and Barbara M. Kennedy (eds.). 2007. *The Cybercultures Reader.* Second Edition. London: Routledge.

Bigge, Ryan. 2006. The cost of (anti-)social networks: Identity, agency and neo-luddites. *First Monday* 11(12). http://firstmonday.org/issues/issue11–12/bigge/index.html (last access: November 22, 2007).

Boase, Jeffrey, John B. Horrigan, Barry Wellman and Lee Rainie. 2006. The strength of internet ties. *Pew Internet and American Life Project.* http://www.pewinternet.org/pdfs/PIP-Internet-ties.pdf (last access: May 20, 2006).

Bolz, Norbert. 1993. *Am Ende der Gutenberg-Galaxis.* München: Fink.

Bourdieu, Pierre and Loïc J.D. Wacquant. 1992. *An Invitation to Reflexive Sociology.* Chicago: University of Chicago Press.

Bourdieu, Pierre. 1991. *Language and Symbolic Power.* Cambridge: Polity Press.

boyd, danah. 2006. Friends, friendsters, and MySpace Top 8: Writing community into being on social network sites. *First Monday.* 11(12). http://firstmonday.org/issues/ issue11–12/boyd/ index.html (last access: 22. 11. 2007).

Bruns, Axel and Joanne Jacobs (eds.). 2006. *Uses of Blogs.* New York: Peter Lang.

Burg, Thomas N. (ed.). 2004. *BlogTalks 2.0. The European Conference on Weblogs.* Krems: Permalink.

Curtis, Pavel. 1997. MUDDING: Social phenomena in text-based virtual realities. In: Sara Kiesler (ed), *Culture of the Internet* 121–141. Mahwah, NJ: Lawrence Erlbaum.

Daft, Richard L. and Robert H. Lengel. 1984. Information richness: A new approach to manage-rial behavior and organizational design. *Research in Organizational Behavior. An Annual Series of Analytical Essays and Critical Reviews* 6: 191–233.

Döring, Nicola. 2002. 1x Brot, Wurst, 5 Sack Äpfel I.L.D.—Kommunikative Funktionen von Kurzmitteilungen (SMS). *Zeitschrift für Medienpsychologie* 14(3): 118–128.

Döring, Nicola. 2003. Sozialpsychologie des Internet. Die Bedeutung des Internet für Kommuni-kationsprozesse, Identitäten, soziale Beziehungen und Gruppen. (Internet und Psycholgie 2.) 2. Auflage. Göttingen: Hogrefe.

Döring, Nicola. 2007. Vergleich zwischen direkter und medialer Individualkommunikation. In: Ulrike Six, Uli Gleich and Roland Gimmler (eds), *Lehrbuch Kommunikationspsychologie und Medienpsychologie*, 297–314. Weinheim: Belt.

Ellison, Nicole B., Charles Steinfield and Cliff Lampe. 2007. The benefits of Facebook "friends": Social capital and college students' use of online social network sites. *Journal of Computer-Mediated Communication* 12(4), article 1: http://jcmc.indiana.edu/vol12/issue4/ellison.html (last access: November 27, 2007).

Floyd, Kory. 1996. Making friends in cyberspace. *Journal of Communication* 46: 80–97.

Geser, Hans. 2007. Me, my self and my avatar. Some sociological aspects of "Second Life". http://socio.ch/intcom/t-hgeser17.pdf (last access: November 27, 2007).

Gscheidle, Christoph and Martin Fisch. 2007. Onliner 2007: Das "Mitmach-Netz" im Breit-bandzeitalter. Grundlagen und Formen aktiver Webnutzung. Ergebnisse der ARD/ZDF-On-line-Studien. 1997. bis 2007. In: *Media Perspektiven* 08/2007: 393–405. Available at: http://www.ard-werbung.de/showfile.phtml/08–2007-gscheidle -fisch.pdf?foi d=22531 (last access: December 12, 2007).

Haas, Sabine, Thilo Trump, Maria Gerhards and Walter Klingler. 2007. Web 2.0: Nutzung und Nutzertypen. Eine Analyse auf der Basis quantitativer und qualitativer Untersuchungen. *Media Perspektiven* 4: 215–222.

Harris, Leslie D. 1994. The psychodynamic effects of virtual reality. *Arachnet Electronic Jour-nal on Virtual Culture* 2(1). http://hegel.lib.ncsu.edu/stacks/serials/aejvc/aejvcv2n01-harris-psychodynamic (last access: November 27, 2007).

Herring, Susan C. (ed.). 1996. *Computer-Mediated Communication: Linguistic, Social, and Cross-Cultural Perspectives.* Amsterdam: John Benjamins.

Herring, Susan C. 2004. Computer-mediated discourse analysis: An approach to researching online behavior. In: Sasha A. Barab, Rob Kling and James H. Gray (eds.), *Designing for Virtual Communities in the Service of Learning*, 338–376. New York: Cambridge University Press.

Höflich, Joachim R. 2003. *Technisch vermittelte interpersonale Kommunikation. Grundlagen—or-ganisatorische Medienverwendung—Konstitution "elektronischer Gemeinschaften".* Opladen: Westdeutscher Verlag.

Höflich, Joachim R. and Julian Gebhardt (eds.). 2005. *Mobile Kommunikation. Perspektiven und Forschungsfelder.* Frankfurt a. Main: Peter Lang.

Huysman, Marleen and Volker Wulf (eds.). 2004. *Social Capital and Information Technology.* Cambridge, MA: MIT Press.

Ingenhoff, Diana, D. Schneider and M. Tanner. 2008. Kommunikationsmanagement im Cyber-space: Der Einsatz von Corporate Blogs und Blog-Monitoring in der Unternehmenskommu-nikation. In: Caja Thimm und Stefan Wehmeier (eds.), *Organisationskommunikation online: Grundlagen, Fallbeispiele, empirische Ergebnisse*, 113–136. (Bonner Beiträge zur Medien-wissenschaft 8.) Frankfurt a. Main/New York: Peter Lang.

Jones, Steven G. (ed.). 1995. *CyberSociety: Computer-Mediated Communication and Community.* Thousand Oaks, CA: Sage Parks.

Keegan, Martin. 1997. A classification of MUDS. *Journal of Virtual Environments* 2. http://www. brandeis.edu/pubs/jove/HTML/v2/keegan.html (last access: November 16, 2007).

Kim, Hyo, Gwang Jae Kim, Han Woo Park and Ronald E. Rice. 2007. Configurations of relationships in different media: FtF, email, instant messenger, mobile phone, and SMS. *Journal of Computer-Mediated Communication* 12(4). http://jcmc.indiana.edu/vol12/issue4/kim.html (last access: July 20, 2007).

Kleinberger, Günther, Ulla and Caja Thimm. 2000. Soziale Beziehungen und innerbetriebliche Kommunikation: Formen und Funktionen elektronischer Schriftlichkeit in Unternehmen. In: Caja Thimm (ed.), *Soziales im Netz. Sprache, Beziehungen und Kommunikationskulturen im Internet*, 270–287. Wiesbaden: Westdeutscher Verlag.

Koch, Peter and Wulf Oesterreicher. 1985. Sprache der Nähe—Sprache der Distanz. Mündlichkeit und Schriftlichkeit im Spannungsfeld von Sprachtheorie und Sprachgeschichte. *Romanistisches Jahrbuch* 36: 15–43.

Lenhart, Amanda and Mary Madden. 2007. *Teens, Privacy & Online Social Networks. How Teens Manage Their Online Identities and Personal Information in the Age of MySpace*. Washington: Pew Internet & American Life Project. http://www.pewinternet.org/ pdfs/PIP-Teens-Privacy-SNS-Report-Final.pdf (last access: July 20, 2007).

Lewis, Cynthia and Bettina Fabos. 2005. Instant messaging, literacies, and social identities. *Reading Research Quarterly* 40(4): 470–501. http://www.reading.org/Library/Retrieve.cfm? D=10.1598/RRQ.40.4.5&F=RRQ-40-4-Lewis.pdf (last access: July 20, 2007).

Lin, Nan. 2001. *Social Capital. A Theory of Social Structure and Action*. (Structural Analysis in the Social Sciences 19.) Cambridge: Cambridge University Press.

Mazer, Joseph P., Richard E. Murphy and Cheri J. Simonds. 2007. I'll see you on "Facebook": The effects of computer-mediated teacher self-disclosure on student motivation, affective learning, and classroom climate. *Communication Education*, 56(1): 1–17.

McKeon, Matt and Susan P. Wyche. 2007. *Life Across Boundaries: Design, Identity, and Gender in SL*. Retrieved December. 2007. from www.mattmckeon.com/portfolio/second-life.pdf.

McLuhan, Marshall. 1962. *The Gutenberg Galaxy. The Making of Typographic Man*. Toronto: University of Toronto Press.

McLuhan, Marshall. 1964. *Understanding Media: The Extensions of Man*. New York: McGraw Hill.

McLuhan, Marshall (with Quentin Fiore). 1967. *The Medium is the Massage. An Inventory of Effects*. Random House.

Quan-Haase, Anabel and Barry Wellman. 2004. How does the internet affect social capital? In: Marleen Huysman and Volker Wulf (eds.), *Social Capital and Information Technology*, 113–135. Cambridge, MA: Massachusetts Institute of Technology Press.

Quan-Haase, Anabel, Joseph Cothrel and Barry Wellman. 2005. Instant messaging for collaboration: A case study of a high-tech firm. *Journal of Computer-Mediated Communication* 10(4). http://jcmc.indiana.edu/ vol10/issue4/quan-haase.html (last access: September 15, 2007).

Rheingold, Howard. 1993. *The Virtual Community: Homesteading on the Electronic Frontier*. Reading, MA: Addison-Wesley.

Runkehl, Jens, Peter Schlobinski and Torsten Siever. 1998. Sprache und Kommunikation im Internet. In: Muttersprache. Vierteljahresschrift für deutsche Sprache 2: 97–109. Available at: http://www.medien sprache.net/de/publishing/publizieren/muster/html-frames / (last access: December 10, 2007).

Schmidt, Jan. 2006. *Weblogs. Eine kommunikationssoziologische Studie*. Konstanz: Universitätsverlag Konstanz.

Schmidt, Jan. 2007. Blogging practices: An analytical framework. *Journal of Computer-Mediated Communication* 12(4). http://jcmc.indiana.edu/vol12/issue4/ schmidt.html (last access: December 10, 2007).

Schneider, Daniel, Sebastian Sperling, Geraldine Schell, Katharina Hemmer, Ramiro Glauer and Daniel Silberhorn. 2005. *Instant Messaging—Neue Räume im Cyberspace. Nutzertypen, Gebrauchsweisen, Motive, Regeln*. München: Fischer.

Schroeder, Ralph. 2002. *Social Life of Avatars: Presence and Interaction in Shared Virtual Environments*. London: Springer.

Siegetsleitner, Anne. 2001. *E-Mail im Internet und Privatheitsrechte*. Freiburg/München: Karl Alber.

Steuerer, Jakob and Jorgen Bang-Jensen. 2002. *Die Dritte Welle der Mobilkommunikation. Business-Visionen + Lebens-Realitäten*. Wien: Springer.

Storrer, Angelika. 2001. Sprachliche Besonderheiten getippter Gespräche: Sprecherwechsel und sprachliches Zeigen in der Chat-Kommunikation. In: Michael Beißwenger (ed.), *Chat-Kommunikation. Sprache, Interaktion, Sozialität und Identität in synchroner computervermittelter Kommunikation*, 3–24. Stuttgart: ibidem.

Thiedecke, Udo (ed.). 2004. *Die Soziologie des Cyberspace. Medien, Strukturen und Semantiken.* Wiesbaden: Verlag für Sozialwissenschaften.

Thimm, Caja (ed.). 2000. *Soziales im Netz. Sprache, Beziehungen und Kommunikationskulturen im Internet.* Wiesbaden: Westdeutscher Verlag.

Thimm, Caja (Hrsg.). 2002. *Unternehmenskommunikation offline / online. Wandelprozesse interner und externer Kommunikation.* (Bonner Beiträge zur Medienwissenschaft 1.) Frankfurt a. Main/New York: Lang.

Thimm, Caja. 2004. Mediale Ubiquität und soziale Kommunikation. In: Udo Thiedecke (ed.), *Soziologie des Cyperspace. Medien, Strukturen und Semantiken*, 51–69. Wiesbaden: Verlag für Sozialwissenschaften.

Thimm, Caja (ed.). 2005. *Netz-Bildung: Lehren und Lernen mit Neuen Medien in Wirtschaft und Wissenschaft.* (Bonner Beiträge zur Medienwissenschaft 5.) Frankfurt a. Main/ New York: Peter Lang.

Thimm, Caja & Sandra Berlinecke. 2007. Mehr Öffentlichkeit für unterdrückte Themen? Chancen und Grenzen von Weblogs. In: Wolfgang Pöttger & Christiane Schulski-Haddouti (eds.), *Vergessen? Verschwiegen? Verdrängt? 10 Jahre Initiative Nachrichtenaufklärung*, 79–99. Wiesbaden: VS Verlag.

Thimm, Caja and Stefan Wehmeier (eds.). 2008. *Organisationskommunikation online: Grundlagen, Fallbeispiele, empirische Ergebnisse.* (Bonner Beiträge zur Medienwissenschaft 8.). Frankfurt a. Main/New York: Peter Lang.

Thurlow, Crispin, Laura Lengel and Alice Tomic. 2004. *Computer Mediated Communication: Social Interaction and the Internet.* London: Sage.

Tidwell, Lisa Collins and Joseph B. Walther. 2002. Computer-mediated communication effects on disclosure, impressions, and interpersonal evaluations: Getting to know one another a bit at a time. *Human Communication Research* 28(3): 317–348.

Trevino, Linda Klebe, Robert H. Lengel, Wayne Bodensteiner, Edwin A. Gerloff and Nan Kanoff Muir. 1990. The richness imperative and cognitive style: The role of individual differences in media choice behavior. *Management Communication Quarterly* 4(2): 176–197.

Turkle, Sherry. 1996. Virtuality and its discontents: Searching for community in cyberspace. *The American Prospect* 24(1): 50–57.

Turkle, Sherry. 1984. *The Second Self: Computers and the Human Spirit.* New York: Simon & Schuster.

Waldvogel, Joan. 2007. Greetings and closings in workplace email. *Journal of Computer-Mediated Communication* 12(2). http://jcmc.indiana.edu/vol12/issue2/waldvogel.html (last access: September 15: 2007).

Walther, Joseph B. 1992. Interpersonal effects in computer-mediated interaction: A relational perspective. *Communication Research* 19: 52–90.

Walther, Joseph B. 1996. Computer-mediated communication: Impersonal, interpersonal, and hyper-personal interaction. *Communication Research* 23: 3–43.

Walther, Joseph B., Jeffrey A. Anderson and David W. Park. 1994. Interpersonal effects in computer-mediated interaction: A meta-analysis of social and antisocial communication. *Communication Research* 21: 460–487.

Wellman, Barry, Anabel Quan Haase, James Witte and Keith Hampton. 2001. Does the Internet increase, decrease, or supplement social capital? Social networks, participation, and community commitment. *American Behavioral Scientist* 45(3): 436–455.

Williams, Dmitri. 2006. On and off the net: Scales for social capital in an online era. *Journal of Computer-Mediated Communication* 11(2). http://jcmc.indiana.edu/vol11/ issue2/williams. html (last access: August 29, 2006).

Wood, Andrew F. and Matthew J. Smith (eds.). 2001. *Online Communication. Linking Technology, Identity, and Culture.* London: Lawrence Erlbaum.

Ziegler, Arne and Christa Dürscheid (eds.). 2002. *Kommunikationsform E-Mail.* (Textsorten 7.) Tübingen: Stauffenburg.

4

Feeling Space: Interpersonal Communication and Spatial Semiotics

Louise J. Ravelli and Maree Stenglin

1. Introduction

In language, a range of resources contribute to interpersonal meanings and relations, and form a key part of our participation in and understanding of social life. Similarly, semiotic systems other than language can be seen to construe comparable meanings in relation to interpersonal communication. In the built environment, for example, spatial semiotics actively construe interpersonal relations between the interactants within and around the space. Buildings make us *feel*: they may seem inviting or intimidating; they may make us feel comfortable or uncomfortable; as if we belong or as if we are intruding. This chapter will explore issues of interpersonal communication in relation to questions of spatial semiotics. Departing from the social semiotic work of Halliday (1978), interpreted in relation to multimodal texts by Kress and van Leeuwen (2006), and drawing on the semiotics of place by Scollon and Scollon (2003), the chapter will demonstrate how it is that many familiar notions from linguistic studies of interpersonal communication—such as issues of power and social distance—can be applied to an understanding of spatial semiotics. This chapter will provide an overview of key literature in the multimodal discourse analysis field and at the same time introduce new systems for describing interpersonal meanings in built spaces, in terms of how affective meanings are construed. These notions will be demonstrated in relation to the *Scientia* building at the University of New South Wales, Sydney, a relatively new landmark building which has been pivotal in reconstruing the visual identity of the University. We will examine how issues such as power, social distance, and affect are evoked through the exterior and interior of the building, and what these mean for relations between the University as an institution and its key stakeholder communities: its students and the general public. In turn, this expanded understanding of interpersonal communication will be turned back to questions of language, considering its relevance to a broader understanding of communication.

The Scientia building[1] has been chosen as a case study for this chapter because of its pivotal role in contributing to the reconceptualization of

---

[1] This is the original name of the building. It was renamed The *John Niland Scientia* in 2006, in honour of the Vice-Chancellor who oversaw its construction.

the identity (visual and discursive) of the University of New South Wales (UNSW). Located in Sydney, Australia, the UNSW is a major national university, albeit one with a relatively short history (it was established in 1949), and one founded in the sciences and technology, which remain its research strengths. A significant program of campus redevelopment in the 1980s and 1990s culminated in the opening of the Scientia in 1999. Designed by MGT Architects, it is a ceremonial building and was awarded a major public architecture award, the 2000 Sir Zelman Cowan Award for Public Buildings, by the Royal Australian Institute of Architects. Described as a "rare, highly refined work" and a "consummate work of public architecture",[2] the Scientia has somehow managed to encapsulate a new identity for the University. It both expresses the power and confidence of the University as an institution, and invites those who enter the campus—students, staff, visitors[3]—to identify with the institution. The purpose of using the Scientia as a case study is to illustrate how a "mere" building can do all this—to explore how spatial semiotics can express meanings such as these, and to examine how we may respond to such meanings.

2. Outline of the Approach: Social Semiotics

To understand how a building such as the Scientia makes meaning, and specifically how it functions interpersonally, we need to clarify the overall approach of this chapter. This chapter is informed by social semiotic theory. Social semiotics focuses on the social dimensions involved in all meaning-making practices. It has been strongly inspired by the research of a group of linguists working with *systemic functional theory*, namely, Halliday (1978, 1985/1994), Halliday and Hasan (1976), Halliday and Matthiessen (2004), Hodge and Kress (1988), Martin (1992), and Matthiessen (1995).

In addition to inspiring a rich theory of language, systemic functional theory has also been used to theorize a wide range of communicative modes as well as multimodal texts:

- visual images (Kress and van Leeuwen 1990, 2006; O'Toole 1994)
- movement (Martinec 1997, 1998a, 1998b, 2000a, 2000b)
- speech, music, and sound (van Leeuwen 1991, 1999)
- architecture/three-dimensional space (Kress and van Leeuwen 2006; Martin and Stenglin 2007; O'Toole 1994, 2004; Ravelli 2000, 2006; Scollon and Scollon 2003; Stenglin 2002, 2004, 2007, in press a, in press b, in press c, in press d; van Leeuwen 1998, 1999, 2005a; White 1994).
- filmic texts (Pun 2005)
- hypermedia texts (Djonov 2005; Lemke 2002).

---

[2] Jury Verdict; Sir Zelman Cowen Award for Public Buildings; Royal Australian Institute of Architects; *Architecture Australia* November/December 2000; accessed 22. 5. 07 at http://www.architectureaustralia.com/aa/aaissue.php?issueid=200011.

[3] Together these shall be referred to as *users*.

The main resource social semioticians have used to theorize all of these communicative modes has been Halliday's metafunctional hypothesis (1978). This hypothesis states that a semiotic system such as language simultaneously fulfils three communicative functions: first, an *ideational function*, in which language constructs representations of human experience; second, an *interpersonal function* which is concerned with our participation in speech situations, and the expression of our attitudes; and third, the *textual function*, the organization of a text into a meaningful whole. The ideational and textual metafunctions will be briefly introduced here, and then the interpersonal metafunction will be introduced in more detail, using examples drawn from both language and visual images, and relating it to spatial semiotics. Following Kress and van Leeuwen (2006), when these functions are extended to spatial semiotics, we will use the terms *representational, interpersonal, and compositional* meanings, equating with the ideational, interpersonal and textual metafunctions respectively. These should be seen to be largely equivalent, and see also Lemke (1998), O'Toole (1994) and Ravelli (2006) for additional options.

2.1. The Ideational Metafunction

The ideational metafunction is concerned with how events are portrayed, including the activities which are construed as taking place, represented in language through particular *Process* types. Events also include what is represented as being involved in those activities, *Participants*, and the *Circumstances* under which these events take place. When looking "at" a spatial text such as a building, it can first be considered in terms of the event being portrayed. The event may be static, represented by *conceptual Processes*, and characterized as being without vectors, or the event may be active, represented by *narrative Processes*, and characterized as having vectors (Kress and van Leeuwen, 2006; see also Ravelli in press). Typically, when looking "at" a building, we generally expect it to be without vectors—buildings should be static, not dynamic! Exceptions to this include the use of vectors pointing upwards, as with skyscrapers, to indicate dynamism and power, or architecturally innovative buildings which use unusual vectors to suggest dynamism in the building. In addition, ideational meanings can be construed in a spatial text through the denotation and connotation of signs, in particular, the materials used in construction, and shapes in the exterior or interior design. For example, in Sydney, Australia, the use of a material such as sandstone connotes both nature, history, and status, as it is an expensive, natural material used in most of Sydney's significant historical buildings.

2.2. The Textual Metafunction

The textual metafunction is concerned with bringing together the disparate elements of a text into a coherent whole, and relating the parts to each other. In language, relevant resources include the complementary patterns of *Theme* and *Information*, enabling a text to construct a particular method of development, and to come to a point of News (Halliday 1994; Martin and Rose 2003). In images, it encompasses five key elements (Kress and van Leeuwen 2006).

Firstly, *information values* can be construed in a text depending on how items are placed in relation to each other. In a building, for example, placement of an important symbol "up high" gives it an *Ideal* information value, whereas the door at entrance level has the value of the *Real* (Kress and van Leeuwen 2006: 260; see this also for further description of other information values). Secondly, some of the componential elements may be made *salient*, through a range of resources such as using large size, a contrasting color, and so on, to make an element stand out. The textual metafunction also encompasses *framing*, that is, the extent to which elements are construed as being the "same", through seamless framing devices, or "different", through strong framing devices, such as a change in design practice, use of a border or space to define elements, and so on. The use of design features may also affect the *reading path* of the text, that is, the likely way a user will take in a visually complex text, and *rhythm* relates to the way in which design features are used to create cohesion. In buildings, placement on the vertical axis is often used to attribute Ideal values to important signifiers, such as religious, national or commercial emblems. The relation of one building to another can be made seamless or distinct, through framing practices (for a full description of all of these aspects, see Kress and van Leeuwen 2006, and Ravelli in press; for a complementary and slightly different perspective on ideational and textual meanings in three-dimensional space, see Stenglin 2004: 447–478, Martin and Stenglin 2007, and Stenglin in press a).

2.3. The Interpersonal Metafunction: Overview

The interpersonal metafunction in systemic functional theory is concerned with participation and interaction, as well as the negotiation of feelings, attitudes, and judgments. In language, for example, we facilitate interaction by taking turns in dialogue, adopting different speech roles, initiating interaction with others as well as responding to such interactions in supportive or confronting ways. We can also use language to describe how we feel, or how we feel about other people or things.

Like language, other semiotics such as visual images also have resources for constituting social interaction. Kress and van Leeuwen's seminal work on images (1990, 2006) is the springboard for much social semiotic analysis of other non-linguistic modes, and aspects of their interpersonal descriptions will be briefly described here, before explaining the extension to spatial semiotics. Kress and van Leeuwen have shown, for example, that the social relations between viewer and the participants represented in an image are determined in the first instance by *contact*: whether the image "demands" visual attention or merely "offers" something for contemplation. Represented participants that enter into direct eye-contact with viewers "demand" visual engagement while those that direct their gaze elsewhere "offer" themselves up for observation. In buildings, contact is realized by whether or not the user can engage with the interior of the building, for example by seeing inside it through windows or glass walls. Where walls are solid, and there are no windows, or they are obscured, the building is an object of contemplation, and does not invite direct contact with it (see Mills 2006).

A second important dimension of the social meaning of images is *social distance*. In language, social distance may be realized by a variety of resources, such as the choice of vocative used in interaction: formal names and titles implying distance, familiar names implying intimacy. The distances people keep from one another depend closely on their social relationships and in images this is reflected in different types of shots. Close shots (including head and shoulders) and very close shots (the head, or part of the face) suggest we have an intimate relationship with the visual subject. Medium close shots (which cut the subject off at the waist) and medium shots (cut off at the knees) suggest social familiarity, but not intimacy. Medium long shots (full figure), long shots (subject occupying approximately half the image), and very long shots (anything wider) suggest we have a public acquaintance with what is being portrayed. In buildings, social distance is also realized by the distance of the viewing position: from what distance it is that we can "see" the building. As Kress and van Leeuwen note (2006: 128):

> We can see a building from the distance of someone about to enter it, in which case we will not see the whole of the building [. . .] We can also see it from the distance of someone who just identified it as his or her destination, and is surveying it for a moment, before moving towards it. In that case the frame will include only the building and leave out the surrounding environment. Or we can see it, so to speak, from behind the gates that keep the public at a respectful distance from the palace, or the fortress, or the nuclear reactor, and in that case the representation will include also the space around the building.

Thus, social distance in relation to buildings is likely to be transformed depending on the nature of the approach to the building.

A third important resource for interaction in images is *power*. Power relates to the relative equality between interactants, and in language, is realized by such features as the reciprocity in use of linguistic options: for example, whether both interactants may initiate speech turns, or whether similar types of vocatives may be used reciprocally (see, for example, Poynton 1989). For both images and three-dimensional objects, power involves some kind of "angle". When we look at objects at our own level (the level angle) they tend to admit a degree of social equality, as the viewing position is reciprocal. If we are positioned higher than what is displayed (high angle), we tend to be in a position of superiority, while standing lower (low angle) usually signals respect or inferiority to what or who is observed. Buildings typically manifest power on the vertical axis, using height to signal this. As Kress and van Leeuwen note (2006: 251): "What towers over us has, by design, power over us, and is, by design, socially distant [. . .]" Further, the variable of power in relation to space may be realized in other ways, such as by particularly large size or solidity on the horizontal axis, giving it a horizontal presence in the visual field. Or, power may be manifested on the horizontal plane in terms of the internal organization of spaces, for example, placing public spaces to the front and more private spaces to the rear. Stenglin (in press b) uses the term *horizontal hierarchy* to refer to such horizontal power relations.

Interaction may also be affected by the nature of the *involvement* one has with the text: in language, direct involvement can be realized by such features as first and second person possessive pronouns, signaling an alignment with what is represented in the text; whereas third person pronouns would realize a more detached perspective, signaling distance (Kress and van Leeuwen 2006: 139). In images and buildings, involvement is realized on the horizontal axis, with different angles signaling different kinds of involvement. The front-on angle realizes direct involvement; the oblique signals detachment. Thus, a door which opens directly to the street invites stronger involvement than one which is placed on an angle.

A further dimension of interaction is *modality*. In language, modality refers to the modification of propositions and proposals, enabling the speaker to "intrude" on the message (Eggins 2004: 172), using such devices as modal adverbs and modal adjuncts. Kress and van Leeuwen extend the notion of modality to interpersonal meanings in images, relating it to how "real" or "truthful" an image is presented as being. Such a measure, however, needs to be evaluated against a specific coding orientation. For example, in a naturalistic coding orientation, "real" images have a wide range of colors, realistic contextual backgrounds, and a mid-level of color saturation. In a sensory coding orientation, in contrast, color differentiation and contextual backgrounds may be more restricted, and very high color saturation is the norm. There is a complex relation between the realization of modality in relation to coding orientation, and Kress and van Leeuwen (2006) should be referred to for further details. When applied to spatial semiotics, the overall coding orientation of the text becomes important. Generally, we expect "real" buildings to be conventional—built in a style which is common for a particular time and place (emphasizing that, as with all these meanings, this is a social-semiotic construction). Buildings which depart radically from convention (the famous "Bilbao effect") draw attention to themselves, raising questions about how "real" they are, and drawing praise or approbation for how "amazing" they are.

To summarize, contact, social distance, power, involvement and modality are some of the important resources for constructing and maintaining *interaction* in linguistic, visual, and spatial texts.[4] With respect to interpersonal meaning and space, Scollon and Scollon (2003) have applied several of the tools developed by Kress and van Leeuwen to their theory of *geosemiotics*. Geosemiotics explores the social meanings of the material placement of signs and draws strongly on notions of represented/interactive participants as well as modality. This is clearly an important starting point for considering spatial semiotics. Extending these notions, this chapter will expand Kress and van Leeuwen's notions of contact, social distance, power, involvement and modality, by applying them to space, in particular, the analysis of the ways interpersonal meanings are organized in the Scientia building.

---

[4] There are also other resources for analyzing interaction in images such as the "pointof-view" dimension (perspective), but it is beyond the scope of this chapter to consider this in depth. See Kress and van Leewen (2006) for more information about perspective (129–140) and for further details on modality see (154–174).

2.4. The Interpersonal Metafunction and Appraisal

An additional dimension of interpersonal meanings, related more to the expression of feelings, attitudes, and judgments, rather than the Mood-related categories that have inspired Kress and van Leeuwen, is that of APPRAISAL. To analyze these, Martin (1997, 2000), Martin and White (2005) and White (1997, 1998, http://www.grammatics.com/appraisal) have developed the APPRAISAL network. APPRAISAL offers systems that describe the semantics of evaluation, that is, how participants are feeling (Affect), the judgments they make (Judgment) and the value they place on the various phenomena of their experience (Appreciation). In language, such meanings are typically realized by a variety of linguistic resources, such as the choice of lexical item, whether it be a verb, noun, adjective, or adverb.

The system of APPRAISAL has recently been extended to the analysis of images (Martin 2001; Painter in press), and it is a particularly important part of the exploration of spatial semiotics. This chapter will draw on APPRAISAL theory, in particular, the system of ATTITUDE to explore how a space can make its occupants or users feel. To do this it will use two recently developed theoretical tools for exploring interpersonal meaning in three-dimensional space. They are *Binding* and *Bonding* (Stenglin 2002, 2004, 2007, in press a; in press b; in press c; in press d; Martin and Stenglin, 2007).

Binding is a scale that organizes spaces along a continuum from extreme openness to extreme closure. Extremes of Binding evoke claustrophobic and agoraphobic responses, whereas median choices produce comfort zones of security and safety, or freedom and possibilities. Binding is realized by a combination of variable elements (such as color and light) and invariable elements (such as walls, floors, and ceilings).

Bonding is concerned with the communing potential of spaces. It is realized in part by bonding icons, social emblems of belonging that people rally around. It is also realized by the hybridization of space—one space designed to serve many social functions and facilitate value transfer. Binding draws strongly on Affect from Appraisal theory, the area concerned with emotions and feelings, in particular, feelings of security and insecurity. Bonding, on the other hand, draws on all three Appraisal systems: Affect, Judgment and Appreciation.

3. Concepts and Theory: Applied to the Scientia

3.1. Introducing the Scientia

Let us first look at the Scientia. Visually, the Scientia dominates the campus, from the point of view of one of its main pedestrian entrances (see Photo 1).[5] It stands at the top of the "University Mall", a central pedestrian link from the main road (Anzac Parade) to the Scientia. As the campus is on a sloping site, the Scientia is literally "up high", as the mall ascends to it. Externally,

---

[5] All photos taken by the authors.

the Scientia consists of two large rectangular shapes, set perpendicular to the mall, divided by a central passage. This passage is constructed of branching arms which thrust up towards the sky, and which enclose a suspended glass structure which spans the two rectangles, but which can be walked through (underneath), to the other side. The rectangular blocks are made of sandstone; the thrusting arms of laminated jarrah[6] poles, tapering at the endpoints, and supporting the glass and steel of the enclosure. It is this central tree-like structure which marks the unique visual identity of the Scientia, and which is now ubiquitous in all aspects of University marketing (see Photo 2).

Importantly, the Scientia changes in identity on approach: at the entrance to the campus, it is visually prominent (because of its size, location, and unusual architecture) but nevertheless distant. It therefore functions somewhat as a

Photo 1. Long shot of the Scientia

---

[6] Jarrah is an indigenous Australian wood, found primarily in Western Australia.

Photo 2.   Medium shot of the Scientia (front side)

"lure".[7] As one approaches it, the size of the Scientia begins to dominate, until, arriving at the threshold, this is maximized to its full potential (see Photo 3). Here, there is perhaps a moment of confusion. There is no entry point to the building on this side, and the passageway is potentially intimidating. However, there is nowhere else to go, with only two poorly indicated alternative paths to the left, and no pathway to the right. On passing through the passage, one ascends steps to the other side, and finds a differently—smaller—scaled Scientia to the rear, with a clearly indicated entry, including an oblique panel which channels users in through the entry (see Photo 4). Thus, as a text, the Scientia unfolds as it is experienced (that is, logogenetically), and the meanings expressed shift according to the point at which one is viewing or experiencing the building.

An additional important feature of the exterior is the inclusion of contrasts, in terms of materials, finishes, and shapes. The heavy sandstone blocks, rectangular and static in shape, contrast with the largely transparent central structure and the dynamic thrust of its upward vectors; natural stone contrasts with manufactured glass and steel; opaque and slightly rough stone contrasts with smooth and transparent glass, and so on. The significance of these contrasts will be elaborated below in relation to Bonding icons.

---

[7] The notion of a spatial *lure* is termed *prominence* in Stenglin (2004) and Stenglin (in press a).

Photo 3.   Close shot of the Scientia (looking up)

Photo 4.   Medium shot of the Scientia (rear view)

Internally, the Scientia primarily consists of a main reception hall (on the left, looking at the front of the building), used for receptions after graduations, and for other functions (as well as for exams sometimes!), and a secondary hall (on the right), used primarily for meetings, and which also houses a temporary restaurant. These two spaces are connected by the entrance vestibule, entered from the rear of the building, and the central atrium. There are a number of other spaces in the building, such as smaller office rooms, and a University cinema facility.

3.2. General Interpersonal Meanings

As with any other semiotic system, spatial semiotic systems operate across the three metafunctions proposed by Halliday for language, as described above. That is, spatially, meaning is made through the ideational function about what is being represented, *representational meanings*; about the nature and organization of parts in relation to the whole through the textual function, *compositional meanings*; as well as about the interactions between participants and their stances and attitudes towards the text, *interpersonal meanings*. Whether in language, image, or space, all of the three metafunctions are simultaneously present in any text, and while operating largely independently, they nevertheless interact in important ways. Our discussion of the Scientia will focus on interpersonal meanings, but it is important to remember that representational and organizational meanings contribute in fundamental ways to the overall meaning of the Scientia as a text. These will be mentioned where appropriate, but see Ravelli (in press) for a discussion of each of the metafunctions in relation to this text; and Martin and Stenglin (2007) and Stenglin (in press a) for an analysis of all three metafunctions in two very different museums.

What we aim to achieve with this analysis is an account of how it is that a building, a concrete, material object, can function to make interpersonal meanings, in a similar way to a linguistic text. We want to consider the interactional relations that are enabled between users, and the building, and hence by implication, with the University as represented by the building. What impressions does it make on those who see it, walk towards it, and—possibly—enter it?

When the variables of power and social distance are considered, it soon becomes evident that the building manifests a motif of contrast, a motif which characterizes the building as a whole.[8] On the one hand, the Scientia is first glimpsed—at the start of the pedestrian mall—as being far away, and while distinctive and interesting, it appears relatively small (see again Photo 1). Thus, at the point of greatest social distance, the Scientia is not necessarily overpowering. As one approaches the building, however, and social distance decreases, the Scientia becomes larger and larger, and its height, solidity, and quality, all become more evident, until at the threshold, the point of least social distance, the power variable is maximized (see again Photo 4). Here, the status and authority of the institution is clearly evoked: users are supposed to be impressed.

At the threshold point (see again Photo 3), where power is maximized, the angle of involvement is frontal. Kress and van Leeuwen (2006: 145) note that this is the angle of "maximum" involvement; hence it can also be maximally confronting for the user, and it is significant that there is no actual entry at this point. Instead, the visitor is lured via the stairs to the rear of the building. From this side, the scale of the building, while still impressive, is significantly reduced, and a polished granite wall is placed on an oblique angle to channel users in to the building. Overall, then, while the power of the institution is clearly asserted on approach, the actual entry itself is made more inviting and welcoming. As a text, the Scientia manifests complex interpersonal meanings, counter-balancing the need to both impress and include.

This counter-balancing of interactional effects is replicated in other interpersonal systems. In terms of contact, parts of the Scientia, such as the sandstone flanks, are solid, preventing any engagement with what is within. Other parts, such as the central structure, are transparent, inviting an inside view. Louvres at the rear may be open or closed, and when open, allow a view through the building to the sky on the other side (see again Photo 4; rear). Thus, the Scientia functions both as an Offer and a Demand, suggesting that it is both an object for contemplation and an object to be engaged with. At the same time, the solid sandstone flanks evoke a naturalistic coding orientation,

---

[8] Again, this is also across each of the metafunctions; see Ravelli (in press).

within which these parts of the building are very "real" and familiar in terms of the local architecture. The central structure, however, with its dynamic and unconventional design, is both low modality ("is that really a building?") and hyper-real ("wow; look at that!").

In three-dimensional spaces, an additional system of interpersonal meaning needs to be considered, that of the *Control* exerted over users, and the relative freedom or restriction of their behavior. Control is realized by the freedom of access to the building and its interior, and the pathways leading to it, and by the absence or presence of restrictions (such as surveillance) on behavior (Ravelli in press).[9] In the Scientia, the strong directionality of the pedestrian mall, combined with the lure of the Scientia at the end of it, implies a Command to users to embark on this pathway. However, the absence of restrictions on this path—there are no fences or gates to negotiate, no security guards to pass—means that the Command functions more as an Invitation: it is the user's choice to embark on this path or not, and once on it, there are possibilities for diversions and alternative destinations on the way (even if these are not made prominent).

Overall, then, in interpersonal terms, the Scientia both welcomes and impresses. It indicates clearly to the user that the University to which the Scientia belongs is an important place, one which should be taken seriously. Simultaneously, it also indicates that the user is welcome to enter, and indeed is invited to do so. Through resources such as those described here, the building and the institution establish their own persona, and indicate appropriate roles and relations for users to take up. In this way, the building functions to create interpersonal meanings between the institution and the users who interact with it.

3.3. Binding and Bonding

In considering interpersonal meanings, it is important to remember that *interaction* also involves *personal* responses. One of the most interesting aspects of interpersonal meanings in relation to spatial semiotics is in terms of how a building makes us *feel*. Is it a space in which we feel comfortable and secure, or at risk and uneasy? Is it a space with which we identify, or a space which alienates?[10] To address such issues in spatial semiotics, the systems of Binding and Bonding, introduced briefly above, have been proposed (Stenglin 2004, 2007, in press a, in press b, in press c, in press d). We will now explore these systems in some detail, and relate them to the exterior and interior of the Scientia.

---

[9] Stenglin (in press a) also explore and analyzes Mood choices in space and the ways different spaces impact on behavior, using Bernstein's concepts of classification and framing (1975). These are particularly relevant to understandings of surveillance.

[10] Responses to spaces can also be provoked by the other metafunctions. For example, textually, a lack of clarity in the layout of a complex spatial text might lead to confusion and disorientation; or representationally, connotations of materials or objects may be positive or negative for a particular user. However, the interpersonal focus here is a more literal sense of "feelings", related to emotions, attitudes, and judgments.

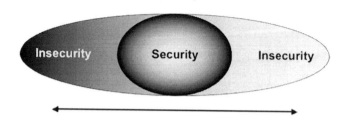

Figure 1. Binding scale: security and insecurity

3.3.1. BINDING. Binding is concerned with the interpersonal relationship between a user and a space, and is determined by the way a space "closes in" or "opens up" around a user. If a space closes in on a person too tightly, for example, that person is likely to feel smothered. In contrast, if a space does not provide enough enclosure, a person may feel dwarfed and overpowered. Thus, Binding is concerned with the feelings of security or insecurity people may experience in a space.

As Binding deals with feelings, which are gradable, it is best represented as a scale or topology. Insecurity lies at both ends of the scale, while security is positioned at the heart of Binding, as illustrated in Figure 1.

Importantly, the categories of security and insecurity are not absolutes, but are subject to cultural, social, and individual variation based on personal experiences of space. Culture, geography and climate influence spatial preferences—in a cold climate, for instance, strongly Bound spaces are likely to be experienced as being more secure. Social factors, such as processes of change, can also influence the experience of space. The first modernist homes of the late 1940's, with full-length glass sliding doors and open plan living areas, provoked strong feelings of insecurity (Andersons 2002), but today would be considered neither radical nor challenging, because such designs have become very familiar (Spigelman 2001: 180). Despite such potential variations in the responses to space, it is nevertheless possible to establish patterns of similarity in the types of spaces that make people feel secure and insecure. It is to these patterns for spatial security that we turn to now.

3.3.1.1. Security. Security, the middle ground for Binding, has two choices, the Bound and the Unbound. Each establishes a relationship of security with users. Spaces that fall within the Bound dimension evoke feelings of comfort, safety, and protection by enveloping around the occupant both horizontally and vertically to create a womb-like enclosure. This is typically provided by vertical enclosures such as walls, which envelop around an occupant in much the same way that a carer's arms may fold around a young child. Horizontal enclosures also provide spatial security and include ceilings (which define the upper limits of a space) and floors (which define its lower limits). The way people feel in a Bound space is encapsulated in the following quote from an architectural reviewer.

> The home has a warm, calm and inviting presence, and it is not just the
> smiling face of owner Ann Godden greeting us that makes us feel welcome.
> It is the house itself (Hayes 2005: 10).

In Unbound spaces, security is experienced as partial freedom from enclosure,
and can be created by receding walls and elevated ceilings which increase the
volume of space around the occupant. This makes the area feel more spacious
and open, and the user feels free and unencumbered. An abundance of natural
light from glass ceilings or glass window walls can achieve the same effect,
because light increases the degree to which users are able to perceive both
depth and volume.

The following quote from a home-owner who has recently completed a
large-scale home renovation captures the essence of feeling Unbound.

> The thing is not the size in terms of floor space, but the size in terms of how it
> makes us feel. It gives us a sense of freedom, a sense of space [. . .] you need
> spaces that are free and comfortable (Burns, SMH Domain, July 14, 2005: 10).

3.3.1.2. Spatial Insecurity. Insecurity may be created by choices which
are Too Bound or Too Unbound. Spaces that are Too Bound set up a smother-
ing, suffocating relationship with their occupants. They include caves, tun-
nels, prison cells, elevators, and mines. Spaces that are Too Unbound do not
provide enough enclosure for occupants. They can be found at the edge of a
cliff or the glass wall of a skyscraper where the floor plane drops away suddenly, or in cavernous spaces that soar vertically high above occupants. Such
spaces are often found in public buildings such as museums and cathedrals,
and may make people feel diminished, vulnerable, and overpowered—especially if users are unaccustomed to such over-scaling.[11]

3.3.1.3. Binding in the Scientia. For reasons of space, our analysis of Binding
in the Scientia will be selective rather than comprehensive, focusing on the rear
entry to the building, the vestibule, and the central atrium (see Photo 4 again).
Generally in the Scientia, we see the same motif of contrast in terms of Binding
that has already been identified in relation to other interpersonal factors. At the
rear of the building, where the actual entrance is located, there are two Bound
spaces. The first is the entry leading into the building (see Photo 5).

In the entry, two solid walls, a sandstone wall on the left and an angled
granite wall on the right, evoke a solid sense of enclosure. As visitors to the
building move past these entrance walls, large glass sliding doors open automatically and visitors are received into the second Bound space: a small vestibule consisting of a low white ceiling and two permeable walls (see Photo 6).
At the same time, large glass window-walls "lure" them into the spaces to their
left and directly ahead (see Photo 7).

---

[11] Again, the potential for variation in responses needs to be remembered. For examples, some
individuals may find strongly Bound spaces (like caves) or strongly Unbound spaces (like cliff
edges) exciting and stimulating, rather than suffocating or overpowering.

Photo 5.   Rear entry to the Scientia

Photo 6.   Vestibule of the Scientia

Photo 7. Transition between Vestibule and Atrium

By clearly delineating the boundaries of both the entrance itself and the vestibule inside, through choices for solid enclosure, a relationship of security is constructed between the spaces and users. Thus, at the point where the power variable is minimized, security is strongly evoked.

In the interior, the Scientia building also contains spaces that are Unbound, such as the central and iconic atrium. This atrium houses a huge triple volume of space. Both the walls and the ceiling are constructed solely from glass. This is a strong choice for Unbinding as it constructs an open, light-filled, diaphanous space that contrasts markedly with the firmly enclosed opaque spaces, which characterize the masonry of the entrance walls and vestibule.

In particular, large sheets of plate glass unbind the interior of the atrium by metaphorically "dissolving" horizontal and vertical planes separating internal from external spaces. The use of glass walls and ceilings thus project the atrium onto the landscape and extend the feeling of spaciousness to include the outdoors: the trees to the rear, the mall and University in front and the sky overhead (see Photo 8). Unbinding in these ways brings interior and exterior spaces into a strong interrelationship. The user therefore experiences security as freedom from firm spatial enclosure.

3.3.1.4. Gradations of Binding. As noted, Binding is represented by a scale, and so finer distinctions may need to be made between spaces which are strongly, weakly, or moderately Bound or Unbound. The entrance vestibule in the Scientia building, for example, would only be weakly Bound, as the space is not enclosed on all four sides, while the atrium would be strongly Unbound as optimal choices for Unbinding are used both vertically and horizontally.

Photo 8.   View from the interior

It is interesting to note that a gradation of choices offers architects and those involved in the design of space a tremendous resource for designing comfortable and secure environments. Environmental psychologist, Anita Rui Olds (1994), argues that people need "small shifts" in the design of spaces to keep them feeling alert and responsive. According to Rui Olds, moderate variations prevent boredom and withdrawal and help people to stay comfortable. It thus seems that slight variation is the key to maintaining feelings of security in three-dimensional spaces as abrupt shifts can overwhelm people.

Having explored the various dimensions of spatial security and insecurity, the Binding scale can now be summarized as seen in Figure 2.

3.3.1.5. Materialization. The next necessary step is to identify how Bound and Unbound spaces are materialized, that is, to identify the resources that are used to create these different feelings of enclosure. In analyzing Binding, it is firstly important to account for the context—particularly the surrounding climactic and geographical conditions—together with information about

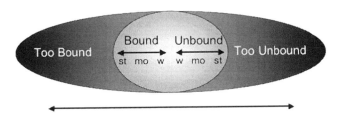

Figure 2. Binding Scale: strongly (st), moderately (mo), weakly (w) Bound and Unbound.

technological innovations and cultural orientations to security (for further information about these contextual factors, see Stenglin 2004: 116–129).

Spaces then need to be analyzed for both variable and invariable elements. The invariables refer to the fixed, structural elements constructing a space, and consist of three intersecting planes: an overhead plane (roof and/or ceiling); wall planes; and a base plane (floor). These define the limits of a space (Ching 1996: 99) and also determine its *Permeability*, that is, the extent to which a space can be penetrated, either physically or visually, by the elements. Permeability may also be materialized by *implying* enclosure, using false ceilings or movable screens, for instance.

The variable elements which materialize Binding are referred to as *Ambience*, that is, the "affordances" that can easily be changed in a space, in particular, color, light, texture and pattern.[12] Together with Permeability, choices for Ambience co-articulate to determine the firmness of enclosure in a three-dimensional space (and see further descriptions in Stenglin 2004: 210–394).

Materialization will now be considered in detail, using the two spaces from the Scientia Building we have already mentioned: the atrium and the entrance together with vestibule. When analyzing the Permeability and Ambience of a space, it is vital to consider these two systems in tandem because they work *together* to construct the feeling of enclosure in a given space.

3.3.1.6. Permeability: Overhead Planes. On the overhead plane, Bound choices shut the environment out by sealing the ceiling from the sky and the elements through choices for *occlusion*. Unbound choices tend to physically seal the elements out but visually open the space to the environment overhead through choices for *diaphany*.

Three main elements need to be considered when analyzing overhead planes: the type of material, the height of the ceiling, and its shape. Opaque materials such as stone occlude a space and make it feel Bound, as we saw in the entrance vestibule to the Scientia building, while diaphanous materials like glass connect the atrium of the Scientia with the sky overhead, making the space feel Unbound (see Photo 9).

---

[12] Interior designers who are vocationally trained to work with Ambience work with a very broad range of elements. They include accessories, scale, fittings, soft furnishings, furniture, and style as well as the elements identified in this chapter: color, light, pattern, and texture. However, only color, light, pattern, and texture were chosen as variables for Ambience in this chapter because they can specifically be used to modify perceptions of how firmly a space is enclosed. Their relevance to Binding is thus most significant.

In terms of height, low ceilings make a space feel Bound, while height makes it feel more expansive. Again, the low height of both entrance spaces to the Scientia (about 2.5–3 meters) is a strong choice for creating a firm enclosure, while the large triple volume of space in the atrium makes the interior feel as though it soars upwards.

Regarding roof shape, there are five common choices for materialization: flat, curved (barrel), raked, pitched, and compound/combination. Of these, a flat or cantilevered ceiling is the most Bound choice, while a raked ceiling unbinds a space by opening it up and outward. The ceiling/roof of the atrium, for example, consists of two raked roofs joined into a "butterfly" shape that creates a trough-like space along the central spine overhead, while both outer perimeters rise upward, and in this way optimize the feeling of being Unbound (see Photo 9 again). The ceiling in the entrance vestibule, in contrast, is flat and provides a firm sense of enclosure over those entering the space.

Photo 9.   Overhead plane in the atrium

Table 1. Summary of Permeability and the overhead plane

Element	Bound (occlusion)	Unbound (diaphany)
material	Solid/opaque eg concrete, thatch	Transparent e.g. glass
height	Human scale	Institutional scale (>5 metres)
shape	Flat (cantilever)	Raked, curved, pitched

3.3.1.7. Permeability: Base Planes. The base plane is the plane of gravity. It anchors the building to the earth and can be divided into two different planes. First, there is a ground plane, which touches the earth and physically supports the building. This can be heavy, "gravitizing" the building (e.g., the pyramids) and is a Bound choice as it signals stability. O'Toole (1994) refers to this as *cthonicity*. Alternately, the ground plane can rest on the earth lightly, like the Eiffel Tower, which only touches the earth at four points, signaling light contact and transience.

As noted, much of the exterior of the Scientia is strongly Bound on the ground plane, by the solid sandstone flanks at the front, and also by a large grey granite platform at the rear on which the entrance to the building sits (see Photos 1 and 4). In contrast, the ground plane of the atrium is elevated approximately two storeys above the ground, using the towering wooden posts as supports. This makes extremely light contact with the earth.

The second half of a base plane is the floor, which may or may not also have covering. The material and height of the floor plane materialize spatial security. Soft, thick carpet that bodies can sink into, for example, creates a Bound feeling. It is comfortable, secure and allows the user to rest their weary limbs. Polished flooring, in contrast, has no resilience or "give", but allows users to glide over it freely, and thus is Unbound. The height of the floor may be varied: level, submerged, or elevated. A level floor is Unbound, as it creates a "level playing field" to glide over. Submerged or elevated floors are Bound choices as both make users feel more enclosed.

Once again, there are contrasts in the flooring chosen for the entrance and atrium of the Scientia building. The entrance has dark grey polished tiles that stretch directly to the window at the opposite end, while the flooring in the atrium consists of polished wooden floorboards. In terms of Binding, both choices for flooring are Unbound as they create a glossy and level platform on

Table 2. Summary of Permeability and the base plane

Plane & element	Bound (occlusion)	Unbound (diaphany)
Ground plane	Heavy contact "gravitises", e.g., stone	Light contact elevates, e.g., stumps, piers
Floor plane: height	Elevated or submerged	Level
Floor plane: material	High resilience to "sink into", e.g. thick carpet	Low resilience to "glide over", e.g. polished tiles

which users can glide into, and around, the building. Finally, the different choices for flooring—tiles and wooden floorboards—also play another important role in visually delineating these two very different spaces.

3.3.1.8. Permeability: Wall Planes. Walls define the *vertical* boundaries of a space and have a great presence in our field of vision (Ching 1996), strongly defining the firmness of enclosure we feel in a space. They can also make a space penetrable or impenetrable depending on the choices for the following variables: visual weight, spatial envelope, and filtering.

Visual weight refers to how heavy or light the walls seem, determined by the opacity or transparency of the materials. Visually heavy walls create a more Bound space than walls that are visually light. In the Scientia, the choice of sandstone and marble for the two walls framing the physical entrance, followed by plaster walls in the entrance vestibule, are choices for occlusion (see Photos 5 and 6 again). In contrast, glass as walling for the atrium is a strong choice for visual lightness and diaphany (see Photo 8).

The spatial envelope refers to the way the walls are constructed to "envelop" a space, either enclosing a space firmly (Bound) or loosely (Unbound). The spatial envelope is determined by the number of walls, their height, and their span. A spatial envelope that completely "wraps around" the occupant creates a firm enclosure, either by using a single wall plane which constructs an organically shaped spatial envelope, such as Frank Lloyd Wright's spherical Guggenheim Museum on Fifth Avenue, New York, or by using four walls that are joined together, creating an envelope that is angular. Open and Unbound envelopes, on the other hand, can be created by combining two walls into an *L*-shape or using one freestanding wall to create partial delineation in a space and optimal openness.

In terms of wall height, most walls stretch from floor to ceiling and create a firm sense of enclosure (Bound), because they occlude visual continuity between adjoining spaces. However, Unbound spaces may be created by reducing the height of the vertical plane, using waist-high walls, for example, to provide a moderate physical sense of separation while maintaining visual continuity between adjoining spaces.

The horizontal span of the wall also contributes to the spatial envelope, with complete wall spans constructing a closed spatial envelope, and freestanding walls constructing more open spatial envelopes.

None of the spaces we have been analyzing in the Scientia in the preceding sections constructs a tight spatial envelope, as the spaces do not have four opaque and enclosing walls (see Photos 5 and 6 again). The entrance comprises a two-sided opaque enclosure while the vestibule is a three-sided enclosure with two opaque walls and one diaphanous one (the glass doors). The result is a vestibule consisting of a three-sided rectilinear envelope with one open end. This openness is important as it prevents the vestibule from feeling oppressive (Too Bound) and allows it to be strongly connected to the adjoining spaces, facilitating the function of the vestibule as a transitional space that welcomes visitors as they move from the exterior to the interior of the building. In addition, the relatively low height of the walls contributes to the feeling of Binding in the space, while their short horizontal span prevents the vestibule from feeling too tightly enclosed.

Table 3.   Summary of Permeability and the wall plane

Element	Bound (occlusion)	Unbound (diaphany)
Visual weight	Heavy materials: opaque, impermeable permanent	Light materials: semi/transparent permeable, temporary/fluid
Spatial envelope: number of walls	1 continuous wall (circle or oval) or 3+ walls	1 or 2 partial-span walls
Height of the walls	Floor-to-ceiling; floor-to-eye level	Waist-high walls; line on the floor
Span	Complete: wall-to-wall	Partial
Filters	Strong filters via minimal openings	Weak filters via large openings

The atrium, on the other hand, contains two different spatial envelopes. The lower section, which is occupied by visitors, consists of *two* enclosing walls while the upper section consists of *four* enclosing walls. The lower section is thus designed as an open, fluid spatial envelope that visitors can move through, while the upper section of the same space is much more strongly delineated and contained. Such strong delineation in the upper regions of the space appears to be important in preventing the space from feeling too open as they provide it with clear upper boundaries.

A further element to consider is the degree to which the walls filter the penetration of elements via openings such as windows and doors. Bound spaces are created by strong filters which "block out" the elements using impermeable materials, small windows, solid doors, and supplementary filters such as blinds and curtains. Unbound spaces are created by weak filters that allow light, air, heat, and the other elements to pass through them. Walls that only allow the penetration of light construct visually Unbound spaces, while walls that allow light, air and/or heat to enter construct visually and physically Unbound spaces, through the use of large openings, louvres, sliding doors, and so forth.

Both of the Scientia spaces we have been analyzing so far have weak filters. The large glass doors at the entrance allow light, air, and heat to enter the vestibule as well as visually connecting it with the outdoors, while the atrium is strongly visually connected to the sky and built environment surrounding it. However, grey blinds have been installed inside the atrium to provide some degree of filtering by reducing the amount of light and heat that enters the space during the periods of intense heat that typify Australian summers.

3.3.1.9. Variables: Ambience. The four key elements to consider when analyzing a space for ambience are color, light, pattern, and texture. In this section, we will briefly consider color and lighting. Warm and dark colors create Bound spaces because they appear to advance and "close" the space "in". Cool and light colors, in contrast, are Unbound because they open a space up and can create the illusion of receding both the walls and the ceiling.

Similarly, light directionality can alter the firmness of enclosure in a space. "Down lighting", for example, closes a space in by appearing to bring the ceiling closer, while "up lighting" can create an illusion of elevating a ceiling, making an area seem more open and spacious.

In applying the notion of Ambience to the Scientia entrance and atrium, we can see that the choices for the variable elements are also significant and carefully balanced. In the entrance, for example, the walls on the right consist of deep reddish brown granite and dark grey plaster (vestibule). To prevent these dark colors from appearing too oppressive, both walls on the left "open" the space somewhat through choices for cool and light colors: cream sandstone and off-white paint. The choices for down-lighting, on the other hand, work to create a firmer sense of enclosure in the entry while the polished texture of the tiles underfoot counters this by increasing light levels. So, in relation to Ambience in the entrance to the building, the design effectively counter-balances choices for diaphany as well as occlusion, to prevent the space from feeling too oppressive, too small, and too "closed in".

As the atrium is primarily made of glass, there are fewer choices for color, nevertheless warm timbers have been chosen for the flooring, contributing to a Bound effect. It is obviously important to create some sense of occlusion in the space; otherwise the occupant would likely feel too exposed. Lighting in the atrium is mainly natural and plentiful, and enters the space from overhead.

In summary, Section 3.1.1 has shown how gradations of Binding, materialized through choices for Permeability and Ambience, work to establish a relationship of security with the occupants of the space. In particular, choices for Permeability and Ambience co-articulate to evoke feelings of security and welcome occupants into the vestibule, a weakly Bound enclosure. Once a relationship of security is established with the user in this way, it is maintained through slight but incremental changes to Permeability and Ambience until the occupants finds themselves in the open, light-filled heart of the building where they feel strongly Unbound. Interaction with a space has the potential to move us in other ways as well, especially with regard to affiliation, which is the focus of Bonding.

3.3.2. BONDING. Bonding is concerned with how we can negotiate solidarity and affiliation in three-dimensional space, through the use of Bonding icons and through the hybridization of a space (Stenglin 2004). Bonding icons are emblems or evocative symbols of social belonging, which have a strong potential for rallying, such as Olympic rings, flags, buildings such as the Sydney Opera House, songs, and so forth. They can also function to establish a visual

Table 4. Summary of Ambience

Element	Bound (occlusion)	Unbound (diaphany)
Color	Warm and dark colors	Cool and light colors
Light directionality	Down lighting	Up lighting
Texture	Rough textures (decrease illumination by absorbing light)	Smooth, shiny textures (increase illumination)
Pattern	—	Vertical and horizontal stripes

identity for an institution such as a university. This is clearly what the Scientia building has accomplished for the University of New South Wales, especially the iconic "tree-like" structure of the central atrium.

3.3.2.1. Bonding Icon: The Scientia Building. The Scientia is clearly a landmark building—what it symbolizes and how it is able to create a new identity for the institution is the concern of Bonding icons. Bonding icons have enormous potential to facilitate empathy, affiliation, and identification through the genesis of shared meanings that evolve amongst members of a community. They do this by crystallizing strong interpersonal attitudes to ideational meanings, as we will now see.

Ideationally, the central part of the Scientia is a tree-like structure with many upward thrusting arms creating vectors pointing to the sky and the heavens beyond. Interpersonally, this tree-like construction evokes many different layers of meaning, including a positive appreciation of abstract values such as dynamism, growth, dreams, and aspirations—both institutional and personal. The central tree also suggests the metaphorical "tree of life", which in turn evokes valuations of appreciation. Such valuations may be positive or negative but their function is to evoke collective understandings or familiar ideas, and in doing so, connect people around shared ideational meaning(s) and mutual attitudes towards them.

Furthermore, in its role as Bonding icon the Scientia evokes many other fused layers of ideational and interpersonal meanings. The materials used, for example, create some very powerful and evocative contrasts. The two large blocks flanking the central tree structure are made of sandstone and are particularly heavy and solid, thereby evoking shared judgments of the permanence and enduring capacity of the building to stand the test of time as well as evoking a shared appreciation of its "consummate" status, reinforced by the use of rarefied materials such as sandstone, jarrah, and *entire walls* of plate glass. Not only are the materials rarefied, they also suggest that the values associated with the building belong to both the natural world (as signified by the sandstone and jarrah) and the industrial, built environment (as signified by the stainless steel and glass).

Again, moreover, a motif of contrast can be seen in relation to the central tree structure, which rests almost delicately on one finely tapered point (see again Photo 3: close up shot). This lack of "gravitas" strongly contrasts with the solid sandstone walls that flank it and by doing so evokes positive judgments of the capacity and giftedness of the architects, engineers, and builders who were able to design and create a structure that appears to defy gravity. Not only are all of these meanings crystallized in the Scientia, they also have the potential to multiply (Lemke 1998; Royce 1998, 2002). Consequently, the materials and contrasts discussed so far function to suggest that the value of the building is simultaneously "traditional" and "ground-breaking", "historical" and "contemporary", "real" and "amazing", "old" and "new", "natural" and "constructed". The synergy that results from such fusion of meanings also has the potential to evoke some very powerful emotions—positive or negative. Positive emotions may include pride and loyalty, while negative feelings could include cynicism and hatred. These shared emotions in turn can evoke affiliation with at least one of two communities: those who identify with the institution and the values it represents, and those who do not.

3.3.2.2. Affiliation and Appraisal. Having explained what and how the building symbolizes, let us now turn our attention to how the building creates communal alignment over time with key stakeholders such as students. To explore how such affiliation is negotiated, we will need to apply Appraisal theory, especially the systems of Attitude: Affect, Judgment, and Appreciation. Shared Affect aligns people around empathy, shared Judgment aligns them around shared principles, while shared Appreciation aligns them around joint tastes and mutual preferences. Although the following account will be a compliant one, we do acknowledge, once again, that the attitudinal alignment evoked by a Bonding icon may be either negative or positive.

In terms of ideational meaning, students attending the University of New South Wales are invited into the Scientia to participate in two main types of activities: examinations and celebrations. During examinations, one can imagine that many students are feeling nervous, apprehensive, and afraid. The building thus no doubt evokes strong feelings of insecurity associated with the passing or failing of examinations—feelings that probably recur over the extended period of time that constitutes student life and only ends after the successful completion of all subjects and the awarding of degrees at graduation ceremonies. At that point, students and their families are invited into the Scientia for celebratory drinks and photographs. On these occasions, the Scientia clearly symbolizes success in education, and this would often evoke very strong feelings of happiness, security, and pride in one's achievements, heightened by the fact that it takes many years of success before one can achieve public recognition.

The strength of such positive and negative emotions would clearly influence the types of judgments students make about the building. This is reflected in the following student comments: "one comes to this building to be at the height of education" and "you have to work hard to get here and graduate."[13] It is not surprising that for many students the building becomes a landmark that also evokes strong judgments associated with social esteem, in particular, their own capacity, tenacity, and normality.

In addition to aligning students around shared feelings and judgments, the building also evokes strong evaluations of appreciation. Appreciation is concerned with the value of objects in a culture. Typically students appraise the composition of the building and its parts in the following ways: "the unusual glass structure", "the unique design" and "the distinctive wooden pole". They also make valuations of the building in terms of its messages or ideologies. These include: "[it] connotes the feeling of grandeur, excellence, prestige" and "[it] is open to all, and embraces knowledge".

By evoking the full range of appraisal in these ways—Affect, Judgment, and Appreciation—the Scientia building is a Bonding icon that over time aligns students into communities of feeling and affinities of collegiality. In this way, it is also able to accrue and crystallize the institutional values embodied by

---

[13] Quotes from students in ENGL2821/LING2530, "Visual Communication", UNSW, 2005.

the University of New South Wales. Another powerful resource for negotiating Bonding is hybridization.

3.3.2.3. Hybridization. The hybridization of spaces facilitates Bonding by transferring the values of one activity to those of another, and vice-versa, thus expanding the potential range for identification with the space (Stenglin 2004). In doing so, it functions in much the same way as a lexical metaphor (Martin 2004b). For example, an art gallery that screens a film from popular culture invites those interested in popular culture into the gallery. Via this, the values of accessibility are transferred to the institution, and the high culture prestige of the gallery is transferred to the film. Similarly, Ravelli's (2000) analysis of a souvenir store for the Sydney 2000 Olympic Games identified that, through hybridization, it was much more than just a retail experience. Via methods of museum-like display, values of the Olympic Games (such as harmony, unity, loyalty) were transferred to the merchandise.

For the Scientia, its functionality is not immediately apparent from the exterior, although its size and design would suggest ceremony. A kind of hybridization does occur on the exterior, however, as students typically sit on the stairs and grass at the front, and at graduations, families take photos with the Scientia as backdrop. Thus the values of everyday life are transferred to the institution, as it forms the backdrop for student activities; similarly, the prestige of the institution is transferred to these activities, giving them significance. Similarly, for the interior, the largely ceremonial spaces could potentially lie empty, a fate mitigated somewhat by using the main hall for receptions (University and private), as well as for exams, and by using the secondary hall as a (temporary) restaurant, with fittings that can be quickly removed, to restore the space for functions or meetings. Again, the prestige of the institution is transferred to these social activities, and the incorporation of a broad range of social activities expands the image of inclusivity of the University.

Bonding therefore involves negotiating communal alignment—either positive or negative—around shared attitudes. In particular, these attitudes include shared affect, appreciation and judgment, and evolve amongst community members over time. As discussed in Section 3.3.2.1., one of the resources for materializing Bonding are icons. Bonding icons crystallize strong interpersonal attitudes to ideational meanings and as a result have the potential to facilitate empathy, affiliation and identification. Another powerful resource for materializing Bonding is hybridization. By facilitating value transfer, hybridization in the Scientia building transfers the prestige of the university to a broad range of social activities while these activities enhance the image of inclusiveness that the institution wishes to project. In these ways, the basic function of Bonding is to align people around shared, communal ideals.

4. Controversial Issues

One of the challenges of a metafunctional approach to any semiotic is to account for both the distinctiveness and the simultaneity of the metafunctions. Our focus in this chapter has been on the interpersonal, but of course, any three-dimensional text is more than just an interpersonal construct. It also functions through the representational metafunction, to construct a sense of "what" is there, and is made to cohere through the textual metafunction. This is also true for the Scientia: what it "stands for", and how it is organized, including in relation to the campus as a whole, are critical to a more comprehensive understanding of the building as a whole. As discussed in Ravelli (in press), the Scientia is made to be, textually, the Centre of the campus. Not a literal centre, but a symbolic one. What it symbolizes in representational terms is captured both by the motif of contrast already identified in relation to interpersonal meanings, namely the contrast of "old" and "new", "natural" and "manufactured", and so on, and by the visual impact of the central structure, with its thrusting arms representing something dynamic and growing, connoting perhaps the tree of knowledge. Thus, the University is represented as a complex institution, grounded in history, dynamically engaging with the present and the future. These aspects are of course semiotic constructs: the Scientia is not literally the Centre of the campus, the University is not particularly old, and any relation to the future is merely speculation. Nevertheless, a three-dimensional space does make meaning across each of these metafunctions, and so a full analysis needs to account for them all, and for their interaction.

At the same time, analysis needs to take account of the potential for different readings of the same text. A text may be read compliantly, resistantly, or tactically (Cranny-Francis 1992), and this chapter has produced what we believe to be a compliant reading of the text. Resistant readings recognize but reject the semiotic thrust of the text (perhaps in the case of the Scientia, something like, "I hate that building!", or else using the stair rails as a slide), whereas tactical readings are less predictable (perhaps for the Scientia, something like "I think I'll use Jarrah in my own home"). Readings are also located socially, culturally, and historically, and thus may vary along any of these dimensions. With the progress of time, for example, something which was initially unconventional and ground-breaking may come to be seen as quite mundane—a process that is also familiar in visual arts discourse (Hughes 1980/1991; Wilkinson 2000).

Perhaps the most fundamental controversy in dealing with three-dimensional spaces is whether or not we want to see such spaces as being semiotic at all: are they really "texts"? Perhaps, after all, a building is just a building? But to such a question we would offer a resounding "no". Three-dimensional spaces of our built environment are indeed texts: they are neither necessary nor natural, but are a "construct of semiosis" (Kress and van Leeuwen 2006: 154). They make meaning socially and culturally, and are produced and read in social and cultural contexts. Sometimes, built spaces within our own culture may be so conventional and familiar that their meanings have become naturalized and are no longer noticed. As Lumley notes (1992: v):

> [. . .] everyone lives and works in buildings of some sort. We all react instinctively to the size and space relationships of architecture because buildings and their surroundings relate to the human figure as we walk in, around and through them. [. . .] When we study architecture, we need to analyse many of the things which we otherwise take for granted, or perhaps like or dislike without knowing why.

Equally, however, anything slightly new or different attracts attention—positive and negative—and highlights the meaning-making potential of these texts. Dramatic new buildings magnify this process, drawing extremes of praise or approbation. Witness, for instance, some of the negative responses to I.M. Pei's pyramid for the Louvre:

> [. . . E]veryday Parisians expressed their disapproval by wearing buttons that asked, *"Pourquoi la Pyramide?"* Pei's daughter, Liane, saw women spit at her father's feet as they passed on the street (Cannell 1995: 17).

Such approbation is not in response to bricks and mortar (or glass and steel, in this case), but to the new and unconventional *meanings* of the pyramid in relation to those of the traditional and familiar Louvre: to its social and cultural contribution.

5. Relation to Applied Linguistics and Research Perspectives

It may still seem strange to be discussing the meaning potential of a building, in a volume which is focused on *applied linguistics*. And yet, as we hope to have shown in the chapter, the connection is not strange at all. Each endeavor shares many of the same features: a concern with texts as communicative constructs, an understanding of meaning as being metafunctional, an understanding of semiotics as being socially situated.

And yet the endeavors are not identical. Kress and van Leeuwen (2006: 122–123 and 139–140, for instance) discuss some of the close parallels between linguistic and visual systems in the interpersonal domain, but also note their divergences. For example, in relation to "image acts", the visual equivalent of linguistic speech acts, they note (Kress and van Leeuwen 2006: 123) that it is more or less impossible for an image to directly offer goods and services: such offers must "take the *form* of an 'offer of information'. It must be *represented*. It cannot be enacted directly." Thus, while other communicative systems can be understood in relation to linguistic communication, they must also be understood in their own terms.

At the same time, however, accounting for the affordances of non-linguistic semiotic systems has the potential, in turn, to feed back into our understanding of language also. In the case of spatial semiotics, Stenglin's newly proposed systems of Binding and Bonding is inspired by work on Appraisal in language, in particular, Martin (2004a). The systems enable a delicate analysis of the resources which enable security, insecurity, affiliation, and exclusion to be negotiated in a three-dimensional space, and the delicacy of this analysis provides the springboard for further reflection on language: what are the ways in which Appraisal and other resources are used in language to align affiliations, create a "secure" sense of belonging, or a distancing effect? We are not suggesting here that such matters have not already been considered within linguistics. We would, rather, like to propose that there is further potential here not only with regard to language, but also the co-deployment of language and visual images, as the research of Caple (2006) and Economou (2006) clearly indicates. Similarly, Martin and Welch (in prep.) are exploring the co-articulation that occurs between language and another modality, facial expressions, and thus furthering our understanding of the multi-dimensional potential of Bonding.

Yet, it is also sometimes the case that work in a new domain does reveal aspects which have otherwise been neglected in a familiar domain. For example, work on visual resources has revealed the meaning potential of the *visuality* of language (through typographic systems, for instance), an aspect which has tended to be ignored in the study of linguistics (van Leeuwen 2005b). Overall then, between applied linguistics and other research directions, there is a dialogic relationship: each research perspective is mutually informing of the other.

Just as with applied linguistics, work on spatial semiotics has the potential for fruitful applications. The enormous descriptive scope of this work provides the opportunity for reflection and critique on spaces that are private, public, and commercial; on spaces that are conventional or ground-breaking. In relation to the interpersonal metafunction, we can explore how spatial semiotics contributes to the establishment, maintenance, and adjustment of social relations, and how they contribute to an individual's sense of security and belonging. Our examination of the Scientia begins to suggest how important spatial semiotics is to the creation of identity for an institution, and there is scope to compare this with other, similar, institutions. Within the University, the interpersonal systems we have described here can be usefully applied to the analysis of the various learning spaces which comprise the institution: the traditional, large lecture halls, with their impersonal, hierarchized layout; smaller tutorial rooms, with their more equalizing potential; and newer "break-out" spaces, allowing for more fluid and informal relationships. Similar issues can be explored in schools (Jones in press), hospitals (Iedema in press), shopping centres (Stenglin 2000), homes (Stenglin in press b) as well as museums and galleries (Martin and Stenglin 2007; Ravelli 2006; Stenglin 2004, 2007, in press a, in press b, in press d). All create important interpersonal relations between institution and user, and can be usefully critiqued.

To undertake such an enterprise requires more than we have outlined here, however. As already noted, the approach needs to be integrated with a crossmetafunctional analysis, to account for the full meaning potential of a three-dimensional text. All of the systems described can be further extended in delicacy, and no doubt application to different instances of texts will reveal the need to adjust these systems. For example, the system of Control proposed above, to account for relative freedoms and restrictions on behavior, needs to be further and more specifically described. Also, there is the potential to apply such systems to other kinds of semiotics, for example, to the relative freedom or restrictions of a user's navigation of the web. As with the relation between linguistic and spatial semiotics, the relation between spatial and other semiotics will not be identical, but can be seen to be analogous.

One particular challenge for further research is to develop models and methods which can account for the logogenetic unfolding of space. Currently, our descriptions of spatial texts can provide synoptic snapshots of different aspects of a complex text (for example, a view of the Scientia from a distance, or up close), but our model cannot yet describe the dynamic unfolding of the text, as it is experienced by users. Dynamically-oriented models exist for aspects of language (see for example, Ventola 1987), but need to be re-thought for spatial semiotics. This is likely to be most challenging for interpersonal meanings generally, as opposed to the other metafunctions, because of the inherently prosodic nature of interpersonal structures (Martin and Rose 2003).

To account for spatial semiotics has much potential, both in understanding the fundamental relations with other communicative systems, such as language, and in extending the approach to account for the wide range of communicative semiotics which characterizes the contemporary world. A focus here on interpersonal meanings allows us to explore some of the ways in which identities, relations, security, and belonging can be created through the resources which comprise our built environment.

References

Andersons, Andrew. 2002. Meet the architects. Unpublished talk, 27 October, Wahroonga, Sydney: Historic Houses Trust, Rose Seidler House.

Bernstein, Basil. 1975. *Towards a Theory of Educational Transmissions: Class, Codes and Control*, Volume 3. 2nd ed. London: Routledge & Keegan.

Burns, Jenna Reed. 2005. A dynamic duo: Two couples, Two semis and two renovations—Under the same roof. *Sydney Morning Herald, Domain Magazine*, July 14, 10–11.

Caple, Helen. 2006. What you see and what you get: The evolving role of images in print newspapers. Talk delivered at the international symposium on "Form and Style in Journalism: Newspapers and the Representation of News 1880–2006", University of Tasmania, 14–15 December 2006.

Cannell, Michael. 1995. *I. M. Pei: Mandarin of Modernism*. New York: Random House.

Ching, Francis D. K. 1996. *Architecture: Form, Space and Order*. 2nd ed. New York: Wiley.

Cranny-Frances, Anne. 1992. *Engendered Fiction: Analysing Gender in the Production and Reception of Texts*. Kensington: University of New South Wales Press.

Djonov, Emilia. 2005. Analysing the organization of information in websites: From hypermedia design to systemic functional hypermedia discourse analysis. Unpublished PhD Thesis; School of English and Department of Linguistics; University of New South Wales.

Economou, Dorothy. 2006. Having it both ways? Images and text face off in the broadsheet feature story. Talk given at an international symposium "Form and Style in Journalism: Newspapers and the Representation of News 1880–2006", University of Tasmania, 14–15 December.

Eggins, Suzanne. 2004. *An Introduction to Systemic-Functional Linguistics*. 2nd ed. London: Continuum.

Halliday, Michael A.K. 1978. *Language as Social Semiotic: The Social Interpretation of Language and Meaning*. London: Arnold.

Halliday, Michael A.K. 1985/1994 *An Introduction to Functional Grammar*. 1st/2nd ed. London: Arnold.

Halliday, Michael A.K. and Ruqaiya Hasan. 1976. *Cohesion in English*. London: Longman.

Halliday, Michael A.K. and Christian M.I.M. Matthiessen. 2004. *An Introduction to Functional Grammar*. 3rd ed. London: Arnold.

Hayes, Babette. 2005. From here to contemporary. *Sydney Morning Herald, Domain Magazine*, September 1, 10–11.

Hodge, Robert and Gunther Kress. 1988. *Social Semiotics*. Cambridge: Polity Press.

Hughes, Robert. 1991. *The Shock of the New*. 2nd ed. New York: Knopf. Iedema, Rick. In press. An essay on the multi-modality, materiality and contingency of organizational discourse. *Organization Studies*.

Jones, Pauline. In press. The interplay of discourse, space and place in pedagogic relations. In: Len Unsworth (ed.), *Multimodal Semiotics and Multiliteracies Education: Transdisciplinary Approaches to Research and Professional Practice*. London: Continuum.

Kress, Gunther and Theo van Leeuwen. 1990. *Reading images*. Geelong, Victoria: Deakin University Press.

Kress, Gunther and Theo van Leeuwen. 2006. *Reading Images: The Grammar of Visual Design.* 2nd ed. London/New York: Routledge.

Lemke, Jay. 1998. Multiplying meaning: Visual and verbal semiotics in scientific text. In: James R. Martin and Robert Veel (eds.), *Reading Science: Critical and Functional Perspectives on Discourses of Science,* 87–113. London: Routledge.

Lemke, Jay. 2002. Travels in hypermodality. *Visual Communication* 1(3): 299–325.

Lumley, Ann. 1992. *Sydney's Architecture.* Melbourne: Longman Cheshire.

Martin, James R. 1992. *English Text: System and Structure.* Amsterdam: Benjamins.

Martin, James R. 1997. Analysing genre: Functional parameters. In: Frances Christie and James R. Martin (eds.), *Genre and Institutions: Social Processes in the Workplace and School,* 3–39. London: Cassell.

Martin, James R. 2000. Beyond exchange: APPRAISAL systems in English. In: Susan Hunston and Geoff Thompson (eds.), *Evaluation in Text: Authorial Stance and the Construction of Discourse,* 142–175. Oxford: Oxford University Press.

Martin, James R. 2001. Fair trade: Negotiating meaning in multimodal texts. In: Patrick Coppock (ed.), *The Semiotics of Writing: Transdisciplinary Perspectives on the Technology of Writing,* 311–338. (Semiotic and Cognitive Studies 10.) Turnhout: Brepols.

Martin, James R. 2004a. Mourning: How we get aligned. *Discourse and Society* 15(2–3) (Special issue on discourse around 9/11: Interpreting Tragedy: The Language of 11 Sep 2001): 321–344.

Martin, James R. 2004b. Sense and sensibility: Texturing evaluation. In: Joseph Foley (ed.), *Language, Education and Discourse: Functional Approaches,* 270–304. London: Continuum.

Martin, James R. and David Rose. 2003. *Working with Discourse: Meaning beyond the Clause.* London: Continuum.

Martin, James R. and Maree Stenglin. 2007. Materialising reconciliation: Negotiating difference in a post-colonial exhibition. In: Terry D. Royce and Wendy L. Bowcher (eds.), *New Directions in the Analysis of Multimodal Discourse.* Mahwah, NJ: Erlbaum.

Martin, James R. and Ariann Welch. In preparation. *Sir William Deane: Symbolising Hope in a Divided Nation.*

Martin, James R. and Peter White. 2005. *The Language of Evaluation: Appraisal in English.* New York: Palgrave MacMillan.

Martinec, Radan. 1997. Towards a functional theory of action. Paper presented to the Multimodal Discourse Analysis workshop, University of Sydney, 15–17 December.

Martinec, Radan. 1998a. Cohesion in action. *Semiotica* 120(1–2): 161–180.

Martinec, Radan. 1998b. Interpersonal resources in action. *Semiotica* 135(1–4): 117–145. Martinec, Radan. 2000a. Rhythm in multimodal texts. Leonardo 33(4): 289–297.

Martinec, Radan. 2000b. Construction of identity in Michael Jackson's 'Jam'. *Social Semiotics* 10(3): 313–329.

Matthiessen, Christian M. I. M. 1995. *Lexicogrammatical Cartography: English Systems.* Tokyo: International Language Sciences Publishers.

Mills, Phillip. 2006. Analysing intersemiosis in the museum: A prototype multimodal analysis. Paper presented to the Australian Systemic-Functional Linguistics Assocation National Conference, Armidale, September 2006.

O'Toole, Michael. 1994. *The Language of Displayed Art.* London: Leicester University Press.

O'Toole, Michael. 2004. Opera ludentes: A systemic-functional view of the Sydney opera house. In: Kay O'Halloran (ed.), *Multimodal Discourse Analysis: Systemic Functional Perspectives,* 11–27. London/New York: Continuum.

Painter, Clare. In press. The role of colour in children's picture books: Choices in ambience. In: Len Unsworth (ed.), *Multimodal Semiotics and Multiliteracies Education: Transdisciplinary Approaches to Research and Professional Practice.* London: Continuum.

Poynton, Cate. 1989. *Language and Gender: Making the Difference.* Oxford: Oxford University Press.

Pun, Betty Oi-Kei. 2005. Intersemiosis in film: A metafunctional and multimodal exploration of colour and sound in the films of Wong Kar-wai. Unpublished PhD Thesis, Department of Chinese Studies and Department of Linguistics, University of New South Wales.

Ravelli, Louise J. 2000. Beyond shopping: Constructing the Sydney olympics in three-dimensional text. *Text* 20(4): 489–515.

Ravelli, Louise J. 2006. *Museum Texts: Communication Frameworks.* London/New York: Routledge.

Ravelli, Louise J. In press. Analysing space: Adapting and extending multi-modal frameworks. In: Len Unsworth (ed.), *Multimodal Semiotics and Multiliteracies Education: Transdisciplinary Approaches to Research and Professional Practice*. London: Continuum.

Royce, Terry D. 1998. Synergy on the page: Exploring intersemiotic complementarity in page-based multimodal text. *Japan Association of Systemic Fucntional Linguistics Occasional Papers* 1(1): 25–48.

Royce, Terry D. 2002. Multimodality in the TESOL classroom: Exploring visual-verbal synergy. *TESOL* Quarterly 36(2): 191–205.

Rui Olds, Anita. 1994. Sending them home. In: Eilean Hooper-Greenhill (ed.), *The Educational Role of the Museum*, 76–80. London: Routledge.

Scollon, Ron and Suzanne Wong Scollon. 2003. *Discourses in Place: Language in the Material World*. London: Routledge.

Spigelman, Alice. 2001. *Almost Full Circle: Harry Seidler*. Rose Bay/Sydney: Brandl & Schlesinger.

Stenglin, Maree. 2000. The bright lights of Broadway: Framing semiotic change. Seminar, Linguistics Circle, Sydney University, 14 March.

Stenglin, Maree. 2002. Comfort and security: A challenge for exhibition design. In: Lynda Kelly and Jennifer Barrett (eds.), *Uncover: Graduate Research in the Museum Sector 1*, 23–30. Sydney: Australian Museum.

Stenglin, Maree. 2004. Packaging curiosities: Towards a grammar of three-dimensional space, Unpublished PhD Thesis, Department of Linguistics, University of Sydney.

Stenglin, Maree. 2007. Making art accessible: Opening up a whole new world. *Visual Communication* 6(2): 202–213.

Stenglin, Maree. In press a. Space Odyssey: A guided tour through the semiosis of three-dimensional space. *Visual Communication*.

Stenglin, Maree. In press b. Binding: A resource for exploring interpersonal meaning in 3D space. *Social Semiotics*.

Stenglin, Maree. In press c. Binding: Hope for bonding. In: Anthony Baldry and Elena Montagna (eds.), Interdisciplinary Perspectives on Multimodality: Theory and Practice. Proceedings of the Third International Conference on Multimodality, Pavia 2006. Campobasso: Palladino.

Stenglin, Maree. In press d. Olympism: How a bonding icon gets its "charge". In: Len Unsworth (ed.), *Multimodal Semiotics and Multiliteracies Education: Transdisciplinary Approaches to Research and Professional Practice*. London: Continuum.

Unsworth, Len (ed.) in press *Multimodal Semiotics and Multiliteracies Education: Transdisciplinary Approaches to Research and Professional Practice*. London: Continuum.

Van Leeuwen, Theo. 1998. Textual space and point of view. Paper presented to the Museums Australia State Conference 'Who sees, who speaks—Voices and points of view in exhibitions', Australian Museum, 21 September.

Van Leeuwen, Theo. 1991. The sociosemiotics of easy listening music. *Social Semiotics* 1(1): 67–80.

Van Leeuwen, Theo. 1999. *Speech, Music, Sound*. London: Macmillan.

Van Leeuwen, Theo. 2005a. *Introducing Social Semiotics*. London: Routledge.

Van Leeuwen, Theo. 2005b. Typographic meaning. *Visual Communication* 4(2): 138–143. Ventola, Eija. 1987. *The Structure of Social Interaction: A Systemic Approach to the Semiotics of Service Encounters*. London: France Pinter. White, Peter. 1994. Images of the shark: Jaws, gold fish, or cuddly toy? An analysis of the Australian Museum's. 1994. shark exhibition from a communicative perspective. Unpublished manuscript, Department of Linguistics, University of Sydney.

White, Peter. 1997. Death, disruption and the moral order: The narrative impulse in mass-media "hard news" reporting. In: Frances Christie and James R. Martin (eds.), *Genre and Institutions: Social Processes in the Workplace and School*, 101–133. London: Cassell.

White, Peter. 1998. Telling media tales: The news story as rhetoric. Unpublished doctoral thesis, University of Sydney.

Wilkinson, Philip. 2000. *The Shock of the Old: A Guide to British Buildings*. London: Macmillan.

Recommended Readings

Baldry, Anthony (ed.). 2000. *Multimodality and Multimediality in the Distance Learning Age: Papers in English Linguistics.*

Campobasso: Palladino. Baldry, Anthony and Paul J. Thibault. 2006. *Multimodal Transcription and Text Analysis.* (Equinox Textbooks and Surveys in Linguistics.) London: Equinox.

O'Halloran, Kay L. (ed.). 2004. *Multimodal Discourse Analysis: Systemic Functional Perspectives.* London: Continuum.

Preziosi, Donald. 1979a. *The Semiotics of the Built Environment.* Bloomington: Indiana University Press.

Preziosi, Donald. 1979b. *Architecture, Language and Meaning: The Origins of the Built World and its Semiotic Organisation.* The Hague/Paris: Mouton.

Royce, Terry D. and Wendy L. Bowcher (eds.). 2006. *New Directions in the Analysis of Multimodal Discourse.* Mahwah, NJ: Erlbaum.

Van Leeuwen, Theo and Carey Jewitt (eds.). 2001. *Handbook of Visual Analysis.* London: Sage.

Ventola, Eija, Cassily Charles and Martin Kaltenbacher (eds.). 2004. *Perspectives on Multimodality.* Amsterdam: Benjamins.

5

Relational Work, Politeness, and Identity Construction

Miriam A. Locher[1]

1. Introduction

As social beings we express, communicate, and, ultimately, negotiate our identity through many different channels: one such channel may be the way we dress, another the way we comport ourselves; yet another important channel is the use of language. We can even claim that the way in which we use language plays a crucial role when enhancing, maintaining, and challenging relationships in interpersonal communication. This use of language has variously been termed *facework*, *identity work*, *relational work* or *rapport management* (cf. Sections 3 and 4 for references). This chapter is intended to explain this use by utilizing some of the literature on identity that follows a postmodernist understanding of the concept of identity as "the social positioning of self and other" (Bucholtz and Hall 2005: 586). In addition, an attempt is made to combine research on the construction of identity by means of language more generally with the linguistic literature that has developed ideas under the keyword *politeness*. It is shown in this chapter that politeness research can fruitfully be combined with research on identity construction. This line of thought has already been pursued to some extent in the field of gender research (cf. Swann 2000),[2] and also in studies on face and identity more generally (cf. Tracy 1990; Spencer-Oatey 2007a,b). The chapter thus focuses on the interpersonal side of communication and further intends to explore the links between identity, face, and politeness. It is organized as follows: In Section 2, I will discuss the interpersonal and the informational aspect of language. In Section 3, I will

---

[1] The author wishes to thank Anne-Françoise Baer-Boesch, Lea Baumann, Derek Bousfield, Nicole Nyffenegger, Lukas Rosenberger, Philipp Schweighauser, and Ariane Studer for their perceptive and critical feedback on early drafts of this chapter, and Gerd Antos, Eija Ventola, Tilo Weber and Richard J. Watts for their comments on the final version of this text. A particular thank you goes to my students Lea Baumann, Manuela Burgermeister, Sonaljeet Kundan and Ariane Studer for sharing their data with me.

[2] Swann (2000) reviews several authors who combine gender with politeness issues, among them Brown (1980), Lakoff (1975), and Holmes (1995). However, these studies are not oriented to the same degree to the *construction* of identity and the role that politeness plays in this process as the present chapter is. More recent work (e.g., Mullany 2004) combines a constructivist approach to gender with politeness research.

move on to link these ideas to identity construction in general. In Section 4, different approaches to politeness will be at the heart of the investigation and will be discussed with identity construction in mind. In Section 5, concluding remarks on the two approaches to interpersonal communication will round off the chapter.

2. The Interpersonal and the Informational Aspect of Language

When engaging in linguistic interaction, people never just exchange factual information but also always reveal information about themselves and their perception of roles in a particular context. The choice of language in different speech situations, in other words, the "register" or "style"[3] the interactants use to accommodate to their addressees and the speech situation, thus always entails interpersonal information, too. The mere fact that individuals have different registers and styles at their disposal and make use of them can be seen as evidence for this need to negotiate roles in interaction.

In the literature, the relationship between the informational and the interpersonal side of communication has been discussed in numerous studies. Watzlawick, Beavin, and Jackson (1967: 54), for example, maintain that "[e]very communication has a content and a relationship aspect such that the latter classifies the former and is therefore a metacommunication." These two parts[4] cannot be disconnected from each other. There are, however, discourses that focus more on the content aspect, such as news broadcasts, or on the relationship aspects, such as rounds of gossip. Kasper (1990: 205) names the former type of interaction *transactional discourse*, in the sense that these exchanges focus on "optimally efficient transmission of information", and the latter *interactional discourse,* in that it "has as its primary goal the establishment and maintenance of social relationships". However, the two types of discourse can never be entirely separated from one another (Fill 1990).

3. Relational Work: Language and Identity Construction

Having generally postulated that there is a content and a relational aspect to acts of communication, we can easily link these ideas to identity construction. In Locher (2004) and Locher and Watts (2005), we have called "the process of defining relationships in interaction" *relational work*. This term is meant to highlight the fact that interlocutors invest "work" into their ways of communicating by adapting their language to different speech events and to the different goals that they might be pursuing. In addition, the term points to the relational aspect of communication in that it highlights the relations the

---

[3] For a detailed discussion of different approaches to style and register in language, see Eckert and Rickford (2001).

[4] Other researchers speak of a tri-partite distinction: the ideational (expressing content), the textual (organizing information into texts), and the interpersonal (Kresta 1993: 32, who bases his approach on Halliday 1976, 1981). The first two are included in the focus on content (transactional) while the latter corresponds to the relational aspect of an utterance (interactional).

interlocutors have with each other. It is important to stress that the term *relational work* does not only refer to polite linguistic behavior, but is meant to cover the entire spectrum of interpersonal linguistic behavior.[5] Polite, refined, and polished language might do a great deal for a person's identity construction, but so does rude, impolite, and aggressive language (cf. also Locher and Bousfield (2008) and Locher and Watts (2008) on linguistic impoliteness).

The construction of identity through linguistic means has been the subject of study in numerous fields. For an excellent and detailed overview of different approaches, I refer the reader to a critical appraisal by Mendoza-Denton (2002). Her general definition of the term is as follows:

> [Identity is] the active negotiation of an individual's relationship with larger social constructs, in so far as this negotiation is signaled through language and other semiotic means. Identity, then, is neither attribute nor possession, but an individual and collective-level process of semiosis. (Mendoza-Denton 2002: 475)

This definition can nicely be tied up with the notion of relational work: relational work refers to the ways in which the construction of identity is achieved in interaction, while identity refers to the "product" of these linguistic and non-linguistic processes. The definition of identity adopted in this chapter is thus one that could be called postmodernist (Swann 2000: 43) in that it sees identity as in flux and not as fixed (cf., e.g., Davies and Harré 1990; Schiffrin 1996; Adelswärd and Nilholm 2000; De Fina 2003; Joseph 2004; Locher 2006a; Locher and Hoffmann 2006).

To exemplify this line of reasoning, I will briefly focus on the issue of *language and gender*. Gender is one aspect of a person's identity that has been studied extensively. Work in this research field also shows how our understanding of identity construction has developed over time. Quite dramatic shifts in focus have taken place from the 1970s until today (Swann 2000, 2002; Bucholtz 2004). According to Bucholtz (2004), we can identify several movements within gender studies. In the 1970s and 1980s, the early feminists were concerned with sexism, misogyny, and the social inequality between men and women, as well as the exercise of power more generally. As an example, Bucholtz discusses the use of generic *he* and feminist attempts to introduce new, non-gendered pronouns to avoid sexism in language.

The next phase in gender research can be labeled the difference and dominance approaches. The dominance approach suggested that men and woman use language differently and that these different styles allow men to exercise power over women. The difference approach was characterized by "a recognition and even celebration of women's own practices" (Bucholtz 2004: 415) and by the claim that women form a different cultural group from men. The studies following this line of thought, however, often remained on a very general

---

[5] The term *facework* is often used by researchers who follow Brown and Levinson's (1987) politeness theory. It has been largely reserved to describe only appropriate and polite behavior with a focus on face-threat mitigation. To avoid confusion and in favor of clarity, the term relational work is adopted to highlight that the negotiation of the relational aspect of language does not only involve mitigating strategies.

level and could be reproached for excluding those men and women who did not fit the general middle-class, heterosexual profile from which most data were derived (Bucholtz 2004: 417). This resulted in more efforts to research gay and lesbian linguistic behavior as well as in studies on non-white and non-middle class speech communities.

Bucholtz ends her review of the literature on gender with a discussion of approaches that focus on "identity in practice and performance". She claims that

> [. . . s]tudies of women of color and of lesbians and gay men have shown the importance of moving away from broad, even universal, categories like gender as the sole explanation for speech patterns and toward other dimensions of identity that enrich and complicate language and gender analyses (Bucholtz 2004: 422).

Bucholtz raises an important issue in this quotation: we have to be aware of the danger of deriving from the variable we are studying (for example *gender*, but also any of the other sociological variables such as *age* or *class*) a monocausal explanation for observed linguistic patterns (cf. Swann 2000, 2002).[6] Bucholtz ultimately puts the emphasis on *agency*, which results in a definition of gender and identity more generally "as *achieved* and *fluid*" (Bucholtz 2004: 422, author's emphasis), rather than being predetermined by social categories.

In Bucholtz and Hall (2005: 586), the authors address the study of identity, "the social positioning of self and other", more generally by reviewing the existing literature in the various fields of study. This framework provides the best current guideline for the study of identity construction. They synthesize the ideas on identity and propose a framework in which this concept should be studied by taking the following five principles into account: the *emergence principle*, the *positionality principle*, the *indexicality principle*, the *relationality principle*, and the *partialness principle*. I will introduce each of these in turn.

The emergence principle is defined as follows:

> 1. Identity is best viewed as the emergent product rather than the pre-existing source of linguistic and other semiotic practices and therefore as fundamentally a social and cultural phenomenon (Bucholtz and Hall 2005: 588).

This principle highlights the emergent and the relational aspect of identity construction. By pointing out that identity is a *product* of interaction, the authors avoid the previously mentioned danger of imposing preexisting categories (such as, e.g., *gender, age, class*) on the text as the only explanatory factors and highlight the social and cultural bases of identity.

The second principle is the positionality principle:

---

[6] In her paper "Yes, but is it gender?", Swann (2002) points out the importance of methodological and theoretical considerations when studying *gender*. One of her many critical comments is that it cannot be enough to study only women in interaction to claim that we are witnessing women's talk, since we first have to find out how much of this women's talk overlaps with men's talk to make such a claim.

2. Identities encompass (a) macro-level demographic categories; (b) local, ethnographically specific cultural positions; and (c) temporary and interactionally specific stances and participant roles (Bucholtz and Hall 2005: 592).

Essentially, this highlights that (a) identity, while being constructed relationally, is also the product of a *combination* of different dimensions, among them the previously mentioned influence of age, class, and sex. In addition, there are (b) factors that can only be discerned when ethnographic work uncovers the meaning of linguistic strategies for the members of a particular social practice, and finally, (c) the authors point out that the emergent participant roles (e.g., *evaluator, joke teller, or engaged listener*) in an ongoing interaction contribute to identity construction.

The third principle is called the indexicality principle. It posits that the interactants' identities are the product of several processes of indexing through language, and thus refers to the actual linguistic mechanisms the interactants use. Bucholtz and Hall (2005: 594) claim that "these processes occur at all levels of linguistic structure and use." Examples are

(a) overt mention of identity categories and labels; (b) implicatures and presuppositions regarding one's own or others' identity position; (c) displayed evaluative and epistemic orientations to ongoing talk, as well as interactional footings and participant roles; and (d) the use of linguistic structures and systems that are ideologically associated with specific personas and groups (Bucholtz and Hall 2005: 594).

The relationality principle entails the crucial point that

[. . .] identities are never autonomous or independent but always acquire social meaning in relation to other available identity positions and other social actors (Bucholtz and Hall 2005: 598).

This principle works on many different levels. One of these relations refers to processes in which similarities with or differences from other perceived groups are constructed by social actors. A further relation is found between *genuineness* and *artifice*. This relation refers to the social process that negotiates "what sorts of language and language users count as 'genuine' for a given purpose" (Bucholtz and Hall 2005: 601) and what is constructed as "crafted, fragmented, problematic or false" (602). The third relation discussed in Bucholtz and Hall (2005: 603) refers to "structural and institutional aspects of identity formation." The notions of authority, hegemony, and power relations more generally are at play here, in that identities are authorized or dismissed by these structures.

The final aspect of the identity framework proposed by Bucholtz and Hall (2005) is the partialness principle. It states that

[a]ny given construction of identity may be in part deliberate and intentional, in part habitual and hence often less than fully conscious, in part an outcome of interactional negotiation and contestation, in part an outcome of others' perceptions and representations, and in part an effect of larger

ideological processes and material structures that may become relevant to interaction. It is therefore constantly shifting both as interaction unfolds and across discourse contexts (Bucholtz and Hall 2005: 606).

The authors stress that *agency* in identity construction should not be understood as a fully rational and always conscious process since there are undoubtedly aspects that are habitual. In addition, identity construction is a composite of processes. Notice the use of "in part" in the quotation above, which points both to the compositionality of identity as well as to the fact that, "[b]ecause identity is inherently relational, it will always be partial, produced through contextually situated and ideologically informed configurations of self and other" (Bucholtz and Hall 2005: 605).

From this brief introduction to the study of identity as proposed by Bucholtz and Hall, we can glimpse how intricate and dynamic such processes of identity construction are. In the next section, the links between research on politeness and identity will be discussed.

4. Relational Work and Politeness Issues

Politeness research is one of the productive research strands that aims at a better understanding of how interactants negotiate the interpersonal side of communication. It is for this reason that different approaches are reviewed here with respect to relational work in general. It is, of course, impossible to give a comprehensive overview of this field here. For such introductions, I refer the reader to the works of Eelen (2001), Watts (2003), and Locher (2004). Two influential works that have appeared during the past few decades will be introduced in this chapter. They are Brown and Levinson's (1978, 1987) concept of *face-saving* and Leech's (1983) *politeness principle*. This is followed by a summary of approaches that highlight social norms and the evaluative character of judgments on linguistic behavior (Watts 2003; Locher 2004; Locher and Watts 2005). Since the notion of *face* is discussed in all of these approaches, the next section is dedicated to explaining this important concept.

4.1. The Notion of Face

Goffman's (1967) notion of *face*,[7] which he derived from Durkheim (1915), is an important concept for the discussion of identity construction and relational work in general. Goffman (1967) defines face as follows:

> The term *face* may be defined as the positive social value a person effectively claims for himself by the line others assume he has taken during a particular contact. Face is an image of self delineated in terms of approved social attributes—albeit an image that others may share, as when a person

---

[7] The notion of *face* has been reproached for being culturally bound and based too much on the individual (Gu 1990: 241–242; Matsumoto 1988: 405). While I agree that the metaphor of *face* is clearly culturally bound, I claim that the theoretical notion of *face* as described in this section is not.

makes a good showing for his profession or religion by making a good showing for himself (Goffman 1967: 5).

In Locher (2004: 52), I suggested that face can be equated with a mask,[8] an image a person gives him- or herself during a particular interaction, and that this face is not fixed but negotiated in *emergent networks*. The notion of emergent network is taken from Watts (1991). He makes a distinction between latent networks and emergent networks. Latent networks comprise the links between social interactants that have been previously established. The emergent network refers to the actual moment in time when interactants engage in a social practice and activate and renegotiate these links (for a discussion, see Locher 2004: 27–30). The recurring negotiation of face in emergent networks implies that a person can have several different faces or masks, depending on the situation. In addition, it is crucial that face depends on the acceptance of others. Goffman (1967: 10) describes this by saying that "it is only on loan to [an individual] from society". Finally, Goffman (1967: 13) maintains that considerations of face will influence interactions between people.

Since this understanding of face implies that interactants always have face, even though the face put on might differ from situation to situation, this means that there is no face-less communication (cf. Tracy 1990: 221; Scollon and Scollon 2001: 48), just as there cannot be any communication without an interpersonal aspect to it. The notions of *face* and *mask* can be linked to an interactant's understanding of a particular identity that he or she wishes to propose in a particular situation. It is this link that allows us to connect politeness research with research on identity construction within a framework of the study of relational work, as long as we do not perceive face to be a fixed construct.[9] On the contrary, we should conceptualize it as a product, emerging in interaction. This is in line with Bucholtz and Hall's (2005: 587) claim that identity "is intersubjectively rather than individually produced and interactionally emergent rather than assigned in an a priori fashion." It also supports Tracy's (1990) position that

> Face is a social phenomenon; it comes into being when one person comes into the presence of another; it is created through the communicative moves of interactants. Whereas face references the socially situated identities people claim or attribute to others, facework[10] references the communicative strategies that are the enactment, support, or challenge of those situated identities (Tracy 1990: 210).

It has to be stressed that the notion of face proposed here is not the same in all the politeness frameworks discussed below. Brown and Levinson (1987) have a more static, bipartite view of face, as explained in Section 4.2, while Spencer-Oatey (2005) uses a more flexible, but also bipartite definition of face in her framework

---

[8] The metaphor of the stage is evoked here where people can put on different masks or faces. However, I do not wish to imply that a person can take off such a mask to reveal an underlying 'true' identity, since there is no face-less communication (cf. Tracy 1990: 221; Scollon and Scollon 2001: 48).

[9] See the discussion of *face* as used by Brown and Levinson (1987) in Section 4.2.

[10] Cf. note 5.

of rapport management, as discussed in Section 4.5.[11] However, it is suggested that the notion of face can stand for identity construction in more general terms and can be useful for both politeness and identity research in this sense.

4.2. Brown and Levinson's Approach to Politeness

Without any doubt, Brown and Levinson (1978/1987) have written the most influential work on politeness in the last few decades. Their work has been enthusiastically received, reproduced, and developed further by many scholars, but has also been extensively criticized by others.[12] In what follows, I will highlight how their study has furthered our understanding of relational work, politeness, and identity construction in general. To do this, I will briefly introduce their main ideas.

Two key terms in Brown and Levinson's framework are *face* and the *face-threatening act*. Face in a Goffmanian sense has already been introduced above. Brown and Levinson (1987: 61) define face as "the public self-image that every member wants to claim for himself". They also maintain that it is made up of two dualistic wants. They introduce the terms *positive face* and *negative face*:

> *negative face*: the want of every "competent adult member" that his actions be unimpeded by others. *positive face*: the want of every member that his wants be desirable to at least some others (Brown and Levinson 1987: 62).

These two sides have also been called the *independence* and *involvement aspects* of face by other researchers (Scollon and Scollon 2001: 48). Brown and Levinson (1987: 62) argue that "face respect is not an unequivocal right", which means that an interactant's face is vulnerable. The authors believe, however, that it is in both the speaker's and the addressee's interest to "maintain each other's face" (1987: 60). This is complicated by the fact that there are acts which intrinsically threaten one or both aspects of an individual's face. These acts are called *face-threatening acts* (FTAs). Brown and Levinson make the following proposition:

> Unless S's want to do an FTA with maximum efficiency [. . .] is greater than S's want to preserve H's (or S's) face to any degree, then S will want to minimize the face threat of the FTA (Brown and Levinson 1987: 62).

The key here is the minimization of the face threat. The authors claim that politeness plays a role as soon as speakers consider each others' face and wish to minimize FTAs. To achieve this minimization, the speakers have several strategies at their disposal, which are mutually known to both speaker and addressee. These strategies range from not committing the FTA at all (strategy 5 in Figure 1) to committing the FTA without mitigation (strategy 1), with intermediate stages that are characterized by making use of different types of redressive means (strategies 2 to 4).

---

[11] See also Ruhi (2007) for a recent discussion and development of the concept *face*.
[12] I refer the reader to Werkhofer (1992), Eelen (2001), Watts (2003), and Locher (2004) for critical reviews of Brown and Levinson's (1978/1987) work.

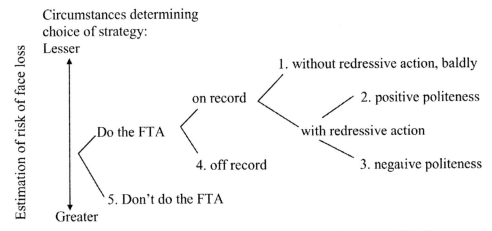

Figure 1.   Possible strategies for realizing FTAs (Brown and Levinson 1987: 60)

The speaker's choice of a strategy depends on several factors that together establish the estimated risk of loss of face, or the "weightiness" of the FTA "x" (W_x). These factors are the value of the distance (D) between the speaker (S) and the hearer (H), the measure of the power that the hearer has over the speaker (P), and the relative ranking of the imposition in its cultural and situational context (R_x). This equation is summarized as follows: $W_x = D(S,H) + P(H,S) + R_x$ (1987: 76). It is best understood as an abstract way of representing the intricate social factors that play a role in interaction.

What does this type of politeness research have to do with relational work and identity construction? An important aspect of identity construction is whether or not we want to project an image of ourselves as someone who is aware of the social norms of behavior that are relevant in a particular social practice. One way of displaying such knowledge is by selecting the type of relational work that is suitable for redressing face-threatening acts in a specific context. Consider, for example, the question of address terms (cf. Brown and Gilman 1960). Anybody who has a language such as French or German as his or her mother tongue knows that there is a difference between the uses of the personal pronouns *tu* and *vous* or *Du* and *Sie*. It is important to pick the right pronouns when addressing an interlocutor since these pronouns index intimacy and distance, as well as hierarchical relationships. It is, in other words, face-threatening to pick a pronoun that is too close (*tu/Du*) or one that is too distant (*vous/Sie*) since this could imply that the relationship between the interlocutors is not as expected.

While one could say that English does not have this problem (since *you* refers to both forms), the English situation is nevertheless far from straightforward. There is an intricate negotiation between calling each other by a nickname (*Bill*), first name (*William*), using a combination of address form and last name (*Mr. Clinton*), or even professional titles combined with last names (*President Clinton*). What combination is used depends on many different factors such as whether the two interactants are related, whether they are friends, whether they are close or distant, whether their relationship is work-related or not, whether they are on the same hierarchical level, etc. Knowledge about which of the address types is appropriate in which context is acquired by socialization into the different social practices.

The fact that we are dealing with face issues can be exemplified by a brief anecdote. Two exchange students from the United States,[13] who participated in our program in the English Department in Berne, Switzerland, addressed the teaching staff with their title (*Dr.*) and seemed not to mind when the teaching staff addressed them by first name. It is, however, customary among the linguists in this department to use only first names to address each other and the students, and to expect the same from the students when addressing staff members. The American students felt uncomfortable adjusting to this custom (even after having been told that it is okay to call their teachers by their first names), and it took them some time to adopt it. What is interesting is that a public usage of "Dr. Locher" in class, such as in a question, always causes raised eyebrows from their fellow Swiss students. To address somebody in a formal way, in a situation where the custom calls for informal usage, thus, reflects on the speaker as well as on the addressee. While the American students wanted to use a respectful term of address, they may have come across as too deferential in the eyes of their peers. It is, of course, also possible to display that one knows the norms and conventions of a particular social interaction and to subvert them. A student might use the term "Dr. Locher" in the context above to question my expertise rather than to confirm it and to show respect.

Recognizing that politeness issues play a role in identity construction, we must acknowledge that some aspects of Brown and Levinson's work are problematic from the perspective that sees identity as being in flux rather than fixed. On the one hand, the notion of face, described as consisting of two wants, is too static to equal *face* with *identity*. I suggest that it is preferable to return to the original Goffmanian sense of the term which makes a link between the two concepts possible. The variables P, D, and R_x can be seen as too simple an explanation for the intricate social processes that take place when interactants engage in social practice and position self and other. There is also a problem with assigning linguistic form to function, as indicated in the linguistic strategies which link linguistic indirectness with the level of politeness, a position that is no longer pursued in many of the more recent works on politeness. Finally, the term *politeness* may actually be a misnomer since Brown and Levinson describe mitigating relational work more generally, without being concerned about whether or not the social agents themselves consider the interaction polite or not. The last two points will be taken up again in Section 4.4. Having said this, Brown and Levinson's work offers us the description of an abundance of linguistic strategies (cf. the indexicality principle introduced in Section 3) that can be identified in social interaction and that can be exploited to discuss the construction of identity in emergent networks.

---

[13] I do not mean to claim that all American students share the same expectations with respect to the use of address terms. The point is that the social practice in question had different norms with respect to the use of address terms than that of the two individuals in question.

4.3. Leech's Politeness Principle

Leech (1983) deals with politeness in connection with his work on *principles of pragmatics* in general. His starting point is Grice's (1975) *cooperative principle*, which is expressed in the following four maxims:

1. Quantity i)   Make your contribution as informative as is required (for the current purposes of the exchange).
          ii) Do not make your contribution more informative than is required.
2. Quality   i)   Do not say what you believe to be false.
          ii) Do not say that for which you lack adequate evidence.
3. Relation i)   Be relevant.
4. Manner   i)   Avoid obscurity of expression.
          ii) Avoid ambiguity.
         iii) Be brief (avoid unnecessary prolixity).
         iv) Be orderly. (Grice 1975: 45–46)

When interactants do not follow one or more of these maxims, they create so-called implicatures, i.e., they create additional meaning.[14] Leech argues that what he calls the *politeness principle* explains the motivation for many of these implicatures. He proposes that the aim of the politeness principle is "to maintain the social equilibrium and the friendly relations which enable us to assume that our interlocutors are being cooperative in the first place" (Leech 1983: 82). For example, an interlocutor might interpret a roundabout way of formulating a request, which constitutes a deviation from the maxim of quantity and the maxim of manner, as being motivated by the speaker's wish not to impose on the addressee. In Leech's understanding, the indirect linguistic realization of the request, which constitutes a departure from the cooperative principle, is motivated by the speaker's wish to appear polite. More generally, we are once more dealing with the positioning of self and other in social practices.

Leech (1983) formulates his politeness principle in the form of the following maxims:

(I)   TACT MAXIM (in impositives and commissives)
    (a)   Minimize cost to *other*
    [(b)   Maximize benefit to *other*]
(II) GENEROSITY MAXIM (in impositives and commissives)
    (a)   Minimize benefit to *self*
    [(b)   Maximize cost to *self*]
(III) APPROBATION MAXIM (in expressives and assertives)
    (a)   Minimize dispraise of *other*
    [(b)   Maximize praise of *other*]

---

[14] This comment refers in fact to a complex set of transgressions that are further discussed in Grice (1975).

(IV) MODESTY MAXIM (in expressives and assertives)
    (a)   Minimize praise of *self*
    [(b)   Maximize dispraise of *self*]
(V) AGREEMENT MAXIM (in assertives)
    (a)   Minimize disagreement between *self* and *other*
    [(b)   Maximize agreement between *self* and *other*]
(VI) SYMPATHY MAXIM (in assertives)
    (a)   Minimize antipathy between *self* and *other*
    [(b)   Maximize sympathy between *self* and *other*] (Leech 1983: 132)

In general, Leech (1983: 133) claims that interactants give "avoidance of discord" more importance than "seeking concord". He also points out that not all the maxims are equally important. The Tact Maxim and the Approbation Maxim are considered to be stronger than the Generosity and Modesty Maxims. As an explanation, Leech maintains that politeness is generally more oriented towards the other than the self.

While Brown and Levinson (1987) remain at a very abstract level when they give us their politeness equation ($W_x = D\,(S,H) + P\,(H,S) + R_x$), Leech focuses more explicitly on the formulation of the "norms" that influence the calculation of the relative ranking of the imposition of the face-threatening act (R_x). It is, however, doubtful whether maxims formulated in this manner are also suitable to capture politeness universally (O'Driscoll 1996: 29). Leech's maxims become more convincing once we argue that they describe culture-specific notions of politeness rather than universal ones. In other words, it may well be that people taking part in a social practice in Britain orient towards these norms both when they are in the role of speakers and of addressees. In analogy, it may well be that other cultures will give more or less importance to some of Leech's proposed maxims, or it may be that they have entirely different ones that constitute polite behavior (cf. Spencer-Oatey 2000: 40; Locher 2004: 66).

With respect to identity construction and relational work, we can say that norms of behavior are clearly at the heart of the issue. The anecdote of the adequate use of address terms in the previous section has given evidence for this. Leech has to be given credit for highlighting this fact even more explicitly than Brown and Levinson did before him.

4.4. The Discursive Approach to Politeness

Building on and sometimes departing from what Brown and Levinson (1978/ 1987) and Leech (1983) have proposed, many other researchers have developed other ideas on politeness (cf., among others, Fraser 1990; Kasper 1990; Holmes 1995; Held 1995). In what follows, however, I will focus on a more recent approach that highlights the discursive notion of the concept of *politeness* as such (Watts 2003; Locher 2004; Locher and Watts 2005, 2008) and claims that politeness is a comment on relational work in particular social practices or *communities of practice*[15] (cf., e.g., Watts 2003; Mills 2003, 2004,

---

[15] For the concept of *community of practice*, consult Eckert and McConnell-Ginet (1992a/b), Wenger (1998), and Meyerhoff (2002).

2005; Mullany 2004, 2008; Schnurr, Marra, and Holmes 2007, 2008; Graham 2007, 2008).

In Locher (2004, 2006b) and in Locher and Watts (2005, 2008), the claim is made that what Brown and Levinson have studied should not be seen as politeness *per se*, but as the description of linguistic strategies to mitigate face-threatening acts within the more general framework of relational work or identity construction. This means that we make a distinction between the term *politeness,* as used in a theory such as Brown and Levinson's, and the understanding of what *politeness* may mean for a lay person. This difference has been called the distinction between first order (lay) and second order (theoretical) conceptions (cf. Watts, Ehlich, and Ide 1992; Eelen 2001; Watts 2005).

This distinction makes it possible to describe the face-threatening character of a linguistic act and to point to the linguistic strategy of mitigation used with the help of Brown and Levinson's framework without *a priori* saying anything about the level of politeness witnessed. Consider, for example, the following well-known constructed sentences that might be uttered during a lunch conversation:

(1) (a) Pass me the salt.
    (b) Could you please pass me the salt?
    (c) Would you be so kind as to pass me the salt?

Depending on the context and the way in which these sentences are uttered, any of them might be appropriate and any might be inappropriate. If you are very close to each other and you generally talk on a very informal basis, an example such as (1a) might be called for, while (1c) might be over the top or even downright insulting. If you are on different hierarchical levels and if you usually talk to each other in a very formal way, you might go for (1c) and find (1a) out of place. The point here is that we cannot easily equate linguistic indirectness with linguistic politeness, or, more generally, linguistic form with linguistic function. On the contrary, we have to be very careful in taking into account the context of the linguistic utterance and any evidence from the interactants themselves that they may have wanted to use relational work in a particular way. For this reason, it is crucial to study the norms of the particular social practice in question. This is in line with Bucholtz and Hall's (2005) positionality principle, as explained in Section 3.

It is clear that a concept such as politeness has an evaluative character and is thus linked to social norms which are negotiated by social beings in interaction over time. This is what is meant by the *discursive nature* of politeness. This approach highlights the importance of social norms even more than Leech's (1983). The difference is that we do not claim to be able to generally state the norms in question in the form of maxims, but we rather wish to stress that the norms as such are constantly in flux and are created, maintained, challenged, and ultimately changed by participants in social practices over time.

By using the term *politeness* again in its lay meaning, we can free it from the overgeneralization that came with its use as a theoretical concept. We claim that polite linguistic behavior is actually only one very small aspect of relational work, namely relational work that is judged by participants *in situ* as appropriate and positively evaluated or marked according to the norms of a social practice (cf. Watts 1989, 1992; Locher 2004, 2006b; Locher and Watts 2005, 2008). The notion of *frame*, i.e., "structures of expectation based on past experience" (Tannen 1993: 53), explains the basis on which these judgments are made. A frame is acquired over time in social practice when interactants categorize the experiences of similar past situations, or draw conclusions from other people's experiences. A frame can contain expectations about action sequences (such as money transactions in a sales situation), but also about role and identity issues (such as the roles of sales assistant and customer). In Locher and Watts (2008: 78), we point out that "[t]he theoretical basis of 'frames' are cognitive conceptualisations of forms of appropriate and inappropriate behaviour that individuals have constructed through their own histories of social practice." Once again, it is important to stress that these norms and expectations are acquired over time and are constantly subject to change. When discussing the emergence principle in relation to identity construction, Bucholtz and Hall (2005) state that

> the property of emergence does not exclude the possibility that resources for identity work in any given interaction may derive from resources developed in earlier interactions (that is, they may draw on 'structure'—such as ideology, the linguistic system, or the relation between the two) (Bucholtz and Hall 2005: 588).

Hence people do not start inventing norms and expectations from scratch every time they meet. On the contrary, the discursive understanding of impoliteness and politeness issues stresses the importance of communities of practice and frames, which means that people draw on their experience and that these concepts entail historicity.

As a consequence of this historicity, as well as the discursive nature of the evaluative notion of politeness, we can say that it is possible that members of different social practices may perceive not only different linguistic behavior as polite, but may also construct the *lexeme* 'politeness' as having slightly different connotations. The meaning of politeness has clearly shifted over time. The *Oxford English Dictionary* (OED) reports "intellectual refinement; polish, elegance, good taste" as obsolete meanings for politeness with quotations from the 17th century. Stein (1994: 8) claims that before the 18th century, politeness referred to "a social ideal, the polite urban, metropolitan gentleman, well-versed in the art of 'polite' conversation, a man about town". By the second half of the 18th century, a new notion of politeness had developed, one that is closely linked to prescriptivism, in that two poles between "correct" (polite) and "incorrect" (impolite) language usage were established and described, for example, in the prescriptive grammars of the time.[16] The modern definition of politeness given in the OED is "[c]ourtesy, good manners, behaviour that is respectful or considerate of others". The entries for the meaning of the adjective *polite* in the OED read as follows:

---

[16] Other studies on the historical concept of politeness in the field of sociohistorical linguistics are Fitzmaurice (1998) and Watts (1999, 2002).

1. a. Smoothed, polished, burnished. *Obs.*
   b. Clean; neat, orderly. *Obs.*
2. a. Of language, the arts, or other intellectual pursuits: refined, elegant, scholarly; exhibiting good or restrained taste.
   b. Of a person, social group, etc.: refined; cultured, cultivated; (also) well-regulated. Now chiefly in *polite society, circles,* etc.
   c. Courteous, behaving in a manner that is respectful or considerate of others; well-mannered.

It would be premature, however, to claim that there is general agreement about the exact connotations of the terms *polite* and *politeness* in all the different social practices (cf. Mills 2002, 2004). It is even possible to argue that the term *politeness* carries negative connotations for some groups of people. This is the case when they consider what others might perceive as socially appropriate behavior as being inappropriate to a certain extent according to their own norms. In Locher and Watts (2008) we suggest that

> this might lead to latently negative evaluative lexemes such as *standoffish, stuck-up, hoity-toity,* etc., thus indicating that an individual who expresses such an evaluation is aware that others would consider the behavior as appropriate, but personally interprets it negatively (Locher and Watts 2008: 98).

Clearly further research is needed to establish the connotations that the lexemes mentioned carry today for different groups of people.

Another advantage of investigating politeness as a first order concept is that we do not perceive its opposite to be impoliteness in general, but allow for the possibility that relational work which is negatively evaluated as breaching social norms may be judged in many different ways by participants in a social practice. The literature on impoliteness is still scarce in comparison to the voluminous literature on politeness. Early approaches took impoliteness as a mirror phenomenon to politeness, often based on an approach similar to Brown and Levinson's (cf., e.g., Lachenicht 1980; Culpeper 1996; Kienpointner 1997). The more recent literature is more diverse both in its methodological approaches as well as in its understanding of impoliteness (cf., e.g., Culpeper, Bousfield, and Wichmann 2003; Culpeper 2005; Bousfield and Locher 2008). The need to steer away from a simple dichotomy between polite and impolite behavior, however, is clearly recognized, and more research is encouraged to study behavior that is face-aggravating in particular social practices.

Let us look at an example in which a metacomment on relational work is being made that was perceived as negative. In (2), taken from Baumann et al. (2006), who studied impoliteness in a small number of family interactions in Switzerland, the metacomment *unhöflech* ('impolite') is mentioned by one of the participants. The conversation took place during a family dinner and was documented immediately after the interaction. The participants are a father and mother, their son, and their daughter, who are in their early twenties. The language is Bernese, the Swiss German dialect spoken by the participants, and is glossed with an idiomatic English translation.[17] The mother asks her son why his girlfriend Rahel, who had left the house only five minutes before the meal, does not have dinner with the family.

(2) 1 Mother: *Wiiso isst de ize d Rahel nid mit üs?*
                  'So how come Rahel doesn't eat with us?'

   2 Son: *Si het doch gseit si wott nid—*
                  'But she said that she didn't want to—'

   3 Mother: *Nei, das hesch du gseit. D Rahel hät nämlech wöue, i has ire agseh.*
                  'No, it was you who said that. Rahel in fact wanted to, I saw it.'

   4 Son: *Das hesch du äuä sicher nid.*
                  'No you surely didn't.'

   5 Mother: (gets louder) *Weisch, si möchte üs vilich ou kennelehre. Sie würd nie eso blöd tue, du tuesch eso blöd.*
                  'You know, she might want to get to know us, too. She would never act this stupidly, you are the one who acts stupidly.'

   6 Son: (gets louder as well) *Tue doch nid eso, hey, ig ma ize nid mit dir über das rede.*
                  'Stop acting like this. Hey, I don't want to talk about this with you now.'

   7 Mother: (even louder) *Ig finge eifach we si jedes Wuchenänd hie verbringt und sich die ganzi Zit vor üs versteckt isch das e chli unhöflech—*
                  'All I'm saying is that, if she stays with us every weekend and hides from us the whole time, then this is somewhat impolite—'

   8 Father: (very loud) *Chöit dir ize über öppis angers rede bitte, es cha doch nid si, dass dir bi jedem znacht schtürmet.*
                  'Could you now talk about something else, please. How can you always be fighting during dinner.'

   9 Mother: (aggressive) *Ach ize wosch du üs scho vorschribe über was mir söue rede.*
                  'Ahh now you even want to tell us what we're supposed to talk about.'

  10 Son: (to father) *Misch di nid i!*
                  'Mind your own business.'

  11 Mother: (to father) *Für wän hautisch di eigentlech?*
                  'Who do you think you are anyway?'

  12 Daughter: *Er isch der Herrgott.*
                  'He's God.'

  13 Father: (in a rather joking way) *I bi schliesslech z Familieoberhoupt.*
                  'After all I am the head of this family.'

---

[17] The transcript in Swiss German was produced by the daughter and mother in the example; the English translation is mine.

14 Daughter: (changing the topic) *auso Ma, wohere göt dir ize id Land-
        schueuwuche?*
        'So Mom, where will you now be going for the school camp?'

In this extract, the mother and the son quarrel about the fact that the son's
girlfriend does not join the family for meals—a behavior which the mother
describes as impolite (7). She also argues that it is really the son who tells his
girlfriend to stay away and that it is not Rahel's own wish (3, 5). The son clearly
does not wish to discuss this issue (6). When the quarrel between mother and
son gets louder and louder, the father interrupts them in an even louder voice
by asking his wife and son to change the topic (8). In addition, he complains
that the two of them are always quarrelling during dinner. This intervention does not go down well with mother and son, as can be seen from the fact
that they immediately turn against the father—now as a joint team. It is the
daughter who answers the aggressive question posed by the mother in line
11 in an ironic way.[18] This tone is taken up by the father, and after that the
daughter takes the opportunity to successfully change the topic entirely.

There are several comments to be made here on relational work and
perceptions of relational work. With respect to frames, i.e., structures of expectations, the mother states that she considers Rahel's staying away from the
dinner table to be a breach of norms. She clearly expects her son's girlfriend to
spend more time with the family and not to "hide". The metacomment 'impolite' thus refers to behavior that was already witnessed earlier as well as at the
time of the interaction, and is now made in the absence of Rahel. Another set of
expectations that we see evidence of in this extract is the father's comment on
the repeated quarrels between his wife and his son (8). He voices his wish that
there should be less *schtürme*, a Bernese expression describing quarrelling
and fighting, derived from 'storm', during dinner time. Finally, there seems to
be a clear idea on the part of the mother and her son that their quarrel is theirs
rather than one that includes all the members of the family. This can be seen
in the content of their immediate reaction to the father's intervention.

Interestingly, there are also several roles and identities explicitly indexed
in this brief extract. In lines 5 and 7 the mother creates a sense of the family
by using the pronoun *üs*/'us' ('You know, she might want to get to know us,
too.'/'hides from us'). This implies that Rahel is not part of this 'us' (yet). While
the mother creates a sense of family including her son, she also creates another
group consisting of her son and his girlfriend Rahel. In line 3, the mother puts
the blame for Rahel's behaviour on her son's rather than on Rahel's shoulders
('No, it was you who said that. Rahel in fact wanted to, I saw it.'). She confirms
this criticism in line 5 ('She would never act this stupidly, you are the one who
acts stupidly.') This is clearly face-aggravating for the son, but saves the girlfriend's face in that direct criticism of her is avoided.

From lines 8 to 13, repeated below from extract (2), the role of the father
is under attack:

---

[18] Here the "Father knows best" ideology, studied by Ochs and Taylor (2001), is evoked in an ironic
fashion.

(3) 8   Father: (very loud) 'Could you now please talk about something else.
                    How can you always be fighting during dinner.'

    9   Mother: (aggressive) 'Ahh now you even want to tell us what we're
                    supposed to talk about.'

   10   Son: (to Father) 'Mind your own business.'

   11   Mother: (to Father) 'Who do you think you are anyway?'

   12   Daughter: 'He's God.'

   13   Father: (in a rather joking way) 'After all I am the head of this
                    family.'

   14   Daughter: (changing the topic) 'So Mom, where are you now going to go
                    for the school camp?'

Once the father has interrupted his wife and his son's quarrel, he is immediately challenged by them for not having the right to do so (9, 10). In line 11, the mother explicitly and aggressively asks the father about his role ('Who do you think you are anyway?'). According to the daughter, who recorded the conversation and commented on it at a later stage when discussing the analysis with me, she wanted to help her father by saying 'He's God'. Her father takes up this ironic mood and evokes the image of patriarch or head of the family.

The face issues in this brief extract are delicate. The attack on the son's face has already been mentioned (lines 3 and 5). The father's face is clearly challenged once his role in the interaction is so bluntly questioned by his wife and son, who were antagonists only seconds before and are now teaming up against him. The daughter finally manages to steer the conversation into calmer waters by means of irony and thus prevents further rounds of aggravating behavior that might have followed if any of the other interactants had tried to answer the aggressive question in line 11. By referring to her mother's occupation in line 14, the daughter highlights her mother's professional face and shifts the attention away from face sensitivities in the family context.

Baumann et al. (2006) stress that the face-threatening acts witnessed in example (2) are in fact not perceived by the participants to be as severe as they might look to analysts not familiar with this particular family and their discursive practice. The conversation indeed proceeded on a neutral tone after the short episode described and did not have any long-term repercussions.

In contrast, extract (4), also taken from Baumann et al. (2006), might look quite unspectacular with respect to the linguistic strategies used, but was experienced as problematic by the daughter with respect to face issues. The episode took place between a father and daughter while preparing the salad for dinner:

(4) 1   Daughter: *Söui die Zibele mit däm Häcksler da schnide?*
                   'Shall I cut the onions with that chopper'

    2   Father: *Ja, das chasch scho.*
                   'Yes, you can do that.'
                   (Father observes Daughter who is obviously struggling with
                   assembling the cutting utensil.)

3   Father: *Nimm doch eifach es Mässer, das geit o!*
              'Why don't you simply take a knife. That would do the trick,
              too!'
4   Daugther: (rather peevishly and aggressively) *Aber weni mit däm wot
              schnide?!*
              'But what if I want to cut with this one?!'
5   Father: *Ja, de isch scho guet!*
              'Yes, all right, go ahead.'

The daughter reports that her father's comment to exchange the fancy chopper
for a simple knife (3) was taken as a face-threatening criticism of and a challenge to her expertise and competence. This resulted in her snapping at her
father in an aggressive way. Her father's reaction, however, points to the possibility that he merely wanted to give advice since he does not react negatively to
the challenge in his daughter's response. Instead he takes her comment literally and supports her in her choice of a chopper. Baumann et al. (2006) point
out that the extent of the face-threatening character in this brief extract can
only be fully explained once it is known that there had been tensions building
up between the father and daughter over quite some time (cf. Bucholtz and
Hall's positionality principle (b), explained in Section 3).

With respect to the terms *politeness* or *impoliteness*, it seems clear that
they refer to the way in which interactants deal with each other, either linguistically or more generally. Judgments on politeness and impoliteness are,
in other words, metacomments made by social interactants on each other's
relational behavior. It may be desirable to be perceived as having the qualities attributed above to one's identity (*polite, elegant, cultured, well-mannered,*
etc.). (Mis)management of relational work that leads to negative perceptions
of relational work and intentionally face-aggravating behavior will equally
reflect on the product of an interactant's construction of identity in an ongoing
emergent network. This is, finally, the link that we can draw between face,
face-threatening acts, and identity construction: since there is no faceless communication, interactants are constantly negotiating face needs and are trying
to deal with face-threatening acts in ways that serve their current interactional goals;[19] since face can be understood as a particular mask or role that an
interactant wants to have confirmed in social practice, we are automatically
dealing with identity construction. To be perceived as polite may then just be
one of the many possible attributes that an interactant wishes to display and
hopes to have accepted as part of his or her identity.

4.5. Relational Work and Rapport Management

The final theoretical approach to be discussed here in the light of the construction of identity and politeness is Spencer-Oatey's (2000, 2005) theory of *rapport
management*, which was developed in research in the field of cross-cultural

---

[19] I do not wish to imply that this interaction always has to be conscious. See Locher and Watts
(2008) for further comments on intentionality.

sociolinguistics. Her framework is discussed here because it shows some useful overlap with the discursive approach to politeness, but also adds further important insights. Spencer-Oatey's (2005) definition of rapport management is similar to the definition of relational work:

> Rapport refers to the relative harmony and smoothness of relations between people, and *rapport management* refers to the management (or mismanagement) of relations between people (Spencer-Oatey 2005: 96; author's emphasis).

Spencer-Oatey (2007b: 647) argues that rapport management should be seen as a more general concept than relational work. I hope to demonstrate in this chapter that dealing with "relational" issues is not reductionist. In fact, I would like to suggest that what Spencer-Oatey defines as rapport management is equal to our understanding of relational work (Locher and Watts 2005). It is important to stress that rapport management, just like relational work, includes not only the negotiation of harmonious relations. Spencer-Oatey (2005) mentions four general types of rapport orientations:

> a *rapport-enhancement* orientation (a desire to strengthen or enhance harmonious relations between the interlocutors), a *rapport-maintenance* orientation (a desire to maintain or protect harmonious relations), a *rapport-neglect* orientation (a lack of concern or interest in the quality of relations, perhaps because of a focus on self), a *rapport-challenge* orientation (a desire to challenge or impair harmonious relations) (Spencer-Oatey 2005: 96; emphasis mine).

Spencer-Oatey's (2005: 97) definition of "(im)politeness" is in line with Watts (2003), Locher (2004), and Locher and Watts (2005) in that she takes "(im) politeness to be the subjective judgments that people make about the social appropriateness of verbal and non-verbal behaviour." However, she does use the term *(im)politeness* as an umbrella term for all kinds of lexemes that index evaluative meanings with positive, negative or neutral connotations, rather than treat it as one of the metacomments.

What is of particular interest to us is that Spencer-Oatey is especially concerned with the *perceptions* and *judgments* of rapport management. She proposes that there are three key elements at the basis of such judgments: "behavioural expectations, face sensitivities and interactional wants" (Spencer-Oatey 2005: 96). The behavioral expectations can be linked to the notion of *frame* previously discussed and stem from the interactants' beliefs about "what is prescribed, what is permitted and what is proscribed" in a particular social practice (2005: 97).[20] Spencer-Oatey uses two different concepts of face to describe face sensitivities. The first type is called *respectability face* and is claimed to be "pan-situational" in that it reflects the interactants' prestige, honor, or good name (based on Ho 1976). *Identity face*, in contrast, is defined

---

[20] Spencer-Oatey (2005: 98–100) describes different aspects that are part of behavioral expectations: contract/legal agreements and requirements, explicit/implicit role specifications, the interactional principles of equity and association, and behavioral conventions, norms and protocols.

as "situation-specific" and highly vulnerable (based on Goffman 1967). I suggest that we can link these two types of face to the notion of latent and emergent networks previously mentioned: respectability face can be argued to be related to the prestige that a person has established in previous encounters or that are given to him or her in relation to the norms and values of the particular social practice in a first encounter. Respectability face thus refers to the latent links in a social network which are closely related to the frame of that particular social practice. These links, however, will be negotiated in an emergent network, in which a person's identity is constructed and his or her face is most vulnerable. The notion of identity face is thus best linked to the emergent network. In her discussion of examples, Spencer-Oatey (2005) concentrates mainly on *identity face*, by linking the linguistic analysis with work on self-aspects and positive social values carried out in the field of social psychology (Schwartz 1992; Schwartz et al. 2001). Such self-aspects can be linked to physical features, roles, abilities, tastes, attitudes, etc. (Simon 2004). Spencer-Oatey (2005: 104) maintains that "people's claims to identity face are based on the positive social values that they associate with their various self-aspects" and that people develop "sensitivities" around them. The third element that Spencer-Oatey identifies as contributing to judgments on rapport management is interactional goals or "wants". She makes a distinction between transactional and interactional goals, similar to the argument presented in Section 2.

While Spencer-Oatey stresses that all three elements influence judgments on rapport management, she claims that interactants make judgments on (im) politeness mainly in relation to behavioral expectations. The other two notions (face sensitivities and interactional wants) interact with these expectations, but are seen to be at the base of judgments on rapport management more generally. Her overall argument is that

> [a]s people interact with each other, they make dynamic judgments as to whether their rapport has been enhanced, maintained or damaged [. . .]. These judgments (conscious or otherwise) are based to a large extent on assessments of the three key bases of perceptions of rapport: interactional wants, face sensitivities, and behavioural expectations (Spencer-Oatey 2005: 116).

These bases of the *dynamic perceptions of rapport* are visualized in Figure 2, reproduced from Spencer-Oatey (2005: 116). What is particularly useful for the present discussion is the mention of emotional reactions in the right hand bottom corner. The discursive approach to the study of politeness and impoliteness claims that interactants make judgments about the appropriateness of behavior in relation to the social norms and expectations of a particular social practice, and that negatively and positively marked evaluations will lead to metacomments such as, for example, *polite* or *impolite*. Spencer-Oatey's figure not only visualizes some of the emotions that are evoked by using the term negatively marked or positively marked, but she also convincingly points out that these reactions are dynamic, based on the perception of self and other and are triggered by different interrelated processes.

How can we link these observations to the ideas on identity construction presented in the previous sections? In Spencer-Oatey's (2005) framework, the notion of identity appears most prominently in her discussion of the concept *identity face*.[21] The process of constructing identity in interaction, however, is clearly entailed in all three elements of behavioral expectations, face sensitivities, and interactional wants. The notion of *role*, for example, can be argued to be of importance in all three realms. This claim is discussed with the help of a constructed example, which is based on the author's own cultural expectations:

(5) Imagine that you are a boss who has to bring the bad news to an employee that he has to be laid off because of financial cuts. You know that the employee in question will be upset and unhappy about that decision and will probably contest it. You are also not happy about having to make this person redundant, whose work you have always valued. Nevertheless, you see no other solution but to go ahead with the dismissal. With respect to your role as boss, the following issues may appear important for the conversation in which you tell your employee the bad news:

- *Behavioral expectations*: As the boss, it is one of your duties to hire employees and make them redundant. You have gone through similar situations before and you can draw on this particular frame here. For example, you plan to invite the employee to your office, you will give him the bad news in a factual way; you will give reasons for the dismissal, and you will offer understanding for the difficult situation that you put your employee in. You will make sure that you fulfil all the legal requirements that may be attached to this activity. From the employee you expect that he recognizes the particular type of interaction and that he orients to it by reacting in a factual rather than an emotional way.
- *Interactional wants*: Your interactional goal is to conduct a factual and efficient conversation. Your interpersonal goal is to be able to conclude the conversation on such a note that your role as boss is not challenged, while you are willing to enhance the employee's face, circumstances allowing, by acknowledging the employee's difficult situation as a result of terminating the work relations.
- *Face sensitivities*: You are sensitive to any challenge of your role as boss (appearing in control, being legitimized to take decisions, etc.) that might come from the upset employee, while you are aware of the face-threatening character of the act of making somebody redundant.

This constructed scenario is admittedly far from accounting for the complexities of real interaction. It has shown, however, that the three elements that Spencer-Oatey identifies are indeed closely related and together will contribute to the identity construction that will be the *product* of the orientations to these three elements once the interaction takes place.

---

[21] In Spencer-Oatey (2007b: 642–644), the author discusses the link between the concept of face and identity explicitly by claiming that the two concepts should be kept apart. However, I argue that we can gain much by equating face with identity, as outlined in this chapter.

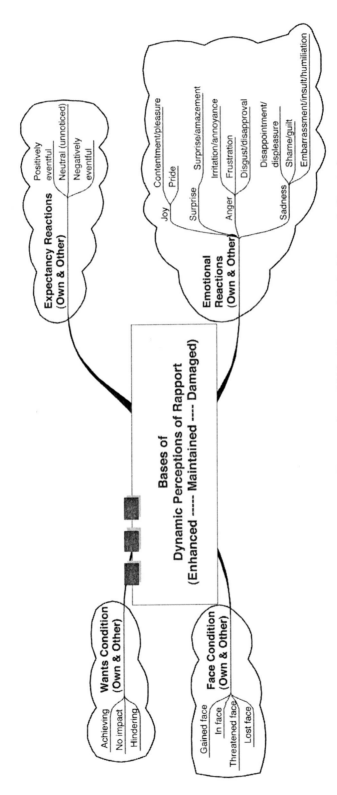

Figure 2. The base of dynamic perceptions of rapport (Spencer-Oatey 2005: 116, copyright by Mouton de Gruyter)

It has to be stressed that Spencer-Oatey deals with the question of *judg-ments* on rapport management in her (2005) paper and explicitly mentions that she is not concerned with "how (im)politeness, face and/or rapport are dynamically managed in interaction" (96). I take this to mean that such a focus is still possible, but not the subject of the paper. The scenario described above was formulated in such a way that it outlined relational concerns at the outset of the interaction. It was meant to illustrate that the three elements that Spencer-Oatey describes as being at the basis of judgments of rapport management will also be crucial in identity construction in general.

5. Concluding Remarks

The aim of this chapter was to link work on the construction of identity in interaction with work on linguistic politeness in order to point out synergies in the two research fields. The recent literature on identity construction has been reviewed with a brief excursion into the issue of language and gender. The literature on politeness was represented by two seminal research traditions, one inspired by Brown and Levinson (1978, 1987), and the other by Leech (1983). In addition, the more recent discursive approach to politeness issues was introduced to indicate new developments in this field of research (Locher and Watts 2005). These approaches were discussed in connection with the con-struction of identity.

I hope to have demonstrated that the view which considers identity as emerg-ing in interaction and the discursive approach to politeness with its focus on relational work can more generally be fruitfully combined in linguistic research which explores interpersonal communication. The overlap in the approaches can be located in the position that there is no communication without a relational aspect, and that "identity is inherently relational" (Bucholtz and Hall 2005: 605). In addition, the understanding of politeness as one of many evaluative concepts, the contents of which are discursively negotiated in social practices over time, highlights the importance of practice or agency that is also crucial to the current postmodernist understanding of identity. The Goffmanian conceptu-alization of the metaphor *face*, being central to politeness research, can also be of use for identity research if it is taken to mean a "role" or "mask" that is being negotiated in an emergent network rather than a predefined set of wants.

Finally, the terms *relational work, facework, identity work,* and *rapport management* have been shown to refer to the same phenomenon—the negoti-ation of relations and identities in interaction, while a particular face or identity is the product of this work. It remains to be emphasized quite clearly that much more empirical research is needed to understand the intricacies of relational work in all its facets. This chapter is meant to encourage such research.

References

Adelswärd, Viveka and Claes Nilholm. 2000. Who is Cindy? Aspects of identity work in a teacher-parent-pupil talk at a special school. *Text* 20(4): 545–568.

Baumann, Lea, Manuela Burgermeister, Sonaljeet Kundan and Ariane Studer. 2006. It really depends on the family: Responses to impoliteness among friends and family members. Unpublished paper, Department of English Languages and Literatures, University of Berne.

Bousfield, Derek and Miriam A. Locher (eds.). 2008. *Impoliteness in Language. Studies on its Interplay with Power in Theory and Practice*. Berlin/New York: Mouton de Gruyter.

Brown, Penelope. 1980. How and why are women more polite: Some evidence from a Mayan community. In: Sally McConnell-Ginet, Ruth Borker and Nellie Furman (eds.), *Women and Language in Literature and Society*, 111–136. New York: Praeger.

Brown, Penelope and Stephen C. Levinson. 1978. Universals in language usage. Politeness phenomena. In: Esther N. Goody (ed.), *Questions and Politeness*, 56–289. Cambridge: Cambridge University Press.

Brown, Penelope and Stephen C. Levinson. 1987. *Politeness: Some Universals in Language Usage*. Cambridge: Cambridge University Press.

Brown, Roger and Albert Gilman. 1960. The pronouns of power and solidarity. In: Thomas Sebeok (ed.), *Style in Language*, 253–276. Cambridge: Massachusetts Institut of Technology Press.

Bucholtz, Mary. 2004. Language, gender, and sexuality. In: Edward Finegan and John Rickford (eds.), *Language in the USA: Themes for the Twenty-first Century*, 411–427. New York: Cambridge University Press.

Bucholtz, Mary and Kira Hall. 2005. Identity and interaction: A sociocultural linguistic approach. *Discourse Studies* 7(4–5): 585–614. Culpeper, Jonathan. 1996. Towards an Anatomy of Impoliteness. *Journal of Pragmatics* 25(3): 349–367. Culpeper, Jonathan. 2005. Impoliteness and 'The weakest link'. *Journal of Politeness Research* 1(1): 35–72.

Culpeper, Jonathan, Derek Bousfield and Anne Wichmann. 2003. Impoliteness revisited: With special reference to dynamic and prosodic aspects. *Journal of Pragmatics* 35,10–11: 1545–1579.

Davies, Bronwyn and Rom Harré. 1990. Positioning: The social construction of self. *Journal for the Theory of Social Behavior* 20: 43–63.

De Fina, Anna. 2003. *Identity in Narrative: A Study of Immigrant Discourse*. Amsterdam: Benjamins.

Durkheim, Emile. 1915. *The Elementary Forms of the Religious Life*. London: G. Allen & Unwin.

Eckert, Penelope and Sally McConnell-Ginet. 1992a. Communities of practice: Where language, gender, and power all live. In: Kira Hall, Mary Bucholtz and Birch Moonwomon (eds.), *Locating Power: Proceedings of the Second Berkeley Women and Language Conference*, 89–99. Berkeley, CA: Women and Language Group.

Eckert, Penelope and Sally McConnell-Ginet. 1992b. Think practically and act locally: Language and gender as community-based practice. *Annual Review of Anthropology* 21: 461–490.

Eckert, Penelope and John R. Rickford (eds.). 2001. *Style and Sociolinguistic Variation*. Cambridge: Cambridge University Press. Eelen, Gino. 2001. *A Critique of Politeness Theories*. Manchester: St. Jerome Publishing.

Fill, Alwin. 1990. Scherz und Streit aus ethnolinguistischer Sicht. *Papiere zur Linguistik* 43(2): 117–125.

Fitzmaurice, Susan. 1998. The commerce of language in the pursuit of politeness in eighteenth-century England. *English Studies* 78: 309–328.

Fraser, Bruce. 1990. Perspectives on politeness. *Journal of Pragmatics* 14(2): 219–236.

Goffman, Erving (ed.). 1967. *Interaction Ritual: Essays on Face-to-Face Behavior*. Garden City, NY: Anchor Books.

Graham, Sage Lambert. 2007. Disagreeing to agree: Conflict, (im)politeness and identity in a computer-mediated community. *Journal of Pragmatics* 39(4): 742–759.

Graham, Sage Lambert. 2008. A manual for (im)politeness? The impact of the FAQ in electronic communities of practice. In: Derek Bousfield and Miriam A. Locher (eds.), *Impoliteness in Language. Studies on its Interplay with Power in Theory and Practice*, 281–304. Berlin/New York: Mouton de Gruyter.

Grice, H. Paul. 1975. Logic and conversation. In: Peter Cole and Jerry L. Morgan (eds.), *Syntax and Semantics, Volume 3, Speech Acts*, 41–58. New York: Academic Press.

Gu, Yuego. 1990. Politeness phenomena in modern Chinese. *Journal of Pragmatics* 14: 237–257.

Halliday, Michael A. K. 1976. *System and Function in Language*. London: Oxford University Press.

Halliday, Michael A. K. 1981. Linguistic function and literary style: An inquiry into the language of William Golding's 'The Inheritors'. In: Donald C. Freeman (ed.), *Essays in Modern Stylistics*, 325–361. London: Methuen.

Held, Gudrun. 1995. Verbale Höflichkeit. Studien zur linguistischen Theoriebildung und empirische Untersuchung zum Sprachverhalten französischer und italienischer Jugendlicher in Bitt- und Dankessituationen. Tübingen: Narr.

Ho, Davis Yao-Fai. 1976. On the concept of face. *American Journal of Sociology* 81(4): 867–884.

Holmes, Janet. 1995. *Women, Men and Politeness*. New York: Longman.

Joseph, John Earl. 2004. *Language and Identity: National, Ethnic, Religious*. Basingstoke: Palgrave Macmillan.

Kasper, Gabriele. 1990. Linguistic politeness: Current research issues. *Journal of Pragmatics* 14(2): 193–218.

Kienpointner, Manfred. 1997. Varieties of rudeness: Types and functions of impolite utterances. *Functions of Language* 4(2): 251–287.

Kresta, Ronald. 1993. Interpersonality and linguistic politeness in English and German linguistic texts. *Papiere zur Linguistik* 48(1): 29–46.

Lachenicht, Lance G. 1980. Aggravating language: A study of abusive and insulting language. *Papers in Linguistics. International Journal in Human Communication* 13(4): 607–687.

Lakoff, Robin. 1975. *Language and Woman's Place*. New York: Harper and Row.

Leech, Geoffrey N. 1983. *Principles of Pragmatics*. New York: Longman.

Locher, Miriam A. 2004. *Power and Politeness in Action: Disagreements in Oral Communication*. Berlin/New York: Mouton de Gruyter.

Locher, Miriam A. 2006a. *Advice Online: Advice-giving in an American Internet Health Column*. Amsterdam: Benjamins.

Locher, Miriam A. 2006b. Polite behavior within relational work: The discursive approach to politeness. *Multilingua* 25(3): 249–267.

Locher, Miriam A. and Derek Bousfield. 2008. Introduction: Impoliteness and power in language. In: Derek Bousfield and Miriam A. Locher (eds.), *Impoliteness in Language. Studies on its Interplay with Power in Theory and Practice*, 1–13. Berlin/New York: Mouton de Gruyter.

Locher, Miriam A. and Sebastian Hoffmann. 2006. The emergence of the identity of a fictional expert advice-giver in an American internet advice column. *Text and Talk* 26(1): 67–104.

Locher, Miriam A. and Richard J. Watts. 2005. Politeness theory and relational work. *Journal of Politeness Research* 1,1: 9–33.

Locher, Miriam A. and Richard J. Watts. 2008. Relational work and impoliteness: Negotiating norms of linguistic behaviour. In: Derek Bousfield and Miriam A. Locher (eds.), *Impoliteness in Language. Studies on its Interplay with Power in Theory and Practice*, 77–99. Berlin/New York: Mouton de Gruyter.

Matsumoto, Yoshiko. 1988. Reexamination of the universality of face: Politeness phenomena in Japanese. *Journal of Pragmatics* 12(4): 403–426.

Mendoza-Denton, Norma. 2002. Language and identity. In: J. K. Chambers, Peter Trudgill and Natalie Schilling-Estes (eds.), *Handbook of Language Variation and Change*, 475–499. Oxford: Blackwell.

Meyerhoff, Miriam. 2002. Communities of practice. In: J. K. Chambers, Peter Trudgill and Natalie Schilling-Estes (eds.), *Handbook of Language Variation and Change*, 526–548. Oxford: Blackwell.

Mills, Sara. 2002. Rethinking politeness, impoliteness and gender identity. In: Lia Litosseliti and Jane Sunderland (eds.), *Gender Identity and Discourse Analysis*, 69–89. Amsterdam: Benjamins.

Mills, Sara. 2003. *Gender and Politeness*. Cambridge: Cambridge University Press.

Mills, Sara. 2004. Class, gender and politeness. *Multilingua* 23(1–2): 171–191.

Mills, Sara. 2005. Gender and impoliteness. *Journal of Politeness Research* 1(2): 263–280.

Mullany, Louise. 2004. Gender, politeness and institutional power roles: Humour as a tactic to gain compliance in workplace business meetings. *Multilingua* 23(1–2): 13–37.

Mullany, Louise. 2008. 'Stop hassling me!' Impoliteness, power and gender identity in the professional workplace. In: Derek Bousfield and Miriam A. Locher (eds.), *Impoliteness in Language. Studies on its Interplay with Power in Theory and Practice*, 231–251. Berlin/New York: Mouton de Gruyter.

Ochs, Elinor and Carolyn Taylor. 2001. The "Father knows best" dynamic in dinnertime narratives. In: Alessandro Duranti (ed.), *Linguistic Anthropology. A Reader*, 431–449. Oxford: Blackwell.

O'Driscoll, Jim. 1996. About face: A defence and elaboration of universal dualism. *Journal of Pragmatics* 25(1): 1–32.

Ruhi, Şükriye and Hale Işık-Güler. 2007. Conceptualizing face and relational work in (im)politeness: Revelations from politeness lexemes and idioms in Turkish. *Journal of Pragmatics* 39(4): 681–711.

Schiffrin, Deborah. 1996. Narrative as self-portrait: Sociolinguistic constructions of identity. *Language in Society* 25(2): 167–203.

Schnurr, Stephanie, Meredith Marra and Janet Holmes. 2007. Being (im)polite in New Zealand workplaces: Maori and Pakhea leaders. *Journal of Pragmatics* 39(4): 712–729.

Schnurr, Stephanie, Meredith Marra and Janet Holmes. 2008. Impoliteness as a means of contesting power relations in the workplace. In: Derek Bousfield and Miriam A. Locher (eds.), *Impoliteness in Language. Studies on its Interplay with Power in Theory and Practice*, 211–229. Berlin/New York: Mouton de Gruyter.

Schwartz, Shalom. 1992. Universals in the content and structure of values: Theoretical advances and empirical tests in 20 countries. In: Mark P. Zanna (ed.), *Advances in Experimental Social Psychology*, 1–65. San Diego: Academic Press.

Schwartz, Shalom, Gila Melech, Arielle Lehmann, Steven Burgess, Mari Harris and Vicki Owens. 2001. Extending the cross-cultural validity of the theory of human values with a different method of measurement. *Journal of Cross-Cultural Psychology* 32(5): 519–542.

Scollon, Ron and Suzanne W. Scollon. 2001. *Intercultural Communication: A Discourse Approach*. 2nd edition. Oxford: Blackwell.

Simon, Bernd. 2004. *Identity in Modern Society: A Social Psychological Perspective*. Oxford: Blackwell.

Spencer-Oatey, Helen. 2000. Rapport management: A framework for analysis. In: Helen Spencer-Oatey (ed.), *Culturally Speaking: Managing Rapport through Talk across Cultures*, 11–46. London: Continuum.

Spencer-Oatey, Helen. 2005. (Im)Politeness, face and perceptions of rapport: Unpacking their bases and interrelationships. *Journal of Politeness Research* 1(1): 95–119.

Spencer-Oatey, Helen. 2007a. Identity, face and (im)politeness. *Journal of Pragmatics* 39(4): 635–638.

Spencer-Oatey, Helen. 2007b. Theories of identity and the analysis of face. *Journal of Pragmatics* 39(4): 639–656.

Stein, Dieter. 1994. Sorting out the variants: Standardization and social factors in the English language 1600–1800. In: Dieter Stein and Ingrid Tieken-Boon van Ostade (eds.), *Towards a Standard English 1600–1800*, 1–17. Berlin/New York: Mouton de Gruyter.

Swann, Joan. 2000. Gender and language use. In: Rajend Mesthrie, Joan Swann, Andrea Deumert and William L. Leap (eds.), *Introducing Sociolinguistics*, 316–353. Edinburgh: Edinburgh University Press.

Swann, Joan. 2002. Yes, but is it gender? In: Lia Litosseliti and Jane Sunderland (eds.), *Gender Identity and Discourse Analysis*, 43–67. Amsterdam: Benjamins.

Tannen, Deborah. 1993. What's in a frame? Surface evidence for underlying expectations. In: Deborah Tannen (ed.), *Framing in Discourse*, 14–56. Oxford: Oxford University Press.

The Oxford English Dictionary. 1989. 2nd edition. Oxford: Oxford University Press.

Tracy, Karen. 1990. The many faces of facework. In: Howard Giles and Peter Robinson (eds.), *Handbook of Language and Social Psychology*, 209–226. Chichester: Wiley.

Watts, Richard J. 1989. Relevance and relational work: Linguistic politeness as politic behavior. *Multilingua* 8(2–3): 131–166.

Watts, Richard J. 1991. *Power in Family Discourse*. Berlin/New York: Mouton de Gruyter.

Watts, Richard J. 1992. Linguistic politeness and politic verbal behaviour: Reconsidering claims for universality. In: Richard J. Watts, Sachiko Ide and Konrad Ehlich (eds.), *Politeness in Language: Studies in its History, Theory and Practice*, 43–69. Berlin/New York: Mouton de Gruyter.

Watts, Richard J. 1999. Language and politeness in early eighteenth century Britain. *Pragmatics* 9(1): 5–20.

Watts, Richard J. 2002. From polite language to educated language: The re-emergence of an ideology. In: Richard J. Watts and Peter Trudgill (eds.), *Alternative Histories of English,* 155–172. London: Routledge.

Watts, Richard J. 2003. *Politeness.* Cambridge: Cambridge University Press.

Watts, Richard J. 2005. Linguistic politeness research: Quo vadis? In: Richard J. Watts, Sachiko Ide and Konrad Ehlich (eds.), *Politeness in Language: Studies in its History, Theory and Practice,* 2nd revised and expanded edition, xi–xlvii. Berlin/ New York: Mouton de Gruyter.

Watts, Richard J., Sachiko Ide and Konrad Ehlich. 1992. Introduction. In: Richard J. Watts, Sachiko Ide and Konrad Ehlich (eds.), *Politeness in Language: Studies in its History, Theory and Practice,* 1–17. Berlin/New York: Mouton de Gruyter.

Watzlawick, Paul, Janet Helmick Beavin and Don D. Jackson. 1967. *Pragmatics of Human Communication: A Study of Interactional Patterns, Pathologies and Paradoxes.* New York: Norton.

Wenger, Etienne. 1998. *Communities of Practice: Learning, Meaning, and Identity.* Cambridge: Cambridge University Press.

Werkhofer, Konrad T. 1992. Traditional and modern views: The social constitution and the power of politeness. In: Richard J. Watts, Sachiko Ide and Konrad Ehlich (eds.), *Politeness in Language: Studies in its History, Theory and Practice,* 155–197. Berlin/New York: Mouton de Gruyter.

6

Humor, Jokes, and Irony Versus Mocking, Gossip, and Black Humor

Alexander Brock

1. Introduction

Humor, jokes, irony, mocking, gossip and *black humor* are labels for a group of communicative activities which are related and yet sufficiently different to earn themselves specific terms. Many other similar ones could be added, including *sarcasm, teasing, banter* and *rumor*. People often make funny remarks, they are ironic or sarcastic, but most of us find it hard to tell exactly what, for instance, the difference between humor and irony is and what specific contribution they make to the ongoing conversation. The term "versus" in the title, moreover, suggests a kind of opposition between some of the categories. Maybe this has to do with the way society commonly evaluates them, crudely speaking: "Humor and irony are good, whereas gossip and mocking are bad." At a closer look, however, things are far less straightforward. The difficulty of defining these categories and analyzing them in context becomes palpable as soon as one looks at a seemingly simple example, like the following. Example (1) shows an extract from a conversation among two 17-year-old school-boys who are strolling around town. Both are relaxed and a little bored:

(1) Holiday Job[1]
Utz:[2] *Ich arbeite vielleicht im Sommer in den ersten paar Wochen in der*
      I   work   maybe   in summer in the first few weeks at the
      "Taverne".
      "Tavern".
      'I might work at the Tavern in the first few weeks of the summer.'
Fred: *Wow, hier in Seblitz? Als was?*
      'Wow, here in Seblitz? As what?'

---

[1] The examples used in this chapter have been taken from two corpora available to the author: private, casual conversation among good friends (Examples 1 and 3) and a phone-in program on a British radio station (Example 2). The data found in both corpora indicate that the phenomena discussed here are common both to the private and public domain.
[2] In the examples from private conversation, all names have been changed in order to protect the speakers' identity.

Utz: *Als äh Besitzer. (Beide lachen)*
        'As erm proprietor. (both laugh)'

Town 2, 1 May, 2004

It is tempting to describe this exchange as harmless joking, because the jocular remark about a school-boy working as a proprietor serves a simple entertainment function, like so many other cases of conversational joking. If, however, Fred were a notorious show-off, then Utz's remark might be interpreted as an echoic comment on Fred's usual conversational behavior, to be classified as ironic teasing. If, on the other hand, the show-off were not Fred, but a common acquaintance of both youths, then Fred might construe Utz's remark as an impersonation of that other person and as a possible introduction to a phase of gossip.

This example shows that even in the simplest of cases, the interpretation of what is going on depends on the context and communicative function as well as the form and content of what is said. It also suggests that, in authentic communication, categories like *joking, teasing, irony* and *gossip* are not always clear-cut and may well overlap in places. Example (2) seems to make an even stronger point. It is taken from a local British radio phone-in program. The DJ, Brian Hayes, discusses people's choice of funeral music with some callers. Then the next caller, Muriel, gives her opinion on the same topic. The extract in Example (2) starts about one minute into Muriel's call:

(2) Funeral Music
Brian: *What are you going to have played at your funeral?*
Muriel: *I don't propose to have one.*
Brian: *Oh I see. Does that mean that you're not going to die?*
Muriel: *No no no. I I've donated my body to science.*

Brian Hayes Show, 27 March, 1986

Brian's question to Muriel may be classified as aggressive humor, as mocking, even as black humor, because it makes fun of somebody else's most intimate arrangements concerning life and death. Non-involved listeners, on the other hand, may just take it as light-hearted fun. So again, several categories suggest themselves, which begs the question of which criteria we use to decide on any of these labels. Other questions arise, too: Why does a DJ use this form of humor in reaction to a caller's statement? And why does the caller react the way she does? In keeping with this volume's orientation, the DJ's remark may be regarded as a kind of problem-solving, which causes a new problem for the caller.

This chapter focuses on the problem-solving aspects of humor, jokes, irony, mocking, gossip, and black humor from an applied-linguistic perspective. Before we can develop this view further, it will be useful to look at the history of research (Section 2) as well as the current research dealing with these everyday categories (Sections 3 and 4). Section (5) provides a summary and an outlook on issues of applied linguistics. The following section gives an overview of research into humor, irony and laughter, as well as into the methods and concerns of text linguistics, pragmatics and sociolinguistics, after which the functional approach will be discussed in more detail.

2. History of the Research Topic and Current Research

The categories named in the title of this chapter show vast differences in their research histories. Some, such as *humor* and *irony*, were recognized two millennia ago by the ancient Greek philosophers as worthy of investigation. This started a research process that continues to this day. Some other categories, such as *mocking* and *gossip,* were long considered too trivial for serious investigation. Hence their research history is considerably shorter. In the following, I sketch out the main traditions in the research history relevant to the categories mentioned in the title of this chapter.

2.1. Humor Research

Humor research goes back to Greek philosophy and rhetoric, where humor was partly seen as an interesting phenomenon in its own right, and partly as a rhetorical device. Suggestions on how to ridicule one's opponent and how to cash in on other people's weaknesses are the forerunners of the modern *superiority/disparagement/aggression theories*, according to which humor arises from a feeling of superiority over others (cf. Hobbes [1651] 1990; Zillman 1983). Another main theory is *incongruity theory*, which states that humor is the reaction to an unexpected, ill-fitting element entering into a frame of expectation. Traces of it can be dated back to Aristotle, and by now it is the most generally accepted theory of humor. Ever since, philosophers (e.g., Hobbes, Kant, Schopenhauer, Nietzsche) have formulated their own humor theory, mostly based on incongruity or superiority. All these attempts were strictly deductive and essentialist, in that the scholars tried to find one central criterion as the explanation for humor. For our Example (1), the scholars would either identify the incongruity of making proprietor a holiday job or the mild aggression which comes with the teasing mentioned before, but not both. In the late 19th century, the two main groups of theories were complemented by *psychological theories*, which concentrated on relief/release of tension caused by suppressed urges. The most famous proponent of these theories is Sigmund Freud ([1905] 1985; cf. Keith-Spiegel 1972: 10–13 for an overview of theories).

The criteria used for defining humor according to the theories mentioned were rarely specified. They range from semantic structure (mostly for incongruity theories) to world-knowledge, flexibility of observation, social status (superiority) and subconscious mental processes (relief/release theories). Systematic verification of the rather intuitive notions only started after 1950. Linguistic humor research first concentrated on phonetic, morphological, and above all semantic issues, looking at puns, ambiguity, semantic scripts and related phenomena (cf. Attardo 1994 for a detailed overview).

By now, humor research has branched out into various traditions connected with linguistics (Attardo 1994), literary studies (Hutchinson 2006), sociology (Kuipers 2006), psychology (Ruch 1998), and some other disciplines. The essentialist approach still exists, but more and more authors now use a combination of theories (cf. Brock 2004), some of which seem also applicable to the category of irony, which would account for the fact that some authors tacitly treat irony as a sub-category of humor (cf. Eggins and Slade 2001: 116).

2.2. Irony

In Greek rhetoric, irony received attention as a type of joking. From the various approaches to irony at the time, subsequent researchers almost exclusively concentrated on the alleged opposition between what is said and what is meant (cf. the criticism in Hartung 1996: 114). Even modern theories are influenced by this approach: Grice's (1975) treatment of irony as based on flouting the quality maxim, Groeben's (1986) speech-act based approach, Clark and Gerrig's (1984) pretense theory of irony where "a speaker is pretending to be an injudicious person speaking to an uninitiated audience" (1984: 121) as well as Sperber and Wilson's echoic-mention theory of irony, in which they formulate:

> [. . .] all standard cases of irony [. . .] involve (generally implicit) mention of a proposition. These cases of mention are interpreted as echoing a remark or opinion that the speaker wants to characterize as ludicrously inappropriate or irrelevant (Sperber and Wilson 1981: 310).

Apart from the difference between saying and meaning, Sperber and Wilson's definition refers to another feature of irony which is usually regarded as constitutive. This feature is a negative evaluation of the target of irony (similar to the superiority/aggression theories of humor), although some authors (Groeben 1986; Long and Graesser 1988) also see positive evaluation as an option.

Both humor and irony can provoke laughter, but as the following section shows, laughter should not be seen as an automatic reaction to humor, and to humor only.

2.3. Laughter

Laughter was long seen as an immediate consequence of humor (cf. Eggins and Slade 2001: 157), so that humor research and laughter research were regarded as much the same thing. This view is exemplified vividly by the fact that Bergson published his influential 1900 essay on humor under the title *Le Rire* (Laughter). Gradually, the awareness of the differences between humor and laughter grew, however, and authors like Plessner identified a number of non-humorous occasions for laughter (Plessner 1993). By now, there is a large body of research focusing on laughter, partly in connection with the growing number of empirical studies on both conversational humor and laughter (cf. Jefferson 1984; Jefferson, Sacks and Schegloff 1987; Schwitalla 2001; Thimm and Augenstein 1996). These studies often identify (non-humor-related) functions of laughter in specific contexts, which makes them particularly useful in establishing laughter as a research object in its own right rather than a mere by-product of humor. Some of the independent functions identified for laughter are:

- establishing transfer from serious to non-serious mode (Jefferson, Sacks, and Schegloff 1987: 160), e.g., to defuse a tense situation
- establishing transfer to non-serious mode before introducing funny material (Schwitalla 2001: 328)
- indicating—e.g. while reporting a personal problem—that the speaker can master his problems, demonstration of emotional self-distance (Jefferson 1984: 351; Schwitalla 2001: 338)
- protection of the recipient's face (Schwitalla 2001: 333)
- threat to the recipient's face (Schwitalla 2001: 335)
- protection of the speaker's own face (Schwitalla 2001: 336)
- introduction of embarrassing topic (Schwitalla 2001: 338)
- reaction to impropriety (Jefferson 1985)
- expression of surprise (Schwitalla 2001: 341)
- laughter as an element of the turn taking system (Jefferson, Sacks, and Schegloff 1987)

The function of defusing a tense situation, like some others, is often directly attributed to humor. It is here at least partly associated with laughter, because this function can be fulfilled without either speaker or recipient being amused or assuming amusement in the other party.

To settle the relationship between humor and laughter, we may want to imagine a scale between two poles. One of the poles represents laughter as a blind, involuntary symptom of humor, the other fully deliberate, symbolic laughter without mirth, which fulfills a number of interpersonal and social functions. This deliberate laughter borrows from humor its expression and puts it to multiple use in social interaction. Other surface manifestations of humor may be borrowed at the same time, e.g., certain formulations, exaggeration, incongruity, aggression, etc. This calculated production of the structural characteristics of humor is a phenomenon that I call *humor presented*. The individual phenomenon of mirth will henceforth be referred to as *humor felt* or *amusement*. Quite clearly, humor presented *may* instigate amusement, but this cannot be taken for granted.

It seems reasonable to assume that most laughter would be situated somewhere between the two poles of laughter as a symptom of amusement and purely social/strategic laughter. This fact should be reflected in scholars' research methods, which is, however, not always the case. Strictly empirical investigations in the tradition of *conversation analysis* should really only be concerned with laughter and humor presented, as these are the only observable phenomena. While there may or may not be amusement behind laughter, its presence or absence is not something the researcher can prove, nor does it have much bearing on its social functionality. The awareness of this fact and its critical methodical reflection would make the study of laughter in the context of humor, joking, gossip, mocking, etc. a far more precise affair. This chapter with its focus on the functional nature of humor in problem-solving deals mainly with humor presented and social/strategic laughter, with the possible exception of some psychological functions (cf. Section 3 below).

2.4. Text Linguistics

Among the research interests of text linguistics are the classification of text types and their precise structural description. These interests are highly relevant to the study of categories like *humor, gossip, mocking,* etc., because the difference between them should somehow be reflected in a good text typology and in structural descriptions of the categories.

Text linguistics has chosen different ways of addressing these problems. Early text typologies (cf. Isenberg 1984) were often deductive, aiming at a strict theoretical demarcation of text types. This kind of approach would not be very successful at describing the situation outlined above for Examples (1) and (2), where several categories seem applicable. The same must be said about strictly structuralist research which often concentrated on the semantic structure of texts (cf. Ulrich 1977: 315 for jokes). Other classifications (cf. Heinemann and Viehweger 1991: 144) aimed less at descriptive homogeneity and more at a linguistic substantiation of why lay people use certain labels for communicative phenomena. In the light of the Examples (1) and (2), this labeling obviously involves some overlap between neighboring categories, as well a certain degree of polysemy of the terms representing categories. One meaning of *mocking,* for instance, seems to be largely synonymous with *hostile teasing,* whereas *friendly teasing* is a near-synonym to one meaning of *banter.* Approaches addressing these challenges include multi-level models, which apply several criteria to identify the relevant properties of text types (cf. Heinemann 2000: 513) as well as prototype models (Sandig 2000), which allow for fuzzy edges between neighboring types and overlaps between them. Morreall (1994: 57), for instance, uses the terms "humorous gossip" and "gossipy humor" (cf. Section 4.5. below).

In the process of modeling laypersons' intuition about text types, text linguistics also opened up to pragmatics, sociolinguistics, and other related disciplines which make the inclusion of contextual features a central concern. With this, text linguistics should be able to handle cases like Examples (1) and (2), where different contexts (perhaps due to differences in background knowledge) produce different interpretations of the material.

2.5. Pragmatics, Modern Sociolinguistics, and Gender Studies

The fields mentioned here look at humor, gossip, etc. in a larger context, including the communicative situation, institutional framing, background assumptions, communicative intentions, status of participants and their relationship to each other, gender, etc. Kotthoff (2006: 4) characterizes humor as a "situated discursive practice". Among other things, scholars from this tradition try to explain why examples like (1) and (2) can be interpreted quite differently, even though the actual wording of the utterance in question remains constant. Studying contextual aspects of phenomena like humor and gossip encompasses an enormous range of valid research problems, so that it is not surprising that currently a great deal of original research comes out of these research fields, with much more yet to be expected (cf. volume 38, 2006, of the *Journal of*

Pragmatics on gender and humor). As pragmatics, sociolinguistics, and gender studies not only investigate the circumstances of producing humor, irony, etc. but also their effects and functions, this research tradition is most relevant to the perspective of this book, i.e., the problem-solving perspective on language adopted here. If, for instance, gossip is not only described in terms of its topic matter, but also as a norm-defining and group-maintaining activity, then this research focuses on gossip as contributing to solving the social problems connected with group stability and norms.

Studies to be mentioned in this connection focus on structures, communicative circumstances and social functions of ironic speech acts (Groeben 1986; Hartung 1996), communicative maxims specific to humor (Attardo 1993; Brock 2004), participants' social background and status, communicative phases (Christmann 1996: 52; Günthner 1996: 83–84; Eggins and Slade 2001: 285), and the technical organization of humorous events (Sacks 1978; Jefferson, Sacks, and Schegloff 1987) as well as gender-specific differences in joking and humor (Coates 1998; Pilkington 1998; Lampert and Ervin-Tripp 2006: 52).

2.6. Summary of Research History: Criteria Used for the Definition of Humor, Jokes, Irony, Mocking, Gossip, and Black Humor

The following summarizes the main criteria so far mentioned to define the above categories. Excluded are their communicative functions, which will be treated in more detail in Section 3 below, as they are of particular concern to this article. I follow a rough chronology of research. The most commonly applied criteria are:

- semantic structure, often text-internal, occasionally in comparison with recipient's knowledge or real world, used for all categories (Ulrich 1977; Raskin 1985)
- morphology and phonetics, used mainly for jokes and puns (Attardo 1994)
- recipient's expectation, used for mainly humor, partly for gossip (Bergmann 1987; Long and Graesser 1988)
- social norms and negative evaluation, used for humor, gossip, and irony (Bergson [1900] 1948; Bergmann 1987; Hartung 1996)
- participation structure (e.g., aggressor, victim, witness), used for humor, gossip, joking, and mocking (Bergmann 1987; Günthner 1996; Brock 2004)
- imitation of somebody's behavior, used for mocking and parody
- degree of privacy, familiarity of participants, shared knowledge, used for humor, gossip, and irony (Bergmann 1987: 69; Hartung 1996: 110–112; Günthner 1996)
- degree of context-dependence, used for the differentiation of jokes and joking (Sacks 1978: 262; Norrick 2001: 1440)
- institutional or social setting (e.g., work and leisure for gossip; Bergmann 1987; Christmann 1996; Coates 1998: 228)

- authorship, used for gossip (Bergmann 1987) and irony (the use-mention distinction in Sperber and Wilson 1981 and the pretense model in Clark and Gerrig 1984; cf. also Hartung 1996)
- breaking of communicative rules, used for humor (Brock 2004)
- communicative phases, used for all categories (Bergmann 1987: 113; Christmann 1996: 52; Günthner 1996: 83–84; Eggins and Slade 2001: 285)
- the contrast between serious vs. non-serious and threatening vs. non-threatening communication (Attardo 1993; Günthner 1996: 81; Brock 2004)
- various surface forms (e.g., simultaneous talk and modality for gossip; Coates 1998), partly as contextualization cues (silly voices; Christmann 1996: 57), gestures, facial expression, laughter used for humor, joking, and irony
- conventionalized opening phrases, such as: "Have you heard this one?" (Attardo 1994).

3. The Functional Approach

Research into the communicative functions of phenomena like humor and gossip directly refers to their problem-solving nature. A communicative problem occurs—such as the need for distraction—and in response, the participants find interactive forms whose function is to deal with the problem in question. The more these forms are conventionalized, the more easily they seem to fulfill their functions, and the more easily participants will recognize them as familiar. This finally leads to labeled categories like *mocking, parody, irony*, etc., which can be identified not only by their functions, but also by certain recognizable forms.

The functional approach is not new. As mentioned in 2.1. and 2.2., humor and irony were treated in ancient Greece and Rome as rhetorical devices, i.e., categories which had to fulfill a communicative function. Some later philosophers also made the communicative function a central defining criterion for categories, notably Bergson ([1900] 1948), who saw laughter as functional in the punishment of human inflexibility. Even though his view was essentialist in that he only saw one function as the essence of the humorous experience, his definition was ground-breaking in that it showed that even humor had to perform a function which went beyond self-sufficiency.

In the last 20 years, numerous articles have been published which look at humor, irony, mocking, etc. from a functional perspective. In the following, I give the most important functions identified in the literature:

Entertainment:
This function should be self-evident for humor, but over the discussion of the more serious functions, some authors lose sight of it. It is, however, stressed by some authors in the context of irony (Hartung 1996: 120), gossip (Bergmann 1987: 154; Pilkington 1998: 255; Ben-Ze'ev 1994: 16), joking (Thimm and Augenstein 1996: 224; Norrick 2001: 1438) and humor (Morreall 1994: 58).

Norm maintenance and social control:
Social group norms are stressed directly or implicitly. This was notoriously claimed by Bergson ([1900] 1948) for humor. See also Long and Graesser (1988: 54), Hay (2000: 719), Norrick (2001: 1448), Kotthoff (2006: 5, 14). For gossip, see Bergmann (1987: 180), Eggins and Slade (2001: 276, 283), and Pilkington (1998: 254).

Group maintenance and solidarity:
By joking, gossiping, and making ironic remarks, an in-group with common values and experiences is created or confirmed. Group membership can be signaled or claimed. See, for gossip, Bergmann (1987: 198), Ben-Ze'ev (1994: 15), Coates (1998: 229), Eggins and Slade (2001: 273, 283), and Morreall (1994: 58); for irony, Hartung (1996: 118), and for humor Long and Graesser (1988: 53–54), Attardo (1993: 555), Eggins and Slade (2001: 155, 159), Norrick (2001: 1439), Hay (2000: 716), and Kotthoff (2006: 10, 15).

Out-group exclusion:
A strong in-group automatically creates an out-group, which is excluded. See Long and Graesser (1988: 53–54) as well as Morreall (1994: 63) for humor.

Reaffirming and strengthening friendship:
Next to influencing group dynamics, humor, gossip, etc. can also be used to build up and maintain individual relationships. See Coates (1998: 229) for gossip. Thimm and Augenstein (1996: 221), Norrick (2001: 1438), as well as Lam-pert and Ervin-Tripp (2006: 53) stress that humor can be instrumental in establishing common ground and intimacy. Kotthoff (2006: 17) points out the role of teasing in relationship management.

Positive politeness:
Some authors, such as Kotthoff (1998: 303) and Norrick (2001: 1440), point to the fact that joking is an activity which requires, produces, and highlights common values and desires. This makes it a positive politeness strategy. Long and Graesser (1988: 54) mention an ingratiation function of humor with a similar definition.

Presenting a personality, enhancing one's self-image:
Norrick (2001: 1438, 1440–1441) points out that humorous activities are part of the personality which an individual builds up and presents to the public.

Information management:
This function is mentioned by many authors and has numerous facets. Bergmann (1987: 202), de Sousa (1994: 33), and Morreall (1994: 56) discuss the informative function of gossip. Attardo (1993: 552) and Morreall (1994) point out that humor, too, may have an information value. Norrick (2001: 1438) claims that humor can be used to demonstrate knowledge. More precisely it may function to exhibit shared knowledge (Norrick 2001: 1439). The *probing* function of humor postulated by Long and Graesser (1988: 53) serves to gather information about other participants' views (cf. also Kotthoff 1998: 254). The

transfer of new information is also emphasized by Norrick (2001: 1438) and Sacks (1978: 268), who formulates: "The joke can [. . .] serve to package information which persons interested in such information can pull out of it." Ben-Ze'ev (1994: 15) mentions that gossip can produce new insight. The *self-disclosure* function of humor described by Long and Graesser (1988: 53) as well as Lampert and Ervin-Tripp (2006: 57) means revealing information about one's views and values to other recipients, while the *decommitment function* of humor (Attardo 1993: 554–555; Long and Graesser 1988: 53) is to free the speakers from the responsibility for an opinion which they do not want to be known to have.

Influencing opinions and emotions:
In addition to the management of information, humor, gossip, and irony may be exploited to influence other people's opinions and feelings, which goes beyond the mere transfer of information.

Exertion of power:
Thimm and Augenstein (1996: 224–226) see two ways in which humor helps to exert power. 1. The unilateral establishment of the humorous mode of communication is an act of controlling the conversation. 2. The recipient may become the object of humorous aggression, which amounts to a face-threatening act. They also state (1996: 233) that speakers may humorously trivialize other participants' position, which is another way of exerting power. Some authors, however, (e.g., Kotthoff 2006: 11) point out that humor may help to *level* power. This is not necessarily a contradiction to Thimm and Augenstein, as Kotthoff clearly describes a different aspect of communication, a temporary suspension of *macro-social* circumstances via humorous communication, whereas Thimm and Augenstein focus on power relations developing within the *micro-setting* of the ongoing communication itself (cf. also Eggins and Slade 2001: 167).

Taylor (1994: 46) sees gossip as powerful talk, and Hay (2000: 724) describes teasing as serving to maintain power. With respect to gossip, Pilkington (1998: 255) refers to speakers who overdo the exertion of power, with the result that the power-play backfires against themselves: "Anyone gaining too much power or overstepping their role leaves themselves open to be gossiped about."

Aggression:
According to superiority and aggression theories, humor should inherently have at least a mildly aggressive component (Norrick 2001: 1438). Aggressive humor may be deliberately and maliciously turned against a victim: either against the immediate recipient or a third person present or absent. This is something not only found in humor in a narrow sense, but also in gossip, mocking, and black humor. It may even be claimed that a considerable degree of aggression is constitutive for mocking (cf. Norrick 2001: 1440; Kotthoff 2006: 13) and some black humor. Norrick (2001: 1443) mentions the production of animosity as a function of sarcasm, while Hay (2000: 721) identifies a conflict-fostering function of humor. Aggression and its target are such an important

aspect of the categories mentioned, that the presence or absence of the target of aggression seems to be a vital aspect for defining some of the categories: *Teasing*, which aims at a reaction, obviously requires the target's presence, whereas *mocking* does not necessarily, and *gossip* even requires the target's absence. This is why, for example, mocking can be used in gossip, but teasing and gossip do not go together simultaneously and with the same target.

In contrast to the research that stresses the aggressive nature of humor, gossip, etc., Attardo (1993: 553) claims that humor may be used to defuse a difficult situation (cf. also Eggins and Slade 2001: 166). Clearly, there are different types of humor, some less aggressive than others. Similarly, Pilkington (1998: 255) mentions that gossip can be used to negotiate differences of opinion, which Hartung (1996: 119) shows to be one of the functions of irony, too.

Resistance and subversion:
Gossip (Goodman 1994: 5) and humor (Kotthoff 2006) are often associated with a subversive function, which is also one of the main aspects in the discussion of carnival traditions. Kotthoff (2006: 10) formulates: "Displaying humor means to temporarily take control of the situation away from those higher up in the hierarchy".

Poetic/aesthetic function:
Morreall (1994: 57) points out that both humor and gossip "primarily please the imagination, making humor and gossip candidates for aesthetic experience." Hartung (1996: 116) claims the same for conversational irony.

Discourse management:
Long and Graesser (1988: 55) as well as Norrick (2001) state that humor and wit can be used to "negotiate openings, closings, topic changes and realignments" (Norrick 2001: 1443). With that, they play an important role not only in the content dimension, but also in the technical organization and the turn-taking system of the conversation.

Psychological function:
Some authors refer to psychological functions of gossip (Goodman 1994) and humor (Hay 2000). The latter may not be surprising in view of the psychological humor theories mentioned in Section 2.1. The therapeutic potential of humor has long been recognized, and there is a large body of research on this issue as well as many therapeutic programs involving humor. The psychological functions of gossip are less well documented. Goodman (1994: 3) mentions coping with one's individual experiences and enhancement of self-esteem, whereas BenZe'ev (1994: 23) and Thomas (1994: 50) see gossip as an outlet for frustration and anger. This establishes another parallel to humor, the release theories of which describe the same function.

Multi-functionality:
In the foregoing explanations, it has become apparent that each of the categories treated in this chapter can perform a number of functions, and it makes sense to assume that they can perform more than one of them at the same

time. Bergmann (1987: 205) emphasizes this fact for gossip, Long and Graesser (1988: 55–56) as well as Hay (2000: 737) do the same for humor.

Institutional functions:
In addition to the multi-functionality mentioned above, yet another factor raises the complexity of a functional analysis. This is the fact that each of the illustrated functions, which we may roughly call *basic* functions, may be used by institutions to fulfill *derived* functions. A politician in a TV-debate, for instance, may use laughter to ridicule his opponent and ingratiate himself with the audience (*basic*) to realize the *derived* function of winning votes; TV stations produce professional comedies to exploit the basic entertaining function of humor for derived financial gains, etc. To take this further, it seems feasible to think of a differentiation of primary and secondary within what I have called the basic functions. All this leads to a fairly complex architecture of functions that humor, irony, gossip, etc. may serve.

The multi-functionality of humor as well as the possibility of serving derived functions can be illustrated with Examples (1) and (2). Utz's remark in (1) about wanting to work as a proprietor certainly fulfills an entertainment function. Considering the fact that neither of the youths has done a holiday job before and that they are both quite inexperienced in this field, we may also assume a solidarity function for the two young men, as well as the psychological function of self-assurance. Brian's question *Does that mean that you're not going to die?* in (2) fulfills the entertaining function, performs information management by asking for elaboration, potentially fosters conflict between himself and the caller, and exerts power by putting the caller under pressure to explain herself and controlling the direction which the conversation is taking. Norm management may also be behind his question, in that it can be interpreted to imply that every person should have a decent funeral. This functional complexity is still enhanced by the fact that the DJ represents a money-making institution. His question therefore serves the derived functions of maintaining the institution's functionality and earning money. For this, the DJ has to stay in control of the commercial product phone-in program and to ensure its entertainment value for the audience in order to get lucrative advertising contracts (cf. Brock 1996).

A third example, though seemingly simple, also shows a complex picture. The situation is a card-game among friends. Fred, Utz, and Kristina are into their second round of *Knack*, a simple card-game. The card constellation that ensures the player an instant victory is also called *Knack*.

(3) Card game
Kristina: *Ach so, was war jetzt hier mit meiner ersten Runde?*
          Oh right what was now here with my   first   round?
          Ich hab'n Knack gehabt.
          I   had a "Knack".
          'Oh right! So what about my first round, then? I won that!'
Fred: *Ich hatte 20 genau.*
          I   had   20 exactly.
          'That's right, I had 20 points.'

Utz: *Ich hatte 27, aber die zählt nicht, war 'ne Einführungsrunde.*
          I   had   27,   but it counts not,   was an   introductory round
          'I had 27 points, but it doesn't count anyway, it was just a warm-up.'
          (conversation continues in jocular tone with mutual mock accusations)

Cards, 2 May, 2004

Utz's attempt at turning the first round into a warm-up which does not count towards the overall score provokes mild amusement. But why are the others amused and not annoyed? What happens is this: nobody would expect Utz to be serious in his transparent attempt to bend the rules of the game. Instead, he produces a fictitious persona who tries to cheat so pathetically. As the fictitious Utz's behavior is an almost automatic reaction to a constellation like this, tried many times over, it may well be interpreted as humor of the mechanical and inflexible kind, after Bergson ([1900] 1948). To this impersonation and the entertainment value it holds, the other players react with amusement. At the same time, the real Utz might be probing for a little lenience or lack of interest on the other players' part to get away with his suggestion after all. This probing would serve the information function as well as the opinion-influencing function. Solidarity among the card-players might also be strengthened, as harmless banter is often one of the main ingredients of card-games, reassuring each other of the friendly relations between the participants.

In my comments on the individual functions, it has become apparent that not only can one category perform a multitude of functions, but also that each function can be carried by more than one category. It is therefore useful to have a closer look at the relationship between the categories treated in this chapter, to look out for similarities and differences that are reflected in different labels for the individual categories.

4. Problem-Solving and the Relationship Between Humor, Jokes, Irony, Mocking, Gossip, and Black Humor

In the light of what has been said so far, simple categories and relationships cannot be expected. If each category can perform several functions and each function can be performed by several categories, then this descriptive dimension is highly complex in itself. Other dimensions such as semantic structure or participation structure are necessary for an adequate description, but they cannot produce clear-cut demarcations of categories either. The participation structure of aggressor, victim, and witness, for instance, has been established for humor, gossip, joking, and mocking (cf. Section 2.6) and therefore cannot serve for sufficient differentiation. In addition to that, researchers do not agree on the definition of each category, which further complicates matters. De Sousa (1994: 27) describes gossip as democratic, "free speech extended to the private sphere", and defines it like this: "Gossip could be defined simply as conversation about other people's private lives" (1994: 26). Coates (1998) and Pilkington (1998) seem to share this positive view of gossip (where the term is used synonymously with *women's talk*), whereas other authors see gossip as "generally malicious" (Thomas 1994: 54) and "moralisch kontaminiert" ('morally contaminated'; Bergmann 1987: 79).[3] The following comments will therefore assume a prototypical organization of categories, and proceed from the general traits of each category. Occasionally, some details will be discussed, too.

4.1. Humor as a Problem-Solving Activity

Humor is the general term for non-serious, playful, non-threatening communicative activities which involve cognitive incongruities, some aggression, psychological relief and some degree of "Witzarbeit" (literally: 'joke work'), to use a term which Freud ([1905] 1985) coined for the technique of a joke. Some authors would also include surprise as a necessary condition. Thus defined, it can serve a very wide range of functions, as illustrated in Section 3, including entertainment, social control, and solidarity building. This potential multi-functionality makes it an extremely efficient communicative device. It can, for instance, be turned to their advantage by speakers who may want to use it to hide their real intentions behind being humorous. If the politician mentioned above is being funny, he may give the impression of simply wanting to entertain people, while his real intention may be to ingratiate himself with the recipients in order to win votes. Thus, humor not only serves the ingratiation function, but it simultaneously covers the tracks of this very strategy. With that, it is a problem-solving activity for the politician in more than one respect. Utz's remark in (1) about working as a proprietor neatly fits into the category of humor and general conversational joking, too, but other interpretations are possible (cf. Section 1).

The wide functional applicability and flexibility of humor as problem-solving is also due to the many kinds and patterns of humor, from light conversational joking to stand-up-comedy and political satire. Each of the comical genres is a different mixture of formal characteristics and cognitive/interpersonal patterns such as incongruities and aggression. Humor with a strong aggressive component may, for instance, be particularly effective in creating in-groups and out-groups as well as exerting power. In the following, I will comment on specific patterns of humor, such as jokes and black humor, as well as the cases of mocking and irony and the related phenomenon of gossip.

As opposed to the relatively free communicative activity of joking, whose only defining requirement seems to be to create a humorous incongruity, the *joke* is a stable communicative genre, studied among other disciplines in text linguistics. It is the joke's pre-formed nature which makes it particularly interesting in terms of functionality and problem-solving. Sacks (1978: 262) points out that jokes "can make their place in a conversation". This means that they are relatively con-text-independent and do not have to be artfully embedded into the flow of conversation. They can simply be announced. Also, in contrast to funny remarks, the turn-taking rules are suspended for the duration of a joke's telling. This way, the teller is free from having to fight for his/her turn. In addition to that, jokes can be planned, and do not require a quick, intuitive

---

[3] Cf. also Eggins and Slade (2001: 278) for different conceptions of gossip.

sense of humor. This reduces the risk of unintentionally hurting someone's feelings, also because the aggression of the joke is at least ostensibly contained in its fictitious world. Serial jokes can create a very strong appreciation of recognition and a feeling of community and solidarity. This is especially prominent in jokes of political resistance. To sum up, the joke is efficient in controlling the flow of conversation and suspending turn-taking. It can be planned and bears relatively low risk of misunderstanding. On the down side, jokes are often predictable, and due to this and their low risk factor they are often considered inferior to free conversational joking.

4.2. Irony and Its Relationship to Humor

As stated in Section 2.2., *irony* has often been described as a form of humor. Hartung (1996: 118) defines it as an indirect negative evaluation which, due to its indirectness, may have a poetic and humorous potential. This definition shows clearly why irony is so closely associated with humor: the indirectness mentioned may produce a kind of incongruity, whereas the negative evaluation may be a form of aggression. If the indirectness highlighted by Hartung involves a certain technique in its production and if we add to the definition the playfulness which Hartung mentions elsewhere (1996: 109), then irony indeed appears as a type of humor. However, not all humor is indirect (some humor draws its incongruous nature from being virtually without technique and bluntly direct, as in the British TV-series *The Young Ones*), and not all humor carries negative evaluation. Likewise, not all irony is playful and light-hearted, particularly when the negative evaluation concerns the participants' vital interests. This results in only a partial overlap of the categories of humor and irony.

It is of little practical relevance for the overlapping cases whether irony uses the forms of humor or humor uses the ironic form. From a problem-solving perspective, these cases of humor and irony fulfill the same social functions— criticism and social control—with much the same means, i.e., indirectness in a creative and light-hearted atmosphere. It is the attraction of irony/humor of this kind to offer a relatively stable, conventionalized, socially accepted, and sometimes entertaining form of social control. As soon as the ingredients or their ratio change—if, for instance, the element of negative evaluation becomes stronger than its playfulness–, humor and irony part ways and begin to solve different communicative problems in different ways.

The relationship between humor and irony shows us not only the subtlety of similarities between the categories, but also that a useful discussion of the categories and their problem-solving nature has to incorporate a discussion of how these problems are solved, i.e., the linguistic form and content.

4.3. Black Humor

Black humor is a case in point. It uses all the techniques of humor and all theories of humor can be successfully applied to it. What makes it special is only its subject matter and the functions it can serve in connection with it: black humor makes fun of topics which are usually considered outside the range of humor—death, mutilation, disease, and other serious threats to the individual. This makes it a potential tool for psychological functions. Framing one's worst fears humorously may be a coping strategy, for both real and imagined threats. This coping function may unite the black humor reportedly popular among the prisoners in Nazi concentration camps with the nauseating details of a slaughter scene in a Monty Python sketch, even though the circumstances are vastly different. Making fear and brutality a topic of humor at the same time turns them from taboo non-topics into topics which society cannot easily avoid. Black humor may thus serve an information and topic management function. Black humor in its many forms is, however, a risky phenomenon, because for some recipients at least it can easily turn into an aggressive, harmful act of communication. If, maybe due to personal experiences, the depiction of threatening aspects outweighs the non-threatening frame within which they are delivered, the humor fades away, and the person is left with the traumatic experience itself. And of course, people can deliberately use black humor to exert power and hurt others. A potential example of black conversational humor can be found in the DJ's question *Does that mean that you're not going to die?* in Example (2).

4.4. Mocking

Mocking is one of the communicative categories which are hard to define, and where people differ considerably in their application of the term. This is not surprising if we look at the constitutive features of mocking: dictionary definitions often stress the imitating, mimicking nature of mocking to show ridicule. Imitation and making fun of people are also humor-related techniques to produce funny incongruities and aggression. This makes humor and mocking similar communicative activities. The crucial difference between them seems to be that in mocking, the ratio of hostility/aggression and light-heartedness favors hostility over the other ingredients. If this is the case, then individual differences in deciding whether something is joking/teasing or cold mockery are a natural result of a) the similarity of the two categories, and b) the individual differences in experiencing degrees of hostility. In the light of this definition, it is easy to see that mocking may function as a means of fostering conflict.

One should not forget, however, that this is not unmitigated hostility. Mocking comes with a technique, which is often imitation, and skillful imitation may have a clear entertainment function. After all, political satire uses very similar techniques, and it may just be a question of one's political affiliation whether something is regarded as healthy political satire or malicious mockery. Also, Norrick (2001: 1447–1448) uses Sperber and Wilson's (1981) *mention* model to show that mocking among good friends may really mean "that the attack is only play and the participants are mutually engaged in a customary joking relationship" which, if anything, strengthens the participants' friendship. This is also the gist of Leech's (1983: 144) banter principle. The question which arises with these meta-communicative uses of mocking is whether we are still really dealing with the phenomenon that deserves the label *mocking*. If hostility is constitutive to mocking, then quoted hostility which is really friendly only borrows the empty carcass of mocking. Leech's definition of *banter* seems to fit this description much better.

4.5. Gossip

Gossip, variously described as malicious talk behind a person's back, seems at first glance to be considerably different from humor. But like humor, it clearly fulfills an entertainment function (Bergmann 1987: 154), for which role-play, exaggeration (Bergmann 1987: 161–162; Morreall 1994: 62; Pilkington 1998: 266; Lampert and Ervin-Tripp 2006: 57), narrative form, and other aesthetic means (Morreall 1994: 57) can be used. Morreall (1994: 56) claims that both humor and gossip provide new and surprising information, and that even gossip is characterized by incongruities (Morreall 1994: 61), as the things we gossip about are often unexpected, ill-fitting and norm-violating. Humor and gossip serve the function of information management (Bergmann 1987: 202). As stated in Section 3 above, both humor and gossip may contain a negative evaluation of somebody's behavior; both have an aggressive component (Hobbes [1651] 1990; Zillman 1983; Bergmann 1987: 199; Eggins and Slade 2001: 278) and are used to vent one's frustration and negative feelings about another person. This aggressive or even malicious (Thomas 1994: 54) aspect seems to me—in contrast to Coates (1998) and Pilkington (1998)—a necessary condition of gossip, because Coates's (1998: 250) definition of gossip as "relaxed informal conversation between equals", which disregards the aggressive and evaluative component, produces an unnecessary synonym to *small-talk*. Humor and gossip both foster group-solidarity, they may exert social control (Bergson [1900] 1948; Bergmann 1987: 193; Ben-Ze'ev 1994: 23), both usually take place in social situations without immediate pressure to perform urgent business (Bergmann 1987), and they can be institutionalized—in the form of comedy programs, plays, books, etc. and in gossip columns. The participation structure for both consists of actor, victim, and witness, and both depend much on their novelty value.

Apart from the many similarities, there are still some aspects which account for the differences in the perception of humor and gossip. First of all, the information management function of gossip is of a specific nature: as Bergmann (1987: 73) points out, gossip derives much of its energy from the tension between what a person makes public and what he/she tries to conceal as private (cf. Morreall 1994: 58), or, in the words of Ben-Ze'ev (1994: 18), the "gap between reputation or conventional behavior and actual behavior is what makes gossip interesting." This is a specification not necessarily shared by humor. There is also a difference in the participation structure: for gossip, the victim usually has to be absent or at least acoustically excluded from the conversation (Bergmann 1987: 67), and all participants should know each other at least reasonably well (Bergmann 1987: 68). However, gossip is less restricted than humor with regard to technique—it *may* use surprise, effective narrative, impersonations, etc., but these are not defining criteria of gossip. And of course, as the novelty value of humor mainly depends on its bringing forth new techniques and forms, the techniques of gossip are extremely limited by comparison, which satisfies its novelty requirement mainly through new information. Also, humor *may* be about real people and their private lives, and it *may* refer to absent people, but there is much humor targeting people present or fictitious characters.

But wherever the conditions for both humor and gossip meet, we encounter a situation which Morreall (1994: 57) describes as "humorous gossip" or "gossipy humor". We may simply call it an overlap of the two categories in an area where they both share the same structural and functional properties. The easy applicability of the patterns of one category in the other testifies to the similarity of functions they have to fulfill.

At this point, a methodological remark seems in place. Morreall (1994: 56) points out that "when gossip is dominated by the spirit of humor, it tends to transcend the pettiness and viciousness that have given gossip such a bad name." In this statement, the positive atmosphere of the gossip described is attributed to humor. This may wrongly lead to the evaluation of light-heartedness as not being a possible property of gossip, but rather of humor or similar phenomena *within* gossip. Similarly, I have talked of one category *borrowing* properties of another. This kind of approach is, strictly speaking, misleading and no more than a handy metaphor, because it disallows for variety within the borrowing categories and reduces them to small and insufficient sets of properties. It is also unnecessary, if one accepts a prototypical organization of categories. They are then defined via clusters of typical functions and conventional structures which they have developed to fulfill these functions. The property of light-heartedness in gossip need not be borrowed from humor, but may be a legitimate property of some gossip, with the only consequence that not everybody would see this as prototypical gossip.

5. Summary: The Role of Applied Linguistics

We have seen in the last section that the similarities between categories are great and the differences in their functional potential for problem-solving are subtle. At the same time, some of the categories treated in this chapter have a better reputation than others, which is signified by the word *versus* appearing in the title, and properties like the malicious nature of some gossip have been discussed here. The similarity of positively and negatively connoted communicative phenomena is not only an academic issue: the picture drawn in the preceding sections is corroborated by observations from communicative reality, where much friction arises from misunderstood banter, humor, or irony. People may unwittingly win themselves a reputation for being arrogant or without a sense of humor. Even in early adulthood, many still lack the communicative mastership over humor, irony, mocking, etc.

This is the point where the problem-solving potential of applied linguistics becomes relevant. Applied linguistics is able to treat communicative problems arising from insufficient competence in the following ways (cf., e.g., Thimm and Augenstein 1996 for an investigation of high practical relevance):

- It can analyze authentic occurrences of problematic categories. With this, it can show how subtle the differences are between harmless joking and insult, or irony and sarcasm. If aggression is common to all these activities, then maybe the *degree* of aggression is crucial. This, however is not only dependent on the speaker's formulation, but also on the recipient's background of expectation. The theoretical background of such an analysis would be pragmatics, sociolinguistics, and the kind of text linguistics outlined in Section 2.4., which models laypersons' intuitions about text types.

- The knowledge thus gained can be used in counseling and communication training to raise the language users' awareness of the possible pitfalls of humor, irony, mocking, etc.
- One of the basic aspects to teach is the fact that due to the interactional nature of communication, a communicative act is not the speaker's exclusive accomplishment, and it is not the speaker's exclusive right to decide on a valid interpretation. The recipient's active role in determining an interpretation becomes obvious in Example (2), where the caller does not react to the humorous or mocking potential of the DJ's question *Does that mean that you're not going to die?* Instead, by responding directly to the propositional content of the question, she turns it into a *bona-fide* question.
- It is vital to point out that the multi-functionality of the categories described is both a blessing and a danger: a blessing, because if properly applied, the categories can do many jobs at the same time, and a danger because this complexity is sometimes hard to control.
- In advanced communication training it should be possible to show that the described overlap of categories may be exploited to the speaker's strategic advantage.
- Above all, it is necessary to raise people's awareness of the fact that every observable function of humor, jokes, irony, etc. is the communicative response to the needs or problems that naturally arise in connection with all human activities, and more specifically with human interaction. This aware-ness-raising is necessary because of the conventional nature of problem-solving via the communicative functions identified. Conventional problem-solving sometimes hides the fact that there was a problem in the first place.

The fact that many people are relatively inept at handling humor, jokes, irony, mocking, gossip, and black humor even at a fairly mature age would suggest that an awareness of these issues should be developed systematically, preferably with the help of educational institutions.

References

Attardo, Salvatore. 1993. Violation of conversational maxims and cooperation. The case of jokes. *Journal of Pragmatics* 19: 537–558.

Attardo, Salvatore. 1994. *Linguistic Theories of Humor*. Berlin/New York: Mouton de Gruyter.

Ben-Ze'ev, Aaron. 1994. The vindication of gossip. In: Robert F. Goodman and Aaron Ben-Ze'ev (eds.), *Good Gossip*, 11–24. Lawrence: University Press of Kansas.

Bergmann, Jörg R. 1987. *Klatsch. Zur Sozialform der diskreten Indiskretion*. Berlin/New York: Walter de Gruyter.

Bergson, Henri. 1948. *Das Lachen*. Meisenheim am Glan: Westkulturverlag Anton Hain. First published as: Le Rire. Essai sur la signification du comique. Paris: La Revue de Paris [1900].

Brock, Alexander. 1996. Symmetrie und Asymmetrie in einem 'phone-in'. *Arbeiten aus Anglistik und Amerikanistik* 21(2): 155–177.

Brock, Alexander. 2004. *Blackadder, Monty Python und Red Dwarf. Eine linguistische Untersuchung britischer Fernsehkomödien*. Tübingen: Stauffenburg.

Christmann, Gabriela. 1996. Die Aktivität des 'Sich-Mokierens' als konversationelle Satire. Wie sich Umweltschützer/innen über den 'Otto-Normalverbraucher' mokieren. In: Helga Kotthoff (ed.), *Scherzkommunikation. Beiträge aus der empirischen Gesprächsforschung*, 49–80. Opladen: Westdeutscher Verlag.

Clark, Herbert H. and Richard J. Gerrig. 1984. On the pretense theory of irony. *Journal of Experimental Psychology: General* 113(1): 121–126.

Coates, Jennifer. 1998. Gossip revisited. Language in all-female groups. In: Jennifer Coates (ed.), *Language and Gender. A Reader*, 226–253. Malden/Oxford/Carlton: Blackwell.

De Sousa, Ronald. 1994. In praise of gossip. Indiscretion as a saintly virtue. In: Robert F. Goodman and Aaron Ben-Ze'ev (eds.), *Good Gossip*, 25–33. Lawrence: University Press of Kansas.

Eggins, Suzanne and Diana Slade. 2001. *Analysing Casual Conversation*. London/New York: Continuum.

Freud, Sigmund. 1985. *Der Witz und seine Beziehung zum Unbewussten*. Leipzig: Gustav Kiepenheuer. First published Leipzig: Deuticke [1905].

Goodman, Robert F. 1994. Introduction. In: Robert F. Goodman and Aaron Ben-Ze'ev (eds.), *Good Gossip*, 1–8. Lawrence: University Press of Kansas. Grice, H. Paul. 1975. Logic and conversation. In: Peter Cole and Jerry L. Morgan (eds.), *Syntax and Semantics 3, Speech Acts*, 41–58. New York: Academic Press.

Groeben, Norbert. 1986. Ironie als spielerischer Kommunikationstyp? Situationsbedingungen und Wirkungen ironischer Sprechakte. In: Werner Kallmeyer (ed.), *Kommunikationstypologie. Handlungsmuster, Textsorten, Situationstypen*, 172–192. Düsseldorf: Pädagogischer Verlag Schwann.

Günthner, Susanne. 1996. Zwischen Scherz und Schmerz. Frotzelaktivitäten in Alltagsinteraktionen. In: Helga Kotthoff (ed.), *Scherzkommunikation. Beiträge aus der empirischen Gesprächsforschung*, 81–108. Opladen: Westdeutscher Verlag.

Hartung, Martin. 1996. Ironische Äußerungen in privater Scherzkommunikation. In: Helga Kotthoff (ed.), *Scherzkommunikation. Beiträge aus der empirischen Gesprächsforschung*, 109–143. Opladen: Westdeutscher Verlag.

Hay, Jennifer. 2000. Functions of humor in the conversation of men and women. *Journal of Pragmatics* 32: 709–742.

Heinemann, Wolfgang. 2000. Textsorte—Textmuster—Texttyp. In: Klaus Brinker, Gerd Antos, Wolfgang Heinemann and Sven F. Sager (eds.), *Text- und Gesprächslinguistik / Linguistics of Text and Conversation. Ein internationales Handbuch zeitgenössischer Forschung / An International Handbook of Contemporary Research* 1, 507–522, Berlin/New York: Walter de Gruyter.

Heinemann, Wolfgang and Dieter Viehweger. 1991. *Textlinguistik. Eine Einführung*. Tübingen: Niemeyer

Hobbes, Thomas. 1990. *Leviathan, or The Matter, Forme & Power of a Common-Wealth ecclesiastical and civil*. Faksimile-Ausgabe Düsseldorf: Verlag Wirtschaft und Finanzen. First published London: Crooke [1651].

Hutchinson, Peter (ed.). 2006. *Landmarks in German Comedy*. Oxford: Lang.

Isenberg, Horst. 1984. Texttypen als Interaktionstypen. *Zeitschrift für Germanistik* 3: 261–270.

Jefferson, Gail. 1984. On the organization of laughter in talk about troubles. In: Maxwell J. Atkinson and John Heritage (eds.), *Structures of Social Action. Studies in Conversation Analysis*, 346–369. Cambridge: Cambridge University Press.

Jefferson, Gail. 1985. An exercise in the transcription and analysis of laughter. In: Teun A. van Dijk (ed.), *Handbook of discourse analysis 3. Discourse and dialogue*, 25–34. London/Orlando/San Diego/New York/Toronto/Montreal/Sydney/ Tokyo: Academic Press.

Jefferson, Gail, Harvey Sacks and Emanuel Schegloff. 1987. Notes on laughter in the pursuit of intimacy. In: Graham Button and John R. E. Lee (eds.), *Talk and Social Organisation*, 152–205. Clevedon/Philadelphia: Multilingual Matters.

Keith-Spiegel, Patricia. 1972. Early conceptions of humor. Varieties and issues. In: Jeffrey H. Goldstein and Paul E. Mc Ghee (eds.) *The Psychology of Humor. Theoretical Perspectives and Empirical Issues*, 3–39. New York/San Francisco/London: Academic Press.

Kotthoff, Helga. 1998. *Spaß Verstehen. Zur Pragmatik von konversationellem Humor*. Tübingen: Niemeyer.

Kotthoff, Helga (ed.). 2006. *Scherzkommunikation. Beiträge aus der empirischen Gesprächsforschung*. Verlag für Gesprächsforschung: http://www.verlag-gespraechsforschung. de/2006/kotthoff.htm. First published Opladen: Westdeutscher Verlag [1996].

Kotthoff, Helga. 2006. Gender and humor. The state of the art. *Journal of Pragmatics* 38: 4–25.

Kuipers, Giselinde. 2006. *Good Humor, Bad Taste. A Sociology of the Joke*. Berlin/New York: Mouton de Gruyter.

Lampert, Martin D. and Susan M. Ervin-Tripp. 2006. Risky laughter: teasing and self-directed joking among male and female friends. *Journal of Pragmatics* 38, 51–72.

Long, Debra L. and Arthur C. Graesser. 1988. Wit and humor in discourse processing. *Discourse Processes* 11: 35–60.

Morreall, John. 1994. Gossip and humor. In: Robert F. Goodman and Aaron Ben-Ze'ev (eds.), *Good Gossip*, 56–64. Lawrence: University Press of Kansas.

Norrick, Neal R. 2001. Jokes and joking in conversation. In: Klaus Brinker, Gerd Antos, Wolfgang Heinemann and Sven F. Sager (eds.), *Text- und Gesprächslinguistik / Linguistics of Text and Conversation. Ein internationales Handbuch zeitgenössischer Forschung / An International Handbook of Contemporary Research* 2, 1438–1449. Berlin/New York: Walter de Gruyter.

Pilkington, Jane. 1998. 'Don't try and make out that I'm nice!' The different strategies women and men use when gossiping. In: Jennifer Coates (ed.), *Language and Gender. A Reader*, 254–269. Malden/Oxford/Carlton: Blackwell.

Plessner, Helmut. 1993. Anlässe des Lachens. In: Steffen Dietzsch (ed.), *Luzifer lacht. Philosophische Betrachtungen von Nietzsche bis Tabori*, 119–175. Leipzig: Reclam Leipzig.

Raskin, Victor. 1985. *Semantic Mechanisms of Humor*. Dordrecht: Reidel. Ruch, Willibald (ed.). 1998. *The Sense of Humor. Explorations of a Personality Characteristic*. Berlin/ New York: Mouton de Gruyter.

Sacks, Harvey. 1978. Some technical considerations of a dirty joke. In: Jim Schenkein (ed.), *Studies in the Organization of Conversational Interaction*, 249–275. New York: Academic Press.

Sandig, Barbara. 2000. Text als prototypisches Konzept. In: Martina Mangasser-Wahl (ed.), *Prototypen in der Linguistik*, 93–112. Tübingen: Stauffenburg.

Schwitalla, Johannes. 2001. Lächelndes Sprechen und Lachen als Kontextualisierungsverfahren. In: Kirsten Adamzik and Helen Christen (eds.), *Sprachkontakt, Sprachvergleich, Sprachvariation. Festschrift für Gottfried Kolde zum 65. Geburtstag*, 325–344. Tübingen: Niemeyer.

Sperber, Dan and Deirdre Wilson. 1981. Irony and the use—mention distinction. In: Peter Cole (ed.), *Radical Pragmatics*, 295–318. New York: Academic Press.

Taylor, Gabriele. 1994. Gossip as moral talk. In: Robert F. Goodman and Aaron Ben-Ze'ev (eds.), *Good Gossip*, 34–46. Lawrence: University Press of Kansas.

Thimm, Caja and Susanne Augenstein. 1996. Lachen und Scherzen in einer Aushandlungssituation oder: Zwei Männer vereinbaren einen Termin. In: Helga Kotthoff (ed.), *Scherzkommunikation. Beiträge aus der empirischen Gesprächsforschung*, 221–253. Opladen: Westdeutscher Verlag.

Thomas, Laurence. 1994. The logic of gossip. In: Robert F. Goodman and Aaron Ben-Ze'ev (eds.), *Good Gossip*, 47–55. Lawrence: University Press of Kansas.

Ulrich, Winfried. 1977. Semantische Turbulenzen: Welche Kommunikationsformen kennzeichnen den Witz? *Deutsche Sprache* 4: 313–334.

Zillmann, Dolf. 1983. Disparagement humor. In: Paul E. McGhee and Jeffrey Goldstein (eds.) *Handbook of Humor Research. Volume 1. Basic Issues*, Chapter 5, 85–107. New York: Springer.

7

Praising and Blaming, Applauding, and Disparaging—Solidarity, Audience Positioning, and the Linguistics of Evaluative Disposition

Peter R. R. White

1. Introduction

Central to much theorizing about the interpersonal functionality of language is a concern with what is often termed *solidarity, contact, bonding, or affiliation*. This, in general terms, is the issue of the connection, communality, or rapport which holds between communicative participants, or, more precisely, the degree of connection, communality, or rapport indicated through the interlocutors' linguistic choices. Do they address each other in friendly or familiar terms, or as strangers? Do they communicate in such a way as to suggest they share beliefs, experiences, expectations, feelings, tastes, and values, or do they seem to be disassociated or at odds? Is their language combative, conciliatory, or amicable? Do they assume agreement or compliance on the part of those they address, or, alternatively, do they anticipate skepticism, resistance, animosity, or ridicule?

Work which has significantly advanced theorizing about the linguistics of solidarity/affiliation includes Brown and Gilman's highly influential *Pronouns of Power and Solidarity* (1960), the very extensive *politeness theory* literature (for example, Brown and Levinson 1987) and, within Systemic Functional Linguistics, Poynton's work on the notions of *contact* and *affect* as parameters of Tenor variation (for example Poynton 1985). This chapter provides an outline of a more recent contribution to theorizing about solidarity/affiliation/bonding provided by work within what is known as the *appraisal framework* (see, for example, Iedema, Feez, and White 1994; Martin 2000; White 2000, 2002; Macken-Horarik and Martin 2003; Martin and White 2005).

Appraisal theory has been developed over the past 15 years or so by linguists working within the Systemic Functional Linguistic (SFL) paradigm of Halliday and his colleagues (see, for example, Halliday [1994] 2004; Martin 1992; Matthiessen 1995). The key insight of Systemic Functional Linguistics for the purposes of this chapter is that there are three broad modes of linguistic meaning-making, what SFL terms *ideational, textual,* and *interpersonal* meaning. Ideational meanings are those by which speakers/writers interpret and reflect on the experiential world, textual meanings are those by which speakers/writers organize their texts and relate them to the context in which the communication is taking place, and interpersonal meanings are those by which speakers/writers adopt subjective positions, take on social roles and identities, and negotiate social relationships.

The focus of appraisal theory is on the last of these three modes of meaning, that of the interpersonal, and the theory picks up on early work in this area by other systemic functional linguists, perhaps most notably the work on Tenor by Martin and by Poynton (see Martin 1992, 1995; Poynton 1985, 1990a,b). The work on appraisal has been directed at extending the SFL-model of interpersonal meaning-making by providing more delicate descriptions of the choices available to speakers/writers as they convey positive and negative assessments and negotiate those assessments with actual or potential respondents. Thus, in simple terms, it is concerned with the ways in which speakers/writers praise or condemn, approve or disapprove, applaud or criticize, empathize or indicate animosity. Under the influence of the Bakhtin-inspired view that all verbal communication is *dialogic* (see, for example, Bakhtin 1982), the appraisal framework perceives attitudinal language to do more than simply self-expressively announce the speaker/writer's viewpoint. Bakhtin's notion, of course, was that even the most "monologic" text involves the speaker/writer in responding in some way to what has been said before on the subject by others and in anticipating in some way how those addressed will themselves react or respond to what it being asserted. Thus in any praising or condemning, applauding or criticizing, there is always more involved communicatively and interpersonally than self-expression. By announcing their own positive or negative viewpoint, speakers/writers indicate where they stand with respect to other members of their discourse community, since these others can be expected to have their own views on the matter, or at least to be in the process of forming a view as the discussion unfolds.

As a consequence of this dialogic perspective, the appraisal framework provides insights into that aspect of solidarity/affiliation which turns on the degree to which communicative participants present themselves as sharing, or failing to share, attitudes, and in the ways in which they manage any apparent differences in these attitudes.

In order to demonstrate this application of appraisal theory, an account is provided in the following sections of how the appraisal framework models the various options available to speakers/writers as they communicate attitudinal meanings, i.e., as they seek to advance or activate positive and negative viewpoints. Three of the key axes of variability in the communication of attitude are:

(i) variation in the type of positive/negative attitude, (ii) variation in the degree of explicitness by which attitudinal assessments are conveyed, and (iii) variation in the degree to which, and the way in which, potential alternative attitudinal positions are entertained or allowed for. Section 2. below provides an overview and discussion of these three axes.

A fourth axis, labeled "graduation" in the appraisal framework, is not considered in this chapter. Graduation is that sub-system of evaluative meanings by which attitudinal assessments are intensified or down-scaled, or by which attitudinal categories can be made more or less precise. For a detailed account, see Martin and White (2005: 135–160) or Hood (2004).

The evaluative arrangements which result from different settings of these parameters of variation can be thought of as constituting particular evaluative stances or dispositions. Thus a speaker/writer who, for example, mostly evaluates by indicating how he/she responds emotionally to phenomena will present a different evaluative disposition from one who typically evaluates by assessing phenomena in aesthetic or ethical terms. Similarly, a speaker/writer who explicitly passes judgement on phenomena will present a different evaluative disposition from one who chooses only to be implicitly or indirectly attitudinal. In Section 3. below, a comparative analysis of the attitudinal workings of two movie reviews is presented in order to demonstrate how the appraisal framework is employed to identify and characterize such evaluative dispositions. The analysis identifies similarities and differences between the two reviews in terms of the types of attitude favored by the writers, the degree to which they favor explicit or implicit attitude, and the ways in which they engage with other voices and alternative viewpoints.

Section 4. concludes the discussion by demonstrating how appraisal-based analyses of evaluative disposition can contribute to our understanding of the ways in which texts position audiences and negotiate solidarity. Towards this end, the section examines the audience positioning effects associated with the evaluative dispositions operating in the two analyzed movie review texts. It is shown that, on account of differences in the modes of evaluation favored by the two reviewers, the two texts construct different "ideal" or "imagined" readers, and negotiate solidarity under different terms.

Before turning to the discussion proper, it needs to be observed that, with some notable exceptions (see, for example, Eggins and Slade 1997: 116–167, Clark, Drew and Pinch 2003), the majority of the work on appraisal and evaluative disposition has, to this point, focused largely on written, single-party texts and not on immediately interactive, conversational, multi-party texts. The material provided below, accordingly, relies largely on insights derived from written texts, takes most of its examples from written texts, and usually refers to the "writer" rather than to the "speaker/writer".

It also needs to be noted that the primary focus of the chapter is upon what can be termed mass communicative texts, i.e., texts where the addressee is some mass grouping not specifically known to the author and not in immediate contact with the author, in this case two movie reviews directed to some general public. In such contexts, the relationship of solidarity/affiliation is essentially a virtual one. That is to say, it is a projected relationship which holds between the authorial voice or persona and the imagined or putative addressee which the text constructs for itself.

2. Axes of Attitudinal Variation

2.1. Attitudinal Subtypes: Feelings, Tastes, and Values

At the broadest level of analysis, the appraisal framework identifies three sub-types or modes of positive/negative attitude: (i) emotional reactions (labeled *affect*), (ii) assessments of human behavior and character by reference to eth-ics/ morality and other systems of conventionalized or institutionalized norms (labeled *judgement*), and (iii) assessments of objects, artifacts, texts, states of affairs, and processes in terms of how they are assigned value socially (labeled *appreciation*), i.e., in terms of their aesthetic qualities, their potential for harm or benefit, their social salience, and so on. Illustrative examples of the different subtypes are provided in the following (relevant lexical items are in bold):

- [Affect (feelings—emotional reaction)]

  (1) I was **unsatisfied** with the characterisation, **underwhelmed** by the mythic pomposity and **bored to tears** by the fight sequences (*Guardian*, January 16, 2001).

  (2) It was, then, with **fury**, that I returned home on Saturday to find my own country rumbling with the mumbles of the peaceniks (*Daily Express*, October 10, 2001).

- [Judgement (values—ethical and other assessments of the social acceptabil-ity or praiseworthiness of human behavior)]

  (3) If the reviewer is too cinematically **illiterate** to appreciate a masterpiece like Crouching Tiger, then it's her loss. Using the film to **belittle** Chinese culture is, at best, **insensitive**. Referring to 'inscrutable' orientals is clichéd **racism**, straight from the nineteenth century (dimsum.co.uk January 19, 2001).

  (4) To see police **brutally manhandling** demonstrators was not only shock-ing but representative of more **repressive** regimes, such as China (*Birming-ham Post*, October 25, 1999).

- [Appreciation (tastes—aesthetic and other social valuations of objects, arti-facts, processes and states of affair)]

  (5) It is a **good** film, **not fantastic**, but **worth watching** (dimsum.co.uk January 19, 2001).

  (6) The new president's speech was **elegant** and **well-woven**, sounding a panoply of themes without seeming **scattered** (*New York Post*, January 21, 2001).

There are a number of motivations for this three-way division. There are lex-ico-grammatical grounds for the division between affect on the one hand and appreciation and judgement on the other—for example, the fact that affect is most directly realized by verbs ("I **loved** this film."; "Mary **annoys** me."), while judgements and appreciations are qualities which attach to entities and actions, and hence are most typically realized as adjectives ("She is **illiterate** and **insensitive**."; "It is a **sweetly** romantic movie.") or adverbs ("The sword is **richly** and **exquisitely** carved and inlaid."). As indicated above, the primary grounds for distinguishing between judgement and appreciation as subcategories of attitude is one of evaluative targeting—judgements are positive/ negative assessments of human behavior by reference to social norms while appreciations do not directly have human behavior as their target, but rather are assessments of objects, artifacts, material states of affairs, and so on.

However, there are also lexical, specifically collocational grounds, for the division between judgement and appreciation, namely the following collocational patterns. Judgement adjectives can typically operate in the following collocational frame:

> It was X (judgement adjective) of Y (human target of judgemental assessment) to do Z.

Examples (7) and (8) below illustrate this.

(7) It was **cruel** of **him** to dump you right around the holidays, especially for things like videogaming (Yahoo! Canada Answers).

(8) It was **foolish** of **Barberella** to have gone out in the rain (elroy online.com).

In contrast, appreciation adjectives are not available for this slot. Thus, "It was thoughtless of you to leave the cat out in the rain." (judgement) is idiomatic and felicitous while "It was elegant of her to wear that outfit." (appreciation) is not. This point can perhaps be more clearly illustrated by reference to a term such as "beautiful". Words of this type are capable of variably acting as judgements or appreciations, according to context. This is illustrated by the following two examples.

(9) [judgement] She has a **beautiful** spirit—she seems very aware of the things that matter in life. I pray to have women strong and wise like that where I live (essence.com). [Her behavior assessed as morally good.]

(10) [appreciation] Helen was an extremely **beautiful** woman, considered one of the fairest that walked the earth (essortment.com). [Helen's appearance— i.e., Helen as an "object"—assessed not by reference to norms of behavioral acceptability but by reference to aesthetic value.]

We note that when terms such as these convey a judgement (i.e., assess human behavior by reference to social norms), the "it was X of Y to . . ." frame is available.

(11) It is **beautiful** of Mary to help out those street kids the way she does [invented felicitous/idiomatic example].

In contrast, when they convey an appreciation (aesthetic assessment) the frame is not available.

(12) *It was **beautiful** of Mary to wear her hair like that [invented infelicitous/unidiomatic example].

The appraisal framework, therefore, provides a three-way taxonomy of attitudinal subtypes. Under this taxonomy, affect is firstly distinguished from judgement/appreciation on the grounds that it is only in the case of affect that the writer directly reports an emotional reaction on the part of some human subject. Secondly, judgement and appreciation are distinguished from each other by reference to the target of the assessment—i.e., the social acceptability of human behavior (judgement) versus social valuations of objects, artifacts, texts, happenings, and states-of-affairs (appreciation). Putting this another way, we can say that feelings (i.e., affectual responses) are central to any attitudinal positioning, but that language makes it possible for these feelings to be externalized and re-construed in more "communal", less immediately subjective terms as qualities which attach to behaviors and entities. This perspective on attitude is illustrated diagrammatically below in figure 1.

In proposing a taxonomy of this type, the appraisal framework represents a significant departure from previous approaches to the semantics of positive/ negative viewpoint. Much of the previous work (see, for example, Ochs and Schiefflen 1989; Biber and Finnegan 1989; Bybee and Fleischmann 1995; Conrad and Biber 2000; Hunston and Thompson 2000) has operated with one broad category encompassing all positive/negative assessment—under terms such as *affect, sentiment, emotion, evaluation,* or *attitudinal stance.* In this, there is an obvious contrast with the appraisal approach. Other work has proposed more delicate taxonomies of evaluative modes or subtypes. For example, Swales and Burke (2003: 5) identified seven types of evaluative adjectives in their work on attitude in academic speech: *acuity, aesthetic appeal, assessment, deviance, relevance, size,* and *strength.* By way of another example, Lemke (1998) has offered the following taxonomy

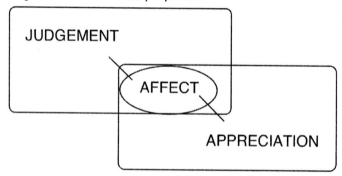

Figure 1.   A three-way taxonomy of attitude sub-types (after Martin and White 2005: 45)

of "evaluative dimensions" in his work on attitudinal meaning: *desirability/inclination*; *warrantability/probability*; *normativity/appropriateness*; *usuality/expectability*; *importance/significance*; *comprehensibility/obviousness*; *humorousness/seriousness*.

The appraisal framework is a departure from this type of work in that it offers a clearly stated lexico-grammatical and semantic rationale for the taxonomic subdivisions which it identifies (see the earlier discussion). As will be demonstrated in Sections 3. and 4. below, the rationale is such as to have enabled appraisal-theory based analyses to discover that particular interpersonal and rhetorical outcomes arise when writers favor particular sub-types of attitude or particular combinations of attitudinal subtypes. (For a full account of the attitudinal sub-types identified by the appraisal framework, see Martin and White 2005: 42–91.)

2.2. Attitudinal Explicitness: Inscription Versus Invocation

The appraisal framework also departs from previous work on evaluation/attitude in systematically recognizing the role of forms of expression which are implicitly or indirectly attitudinal, in opposition to forms of expression which overtly or explicitly convey a positive or negative viewpoint. Explicitly attitudinal expressions are those where the attitudinal value (positive or negative assessment) is largely fixed and stable across a wide range of contexts—for example, via lexical items such as *corrupt, virtuously, skillfully, tyrant, coward, beautiful, abused, brutalized*. Under the appraisal framework, this type of attitudinal expression is termed *inscription* and is contrasted with formulations where there is no single lexical item which, of itself and independently of its current co-text, carries a specific positive or negative value. Rather, the positive/negative viewpoint is activated via various mechanisms of association and implication. This is illustrated by invented example (13) below:

(13) He only visits his mother once a year, even though she is more than 90 years old.

Under the appraisal framework, the term attitudinal *invocation* (and also attitudinal *token*) is used of such forms of attitudinal expression.

Within formulations which indirectly "invoke" attitude in this way, appraisal theory makes a further distinction between formulations which contain no evaluative lexis of any type and those which contain evaluative material but not of an explicitly positive/negative type. In the first instance, the positive or negative assessment is "evoked" via purely experiential (i.e., factual) material which, as a result of being selected and brought into focus within the text, has the potential to trigger a positive or negative reaction in the reader via processes of attitudinal inference. In the second instance, the positive or negative assessment is "provoked" via material which, while evaluative, is not of itself positive or negative—for example, via intensification, comparison, metaphor, or counter-expectation. These possibilities are illustrated by examples (14) and (15) below:

Attitudinal invocation exemplified (evocation and provocation)

(14) [evocation—triggering positive/negative responses by means of a focus on purely informational content:] George W. Bush delivered his inaugural speech as the United States President who collected 537,000 fewer votes than his opponent (*Observer* newspaper, January 21, 2001).

(15) [provocation—triggering positive/negative responses by means of formulations which contain evaluative material but have no lexical item which explicitly, and of themselves, convey negative or positive assessments:] Telstra has withdrawn sponsorship of a suicide prevention phone service—**just days after** announcing a $2.34 billion half-yearly profit (*Sunday Mail*, July 23, 2005).

In (15) above, the expression "just days after" construes surprise on the part of the journalist author—the action by Telstra, Australia's primary, government-controlled telecommunications provider, is assessed as unexpected, or at least as coming sooner than would be expected. Such expressions are not of themselves positive or negative, but nonetheless have a clear potential to "provoke" in the reader an attitudinal response, in this case a negative assessment of Telstra's actions.

It is a feature of attitudinal invocations that they are typically conditioned by the co-text and will often be subject to the beliefs, attitudes, and expectations readers bring to their interpretations of the text (i.e., their reading position). Thus, for example, a US supporter of the Republican Party may not interpret the above proposition that Mr Bush received "537,000 fewer votes than his opponent" as signifying anything untoward or wrongful with regard to Mr Bush's presidency. Similarly, it is highly likely that such a proposition would not be presented in attitudinal isolation and that there will be other indicators elsewhere in the text as to the attitude being taken towards Mr Bush's election. These indicators will act to indicate how this particular piece of information is meant to be interpreted evaluatively.

In attending to this explicit (inscription) versus implicit (invocation) distinction, appraisal theory is concerning itself with issues which have been taken up by theorists interested in what is seen as the distinction between "saying" and "meaning", or between "encoding" and "implicating", and even more broadly the distinction between "semantics" and "pragmatics" (see, for example, Sperber and Wilson 1995; Levinson 2000; Carston 2002). None of this prior work has, however, been specifically concerned with the implication or indirect activation of attitudinally positive/negative meanings, and appraisal theory is novel in identifying the distinction between attitudinal *evocation* (attitudinal positioning via purely informational or factual meanings) and attitudinal *provocation* (attitudinal positioning through meanings which are evaluative but not explicitly positive or negative).

2.3. Dialogic Engagement: Recognition of Alternative Voices and Positions

The third key axis of evaluative variability turns on the degree to which, and the ways in which, writers acknowledge and engage with other voices and alternative positions as they advance their own evaluative viewpoint. Thus, for example, writers may choose either to acknowledge or to ignore prior utterances on the same topic by earlier speakers. If they do acknowledge prior utterances, they may present themselves as aligned with, at odds with, or neutral with regards the earlier utterance. Similarly, writers have a range of options when it comes to signaling how they expect those addressed will react or respond to the current proposition. They can, for example, present themselves as anticipating agreement, compliance, surprise, skepticism, or resistance on the part of the addressee.

The appraisal framework characterizes a broad range of meanings and expressions as having this *dialogic* function. Labeled *engagement* in the appraisal framework, these resources include attribution, modals of probability and evidentials, negation, adversatives and concessives, adverbials such as *of course*, *naturally*, and intensifications by which alternative positions are fended off or rejected (for example, *the facts of the matter, I contend that*). The key insight here is that all these meanings are *dialogic* in the Bakhtinian sense and act to recognize that the communicative context in which the utterance operates is one with multiple voices and viewpoints. Utterances which employ any of these meanings are thus classed as "heteroglossic".

Set against these "dialogically engaged" formulations are utterances formulated as bare, categorical assertions, i.e., ones from which any form of modalization, qualification, authorial reinforcement, counter-expectation, or justification has been omitted. Example (16) below, taken from one of the movie review texts which will be discussed below in Section 3., illustrates this "bare assertion" category.

(16) [The movie] is a sublime piece of work; a marriage of old and new so perfectly managed that it results in something altogether rich, strange and unusual.

Under the influence of Bakhtin's view of all language as dialogic, the bare assertion is not regarded as a default or an interpersonally neutral option. Rather it is seen as but one choice among a range of options by which the writer takes a stance with regard to the proposition and with regard to potential respondents to the current communication. Thus, it is just one option within a system of choices as to stance which include the following (all invented examples):

(17) **Of course** *The Matrix* is the best movie of all time.

(18) **The facts of the matter** are that *The Matrix* is the best movie of all time.

(19) *The Matrix* is **undoubtedly** the best movie of all time.

(20) **In my view**, *The Matrix* is the best movie of all time.

(21) *The Matrix* is **probably** the best movie of all time.

(22) *The Matrix* **could** be the best movie of all time.

(23) **A number of critics have declared** *The Matrix* to be the best movie of all time.

(24) *The Matrix* is the best movie of all time. [bare assertion—monoglossic]

The appraisal framework observes that, by choosing not to modalize, justify, reinforce, or otherwise qualify the bare assertion, the speaker/writer presents the proposition as not needing any form of support or interpersonal management in the current communicative context. The bare assertion is revealed as the means by which the proposition is presented as dialogically unproblematic or uncontentious, as not at odds or in tension with some alternative viewpoint. Such formulations are classified as *monoglossic*, in recognition of the fact that they involve only the single voice of the writer and ignore the multiplicity of alternative views and voices likely to be in play in the current communicative context. (For a full account, see Martin and White 2005: Chapter 3).

This perspective leads appraisal analysts to take a particular view of modals of probability, evidentials, and related formulations (e.g., *may, might, could, seems, appears, perhaps, probably, in my view, I think, personally*, etc). Such formulations have traditionally been seen to convey uncertainty, equivocation, or lack of commitment on the part of the speaker/writer (see, for example, Lyons 1977: 452). While the appraisal framework allows that such meanings may, on some occasions, be in play, it holds that these locutions more generally function dialogically to acknowledge that the current proposition is in tension with alternative propositions and potentially puts the speaker/writer at odds with other, dissenting voices.[1] Under the appraisal framework, such formulations are said to "entertain" or allow for other viewpoints and are understood to be *dialogically expansive* in this openness to alternative voices and positions.

3. Demonstration: The Appraisal Framework and the Analysis of Evaluative Disposition

In this section, a detailed appraisal analysis is provided of the two movie review texts mentioned previously. As already indicated, the purpose is to provide a demonstration of the kinds of insights which have been made available by the appraisal framework, more specifically, a demonstration of how the framework provides for the identification and characterization of particular evaluative dispositions. Both reviews are concerned with *Crouching Tiger, Hidden Dragon,* an extremely successful 2001 film by Chinese director Ang Lee. It must be stressed that the texts, of themselves, are not the primary point of interest. The overriding point of the analysis is to demonstrate a methodology for the investigation of attitudinal disposition which is applicable to texts of all types. These two particular texts have been chosen, because they are rich in attitudinal meanings and because they provide for usefull contrasts between different evaluative dispositions.

The first review, by Xan Brooks, is from the arts pages of the leading British broadsheet newspaper, *The Guardian.* The second is by a contributor to www. epinions.com, a website which enables members of the public to post reviews and

---

[1] The notion that such formulations are "dialogic" in this sense has previously been advanced by writers such as Myers and Hyland. Myers, for example, has observed that one purpose of such locutions is not to mark knowledge claims as uncertain, but rather to mark the claim as "unacknowledged by the discourse community" (Myers 1989: 12). Similarly, Hyland has argued that that "hedges" (which include low intensity modals) sometimes act to convey "deference, modesty or respect" rather than to convey uncertainty (Hyland 2000: 88).

engage in online discussion about movies. Analyses of the two texts are provided below in Sections 3.1. and 3.2. The following Sections 3.3. through 3.5. provide discussions of different aspects of these analyses.

3.1. Analysis of Review Text 1 (the Guardian newspaper)

The first review (*Guardian*, January 5, 2001) is provided below in figure 2. The following text decorations have been employed to indicate different sub-types of attitude:

- boxed for inscribed affect,
- *italics* for inscribed judgement,
- **<u>bold underlining</u>** for inscribed appreciation

<u>Perfectly</u> positioned at the cusp of the year, Ang Lee's latest film proves to be a bit of a Janus itself. On the one hand Couching Tiger, Hidden Dragon points forward, with its **<u>state-of-the-art</u>** stunt work and **<u>seamless weave</u>** of special effects. On the other it faces the past - dusting off a mythic adventure plotline that could have sprung from the pen of some 12th century calligrapher. What we have here, then, is a **<u>sublime</u>** piece of work; a marriage of old and new *so perfectly managed* that it results in something altogether **<u>rich</u>**, **<u>strange</u>** and **<u>unusual</u>**. All hail the first **<u>great</u>** film of 2001.

Returning east after a profitable sojourn in the States (where he filmed The Ice Storm and Ride With the Devil), Lee contrives to rustle up a narrative that is at once **<u>grand scale</u>** and **<u>intimate</u>**; **<u>disciplined</u>** and **<u>extravagant</u>**. Its Chinese-language tale centres around three principal characters: *upright* warrior Li Mu Bai (Chow Yun-Fat), his aquiline partner Yu Shu Lien (Michelle Yeoh) and Jen (Zhang Ziyi), a *spoilt* little rich girl who has schooled herself in the arts of combat and *wavers in a kind of limbo between light and dark*. For good measure, Lee also throws in a *renegade* bandit (cueing a lengthy desert-set interlude), a *wicked* witch and a magical, Excalibur-style sword.

In the meantime the tale swoops and sways between **<u>keening romance</u>**, **<u>tense adventure</u>** and near slapstick comedy; oiling the costume changes with moments of **<u>breathtaking</u>** action. Choreographed by Yuen Wo Ping (who devised the fight scenes in The Matrix), Crouching Tiger **<u>blooms</u>** into **<u>fantastical</u>** life in its gravity-defying showdowns, as its combatants glide urgently across rooftops (their slippered feet pitter-pattering faintly on the tiles) or face off astride the elastic tips of fir trees. In *cruder* hands, the whole thing would be **<u>too ridiculous</u>** for words. Here you find yourself relishing every moment.

In the end, perhaps, Lee has created a **<u>bracing</u>** new sub-genre with this **<u>gorgeous firework display</u>** of a picture. Crouching Tiger is a martial arts movie that arrives pruned of both the **<u>melodrama</u>** of the style's early manifestations and the irony that has lately **<u>infested</u>** it. It is **<u>unapologetically serious</u>** at certain moments, **<u>unashamedly flamboyant</u>** at others. It's a film of **<u>exquisite grace under fire</u>**; a work so **<u>lush</u>**, **<u>giddy</u>** and **<u>beautiful</u>** it has you giggling in the aisles.

Figure 2.   Analysis of *Guardian* newspaper review, Xan Brooks, January 5, 2001.

Instances of invoked (implied) attitude are not identified in the analysis but are discussed later in Section 3.4.

3.2. Analysis of Review Text 2 (www.epinions.com)

An analysis of the second review text is provided below in Figure 3. The same text decorations have been used to indicate attitudinal sub-types.

- boxed for inscribed affect,
- *italics* for inscribed judgement,
- **bold underlining** for inscribed appreciation

Look! I like **a foreign film! I'm** *intelligent*!

People seem to like subtitled films. Perhaps it justifies their *intelligence* if they can claim that they enjoyed a movie in another language. Personally, I dislike subtitled films because you always end up looking at the bottom of the screen, trying to decipher the plot, when something important happens. Someone always ends up walking in front of you in the middle of an important conversation between the two key characters.

The scenery seems to be very **beautiful** throughout the entire film. I believe this is because the American audience has never seen it before. The public has seen the Grand Canyon and the Rocky Mountains before. We have never seen central China, and we enjoy the change.

Now to get to the plot. The first and **biggest problem** is the annoying effect that has people flying across rooftops and running up walls. I heard that the same person did the effects for The Matrix. I could believe that. This movie had that exact same "run up the walls" effect as The Matrix, only it happened in every scene. Also, the ability the main characters have is never explained. Why can they fly, while everyone else is forced to walk? Also, when some situations that could be avoided by flying away aren't, I wondered if their abilities are only available in certain situations. Again, this is never explained. By the end of this long movie, this has become unbearably annoying.

Take your generic Jackie Chan movie. The karate that happens is **goofy** and very fast. Rewind to ancient China, and you have Crouching Tiger, Hidden Dragon. There is only one difference: In Crouching Tiger, the karate happens so fast that it is impossible to see. I like to see the punch that breaks the bad guys jaw. The only signal the viewer gets in this movie is when one of the people falls down.

If you want to see kung-fu, go rent a Jackie Chan movie. If you want a **deep** plot, rent The Usual Suspects. Just don't **waste any more money** on this movie.

Figure 3.   Analysis of www.epinions.com review, by user-name "demon5974", February 19, 2001

3.3. Discussion: Authorial Preferences as to Attitudinal Sub-type

3.3.1. REVIEW TEXT 1 (THE *GUARDIAN*). In terms of the attitudinal subtypes employed in the texts, it is clear that the author of review text 1 overwhelmingly favors appreciation (specifically aesthetic assessments of the film as artifact) over judgement and affect when adopting an attitudinal position towards the movie. Thus, most of the attitudinal work is done by appreciating formulations such as (partial quotations from review text 1),

(25) **a seamless weave** of special effects

(26) a **sublime** piece of work

(27) something altogether **rich**

(28) a **gorgeous firework display** of a picture

(29) a **bracing** new sub-genre

In terms of judgements directed at the film itself, these are confined to just the two instances:

(30) a marriage of old and new **so perfectly managed**

(31) **cruder** hands.

Both of these assessments construe the director's behavior as highly skilled and competent. The remaining judgements are directed at the fictional characters—i.e., "**upright** warrior", "a **spoilt** little rich girl"—and hence have a very different rhetorical function from judgements of real-world human targets such as the director or the actors. Most importantly in the current context, they do not of themselves act to signal where the writer stands attitudinally with regards the movie. Similarly, instances of affect are limited, again to just two instances.

(32) you find yourself **relishing** every moment

(33) it has you **giggling** in the aisles

One of the key insights of the appraisal framework is that there is something significant in terms of interpersonal positioning and potential rhetorical effect when a writer chooses one of the attitudinal modes rather than another (i.e., appreciation versus judgement versus affect). Consider the following invented examples as available choices for a writer wanting to indicate a positive disposition towards a movie.

(34) [affect] I **loved** the movie.

(35) [appreciation] It's a **brilliant** movie.

(36) [judgement] In this movie, Ang Lee shows himself to be **at the height of his powers** as a director.

By taking up the affect option, the writer/speaker chooses to present the evaluation as entirely personal, as a matter of his/her own individual response. In contrast, both the appreciation and judgement options externalize the evaluation in that it is presented as a quality inhering in the evaluated entity itself, rather than in the evaluator. In the case of affect, the appeal is only to the individual who has experienced the phenomenon in question, while, as discussed briefly above in Section 2.1., in the case of appreciation and judgement the appeal is to some communal or institutionalized norm of assessment. Of course, it can be argued that an affectual response is involved in all these options, that a sense of "I loved" is involved in all three. The point, however, is that through appreciation and judgement the speaker/writer can choose to construe the attitude in different terms, to present the attitudinal position not as an individual emotional response, but as a property of the evaluated entity itself which has been identified by the application of communal standards of taste or value.

With respect to judgement versus appreciation, the choice is between assessing the human agent (judgement) and assessing his/her work (appreciation). This is interpersonally and rhetorically significant, because to assess the human agent (judgement) puts most at stake interpersonally since the assessment goes most directly to the human agent and their standing and character in the community. In contrast, appreciation of a text or other artifact puts the assessment at one remove from its human creator. To criticize the movie, for example, is only indirectly to criticize the director, hence putting less at stake interpersonally. Thus, the judgement "New Yorkers are unfriendly." puts more at stake interpersonally than the appreciation, "New York is an unfriendly place.".

The very strong preference shown above by this reviewer for appreciation over affect and judgement can thus be seen to have clear interpersonal consequences. The evaluative stance is not that of an individual reporting his/her own emotional responses to the movie. Tellingly, on the two occasions when an affectual response is offered, it is not the reaction of the writer himself (i.e., not "I") but rather the impersonal *you* (i.e., "you find yourself relishing every moment"). Similarly the writer presents himself as not much interested in direct assessment of the director's or the actors' behavior—with just the two instances where the film maker is directly praised for his competence. Rather, for this writer, movie reviewing is very largely a matter of responding to the movie as artifact and bringing to bear a system of sophisticated aesthetic norms against which the movie can be measured.

3.3.2. REVIEW TEXT 2 (WWW.EPINIONS.COM). These findings will probably come as no surprise to those familiar with how film reviewing is typically conducted in more "highbrow" English-language newspapers and magazines. It is usual for professional reviewers of this type to adopt this particular aesthetics-oriented evaluative arrangement. However, the analysis of review text 2 (Figure 3 above) indicates that this is an option as to evaluative disposition which is not taken up by the epinions.com contributor. His review is strikingly different from review text 1 in the much reduced use it makes of appreciation, with the first instance not occurring until the second paragraph ("beautiful scenery") and subsequent instances occurring at a rate of only about one per paragraph. Additionally, only two of the text's five appreciations (i.e., "biggest problem", "don't waste any more money on this movie") act to convey the writer's attitude towards the movie.

Equally important, in terms of the contrast with the previous text, is the much enhanced role played by affect in review text 2 as the writer reports his own "dislike" and "annoyance" with the movie and indicates animosity towards those who "like" foreign films of this kind. In broad terms, then, review text 2 operates with an evaluative disposition under which film criticism is very personal, a matter of individual likes and dislikes. It is an arrangement by which the writer makes virtually no claim to having access to the institutionalized norms of aesthetic assessment associated with professional film criticism of the type exemplified by review text 1 (Figure 2). Reacting to movies is a matter of individual feelings, not of appreciative norms and the only claim the writer makes to aesthetic expertise is in his use of the term "deep" to positively appraise certain types of plot (though not necessarily the type of plot which the writer himself favors).

3.4. Discussion: Authorial Preferences as to Inscribed Versus Invoked Attitude

A second important evaluative difference between the two texts is the much greater use the author of review text 2 makes of invoked attitude. Review text 1 includes only one clear cut case of attitudinal invocation—the observation that the movie's plotline "could have sprung from the pen of some 12th century calligrapher". The potential implication here is that springing from the pen of 12th century calligrapher is a positive for a plotline. However, so densely surrounded is this observation by explicit positive evaluations of the movie that there is little at stake rhetorically should a reader fail to provide this attitudinal inference.

In contrast, attitudinal invocation has a much more substantial role to play in review text 2. Firstly, there is the headline with which the review begins (partial quotation from review text 2).

(37) Look! I like a foreign film! I'm intelligent!

This functions to position the reader to take a negative view of people who claim to like foreign films, such as *Crouching Tiger, Hidden Dragon,* and therefore to take a negative view of the movie itself. The implication being activated is that such people are dissemblers who only make such claims because they think it will impress others. Since this is invocation rather than inscription of attitude, the headline does not include any overt assertion of negativity towards lovers of subtitled movies. The writer does not, for example, explicitly declare those who say they enjoyed the movie to be "bogus", "fake", or "dissembling". Rather it is left up to the readers to draw these evaluative conclusions from the material presented. This is actually a rather complicated instance of attitudinal invocation in that, for the implication to arise, the reader must read these, not as the words of the reviewer himself, but as the reported words or thoughts of some other speaker, specifically a foreign film lover.

The first sentence of the review functions attitudinally in a similarly indirect way:

(38) People seem to like subtitled films. Perhaps it justifies their intelligence if they can claim that they enjoyed a movie in another language.

Later, there are attitudinal invocations directed at positioning the reader to take a negative view of subtitled movies generally. For example,

(39) [With subtitled films] you always end up looking at the bottom of the screen, trying to decipher the plot, when something important happens. Someone always ends up walking in front of you in the middle of an important conversation between the two key characters.

The obvious implication is that viewing subtitled, foreign movies is annoying and unsatisfactory. It is noteworthy that the repeated use of the hyperbolic "always" here acts as a signal that the material is attitudinally loaded. This is followed soon after, by example (40):

(40) The scenery seems to be very beautiful throughout the entire film. I believe this is because the American audience has never seen it before. The public has seen the Grand Canyon and the Rocky Mountains before. We have never seen central China, and we enjoy the change.

Out of context, the material suggests a positive view of the movie, since it is presented as involving "beautiful" scenery and providing "enjoyment" for the American viewing audience. In context, however, a negative viewpoint is invoked, specifically a negative assessment of the critical capabilities of those who have been praising the movie, implying that they favor the movie, not on account of its intrinsic cinematic properties, but only on account of their naïve enjoyment of the unfamiliar scenery.

Several further invocations with a similar attitudinal functionality follow. For example,

(41) This movie had that exact same "run up the walls" effect as The Matrix, only it happened in every scene.
(42) Also, the ability the main characters have is never explained. Why can they fly, while everyone else is forced to walk?

From this discussion, it becomes clear that use of attitudinal invocation is an important element in the attitudinal arrangement by which the second reviewer disposes himself attitudinally towards the movie and positions his readers to share his viewpoint. The contrast with review 1 is a marked one.

3.4.1. INVOKING VERSUS INSCRIBING ATTITUDE: POTENTIAL COMMUNICATIVE CONSEQUENCES. To understand the potential communicative consequences of this difference (i.e., between invocation and inscription) it is necessary to consider again what is involved interpersonally in the use of attitudinal invocation. There are two aspects of the functionality of invocations of the type which occur in review text 2 which are important here. In review text 2, these invocations do not, of course, operate in isolation. The writer's evaluative position has been made explicitly very clear elsewhere in the text via his inscribed attitudinal assertions, i.e., his announcement that he "dislikes" subtitled movies, that he found the effects used in the movie "unbearably annoying" and that the reader should not "waste any more money on this movie". The attitudinal invocations, therefore, operate against this backdrop. Accordingly, unless there are counter-indicators, readers will bring to their interpretation of the invocations an expectation that, by implication, these too will be conveying a negative view of the movie. They will expect to find assumptions at work which lead to negative conclusions about the move. Thus in example (41), it is possible to discover an assumption on the part of the writer that repeated use of the "run up the walls" effect from *The Matrix* is cinematically ill conceived and annoying. Similarly in example (42), it is possible to discover the assumption that it is unsatisfactory and cinematically damaging for there to be no explanation of why some characters can fly and others cannot. This is the first important aspect of the functionality of invocations of this type, i.e., that they rely on the reader discovering certain assumptions on the part of the writer.

The second important aspect is that the invocations rely on the reader sharing these assumptions or regarding them as reasonable. Thus example (41) above will only operate to activate a negative view of the movie should the reader share with the writer the assumption that repeated use of the "running up the wall" effect is cinematically flawed. A reader who thoroughly enjoys the "running up the wall" effect will not be positioned by this to regard the movie negatively and will find it incongruous or rhetorically dysfunctional that the writer should offer this as evidence against the movie. Similarly, example (42) above will only operate to activate a negative view should the reader share the view that movies of this type must explain why some characters can fly and others cannot. Without this agreement, such invocations become communicatively incongruous, since they provide information which is clearly intended to support a particular value position but which, in the end, fails to achieve this outcome. Invocations of the type found in this text, therefore, involve the writer making assumptions about the attitudinal implications of the material presented in the invocation, and then taking for granted that these are assumptions which will unproblematically be shared by the reader.

The ultimate communicative effect of these twin aspects of functionality is for the text to construct an "imagined" or "ideal" reader who shares and takes for granted the writer's own evaluative assumptions. Thus, the regular use of such invocations results in an evaluative disposition in which the writer assumes a substantial degree of attitudinal alignment with the reader, even before the reader completes his/her reading of the text. The disposition is thus one of assumed attitudinal like-mindedness.

3.5. Discussion: Authorial Preferences as to Modes of Dialogic Engagement

The final evaluative difference between the two texts to be considered is a matter of dialogic engagement—i.e., variation in the degree to which the authors present themselves as responding to prior utterances and in the degree to which they present their propositions as potentially in tension with alternative viewpoints.

3.5.1. REVIEW TEXT 1. The author of review text 1 almost exclusively employs bare, unqualified categorical assertions as he advances his assessment of the movie. The following examples of bald evaluative assertion are typical of the text (partial quotations from review text 1).

(43) [. . .] Couching Tiger, Hidden Dragon points forward, with its state-of-the-art stunt work and seamless weave of special effects.

(44) What we have here, then, is a sublime piece of work; a marriage of old and new so perfectly managed that it results in something altogether rich, strange and unusual.

(45) Lee contrives to rustle up a narrative that is at once grand scale and intimate; disciplined and extravagant.

(46) It's a film of exquisite grace under fire; a work so lush, giddy and beautiful it has you giggling in the aisles.

There is only the one rhetorically significant instance where a dialogically expansive formulation is employed to signal recognition that an alternative viewpoint is possible—in the final paragraph:

(47) In the end, **perhaps**, Lee has created a bracing new sub-genre with this gorgeous firework display of a picture.

Otherwise, the reviewer's observations and evaluations are presented as dialogically unproblematic and hence able to be announced without qualification, reinforcement or justification. In terms of the categories of the appraisal framework, review text 1 is almost exclusively monoglossic.

3.5.2. REVIEW TEXT 2. In contrast, review text 2 does include some rhetorically significant engagement with alternative viewpoints, at least in its opening stage. Formulations which serve this function have been indicated in bold in example (48) below.

(48) [i] People **seem** to like subtitled films. [ii] **Perhaps** it justifies their intelligence if they can claim that they enjoyed a movie in another language. [iii] **Personally**, I dislike subtitled films because you always end up looking at the bottom of the screen, trying to decipher the plot, when something important happens. Someone always ends up walking in front of you in the middle of an important conversation between the two key characters.

The effect is to signal an acknowledgement by the writer that his beliefs about people who say they like foreign movies may be subject to contestation, i.e., he allows for the possibility that there are other reasons why people say they like subtitled movies. In sentence [iii], the use of "personally" acts to explicitly acknowledge that these are his own subjective views and accordingly just one position among a range of possible viewpoints. This opening, then, can be characterized as involving a degree of dialogic expansiveness, as the writer acknowledges the contentiousness of his various viewpoints and thereby entertains the possibility of dissenting views. His negative assessment of foreign movies is thus located in a heteroglossic environment of multiple value positions.

The remainder of review text 2, however, is very largely monoglossic as the writer uses bare assertion to explicitly evaluate this and other movies, or advances observations which are implicitly evaluative. Thus, for example, all the following propositions are advanced via bare assertion (partial quotations from review text 2).

(49) The first and biggest problem is the annoying effect that has people flying across rooftops and running up walls. [inscription—explicitly attitudinal]

(50) This movie had that exact same "run up the walls" effect as The Matrix, only it happened in every scene. [invocation—implicitly attitudinal]

(51) By the end of this long movie, this has become unbearably annoying. [inscription—explicitly attitudinal]

(52) Take your generic Jackie Chan movie. The karate that happens is goofy and very fast. [inscription—explicitly attitudinal]

(53) There is only one difference: In Crouching Tiger, the karate happens so fast that it is impossible to see. [invocation—implicitly evaluative]

(54) Just don't waste any more money on this movie. [inscription—explicitly attitudinal]

The two texts have thus been shown to be similar with respect to dialogic engagement, to the extent that both authors frequently employ bare assertion in advancing their evaluative propositions. They thereby frequently choose to signal either the assumption that their viewpoint is not in tension with any alternative position or, alternatively, the assumption that any such alternative viewpoints do not need to be recognized or engaged with in the current communicative context. Against this, the two texts differ dialogically in that review text 2 is less consistently monoglossic, and does, at least in its opening stages, make dialogic space for alternative voices and viewpoints.

3.6. Mapping Evaluative Disposition

The findings as to evaluative disposition outlined above are summarized in the following tabular presentation.

Table 1. Patterns of evaluative preference

	Review text 1 (*Guardian*)	Review text 2 (epinions.com)
[attitudinal subtype]	Strong preference for appreciation over judgement and affect	Values of all three subtypes employed, although affect afforded a central role
[attitudinal targeting]	Strong preference for the movie to serve as the target of evaluation	Multiple targets of evaluation—the film itself, foreign films generally, people who say they like foreign films
[explicitness/ implicitness]	Strong preference for inscription over invocation	Both inscriptions and invocation. Judgement (of people who like foreign films) only via invocation
[dialogic engagement]	Strong preference for monoglossic bare assertion over any of the heteroglossic options	Mixed—evaluative utterances formulated in both heteroglossic and monoglossic terms, although monoglossic expression predominates

4. Evaluative Disposition, Audience Positioning, and Solidarity

With this analysis of evaluative disposition in place, it is possible to address the other key concern of the chapter chapter: the application of such appraisal-based analyses to the investigation of how such texts construct relationships with those addressed and establish terms under which solidarity may obtain with this "ideal" or "putative" readership. In order to advance such investigations, it is necessary to consider the interpersonal and dialogic potential of the choices which constitute a given evaluative disposition. Thus it is necessary to consider the communicative consequences of, for example, an author favoring one of the subtypes of attitude, or of the author employing attitudinal invocation rather than inscription at a particular point in the text, or making extensive use of a particular engagement option, and so on. Even further, it is necessary to consider the communicative consequences which may flow from particular patterns of evaluative co-selection—for example, the co-selection of particular types of attitude, particular options as to implicitness/explicitness, and a particular orientation to dialogic engagement. In the following discussion, this type of investigation will be demonstrated by reference to the evaluative arrangements identified as operating in the two movie review texts.

4.1. Review Text 1

As outlined above in Section 3., the author of review text 1 offers enthusiastic praise for the movie, conveying his high regard for it largely via the categorical, monoglossic assertion of explicit appreciation. The categorical, bare assertion is, of course, the usual option for material which is treated as factual or established knowledge in a given communicative setting, since in such cases it makes pragmatic sense to treat such material as uncontentious and not at odds with some alternative position—for example, "Ang Lee was the director of *Crouching Tiger, Hidden Dragon*". But the author's explicit appreciations of the movie will not, of course, be seen as factual or as knowledge in this sense, and accordingly the combination of explicit attitude and categoricality has a different function. The effect is to construct for the text a particular imagined audience or putative addressee for whom the proposition will be not so much factual as unproblematic, and who will agree with the evaluative proposition or at least find it plausible, reasonable, or otherwise acceptable. In terms of the negotiation of solidarity, the effect is to construct conditions under which a sense of rapport, connection, or affiliation is only available to those readers who accept these bald, unqualified, and unjustified "expert" adjudications without quibble or questioning. The effect is to construct an unoppositional audience, ready to be instructed in the aesthetic merits of a movie about which they have not yet formed a view.

4.2. Review Text 2

Review text 2 is substantially more complicated in terms of interpersonal positioning and the negotiation of solidarity. Firstly, as discussed above in Section

3.3., there is the writer's preference for affect. By this, he presents his position as primarily a matter of his own emotional responses, offering declarations such as "I dislike . . ." and "I like to see . . .". Thus, the assessments are very clearly grounded in the contingent, individual subjectivity of the writer himself, thereby opening up dialogic space for alternative viewpoints. It is possible for readers to accept that these are valid emotional responses on the part of the writer while not necessarily having the same response themselves. Further enhancing this sense of dialogic openness, at least in the opening stage of the review, is the writer's use of the dialogically expansive, "seem", "perhaps", and "personally" to further acknowledge the subjective, contingent nature of his value position.

At the same time, it is noteworthy that the reviewer does not simply announce his various attitudinal assessments. At several key points in the text, he also offers the reader argumentation in support of these assessments. For example, he does not simply declare a dislike of subtitled movies but rather offers several sentences in which he sets out reasons why this dislike is justified—i.e., the tendency to miss important developments due to having to look at the bottom of the screen, and so on. Similar argumentative support is provided for his contention that the film's "running up walls" special effects are "unbearably annoying". By this, the writer presents himself as involved in persuasion and thus constructs a reader who may need convincing—otherwise there would be no need to justify the evaluations in this way.

The effect is to construct a reader/writer communality which is less constrained than that which obtains in review text 1. In anticipating a reader who may not agree and hence who may need to be persuaded, the writer makes allowances for and, in a sense, legitimizes potentially divergent viewpoints, or at least acknowledges that they have a place in the unfolding "conversation" around the movie. The dialogic conditions under which solidarity is offered to the reader are such as to allow for resistance and difference of viewpoint.

Against this more dialogically open orientation, however, is the author's negative stance towards people who say they like subtitled foreign movies such as *Crouching Tiger, Hidden Dragon*. As discussed in some detail above in Section 3.4., here, through the exclusive use of attitudinal invocation rather than inscription, the writer takes the reader for granted attitudinally, assuming he/she will share and find unproblematic the writer's conviction that such people are boastful dissemblers. This is especially the case with the text's headline where the invoking material is baldly asserted.

(54) Look! I like a foreign film! I'm intelligent! (repeated above as example 37)

Such taking-for-granted results in highly constrained opportunities for writer/reader communality, since for the reader to resist such a viewpoint is to reject what the writer presents as "natural" and "commonsensical" and hence not subject to any form of debate or negotiation. In terms of his negotiation of solidarity and audience positioning, then, the author of review text 2 is not consistent, or at least demonstrates variability in the stance he takes. In his critique of the movie itself, he acknowledges the contentiousness of his own position and leaves dialogic space for a reader who may disagree. In his contempt for people who go about declaring how much they like such movies, he makes no such allowances, assuming a like-minded reader who is similarly contemptuous.

5. Conclusion

It is clear that an understanding of how positive and negative attitudes are conveyed and negotiated is crucial for those with an interest in the interpersonal functionality of language. By the attitudes we express, we not only forge identities and personas for ourself but enter into relationships of affiliation or dis-affiliation with the communities of shared feelings, tastes, and values which invariably operate in any society. Thus, it is via our expressions of attitude that we announce who we are, in social, cultural terms and develop the various personal and professional alliances upon which we are so fundamentally reliant.

As demonstrated by the analyses set out in the chapter, the appraisal framework provides a theoretical basis and an analytical methodology for investigations of the nature of the attitudinal meanings and the mechanisms by which these are activated linguistically. Appraisal theory is, of course, concerned with issues which have been taken up elsewhere in the linguistics, discourse analysis, and pragmatics literature under such headings as "attitude/evaluation", "affect", "modality", "evidentiality", "hedging", "stance" and "metadiscourse".[2] The appraisal-theory approach constitutes a significant development of this earlier work in that it offers a delicate taxonomy of attitudinal meanings and the formulations by which writers engage dialogically with prior speakers and potential respondents. Perhaps most significantly, as the chapter has demonstrated, it provides an account which attends to patterns of co-occurrence and interaction in texts between the different appraisal systems and thereby makes possible conclusions as to the communicative outcomes likely to be associated with the particular evaluative disposition in operation in a text. By this, it becomes possible to develop linguistically principled accounts of the mechanisms by which written texts construe for themselves ideal or imagined addressees, and by which virtual relationships of solidarity/communality are constructed with this putative readership.

Sources of Citations

Birmingham Post, October 25, 1999, leading article.
Daily Express, October 10, 2001, Sarler, Carol, Damn the Peaceniks for their faint hearts Feature Pages, *Daily Express* (UK).
dimsum.co.uk January 19, 2001, articles and online discussion of *Crouching Tiger, Hidden Dragon*, www.dimsum.co.uk. accessed February 25, 2001.
elroyonline.com, web blog, www.elroyonline.com/p43093500.htm, accessed August 12, 2007.

---

[2] For attitude/evaluation and stance, see Ochs and Schiefflen (1989), Biber and Finnegan (1988), Conrad and Biber (2000), and Hunston and Thompson (2000); for modality, see Palmer (1986) or Bybee and Fleischmann (1995); for evidentiality, see Chafe and Nichols (1986); for hedging, see Myers (1989), Markkanen and Schroder (1997), and Hyland (1996); and for metadiscourse, see Crismore (1990) and Hyland (2006).

essence.com, web discussion list, www.essence.com/essence/lifestyle/voices/ 0,16109, 1227093,00. htm, accessed October 1, 2007.

essortment.com, general information website, www.ctct.essortment.com/ legendtrojanwarhss. htm, accessed November 3, 2007.

Guardian, January 16, 2001, Raven, Charlotte Crashing bore, wooden drama/ Arts pages film review.

New York Post, January 21, 2001, op-ed page editorial.

Observer newspaper (UK), January 21, 2001, leading article.

Sunday Mail (Australia), July 23, 2005, news item.

Yahoo! Canada Answers, discussion list website, http://ca.answers.yahoo.com/answers2/ frontend.php/question?qid=20071227143307AAc4Mpi, accessed August 12, 2007

References

Bakhtin, Mikhail M. 1982. *The Dialogic Imagination*. Austin: University of Texas Press.

Biber, Douglas and Edward Finegan. 1988. Adverbial stance types in English. *Discourse Processes* 11(1): 1–34.

Brown, Roger and Albert Gilman. 1960. The pronouns of power and solidarity. In: Thomas A. Sebeok (ed.), *Style in Language*, 253–276. Cambridge, MA: Massachusetts Institute of Technology Press.

Brown, Penelope and Stephen Levinson. 1987. *Politeness: Some Universals in Language Usage*. Cambridge: Cambridge University Press.

Bybee, Joan L. and Suzanne Fleischman. 1995. *Modality in Grammar and Discourse*. Amsterdam/Philadelphia: John Benjamins.

Carston, Robyn. 2002. *Thoughts and Utterances: The Pragmatics of Explicit Communication*. Malden, MA/Oxford: Blackwell.

Coffin, Caroline. 1997. Constructing and giving value to the past: An investigation into Second School history. In: Frances Christie and James R. Martin (eds.), *Genre and Institutions: Social Processes in the Workplace and School*, 196–230. London: Cassell.

Coffin, Caroline. 2003. Reconstruals of the past—Settlement or invasion? The role of JUDGEMENT analysis. In: James R. Martin and Ruth Wodak (eds.), *Re/reading the Past: Critical and Functional Perspectives on Discourses of History*, 219–246. Amsterdam/Philadelphia: John Benjamins.

Conrad, Susan and Douglas Biber. 2000. Adverbial marking of stance in speech and writing. In: Susan Hunston and Geoff Thompson (eds.), *Evaluation in Text: Authorial Stance and the Construction of Discourse*, 56–73. Oxford: Oxford University Press.

Eggins, Suzanne and Diana Slade. 1997. *Analysing Casual Conversation*. London: Cassell.

Halliday, Michael A.K. 2004. *An Introduction to Functional Grammar*. 3rd edition revised by Christian M.I.M. Matthiessen. London: Hodder Arnold.

Hunston, Susan and Geoff Thompson (eds.). 2000. *Evaluation in Text:. Authorial Stance and the Construction of Discourse*. Oxford: Oxford University Press.

Hyland, Ken. 2000. *Disciplinary Discourses: Social Interactions in Academic Writing*. London: Longman.

Iedema, Rick, Susan Feez and Peter R.R. White. 1994. *Media Literacy (Write it Right Literacy in Industry Research Project—Stage 2)*. Sydney: Metropolitan East Disadvantaged Schools Program.

Lemke, Jay L. 1998. Resources for attitudinal meaning: Evaluative orientations in text semantics. *Functions of Language* 5(1): 33–56.

Levinson, Stephen C. 2000. *Presumptive Meanings*. Cambridge, MA: Massachusetts Institute of Technology Press.

Macken-Horarik, Mary and James. R. Martin (eds.). 2003. *Negotiating Heteroglossia: Social Perspectives on Evaluation*. Special issue of *Text* 23(2).

Martin, James R. 1992. *English Text: System and Structure*. Amsterdam/Philadelphia: John Benjamins.

Martin, James R. 1995. Interpersonal meaning, persuasion and public discourse: Packing semiotic punch. *Australian Journal of Linguistics* 15(1): 33–67.

Martin, James R. 2000. Beyond exchange: Appraisal systems in English. In: Susan Hunston and Geoff Thompson (eds.), *Evaluation in Text. Authorial Stance and the Construction of Discourse*, 142–175. Oxford: Oxford University Press.

Martin, James R. and Peter R.R. White. 2005. *The Language of Evaluation: Appraisal in English.* London/New York: Palgrave/Macmillan.

Matthiessen, Christian M.I.M. 1995. *Lexicogrammatical Cartography: English Systems.* Tokyo: International Language Sciences Publishers.

Myers, Gregory. 1989. The pragmatics of politeness in scientific articles. *Applied Linguistics* 10: 1–35. Poynton, Cate. 1985. *Language and Gender: Making the Difference.* Geelong, VIC: Deakin University Press.

Poynton, Cate. 1990a. Address and the semiotics of social relations: A systemic-functional account of address forms and practices in Australian English, PhD. Thesis. Department of Linguistics, University of Sydney.

Poynton, Cate. 1990b. The privileging of representation and the marginalising of the interpersonal: A metaphor (and more) for contemporary gender relations. In: Terry Threadgold and Anne Cranny-Francis (eds.), *Feminine/Masculine and Representation*, 231–255. Sydney: Allen & Unwin.

Sperber, Dan and Deidre Wilson. 1995. *Relevance Communication & Cognition.* 2nd edition. Cambridge, MA/Oxford: Blackwell.

Swales, John and Amy Burk. 2003. "It's really fascinating work": Differences in evaluative adjectives across academic registers. In: Pepi Leistyana and Charles F. Meyer (eds.), *Corpus Analysis—Language Structure and Language Use*, 1–19. Amsterdam/New York: Rodopi.

White, Peter R.R. 2000. Dialogue and inter-subjectivity: Reinterpreting the semantics of modality and hedging. In: Malcolm Coulthard, Janet Cotterill and Frances Rock (eds.), *Working With Dialogue*, 67–80. Tübingen: Niemeyer.

White, Peter R.R. 2002. Appraisal: The language of evaluation and stance. In: John Verschueren, Jan-Ola Östman, Jan Blommaert and Chris Bulcaen (eds), *Handbook of Pragmatics* (2002 Installment), 1–27. Amsterdam: John Benjamins.

White, Peter R.R. 2003. Beyond modality and hedging: A dialogic view of the language of inter-subjective stance. *Text*—Special Edition on Appraisal: 259–284.

White, Peter R.R. 2005. Subjectivity, evaluation and point of view in media discourse. In: Caroline Coffin and Kieran Halloran (eds), *Grammar, Text & Context: A Reader*, 229–257. London/New York: Arnold.

White, Peter R.R. 2006. Evaluative semantics and ideological positioning in journalistic discourse. In: Inger Lassen (ed.), *Image and Ideology in the Mass Media*, 45–73. Amsterdam/Philadelphia: John Benjamins.

White, Peter R.R. and Motoki Sano. 2006. Dialogistic positions and anticipated audiences: A framework for stylistic comparisons. In: Karin Aijmer and Anne-Marie Simon-Vandenbergen (eds.), *Pragmatic Markers in Contrast*, 189–214. Frankfurt/M.: Elsevier.

White, Peter R.R. 2008. Appraisal web site: www.grammatics.com/appraisal.

Part II

Applied Interpersonal Communication

8

Everyday Communication and Socializing

Tilo Weber

1. Introduction

Since the 1960s, spoken discourse has been established as a (if not *the*) main research focus of functionally and typologically oriented linguistics and related disciplines including sociology and social psychology. The primary realm of the study of spoken discourse is ordinary life outside professional and highly formalized circumstances, i.e., everyday communication.

But what *is* everyday communication? What are its defining properties? Is this type of communication distinguishable from other kinds of discourse and, if so, according to which criteria? To answer questions like these has become increasingly important for linguists who have become aware of the fact that speakers are not just members of a homogeneous speech community that unites "competent" users of a single language. Rather, speakers master different registers, styles of speech, degrees of formality, genres, etc. and are able to switch between them according to contextual needs. This variability pertains to all linguistic levels, ranging from phonetic and phonological structure up to activity types and genres.

At first sight, *everyday communication* appears to be the most natural, mundane, and non-technical term that modern linguistics and social sciences have to offer to refer to this type of social interaction. As members of Western cultural communities, we have no problems listing typical instances of everyday communication: phone conversations with friends, family dinner conversations, and occasional exchanges with strangers asking their way through our neighborhood. Also socializing, in the sense of non-goal oriented "small talk", can be included in this list of examples of everyday communication. If pressed to specify what all of these discourses have in common and what makes them examples of everyday conversation, we may consider, among others,[1] the following features: they are ordinary and usually informal, spoken rather than written, private rather than public. What is also common

---

[1] Sacks, Schegloff, and Jefferson (1974: 700–701) provide a more detailed, but not meant to be exhaustive, list of "grossly apparent facts" about "any conversation" to constrain their area of study (cf. also Nofsinger 1992: 1).

to all of them is that what is talked about is not fixed in advance. But, as with many other concepts relevant to the study of language (e.g., *word, a (particular) language, meaning*), it is much easier to enumerate *prototypical* examples of everyday communication, such as chatting, and *prototypical* properties of these examples, such as informality, than to define the concept in a way that would make it possible to draw a sharp line between instances and non-instances of the category.

One aim to be pursued in the present chapter is to offer convincing arguments to the effect that everyday communication is a *prototype category* which originates in a folk- or ethnocategory and is never in need to be defined for the practical purposes of the mundane interactional circumstances in which it is usually employed. Even though the radial nature of this category does not allow for an Aristotelean definition, it is argued here that the concept should not be prematurely abandoned on account of its vagueness, but that it can indeed be useful in linguistics and social studies. First, as ordinary discourse participants, we use expressions of the form *everyday + x* (where "x" may be substituted by words like *language, communication, life, phenomenon,* etc.) as elements of our standard language. But for linguists, this raises the question as to what are the intuitions that underlie the use of these terms, or, in other words, as to what "everydayness" means from the perspective of ordinary speakers.

Scholars working within various research paradigms seem to agree that it is necessary to look at an intermediate level of categorization between the superordinate level and the different subordinate levels of genres of spoken discourse. If this assumption is considered plausible, the question then arises as to which categories are to be distinguished at this intermediate level and as to whether *everyday communication* (as opposed, e.g., to *institutional discourse*) is a candidate for being included in the list of these categories.

These introductory remarks lead up to the conclusion that *everyday communication* is a relevant and, at the same time, problematic category in interpersonal communication research. Proceeding from this starting point, the remainder of this chapter will elucidate everyday communication in five stages.

Section 2 reconstructs the "pre-history" of research in everyday communication apropos of four different approaches to language and social interaction. The aim here is to demonstrate that there are particular empirical findings and theoretical problems that lead scholars to turn their primary attention away from written sentences and texts, on the one hand, and ideal language, on the other hand, in order to focus on ordinary discourse. Section 3 shows how, on this basis, conversation analysis and systemic functional linguistics from the very beginning on have made everyday conversation their main object of study. Following this, Section 4 suggests that *everyday communication* is a prototype category and explores six dimensions as to which typical instances of everyday communication are defined and how they can be distinguished from other types of interaction. Section 5 highlights several potential research directions which appear to be the most urgent and promising to pursue at present, and Section 6 provides a brief summary.

2. The Pre-History of Studies in Everyday Communication and Socializing

Everyday communication today has become a legitimate empirical base not only for the analysis of social processes but also for such classical areas of linguistics as morphology and syntax. This is the result of a rather recent development both in the social sciences and in linguistics. For millennia up to the 19th century and outside the tradition of rhetorics, linguistic "data", in the sense that we have used this term in the Western tradition of studying language, has been mainly limited to two types:

- isolated morphemes, words, and sentences constructed by philosophers, philologists, or grammar teachers; these constructs reflected the (native) speaker intuitions of their authors more than the actual language use
- formal, often literary, sentences quoted from written texts.

In the work of grammarians, for example, this was reflected by a strong bias in favor of written and "highly valued" varieties of languages and a neglect of oral language use and varieties of languages other than the standard ones.

The reasons that changed this situation are of a primarily theoretical nature. However, for those researchers who shifted their interest from the literary European languages to native cultures in the Americas or in Southern Asia, it was a matter of practical necessity to take into account oral and everyday communication where written and formal or literary communication either was not present at all or not easily accessible to ethnographers and linguists.

Regarding the theoretical and methodological groundwork that paved the way for turning attention to everyday communication as an object of empirical studies, four approaches have been particularly influential:

1. Bronisław Malinowki's (1923, 1927) field work investigations on what he called "primitive languages" and his "pragmatic" view of meaning,
2. Karl Bühler's *organon model* of the linguistic sign ([1934] 1999) together with its adoption by Roman Jakobson (1961),
3. *ordinary language philosophy* the proponents of which, in line with the later work of Ludwig Wittgenstein, maintained that ordinary language not only is a worthy *object* of study, but it is also the most fundamental *means* (or metalanguage) of philosophical and linguistic analysis,
4. Harold Garfinkel's ([1967] 1984a) ethnomethodology which is based on the doctrine that social interaction is both indexical and reflexive.

2.1. Malinowski's Functional Approach to Culture and Language

This section presents Bronisław Malinowski as a researcher who 1) defined an empirical point of view from which everyday communication became the focus of attention for anthropologists and linguists, 2) introduced the method of participant observation, and 3) coined concepts that today are crucial for the elucidation of language use, including *phatic communion, context of situation,* and *pragmatic character of language.*

Malinowski was a pioneer of social anthropology. His field trips, the most extensive of which lead him to the Trobriand islands of the South Pacific (1914–1918), gave rise to a series of studies that were innovative both at the theoretical level as well as having new methodological implications: theoretically, Malinowski ([1922] 1990) insisted that the anthropologist investigating a foreign culture has to approach his/her objects from a certain point of view using categories deeply rooted in the observed culture itself rather than criteria being applied to the particular culture from the external perspective of Western science. The approach that Malinowski developed for studying foreign, "primitive" societies, was later on generalized and radicalized. This was the case, e.g., when ethnomethodologists, following Harold Garfinkel (1967), and without being directly influenced by Malinowski, demanded the use of *participant categories* as the only legitimate type of research category for the analysis of social structures and processes.

Malinowki's methodological principles are direct consequences of his theoretical approach. From the latter, it follows that social interaction among members of foreign social communities cannot be done justice to on the mere basis of *apriori* theoretical axioms nor by means of concepts readily available from the standard scientific toolbox. Rather, research questions, concepts, and analytic categories have to be developed that are demonstrably relevant from the point of view of the target community (even though its members may not be consciously aware of them); and as such these categories are outcomes of, rather than prerequisites to, inductive processes based on minute and extensive observation. This research strategy can only be successful to the extent that the researcher may gain intimate access to the daily lives of those individuals that s/he is observing. This is achieved by becoming a temporary member of their social communities—a method of doing field work that has since been established in the social sciences under the name of *participant observation* (cf., e.g., Kawulich 2005).[2]

Malinowski's study that had the most significant impact on linguists was published as a supplement chapter to Charles K. Ogden and Ivor A. Richards' (1923) famous monograph on *The Meaning of Meaning.* In his chapter *On the problem of meaning in primitive languages,* Malinowski argued convincingly that the meanings of sentences in "primitive" languages cannot be accounted for adequately by translating them word by word or even morpheme by morpheme into English, German, or any other idiom used by linguists as a metalanguage. Quoting just one of his examples suffices to demonstrate that this claim is plausible:

(1) *Tasakaulo*   *kaymatana*   *yakida;*
    We run   front-wood   ourselves;
    tawaoulo   *ovanu;*   *tasivila*   *tagine*
    we paddle   in place   we turn   we see

---

[2] Besides Malinowski and the so called British functionalists, Franz Boas ([1938] 1965) and his students were pioneers of this method.

soda;	*isakaulo*	*kc' u'uya*
companion ours;	he runs	rear-wood
oluvieki	*similaveta*	*Pilolu*
behind	their sea-arm	Pilolu

(Malinowski 1923: 300–301)

Malinowski does not provide an idiomatic translation of the utterance in (1), the verbatim gloss of which does indeed read like "a riddle or a meaningless jumble of words" (Malinowski 1923: 301). According to Malinowski, the utterance is not at all without meaning and communicational significance. However, in order to be able to appreciate what the Trobriand speaker meant when uttering the above quoted sentence, one has to take into account, among other things, "the situation in which these words were spoken" as well as "a set of customs" to which utterance (1) "corresponds". In the particular case quoted above, the context of situation seems to be defined by a speaker reporting on "an overseas trading expedition [. . .], in which several canoes take part in a competitive spirit". Obviously, this context information is too thin even to resolve the references of expressions glossed as "front wood" or "companions ours" that—as we have to believe Malinowski—are used metaphorically here. To be able to appreciate the "competitive spirit" of the event and its significance for speakers and hearers that make it worth reporting, etc., one would have to know many other facts that we may subsume under the broad category of "culture". Without claiming exhaustiveness, Malinowski mentions the following items:

- "competitive activities for their own sake" that are of high significance for the Trobriand people
- their "tribal psychology in ceremonial life, commerce and enterprise"
- "the geographical feeling of the natives"
- "their use of imagery as a linguistic instrument" (all quotes from Malinowski 1923: 301).

This extensive example is taken from a language and a culture that, probably, are as strange to the reader of this chapter as they were for Malinowski himself when he first got in contact with the Trobriand islanders. The sense of strangeness that at first appears to be a disadvantage, turns out to be an advantage because the experience of bewilderment illustrates one of the central ideas defining Malinowki's theory of language: the description and analysis of "exotic" (i.e., for us, other than Indoeuropean) languages is possible only if we explicitly build on the presuppositions concerning the cultural background of the speakers. Malinowski, then, extends this view to language in general and states:

> Exactly as in the reality of spoken or written languages, a word without *linguistic context* is a mere figment and stands for nothing by itself, so in the reality of a spoken living tongue, the utterance has no meaning except in the *context of situation* (Malinowski 1923: 306; author's emphasis). [. . .] What I have tried to make clear by analysis of a primitive linguistic text is that language is essentially rooted in the reality of the culture, the tribal

life and customs of a people, and that it cannot be explained without constant reference to these broader contexts of verbal utterance (Malinowski 1923: 305).

What makes Malinowki's doctrine so interesting and consequential for his scientific successors is its radically pragmatic nature[3] according to which language is based on language use and language use is fundamentally indexical, i.e., "essentially" rooted in situational and cultural contexts. From this, he concludes that the idea of context-free, i.e., timeless conventional, meaning is "fictitious and irrelevant" (Malinowski 1923: 307).

Based on this approach to language, Malinowski's interest in everyday communication is theoretically motivated, but, at the same time, it is also a matter of practical necessity and this is directly implied by the research strategy of participant observation. Because linguistic meaning can only be accounted for on the basis of detailed cultural knowledge, the linguistic field worker has to become acquainted with the culture in focus. A "culture", however, is neither a well-defined object, easily amenable to observation, nor is it accessible to direct reflection by those who share it and who could be questioned about it. Rather, it is realized in the totality of practical and interactive activities and products of the community members. In order to move towards an account of this totality, the researcher has to gain access to the culture from within, which is best accomplished by temporarily sharing the everyday lives of the members of that culture and engaging in participant observation. Once the investigator has been granted access and some trust in his/her intentions has been built up, s/he may be permitted to audio- and videotape authentic interactions.

To summarize, it can be stated that everyday communication and, specifically, socializing—taken here in the common-sense understanding of these terms—is the most relevant kind of data for the Malinowskian linguist because it best reflects the cultural foundations in which language use is embedded in any given speech community and because it is easily accessible to the researcher.

In addition to his enormous impact on anthropology and on many modern practitioners of field work (Firth [1957] 1970), Malinowki's pragmatic approach has, in the field of linguistics, both directly and indirectly proved to be a source of inspiration for a variety of scientific schools as well as for individual scholars. They all share a contextual theory of language and pursue an interest in actual language use rather than in abstract linguistic systems and structures of the Saussurean and, later, the generativist type. Amongst those who have come under his influence, his student John Rupert Firth (e.g., 1937, 1957) has to be mentioned in the first place as a researcher who became a central figure in British functionalism. Firth's most influential followers include Michael A.K. Halliday (2007), known above all for his development of *systemic functional linguistics* (SFL; e.g., Halliday 1973; Halliday and Matthiessen 2004) and his social semiotics (Halliday 1978). Malinowki's program that originated from

---

[3] "To restate the main position arrived at in this section we can say that language in its primitive function and original form *has an essentially pragmatic character*; that it is a mode of behaviour, an indispensable element of concerted human action" (Malinowski 1923: 316; emphasis mine, T.W.).

an interest for non-Indoeuropean languages and cultures, has proven its universality, particularly in view of the fact that the proponents of the functional paradigm redirected their focus on *casual conversations* (Ventola 1979; Eggins and Slade 1997) in European languages. To study any language, regardless of its typological kind or origin, means to study its use by speakers within particular *contexts of situation* and under specific cultural circumstances.

Malinowski's legacy for the study of everyday communication and socializing as a communicative activity lies in the fact that he had introduced these as legitimate objects of research into the fields of cultural studies and social sciences. Rather than seeing language serving merely as a means by which speakers refer to objects and facts and exchange information Malinowski's insight that language is used to establish, maintain, and negotiate social relations is commonplace today. Accordingly, *phatic communion*—a term "actuated by the demon of terminological invention" (Malinowski 1923: 315)—is defined as

> [. . .] a type of speech in which ties of union are created by a mere exchange of words. [. . .] They fulfil a social function and that is their principal aim, but they are neither the result of intellectual reflection, nor do they necessarily arouse reflection in the listener. Once again we may say that language does not function here as a means of transmission of thought (Malinowski 1923: 315).[4]

In this view, what today is called *small talk* or "mere" *socializing* appears an activity type that realizes a linguistic function that, as such, is of no less value and is no less worthy of investigation than "the transmission of thought".

2.2. Phatic Communication From the Point of View of Bühler's and Jakobson's Semiotic Conceptions

Unlike Malinowski, neither Karl Bühler ([1935] 1999) nor Roman Jakobson (1960) were ever involved in the empirical study of language use in its natural "habitat" of everyday communication. In spite of this, they may rightly be listed among those who have paved the (theoretical) way for research in everyday talk in general and socializing as a communicative activity in particular. This is true mainly because Bühler puts forward a proclaimed functionalist view of language, i.e., of the linguistic sign that is defined by three functions: expression, representation, and appeal. It was Jakobson (1960) who, building up on and elaborating this conception, used Malinowki's term *phatic* to distinguish the particular function that is of particular interest in the context of the present chapter.

Bühler and, later, Jakobson approach language from a perspective which is quite different from that of Malinowski. The latter arrived at his pragmatic view when he had to deal with the practical problems of being a radical foreigner to a culture to which he found himself exposed and of a fieldworker who

---

[4] In order to emphasize the pioneering character of the ideas thus expressed, it may be noted that this view is formulated at the same time at which philosophers of language including Bertrand Russell, Ludwig Wittgenstein, and the proponents of the Vienna Circle are devoting their research to the concept of an *ideal language* and pursuing the most influencial research program of logical semantics that is based on assumptions contrary to Malinowki's.

was confronted with linguistic facts that forced him, in order to make any sense of them at all, to rely on his own interpretation of both the communicational co-text and the cultural context. The contextualist framework directly reflects this very experience. Bühler's approach, even though occasioned by concrete instances of language use, is motivated theoretically. It arises within a general theory of science and is characterized by its author as *axiomatic reasoning* (cf. Hilbert 1918, quoted after Bühler 1934: 20), i.e., a way of arguing that proceeds from fundamental constitutive assumptions. The first and the most famous of Bühler's four axioms is represented by his organon model that is intended as a model of the "concrete speech event" in those circumstances "in which it quite regularly occurs" (Bühler 1999: 24; translation mine, T.W.).

Following de Saussure ([1916] 1990), Bühler takes language to be a semiotic system, a system of linguistic signs (Bühler 1999: 9, 33). Quite interestingly, however, and in contrast, to many structuralist and, later, generativist views originating from Saussure's doctrine, the linguistic sign, for Bühler, is a dyad of form and *function*, rather than form and *content/meaning/intension*/etc. This semiotic conception is consequential because it broadens the view of the linguistic sign as a *multi*functional phenomenon rather than a mere means of reference (as understood by the logical empiricists of that time). Almost in passing and quoting Saussure, Bühler introduces his essentially functionalist view:

> [. . .] that "linguistic phenomena always present two complementary facets, each depending on the other" (Saussure 1922:23 [1983:8; 1959:8; 1931:9]). Of course; but a specialist certainly does not need to be told that sound and function belong to the entirety of a concrete language phenomenon (Bühler [1934] 1990: 8).

It is worth emphasizing, however, that Bühler's functionalism represents a theory of the sign rather than a communication theory. Auer (1999a: 22) points out that the organon metaphor together with the invocation of Plato's *Kratylos* are rather infelicitous with regard to Bühler's own intention. This is because Bühler's model does not suggest that the sign is a ready made *tool* used by a speaker in the same way that a hammer is used by a craftsman for the realization of a certain preset goal or purpose. According to the model, the association of form and functions, which constitutes the sign, depends on the threefold relation of the sign to a speaker, a hearer, and an object/state of affairs in a particular context of situation. By the same token, the sign is the 'medium' (*Mittler*) that uniquely establishes the relations between speaker, hearer, and the world to each other.[5]

---

[5] In spite of this contextualistic character of the organon model, which is the basis of his entire linguistic theory, Bühler insists that there are uses of language that are 'removed from any specific situation' (*situationsfern*; Bühler 1934: 21). His prime examples for this include written texts and phraseologisms. For the purposes of the present chapter, it suffices to point out the functionalist nature of Bühler's view. It is, therefore, neither necessary nor possible here to elucidate the non-trivial question of how the organon model is to be interpreted in the light of Bühler's distinction between 'subject [and context] related' (*subjektsbezogene*) and 'subject [and context)] free and intersubjectively fixed' (*subjektsentbundene und dafür intersubjektiv fixierte*) phenomena (Bühler 1999: 49; for a discussion, cf. Auer 1999a: 25–29).

It was Roman Jakobson who, in his paper on *Linguistics and poetics* (1960), suggested a semiotic model that was inspired by the organon model and introduced further differentiations. According to Jakobson, the linguistic sign was defined by six functions, which his model arranged in the following manner:

REFERENTIAL

(cf. Bühler's *representation*)

EMOTIVE   POETIC   CONATIVE

(cf. Bühler's *expression*)   PHATIC   (cf. Bühler's *appeal*)

METALINGUAL   (cf. Jakobson 1960: 356)

Jakobson's explication of the semiotic nature of language is in two regards relevant to the study of everyday communication. First, he (re-)introduces the notion *phatic function of language* into semiotics. Second, he—like Bühler before him—points out that not all language use realizes all these functions equally, at the same time to the same extent. Rather he suggests that different linguistic genres are defined by which one(s) of the functions is (are) realized by speakers or writers.

The relevance of this conceptual framework for identifying socializing as an interactional genre most prototypical of everyday communication is revealed in the following quote:

> There are messages primarily serving to establish, to prolong, or to discontinue communication, to check whether the channel works ("Hello, do you hear me?"), to attract the attention of the interlocutor or to confirm his continued attention ("Are you listening?" or in Shakespearean diction, "Lend me your ears!"—and on the other end of the wire "Um-hum!"). This set for CONTACT, or in Malinowski's terms PHATIC function [. . .], may be displayed by a profuse exchange of ritualized formulas, by entire dialogues with the mere purport of prolonging communication. [. . .] (Jakobson 1960: 355).

By focusing on the phatic semiotic function, Jakobson draws attention to the fact that language use is mostly *communicative* language use and that communication is not possible unless there is *contact* established between the participants. Interactive language use necessarily serves this function to some degree or other. Hence, *small talk* or *socializing* can be conceived as a genre of interaction in which the phatic function is the one that motivates the exchange in the first place, but this function is also present in communications of other types.

2.3. Ordinary Language Philosophy and Everyday Communication

Rather than aiming at an account of what ordinary language *is* in terms of linguistic means and structures, ordinary language philosophy originated from an interest in what the appropriate *role* of this type of language is in the realm of philosophical analysis; that is, ordinary language is looked at from the perspective of philosophical methodology (cf. Hanfling 2000: Chapter 2). This method of philosophizing developed as an offspring and by way of a critique[6] of the most prevalent philosophical paradigm in the Anglosaxon world of the 1940s and 1950s, i.e., analytic philosophy as represented by authors like Bertrand Russell and the Vienna circle lead by the logical positivists Rudolph Carnap and Hans Reichenbach.

That ordinary language philosophy represents a method of philosophizing is, *ex negativo,* expressed quite clearly in a quote from one of the most prominent and determined opponents of this approach. Bertrand Russell rightly attributes to philosophers including his former student Ludwig Wittgenstein (1953), John L. Austin (1962, 1964), Gilbert Ryle (1949), and Peter Strawson (1950) the conviction

> [. . .] that common speech is good enough, not only for daily life, but also for philosophy. [. . .] I, on the contrary am persuaded that common speech is full of vagueness and inaccuracy [. . .]. Everybody admits that physics and chemistry and medicine each require a language which is not that of everyday life. I fail to see why philosophy, alone, should be forbidden to make a similar approach towards precision and accuracy (Russell 1959; quoted after Hanfling 2000: 1–2).

Several aspects of ordinary language philosophy are alluded to in this quotation. Ordinary language is equated with the language of "everyday life", i.e., of everyday communication. Furthermore, Wittgenstein and others suggest that the language of everyday communication alone is sufficient for philosophical purposes. In addition, they argue that ordinary language *by necessity* is the fundament and ultimate means of philosophy. Even if one designed—as conceived by, e.g., Russell, Carnap, and the early Wittgenstein ([1921] 2002]—an ideal language of science, there would be no other way to explicate the meaning of its concepts than by means of ordinary language. Ordinary language, hence, proves to be the most basic metalanguage. The observation that this metalanguage is "full of vagueness" may (or may not) be considered problematic from the point of view of science; it does not, however, support any counter-argument against the doctrine suggested by ordinary language philosophy. Austin himself formulates:

> [. . . O]ur common stock of words embodies all the distinctions men have found worth drawing, and the connexions they have found worth marking, in the lifetimes of many generations: these surely are likely to be more numerous, more sound [. . .] than any that you or I are likely to think up in our arm-chairs of an afternoon (Austin 1961; quoted after Hanfling 2000: 26).

The philosophical implications of this view are outside the scope of this chapter. However, for attempts at elucidating the nature of the meaning of linguistic expressions, i.e., for semantic analysis in general, the consequences

---

[6] The emergence of ordinary language philosophy out of logical semantics is nicely illustrated by the *Russell-Strawson*-debate on definite descriptions (Russell 1905, 1957; Strawson 1950; for a review, cf. Hanfling 2000: 170–175).

are concisely expressed in the famous 43rd paragraph from Wittgenstein's *Philosophical Investigations*:

> For a *large* class of cases—though not for all—in which we employ the word "meaning" it can be defined thus: the meaning of a word is its use in the language (Wittgenstein 1953: §43).

From a linguistic point of view, the question immediately arises of how the use of a word "in the language" can be determined. The adherents of *speech act theory* (Austin 1962; Searle 1969), the most direct "heirs" of ordinary language philosophy that have influenced linguistics, seem to have answered this with reference to introspection. Accordingly, ordinary language is what speech act theorists, provided they are native speakers of that language, consider to be ordinary language. Typical linguistic "data", then, include one-sentence utterances (*The cat is on the mat.*; *Would you pass me the salt, please.*; etc.) selected or even constructed by the linguist and analyzed by him/her on the basis of linguistic intuitions presupposed to be shared by all competent members of the speech community. The overall deductive nature of speech act theory is an inheritance from its analytic predecessor.

There are, however, approaches to pursuing a Wittgensteinean semantic program in linguistics that are more empiristic in kind, i.e., data-driven or even corpus-based. One example is provided by Franz Hundsnurscher (1995) who explicates the meaning of the German adjective *alt* ('old') by giving a 'usage profile' (*Gebrauchsprofil*) that is the result of a corpus analysis. More recently, the volume by Deppermann and Spranz-Fogazy (2002) presents data-based empirical studies on the emergence of meaning in conversation.

In sum, it can be stated that ordinary language philosophy has provided arguments that direct the attention of linguists and, more specifically, semanticists to the actual use speakers make of language in everyday communication.

2.4. Ethnomethodology

Ethnomethodology, an approach to sociology closely associated with the names of Harold Garfinkel ([1967] 1984a) and his students, is the fourth important source that lead to the study of everyday communication in linguistics. Garfinkel arrived at his major claims on the reflexive and indexical nature of social interaction under the influence of Husserlean phenomenology and, especially, of Alfred Schütz, on the one hand, and as the result of his critique of Talcott Parsons' way of doing sociology on the other. The relevance of ethnomethodology for the study of everyday communication is obvious from the fact that conversation analysis (see below Section 3.1.) is its direct offspring. Like Malinowski, but in contradistinction to speech act theory and Bühler's semiotics, ethnomethodology is emphatically empiricist in nature (Weber 2003). And similar to Malinowski's, Garfinkel's and his most influential student's, Harvey Sacks', approaches, his interest in language use and communication was also of a secondary and rather indirect nature. This is illustrated by the following statement by John Heritage:

The term 'ethnomethodology' thus refers to the study of a particular subject matter: the body of common-sense knowledge and the range of procedures and considerations by means of which the ordinary members of society make sense of, find their way about in, and act on the circumstances in which they find themselves (Heritage 1984: 4).

The (ethno-)methods by which the members of a community make sense of each other's activities and their environment, thus, are the ethnomethodologists' primary objects of interest. Language use and communication are drawn into their focus because linguistic social interaction is a major, though not the only, kind of activity by which individuals collaboratively perform and display their sense makings to each other and—which is most important from a methodological point of view—to outside observers and analysts.

Garfinkel's radical empiricism and anti-apriorism is based on two main theoretical assumptions:

1. *indexicality*: the meaning of any given social behavior (whether linguistic or otherwise), rather than being determined by the conventional type-meanings of the tokens produced, is interactively and collaboratively constructed by the participants in the ongoing interaction.
2. *reflexivity*: "[. . . T]he activities whereby members produce and manage settings of organized everyday affairs are identical with members' procedures for making those settings "account-able" (Garfinkel 1984b: 1).[7]

In other words, Garfinkel suggests that participants in interaction not only produce sense by their social activities, but they also *display* to their co-interactants that they are doing so.

From these two basic assumptions, which are grounded in the traditions of phenomenology, a radically empiricist approach to social interaction follows. If sense is not an *apriori* property of semiotic types but emerges in the *hereandnow* of social interaction, it cannot be adequately accounted for on the basis of an analyst's own native speaker competence which reflects the necessarily de-contextualized outcome of his/her linguistic socialization within a speech community. Hence, ethnomethodologists consider Husserl's *epoché*, i.e., the "bracketing" or suspension of one's own "prejudices" with regard to the objects of study, the first step to any sound data analysis.

However, what criteria can be applied for the interpretation of utterances if the interpreter's intuitions are excluded? Garfinkel's answer is closely related to his concept of *reflexivity* and presupposes a priority of the participants' perspective to the analyst's with regard to the analysis of discourse. Accordingly, an analyst is able to *observe* what a particular utterance means, because the participants *display* their understandings of each other's contributions by reacting to them *as* to activities of certain types. Paul, for instance, may utter "It's 5 o'clock" in response to Cynthia's "Excuse

---

[7] Garfinkel (1984b) advances this "central recommendation" of reflexivity right at the beginning of his programmatic paper on *What is ethnomethodology?*.

me, what time is it?" and, thus, react to it *as* if to a question for the time. In turn, Cynthia's behavior (e.g., her uttering "Thanks" or her nodding) will indicate to Paul that he interpreted Cynthia's utterance correctly. "Correctly", however, does not imply that Paul "really" understood, what Cynthia thought and intended by what she said. For the ethnomethodologist (as for everybody else), other minds are opaque; what the observer and Paul alike may conclude from Cynthia's interactive behavior, however, is that Paul's understanding was *sufficiently* in line with Cynthia's intention to meet *the practical purposes* of the ongoing interaction (cf. Garfinkel 1984a: 7). This conclusion is justified by the assumption that speakers are *accountable* for what they say[8] and for how it is reacted to by their interlocutors. In those cases where they notice a misunderstanding or another communicational problem, they are expected to take measures to account for what they meant and, thus, to fix the problem at least to an extent necessary for the ongoing exchange. From a methodological point of view, the argument reconstructed above suggests a radically empiricist research strategy.

2.5. Summary

At the beginning of the 20th century, everyday communication and, especially, an empirical account of authentic everyday communication were far outside the scope of linguistics. The review of the theoretical and empirical findings, and arguments has shown how scholars changed their perspectives and turned to consider speaking and listening in ordinary circumstances of everyday life more than just an epiphenomenon of speakers' putting the language system into use. The objective of this discussion was to show that, while having started from very different premises, the proponents of the four approaches discussed arrived at conclusions that are remarkably similar with regard to the aspects relevant to the issues discussed here. All four accounts argue in favor of a *functional* view which considers language to be inextricably related to language *use* and social *interaction*. This theoretical reason makes everyday communication, by which participants typically realize social interaction, the obvious focus of linguistic interest. The *empirical* nature of this interest is a consequence of the insight that meaning (Malinowski), semiosis (Bühler), or sense-making (Garfinkel) is essentially indexical, i.e., it comes about only under the special conditions of particular contexts of situation.

   After this reconstruction of the pre-history, the next section introduces two research paradigms, conversation analysis and systemic functional linguistics, proponents of which explicitly turn their research attention to the empirical analysis of discourse and, in particular, everyday communication.

---

[8] Within ethnomethodology, this doctrin plays a similar role as, in the Gricean paradigm, the assumption that the presumption of rationality is taken for granted by all rational interactants. According to this assumption, meaningful interaction is utterly impossible unless the participants mutually attribute rationality to each other (cf. Grice [1967] 1989: 29–30).

3. Everyday Conversation in the Focus of Empirical Discourse Analysis

This section presents two approaches, conversation analysis and systemic functional linguistics, that have focused either directly or indirectly on the "everydayness" of everyday communication as distinct from other modes of interaction. Furthermore, brief reference will be made to a few other works which have contributed to research on everyday communication, but which are not closely associated to either of the two paradigms mentioned above.

3.1. Conversation Analysis (CA)

As we saw in the previous section, ethnomethodology provided the theoretical arguments to convince scholars that social order, the principles of interaction, and the coming about of sense should be studied empirically. As the initial step in a valid research strategy, the focus should be on authentic *given*, rather than *made up, data* that occurred uninfluenced by the analyst. Introspection and the analyst's intuitions, which are based on his/her experiences as a member of the community under observation, are to be excluded from the analytic process as far as possible.[9]

At the beginning of the 1960s, it was an ethnomethodological background together with a number of technical innovations that were conducive to the rise of a research program which explicitly concerned itself with the study of spoken discourse: conversation analysis.[10] As noted above, social interaction is mainly realized by way of interactants' engaging in talk. The telephone as a widespread medium of communication and the availability of recording devices—audio-recorders and, from the 1970s onwards, video-cameras—enabled researchers to realize the empiricist programs formulated earlier by ethnomethodologists but also by other empirically minded linguists. It was Michael A.K. Halliday, the initiator of systemic functional linguistics, who acknowledged this fact when he stated:

> Perhaps the greatest single event in the history of linguistics was the invention of the tape recorder, which for the first time has captured natural conversation and made it accessible to systematic study (Halliday 1994; quoted after Eggins and Slade 1997: 1).

Up to this point, scholars had to rely on field notes they took at the same time they were observing their research objects, or in retrospect. Discourse analysts were now able to preserve their data in a way that allowed for multiple

---

[9] The limits of this methodological doctrine have often been pointed out. Most consequential is William Labov's (1972: 209) discussion of the so called *observer's paradox*. For a review of the consequences following from this problem and related ones for the methodology of conversation analysis, cf. Weber (2003).

[10] Introductory monographs on conversation analysis are numerous and include Psathas (1995), Hutchbe and Wooffit (1998), Silverman (1998), Have (1999), and Markee (2000). German readers may be referred to the canonical introductory articles by Kallmeyer und Schütze (1976) and Bergmann (1981, 1994).

replays. They were able to do fine-grained analyses on a multiplicity of details that generally pass unnoticed when the observer has the chance to listen to and watch a verbal exchange only once.

A look at the early work in conversation analysis (Sacks 1995[11]; Schegloff and Sacks 1973; Schegloff 1968, 1972; Sacks, Jefferson, and Schegloff 1974; Schegloff, Sacks, and Jefferson 1977) reveals that *conversation* is, here, understood in the sense of *authentic oral social interaction* which is set off from made-up, written, and/or monological texts. The data available for recording and, subsequently, for analysis include exchanges as different as therapy sessions, telephone calls from a suicide prevention center, and private phone conversations. Only the latter would, in the still intuitive sense in which the term has been used so far, qualify as a typical kind of everyday communication.

The properties that characterize specific modes or genres of spoken discourse and distinguish them from one another have not yet been explicitly focused upon in this approach. Rather, conversation analysts identify and describe structures and mechanisms that seem to be constitutive of conversation in the broad understanding. Most influential for subsequent research has been Sacks, Jefferson, and Schegloff's (1974) paper on *A simplest systematics for the organization of turn-taking for conversation* that explores the so called "turn-taking machinery". Based on conversational data of various types and origins, the authors argue that the constitutive process that underlies verbal interaction, i.e., the *abab*-alternation of the participants' turns-at-talk, is regulated by a relatively simple mechanism that is applied recursively by the speakers. Other phenomena identified as central to conversation are:

- *adjacency pairs* and *conditional relevancy* (e.g., Sacks 1987; Schegloff 1968; Kallmeyer 1976)
- *preference structures* (e.g., Schegloff, Sacks, and Jefferson 1977; Pomerantz 1986; Bilmes 1988)
- *repair activities* (e.g., Schegloff, Sacks, and Jefferson 1977; Schegloff 1979b; Egbert 2002; Weber 1998)

Among other things, conversation analysts are credited for having demonstrated that one of the most mundane and everyday activities mastered by virtually all members of a social community, i.e. conversation, depends on activities the successful performance of which is a true *accomplishment*. Hence, seemingly trivial activities, like turn-taking or the closing of a conversation, are liable to problems or even to complete failure which interactants have, but may fail to be able, to avoid or to overcome by their communicative activities.

It was only later that conversation analysts started to focus more on different sub-types of what until then had been studied under the general heading of conversation. Everyday communication, it seems, is now referred to as a kind of default case providing the background against which discourse of

---

[11] It is one of the pecularities of conversation analysis as a scientific paradigm that much of the work authored and co-authored by Harvey Sacks was edited and "officially" published after the death of this charismatic scholar in 1975. For the editing history of Sacks' early lectures, cf. Schegloff (1995).

other kinds is profiled. Paul Drew and John Heritage's (1992: 21–22) section on *Institutional talk and ordinary conversation* in the introduction to their volume on *Talk at Work* is typical of this strategy. At its onset, they state:

> In the following discussion, we will address some aspects of interaction which are often cited when analysts seek to distinguish "institutional talk" from "ordinary conversation" (Drew and Heritage 1992: 21).

By subsequently stating what *talk at work* is, which the authors equate with institutional talk, they—*ex negativo*—define also their concept of ordinary conversation. Accordingly, ordinary conversation typically

- is *not* "normally informed by *goal orientations* of a relatively restricted conventional form"
- does *not* "involve *special and particular constraints* on what one or both of the participants will treat as allowable contributions to the business at hand"
- is *not* "associated with *inferential frameworks* and procedures that are particular to specific institutional contexts" (all quotes from Drew and Heritage 1992: 22; authors' emphases).

The quotation of this "definition" would not be complete without the following qualification by which the authors

> [. . .] stress that we do not accept that there is necessarily a hard and fast distinction to be made between the two in all instances of interactional events, nor even at all points in a single interaction event (Drew and Heritage 1992: 21).

From this, it can be concluded that everyday communication, at least from the point of view of conversation analysts, does not *tend* to be goal-oriented, specifically constrained with regard to allowable moves, and associated with particular inferential frameworks. However, it is well conceivable that one or several of these features may be displayed by (rather untypical) instances of everyday communication. An example in point is provided by family dinner table conversations among the members of traditional European families where the contributions allowed to the various participants seem very much conventionalized (Keppler 1995).

The success of conversation analysis in defining everyday communication as opposed to institutional discourse remained somewhat vague. Another strategy to explicate the notion of everyday communication is to look more specifically at what activity types or genres discourse analysts have analyzed under two different headings. The list of institutional—and, thus, non-everyday—genres explored as such by conversation analysts is very long and beyond the space available here (cf. the contributions to Drew and Heritage 1992; Boden and Zimmerman 1991; Arminen 2005); it includes medical discourse (Have 2006; Heritage and Maynard 2006; Lehtinen 2007), job interviews (Botton 1992; Birkner 2001), court proceedings (Atkinson and Drew 1978; Atkinson 1992; Drew 1992), educational discourse (Hester and Francis 2000), and many more. As for clear examples of everyday genres explored within conversation analysis, the list is much shorter, which is in line with the observation formulated above that everyday discourse is to be defined *sui generis* rather from a merely negative point of view. Everyday genres that have attracted the attention of researchers influenced by conversation analysis include dinner table conversations (Weber 1998) and small talk (Schneider 1988; Coupland 2000).

3.2. Casual Conversation From the Point of View of Systemic Functional Linguistics (SFL)

As expressed by Halliday's statement given earlier, practitioners of systemic functional linguistics have been using authentic oral discourse as data right from the moment at which this was technically feasible. While, from a CA perspective, *everyday communication* has to be reconstructed as a participant category by means of an empiricist methodology, systemic functionalists pursue a different approach. Their starting point—within a broader theoretical framework that includes the concepts of *genre* and *register*—is a presupposed notion of *casual conversation*. Eggins and Slade introduce their research object along these lines:

> Very often we talk to other people to accomplish quite specific, pragmatic tasks: we talk to buy and to sell, to find out information, to pass on knowledge, to make appointments, to get jobs, and to jointly participate in practical activities.
>
> At other times we talk simply for the sake of talking itself. An example of this is when we get together with friends or workmates over coffee or dinner and just "have a chat". It is to these informal interactions that the label **casual conversation** is usually applied (Eggins and Slade 1997: 6; authors' emphasis).
>
> [. . .] We will define casual conversation functionally and, initially at least, negatively, as talk which is NOT motivated by any clear pragmatic purpose (Eggins and Slade 1997: 19; authors' emphasis).

Much like conversation analysts, Eggins and Slade, first, set off casual conversation against goal-oriented discourse. It seems, however, that their concept is narrower and excludes more than just institutional talk in the CA sense. If all interaction that pursues "quite specific, pragmatic tasks" is beyond the realm of the casual, asking a passerby for the time or the shortest way to the railway station does not qualify as casual conversation. Furthermore, if one considers complex genres, e.g., dinner table interactions or job interviews, casual and "pragmatic" activities occur alternately. Thus, it appears that what systemic functionalists put into focus are those aspects of communication that, using Malinowski's and Jakobson's term, can be qualified as *phatic* interaction. And if this is a fair description, *socializing* may be regarded a more appropriate term given that, e.g., the exchange of greeting formulas at the beginning of a job interview serves phatic purposes, but is certainly not casual.

Eggins and Slade's view is indeed compatible especially with Jakobson's model according to which the linguistic sign is functionally motivated in six regards. Different kinds of language use, then, differ from each other according to which of the functions is the primary—and not necessarily the only—one (cf. above Section 2.1.2.). In casual conversation, then, the phatic function is the participants' main motivation to interact. Ventola expresses the idea that casualness is a matter of degree:

> *Casualness* may be a part of any encounter, but there are particular face-to-face encounters which are marked by this feature namely *casual encounters* (Ventola 1979: 267; author's emphasis).

Given this functional view, the description of casual conversation as "talk simply for the sake of talking itself" appears somewhat misleading, which is also clear when Eggins and Slade state:

> [. . . C]asual conversation is a critical linguistic site for the negotiation of such important dimensions of our social identity as gender, generational location, sexuality, social class membership, ethnicity, and subcultural and group affiliations. In fact, we will be arguing in this book that casual conversation is concerned with the joint construction of social reality (Eggins and Slade 1997: 6).

It follows from the discussion above, that *casual conversation* is much narrower a concept than *everyday communication*. Furthermore, casual encounters are found also beyond the realm of everyday interaction and do occur in the context of "talk at work", i.e., of institutional exchanges. Apparently, systemic functional linguists like Ventola, Eggins, and Slade focus on a somewhat different research object than conversation analysts. There is, however, a close relationship between the two perspectives, an intersection that is represented by small talk or socializing. Socializing can be conceived of as the prototypical everyday speech activity or discourse genre because its participants primarily engage in realizing the phatic semiotic function, that is, in casual conversation.

The systemic functional perspective, thus, does not provide us with an intensional understanding of what constitutes the "everydayness" of everyday communication. However, it directs our attention to the center of this fuzzy category as one of its prototypes. An advantage of this approach is that it relies on a single positive criterion only, which makes it feasible to identify stretches of casual talk even when they are embedded in structurally and functionally more complex interactions. Collections of plausible examples of socializing, which are offered both by Ventola as well as by Eggins and Slade, serve as data on the basis of which further questions may be answered. Within the limited realm of this chapter, only an inexhaustive list of relevant issues can be given:

- What is the structure of casual conversation (Ventola 1979)?
- Are there types of casual conversation?
- Is there a specific grammar of casual conversation (Eggins and Slade 1997: Chapter 3)?
- What is the semantics of casual conversation (Eggins and Slade 1997: Chapter 4)?

etc.

3.3. Further Contributions to Research on Everyday Communication

In the preceding sections, conversation analysis and systemic functional linguistics were presented as two research paradigms on the basis of which scholars have contributed to our understanding of everyday communication. From this systematic point of view, however, it is easy to overlook work that is not readily associated with either of the two approaches.

In this regard, Robert E. Nofsinger's introductory textbook on *Everyday Conversation* (1991) should be mentioned. The aim of this author is not so much to align himself with a particular paradigm and to develop, on this basis, an innovative theory of a particular genre, but rather, to present to his readers what scholars from different, and not necessarily mutually compatible, theoretical backgrounds have contributed to his topic. Accordingly, Nofsinger introduces speech act theory and Gricean pragmatics as having laid the foundations that made research in everyday communication possible. The larger portion of his monograph is, then, concerned with those findings of conversation analysts that pertain to the study of everyday communication. In sum, Nofsinger provides a thorough and easily accessible introduction to the topic without discussing the theoretical details and problems that go along with it.

Finally, I would like to refer to two studies on dinner talk, one by Angela Keppler (1995) and one by Shoshana Blum-Kulka (1997; cf. also Tannen [1984] 2005). Even though they do not explicitly concern themselves with definitorial problems, their analyses of participants' activities from a sociological point of view are relevant for linguists interested in ordinary social interaction because dinner table conversations represent an interactive genre that seldom is missing in lists of exemplary cases of everyday communication.

3.4. Summary

The purpose of Section 3 was to demonstrate that conversation analysts and systemic functionalists both concern themselves with everyday communication, but their perspectives are different. Conversation analysts approach everyday communication as a special case of discourse that is to be distinguished from institutional interactions. In contrast, systemic functional linguists focus more specifically on casual conversation as a prototypical type of everyday communication. Both accounts go along with specific strengths and weaknesses; and they also share a common property. While conversation analysts propose a more global account of everyday communication, their concept remains rather vague; on this basis, it would be difficult to collect undisputable examples of everyday interaction that go beyond the well known and often listed prototypes. On the other hand, Ventola (1979) and Eggins and Slade (1997) define casual communication, or socializing, as a class of everyday interactions elements of which are characterized by a common primary function: phatic communion. While casual conversation is without doubt a prototypical case of everyday communication, the latter concept is commonly used in a much broader sense. It includes, e.g., dinner table conversations that are both structurally and functionally more complex than casual conversations. Ventola, Eggins, and Slade, thus elucidate a particular type of everyday communication; however, they do not say what everyday communication in the broad sense is.[12]

Hence, conversation analysts as well as systemic functional linguists are not alone in struggling to find a well defined account of everyday communication. What, on first sight, seems unsatisfactory, appears less surprising when two factors are considered: first, *everyday communication*, above all, is an ethnocategory used by speakers on an intuitive basis in—well—everyday communication. What suits the practical purposes of ordinary interaction is not necessarily apt in scientific contexts. Second, *everyday communication* refers to an intermediate level of categorization that is rather abstract. Other than for both the superordinate category (i.e., spoken discourse) and the subordinate categories (e.g., socializing, dinner table conversations, etc.), in the case of everyday communication, it is impossible to identify specific properties that all members share and all non-members do not show.

In conclusion, everyday conversation is a category that seems best defined with reference to prototypical members and prototypical properties featured by these members. This gives rise to more systematic considerations presented in the following section.

4. *Everyday Communication* as a Prototype Category With *Socializing* as Its Central Member

Confronted with conceptual and methodological problems like the ones discussed above, Petra Lindemann (1990: 206, 219) suggests that the concept of 'everyday conversation' (*Alltagsgespräch*) should be completely dispensed with. However, this radically "therapeutic" approach is not recommended here for two reasons: first, *everyday communication* and its relatives, including *everyday language, everyday situation,* and *everyday life,* are ethnocategories that are frequently referred to by speakers outside of scientific discourse; empirically minded social scientists and linguists cannot ignore this fact and have, therefore, to account for it by explicitly reconstructing the tacit intuitions which underlie these common, if problematic, concepts. Second, the contrast between everyday and institutional communication, which has been proven useful by proponents of rather different research paradigms, suggests that there is a relevant *intermediate level of categorization* between the superordinate level of oral discourse and particular everyday genres or activity types, such as small talk or job interviews.

Taking into account the problems discussed above whilst at the same time retaining this concept is possible only if the prototypical nature of this particular category is given its due weight. On the one hand, it is feasible, on this basis, to account for the observation that the transition from ordinary to institutional communication (Drew and Heritage 1992: 21) or from casual to noncasual discourse (Ventola 1979; Eggins and Slade 1997) is continuous rather

---

[12] In her study on *The Structure of Social Intraction*, Ventola (1987) shows how participants switch between genres thus realizing everyday interactional activities also in institutional settings.

than discrete. On the other hand, it allows us to understand why *socializing* or *small talk* is almost always mentioned when concrete examples of everyday communication are listed; and also, why it is plausible to state that not all small talk is casual (e.g., in the context of job interviews) and institutional discourse is not necessarily formal and goal-oriented (e.g., the exchange of greetings among colleagues in the morning).

In the following, this proposal is spelled out by brief reviews of six properties that characterize typical cases of everyday communication: these are *ordinary, authentic, oral, private, informal,* and *lacking goal-orientation/phatically motivated*.

- *Ordinariness*: Everyday communication is, in the first place, communication that happens every day or, at least, frequently. It represents a type of ordinary, mundane social interaction. Several times a week, most—but probably not all—of us are involved in dinner table conversations or chats in the street, in the office, in the supermarket, or in some other place. It is obvious however, that ordinariness is also the mark of interactions that, even though they occur daily, are not everyday communications in the sense discussed in the present chapter. Primary or high school teachers, for instance, spend many hours a day communicating with students during lessons; still, we do not want to include teaching or class discourse into the category of everyday communication. In contrast, telephone chats are considered ordinary language use even though many people in Western societies do not phone regularly with their friends or relatives.

- *Authenticity*: Conversation analysts have insisted against traditional linguists, but also against other pragmatically minded scholars, such as the proponents of speech act theory, that admissible data for linguistic analysis ought to be "authentic". Accordingly, the interactions included in an ideal data base are independent of the analyst in all regards, e.g., in terms of their selection, occasion, participants, structure, topics, etc. The discussion, initiated by William Labov (1972: 206), on the so called *observer's paradox* has demonstrated, however, that data authenticity in the empirical social sciences and in linguistics can at best be approximately realized and, thus, is a matter of degree. The preference, for instance, in early CA studies for exchanges between family members, friends, and students was, in addition to theoretically well justified reasons, in part due to the fact that these data were readily available to the researchers.

- *Orality*: Everyday communication overwhelmingly is spoken discourse. This is trivially and exclusively true for oral societies and for early childhood. But also in Western cultures and in later periods of the life, the role of writing outside professional contexts, for most, is of rather minor significance. Or so it used to be. In recent years, the rise of new communicative means and platforms, ranging from e-mail to social networking sites and virtual worlds on the internet, have created a kind of social reality that is very much based on writing rather than or in addition to speaking. To date, it is still a minority of members even in developed societies that make extensive use of these media and platforms. Their example illustrates, however, that the possibility of leading an everyday life that is very much rooted in the "virtuality" of electronic media and based primarily on writing has left the realm of science fiction literature and entered the "actual" reality with many concrete (e.g., cognitive, financial, and societal) consequences.

- *Privateness*: Conversation analysts like Drew and Heritage (1992) have equated institutional communication with "talk at work". In contrast then, everyday communication is "talk at home" or in private circumstance. This is obviously true for our prototype of socializing and for dinner table talk among friends and family members. Talk shows on TV, however, the success of which to a large extent is dependent on an atmosphere of privateness, mundaneness, and authenticity, are not at all private. However, they feature several other properties considered characteristic of everyday communication, including informality, the range of intimate topics, etc.

- *Informality*: Socializing among friends typically is informal and casual. At first sight, phatic interaction appears hardly to be regulated by constraints on admissible behavior. However, even small talk at a neighborhood barbecue may not allow for all conceivable topics of conversation (e.g., sexual preferences, severe financial problems), and may also require the use of formal terms of address (e.g., of honorifics or—in languages like German and French—the formal *Sie/vous* (3rd/2nd person plural pronoun) rather than the familiar *du/tu* (2nd person singular pronoun)), etc. *Politeness* and *face* (Goffman [1955] 1967) are categories, interactants orient to in discourse of all types. Independently of the discourse genre, the degree of informality decreases, the more formal the setting is, in the context of which the genre is realized.

- *Lack of goal-orientation/phatic motivation*: "Talk simply for the sake of talking itself" (Eggins and Slade 1997: 6), i.e., chat or socializing interaction, may be rightly characterized as lacking an orientation to intentionally pursued pragmatic goals. Even in the context of dinner talk, however, participants will ask each other to pass the salt or a dish of vegetables, which clearly is a goal-oriented activity. A couple making plans for the weekend or asking one's spouse whether he can take the kids to school both represent everyday, mundane, and even casual communications, and still speakers pursue quite specific goals by performing them.

This section has elaborated on the prototype character of everyday communication as a linguistic category. Accordingly, everyday communication may be modeled as a radial or, rather, multi-dimensional category in the center of which we find the prototype(s) that are characterized by the six features presented above. This model allows us to account for the fact that socializing almost unanimously is considered a prototype case of everyday communication and, at the same time, to include as peripheral members cases that are lacking one or several of the characteristic properties.

5. Research Perspectives

After almost a whole century of research and since Malinowki's ethno-graphic field-studies on "primitive" cultures, everyday communication has been established as a research object and an indispensable kind of data base both in the social sciences and in empirically oriented linguistics. Progress in these fields has always been stimulated by theoretical, empirical, and technological developments. At present, several directions can be identified in which research in everyday communication will proceed in the near future. Four of those potential developments are briefly characterized in the following.

It was Michael A.K. Halliday who rightly pointed out the impact made by the audio recorder on empirical linguistics. For some time now, linguists have used increasingly sophisticated technologies including (multiple) digital cameras, eye trackers, etc. Along with these technological innovations goes an understanding that "natural" communication is not limited to the verbal and, so called, "para-verbal" levels, but is *multimodal*. Simultaneous video recordings from various perspectives, the possibility to manipulate the video tapes (slow motion, zoom), etc. allow discourse analysts to investigate different semiotic levels of everyday communication and their interaction, including gestures and mimics, eye gaze, body posture, proxemics, and others. The fact that research in this direction is soaring is indicated by the large number of recent and upcoming publications (e.g., Poggi 2007), conferences (cf., e.g., All-wood, Dorriots, and Nicholson 2006), and new journals (e.g., *GESTURE*. John Benjamins).

While, for a long period of time, the analysis of everyday communication was regarded relevant mainly for scholars of language usage (or *parole*), more recently, functionally oriented linguists have insisted that natural and, by implication, everyday communication is the primary locus of structures and dynamics on *all* linguistic levels and, thus, has to be studied also by pho-nologists, grammarians, and semanticists. On the basis of an empiricist view of language, proponents of this approach have published work under various labels, including *discourse functional linguistics* (e.g., Ford, Fox, and Thompson 2001) and *interactional linguistics* (Selting and Couper-Kuhlen 2001).

From the perspective of *applied linguistics*, another stimulus for research in everyday communication may originate from the popularity of this topic in the areas of commercial and popular consulting, training, coaching, etc. The list of practically oriented monographs, training manuals and videos, week-end seminars, etc. is very long. These contributions to what Antos (1995) has called 'lay-linguistics' (*Laien-Linguistik*) hold out the prospect for their clients to improve their small talking and other special communication skills that are considered indispensable for private and professional success. For a number of reasons (cf. Weber 2005), these products are at best indirectly informed by linguistic research (e.g., via Schultz von Thun's (2007) 'model of the four ears' (*Vier-Ohren-Modell*) that is based on Bühler's organon model). If the cultural differences between social scientists on the one hand and prac-tically (and commercially) oriented trainers and consultants, on the other, could be bridged, the potential profit would be mutual. From the point of view of linguists, this would, e.g., include access to data that otherwise are not easily available.

As mentioned in Section 4 above, the implication that authentic communication, by default, is oral communication has to some degree lost its status as an unquestionable truism with the rise of electronic media and the internet in recent years. These technological innovations have brought with them rapid changes and are at the moment causing dramatic consequences for the ways an increasing number of people in developed and developing societies communicate. While more recently introduced means of written communication, including e-mail, short message system (SMS) services, instant messaging, internet chats and forums, allow users to realize many of the functions formerly limited to oral and mostly to face-to-face interactions, social networking sites, e.g., *facebook* (www.facebook.com), and virtual worlds, e.g., *Second Life* (www.secondlife. com), for some, have redefined and, very likely, will redefine in the future what is to be considered *ordinary* or *everyday* (cf. Chapter 3, this volume). This means that at the moment, for students of everyday communication, an entirely novel research domain is emerging.

6. Concluding Remarks

In this chapter, everyday communication was approached in four major steps. First, the emergence of everyday communication as a linguistic research object in the first half of the 20th century was reconstructed (Section 2). It was demonstrated that scholars as different as Bronisław Malinowski (1923), Karl Bühler (1934), John Austin (1962, 1964), and Harold Garfinkel (1984) put forward arguments and findings that converge on a common conclusion: questions on the grammatical structure and meaning of linguistic expressions and utterances cannot be answered without reference to authentic data from everyday communication in their situational and cultural contexts. Following this summary of the scientific "prehistory", Section 3 introduced *conversation analysis* and *systemic functional linguistics* as two research paradigms that approach everyday communication in specific manners respectively. Whereas conversation analysts, from a more global perspective, look at everyday communication as at a type of discourse that is in contrast with institutional talk, systemic functional linguists have concerned themselves primarily with one of its prototypes, i.e., *casual* or *phatic* interaction.

Up to this point of the discussion, a picture of everyday communication as an important concept in linguistics had emerged that displays the structure of a *prototype category*. This radial category, it was argued further, is derived from an ethnocategory or, rather, an entire family of ethnocategories. Section 4 presented a more systematic look at the prototype nature of everyday communication. One of its central members, *socializing* or *small talk*, was characterized by six properties: *ordinariness, authenticity, orality, privateness, informality,* and *a lack of goal-orientation*. It was further stated that the prototype conception of everyday communication also implies the notion of peripheral category members which are marked by a lack of one or the other of the characteristic properties. Finally, Section 5 highlighted perspectives on current and future research in everyday communication.

References

Alberts, Jess K., Christina G. Yoshimura, Michael Rabby, and Rose Loschiavo. 2005. Mapping the topography of couples' daily conversation. *Journal of Social and Personal Relationships* 22: 299–322.

Allwood, Jens, Beatriz Dorriots, and Shirley Nicholson (eds.). 2006. *Multimodal Communication. Proceedings from the Second Nordic Conference on Multimodal Communication. Gothenburg 2005.* (Gothenburg Papers in Theoretical Linguistics 92.) Gothenburg: Göteborgs Universitet.

Andersch, Elizabeth G., Lorin C. Staats, and Robert N. Bostrom. 1969. *Communication in Everyday Use.* New York: Holt Rinehart & Winston.

Antos, Gerd. 1996. *Laien-Linguistik. Zum Verhältnis von Laien und Experten in der Sprachwissenschaft. Studien zu Sprach- und Kommunikationsproblemen im Alltag am Beispiel von Sprachratgebern und Kommunikationstrainings.* Tübingen: Niemeyer.

Atkinson, J. Maxwell. 1982. Understanding formality. Notes on the categorization and production of "formal" interaction. *British Journal of Sociology* 33: 86–117.

Auer, Peter. 1999a. Ausdruck—Appell—Darstellung (Karl Bühler). In: Peter Auer. *Sprachliche Interaktion. Eine Einführung anhand von 22 Klassikern*, 18–29. (Konzepte der Sprach- und Literaturwissenschaft 60.) Tübingen: Niemeyer.

Auer, Peter. 1999b. Sprachfunktionen. Roman Jakobson. In: Peter Auer. *Sprachliche Interaktion. Eine Einführung anhand von 22 Klassikern*, 30–38. (Konzepte der Sprach- und Literaturwissenschaft 60.) Tübingen: Niemeyer.

Austin, John L. 1962. *How to Do Things with Words.* Oxford. Austin, John L. 1964. *Sense and Sensibilia.* Reconstructed from the manuscript notes by Geoffrey James Warnock. Oxford: Oxford University Press.

Bergmann, Jörg R. 1981. Ethnomethodologische Konversationsanalyse. In: Peter Schröder and Hugo Steger (eds.), *Jahrbuch. 1980. des Instituts für deutsche Sprache. Dialogforschung*, 9–51. Düsseldorf: Schwann.

Bergmann, Jörg R. 1994. Ethnomethodologische Konversationsanalyse. In: Gerd Fritz and Franz Hundsnurscher (eds.), *Handbuch der Dialoganalyse*, Tübingen: Niemeyer.

Bergmann, Jörg R. and Thomas Luckmann. 1995. Reconstructive genres of everyday communication. In: Uta Quasthoff (ed.), *Aspects of Oral Communication*, 289–304. Berlin, New York: de Gruyter. Bilmes, Jack. 1988. The concept of preference in conversation analysis. *Language in Society* 17: 161–181.

Birkner, Karin. 2001. *Bewerbungsgespräche mit Ost- und Westdeutschen. Eine kommunkative Gattung in Zeiten gesellschaftlichen Wandels.* Tübingen: Niemeyer.

Blum-Kulka, Shoshana. 1997. *Dinner Talk. Cultural Patterns of Sociability and Socialization in Family Discourse.* Mahwah, NJ/London: Lawrence Erlbaum. Boas, Franz. 1965. *General Anthropology.* Boston: Heath. First published Boston [1938].

Button, Graham. 2000. The ethnographic tradition and design. *Design studies* 21: 319–332.

Bühler, Karl. 1990. *Theory of Language. The Representational Function of Language.* Translated by Donald Fraser Goodwin. Amsterdam/Philadelphia: John Benjamins.

Bühler, Karl. 1999. *Sprachtheorie: Die Darstellungsfunktion der Sprache.* Mit einem Geleitwort von Friedrich Kainz. 3rd edition. Stuttgart: Lucius & Lucius. First published Jena: Fischer [1934].

Deppermann, Arnulf and Thomas Spranz-Fogasy (eds.). 2002. *Be-deuten. Wie Bedeutung im Gespräch entsteht.* Tübingen: Stauffenburg Verlag. Drew, Paul and John Heritage (eds.). 1992a. *Talk at Work. Interaction in Institutional Settings.* (Studies in interactional sociolinguistics 8.) Cambridge: Cambridge University Press.

Drew, Paul and John Heritage. 1992b. Analyzing talk at work: an introduction. In: Paul Drew and John Heritage (eds.), *Talk at Work. Interaction in Institutional Setting*, 3–65. Cambridge: Cambridge University Press.

Duranti, Alessandro and Charles Goodwin. 1992. Rethinking context. An introduction. In: Alessandro Duranti and Charles Goodwin (eds.), *Rethinking Context. Language as an Interactive*

Phenomenon, 1–42. (Studies in the social and cultural foundations of language 11.) Cambridge: Cambridge University Press.

Egbert, Maria. 2002. Der Reparatur-Mechanismus in deutschen und interkulturellen Gesprächen. Unpublished Habilitationsschrift. Oldenburg: Carl von Ossietzky Universität Oldenburg.

Eggins, Suzanne and Diana Slade. 2004. Analysing Casual Conversation. London: Continuum.

Erickson, Frederick. 2004. Talk and Social Theory. Ecologies of speaking and listening in everyday life. Cambridge: Polity Press.

Firth, Alan. 1994. The Discourse of Negotiation. Studies of Language in the Workplace. Oxford: Pergamon.

Firth, John Rupert. 1937. The Tongues of Men. London: Watts.

Firth, John Rupert. 1957a. Papers in Linguistics: 1934–1951. London: Oxford University Press.

Firth, John Rupert. 1957b. Studies in linguistic analysis. Oxford: Blackwell.

Firth, Raymond (ed.). 1970. Man and Culture. An Evaluation of the Work of Bronislaw Malinowski. London: Routledge and Kegan Paul. First published London [1957].

Ford, Cecilia E., Barbara A. Fox, and Sandra A. Thompson (eds.). 2002. The Language of Turn and Sequence. New York: Oxford University Press.

Furchner, Ingrid. 2002. Gespräche im Alltag—Alltag im Gespräch: die Konversationsanalyse. In: Horst M. Müller (ed.), *Arbeitsbuch Linguistik*, 306–327. Paderborn: Schöningh.

Garfinkel, Harold. 1984a. *Studies in Ethnomethodology*. Cambridge: Polity Press. First published Englewood Cliffs, NJ: Prentice-Hall [1967].

Garfinkel, Harold. 1984b. What is ethnomethodology? In: Harold Garfinkel. *Studies in ethnomethodology*, 1–34. Cambridge: Polity Press.

Goffman, Erving. 1967. On face-work. An analysis of ritual elements in social interaction. In: Erving Goffman. *Interactional Ritual. Essays on Face-to-face Behavior*, 5–45. Garden City, NY: Doubleday. First published in *Psychiatry* 18(3): 213–231 [1955].

Goss, Blaine. 1983. *Communication in Everyday Life*. Belmont, CA: Wadsworth Publ. Co. Grice, H. Paul. 1989. Logic and conversation. In: Paul Grice. *Studies in the Way of Words*, 1–143. Cambridge, MA: Harvard University Press.

Halliday, Michael A. K. 1973. *Explorations in the Functions of Language*. London: Arnold.

Halliday, Michael A.K. 1978. *Language as Social Semiotic. The Social Interpretation of Language and Meaning*. London: Arnold.

Halliday, Michael A.K. 2007. *The Collected Works of M.A.K. Halliday*. Edited by Jonathan James Webster. 10 volumes. London: Continuum.

Halliday, Michael A.K. and Christian M.I.M. Matthiessen. 2004. *An Introduction to Functional Grammar*. 3rd edition. London: Arnold.

Hanfling, Oswald. 2000. *Philosophy and Ordinary Language. The Bent and Genius of Our Tongue*. London: Routledge.

Have, Paul ten. 1999. *Doing Conversation Analysis. A Practical Guide*. London: Sage. Heritage, John. 1984. *Garfinkel and Ethnomethodology*. Cambridge: Polity Press.

Hester, Stephen and David Francis. 2001. Is institutional talk a phenomenon? Reflections on ethnomethodology and applied conversation analysis. In: Alec McHoul and Mark Rapley (eds.), *How to Analyse Talk in Institutional Settings: A Casebook of Methods*, 206–217. London: Continuum.

Houtkoop, Hanneke and Harry Mazeland. 1985. Turns and discourse units in everyday conversation. *Journal of Pragmatics* 9: 595–619.

Hundsnurscher, Franz. 1995. Das Gebrauchsprofil der Wörter. Überlegungen zur Methodologie der wortsemantischen Beschreibung. In: Ulrich Hoinkes (ed.), *Panorama der Lexikalischen Semantik. Thematische Festschrift aus Anlaß des 60. Geburtstags von Horst Geckeler*, 347–360. Tübingen: Gunter Narr.

Hutchby, Ian and Robin Wooffitt. 1998. *Conversation Analysis*. Oxford: Blackwell.

Jakobson, Roman. 1960. Linguistics and poetics. In: Thomas A. Sebeok (ed.), *Style in Language*, 353–357. Cambridge, MA: M.I.T. Press.

Jefferson, Gail. 1996. On the poetics of ordinary talk. *Text and Performance Quarterly* 16: 1–61.

Kallmeyer, Werner. 1977. Verständigungsprobleme in Alltagsgesprächen. *Deutschunterricht* 19 (6): 52–69.

Kallmeyer, Werner and Fritz Schütze. 1976. Konversationsanalyse. *Linguistische Berichte* 1: 1–28.

Kawulich, Barbara B. 2005. Participant observation as a data collection method [81 paragraphs]. *Forum Qualitative Sozialforschung / Forum: Qualitative Social Research [On-line Journal]* 6(2). http://www.qualitative-research.net/fqs-texte/2–05/05–2-43e.htm (last access: November 23, 2007).

Keppler, Angela. 1995. *Tischgespräche. Über Formen kommunikativer Vergemeinschaftung am Beispiel der Konversation in Familen.* Frankfurt, M.: Suhrkamp.

Labov, William. 1972. *Sociolinguistic Patterns.* Philadelphia: University of Pennsylvania Press.

Langs, Robert. 1993. *Unconscious Communication in Everyday Life.* Northvale NJ: Aronson.

Lappé, Winfried. 1983. *Gesprächsdynamik. Gesprächsanalytische Untersuchungen zum sponanten Alltagsgespräch.* Göppingen: Kümmerle Verlag.

Larson, Charles U. 1981. *Communication. Everyday Encounters.* Prospect Heights, IL: Waveland Press Inc.

Leeds-Hurwitz, Wendy. 1990. *Communication in Everyday Life. A social Interpretation.* Norwood, NJ: Ablex Publ.

Levinson, Stephen C. 1992. Activity types and language. In: Paul Drew and John Heritage (eds.), *Talk at Work. Interaction in Institutional Settings,* 66–100. Cambridge: Cambridge University Press.

Lindemann, Petra. 1990. Gibt es eine Textsorte *Alltagsgespräch? Zeitschrift für Phonetik, Sprachwissenschaft und Kommunikationsforschung* 43: 201–220.

Malinowski, Bronisław. 1923. The problem of meaning in primitive languages. In: Charles Kay Ogden and Ivor Armstrong Richards (eds.), *The Meaning of Meaning. A Study of the Influence of Language upon Thought and of the Science of Symbolism.* With an introduction by J.P. Postgate, 296–336. London: Kegan Paul, Trench, Tubner & Co. First published London: Routledge & Kegan Paul [1923].

Malinowski, Bronisław. 1999. Argonauts of the Western Pacific. An account of native enterprise and adventure in the Archipelagoes of Melanesian New Guinea [Robert Mond expedition to New Guinea 1914–1918] (1922). London: Routledge. First published New York: E.P. Dutton [1922]

Malone, Martin J. 1997. *Worlds of Talk. The Presentation of Self in Everyday Conversation.* Cambridge: Polity Press.

Markee, Numa. 2000. *Conversation Analysis.* Mahwah, NJ: Lawrence Erlbaum. Nofsinger, Robert E. 1991. *Everyday Conversation.* Newbury Park: Sage.

Philips, Susan U. 1992. The routinization of repair in courtroom discourse. In: Alessandro Duranti and Charles Goodwin (eds.), *Rethinking Context. Language as an Interactive Phenomenon,* 311–322. Cambridge: Cambridge University Press.

Poggi, Isabella. 2007. *Mind, Hands, Face and Body. A Goal and Belief View of Multimodal Communication.* Berlin: Weidler Buchverlag.

Psathas, George (ed.). 1979. *Everyday Language. Studies in Ethnomethodology.* New York: Irvington.

Rothenbuhler, Eric W. 1998. *Ritual Communication. From Everyday Conversation to Mediated Ceremony.* Thousand Oaks: Sage.

Russell, Bertrand. 1905. On denoting. *Mind. A Quarterly Review of Psychology and Philosophy.* New Series XIV: 479–493.

Russell, Bertrand. 1957. Mr. Strawson on referring. *Mind. A Quarterly Journal of Psychology and Philosophy.* New Series. LXVI: 385–389.

Sacks, Harvey. 1987. On the preference for agreement and contiguity in sequences in conversation. In: Graham Buttonand John R.E. Lee (eds.), *Talk and Social Organisation,* 54–69. Philadelphia: Multilingual Matters.

Sacks, Harvey. 1995. *Lectures on Conversation.* Edited by Gail Jefferson, with an introduction by Emanuel A. Schegloff. Oxford: Blackwell.

Sacks, Harvey, Gail Jefferson, and Emanuel A. Schegloff. 1974. A simplest systematics for the organization of turn-taking for conversation. *Language* 50(4): 696–735.

Saussure, Ferdinand de. 1990. *Course in general linguistics.* Edited by Charles Bally and Albert Sechehaye with the collaboration of Albert Riedlinger. Translated and annotated by Roy Harris. London: Duckworth.

Schegloff, Emanuel A. 1968. Sequencing in conversational openings. *American Anthropologist* 70: 1075–1095.

Schegloff, Emanuel A. 1979a. Identification and recognition in telephone conversation openings. In: George Psathas (ed.), *Everyday Language. Studies in Ethnomethodology*, 23–78. New York: Irvington.

Schegloff, Emanuel A. 1979b. The relevance of repair to syntax-for-conversation. In: Talmy Givón (ed.), *Discourse and Syntax*, 261–286. (Syntax and semantics 12.) New York: Academic Press.

Schegloff, Emanuel A. 1995. Introduction. In: Harvey Sacks. *Lectures on Conversation*, ix–xliv. Oxford: Blackwell.

Schegloff, Emanuel A., Harvey Sacks, and Gail Jefferson. 1977. The preference for self-correction in the organization of repair in conversation. *Language* 53(3): 361–382.

Schneider, Klaus P. 1988. *Small Talk. Analysing Phatic Discourse*. Marburg: Hitzeroth.

Schulz von, Friedemann. 2007. Miteinander reden 1. Störungen und Klärungen. Allgemeine Psychologie der Kommunikation. 45. Auflage. Reinbek: Rowohlt. First published Hamburg [1981].

Selting, Margret and Elizabeth Couper-Kuhlen (eds.). 2001. *Studies in Interactional Linguistics*. (Studies in discourse and grammar 10.) Amsterdam/Philadelphia: John Benjamins.

Silverman, David. 1998. *Harvey Sacks. Social Science and Conversation Analysis*. Oxford: Oxford University Press. Strawson, Peter F. 1950. On referring. *Mind. A Quarterly Journal of Psychology and Philosophy*. New Series. LIX: 320–344.

Tannen, Deborah. 2005. *Conversational Style. Analyzing Talk among Friends*. Revised edition. Oxford: Oxford University Press. First published Oxford [1984].

Ventola, Eija. 1978. Structural study of casual conversation. In: M. Leiwo and A. Räsänen (eds.), *AFinLA—Finnish Applied Linguistics Association Yearbook 23*, 105–117.

Ventola, Eija. 1979. The structure of casual conversations in English. *Journal of Pragmatics* 3(3/4): 267–298.

Ventola, Eija. 1987. *The Structure of Social Interaction: A Systemic Approach to Semiotics of Service Encounters*. London: Pinter publishers.

Weber, Tilo. 1998. Shared background and repair in German conversation. Boulder, CO: University of Colorado, Boulder.

Weber, Tilo. 2002. Reparaturen—Routinen die Gespräche zur Routine machen. *Linguistische Berichte* 192: 419–454.

Weber, Tilo. 2003. There is no objective subjectivity in the study of social interaction. *Forum Qualitative Sozialforschung/Forum: Qualitative Social Research [On-line Journal]* 4 (53 paragraphs). http://www.qualitative-research.net/fqs-texte/ 2–03/2–03weber-e.htm (last access, November 27, 2007).

Weber, Tilo and Gerd Antos. 2005. Kommunikationstrainer/innen und Linguistik. Einseitige Betrachtungen zu einem wechselseitigen Isolationsverhältnis. In: Gerd Antos and Sigurd Wichter (eds.), *Transferwissenschaft. Wissenstransfer durch Sprache als gesellschaftliches Problem*, 57–74. (Transferwissenschaften 3.) Frankfurt, M.: Peter Lang.

Wittgenstein, Ludwig. 2002. *Tractatus logico-philosophicus*. German text with an Englisch translation 'on regard' by Charles Kay Ogden. London: Routledge. First published as *Logisch-philosophische Abhandlung*. Leipzig [1921].

Wittgenstein, Ludwig. 1953. *Philosophical Investigations*. Translated by Gertrude E.M. Anscombe. Oxford: Blackwell.

Wittgenstein, Ludwig. 1969. *The Blue and Brown Books. Preliminary Studies for the Philosophical Investigations*. Oxford: Blackwell.

Wood, Julia T. 2007. *Interpersonal Communication. Everyday Encounters*. Belmont, CA: Thomson/Wadsworth.

Wooffitt, Robin. 2006. *Conversation Analysis and Discourse Analysis. A Comparative and Critical Introduction*. London: Sage.

9

Counseling, Diagnostics, and Therapy

Peter Muntigl

1. Introduction

Over the years, linguistics seems to have been gaining a stronger foothold in psychotherapy research. By this I mean to say that discourse structures are increasingly being taken into account to help describe and explain how the production and evolution of meanings is realized in psychotherapeutic inter-actions. Whereas some researchers have suggested links between language and client narratives (Angus and McLeod 2004; McLeod 1997; White and Epston 1990) or language and levels of intended meanings (Stiles 1986), other researchers have made the more general argument that therapeutic activi-ties are primarily constructed in language (Anderson and Goolishian 1992; Meares 2004; McNamee and Gergen 1992).

But for all this (recent) attention given to language and the social con-struction of meanings, a brief glimpse of any of the above-mentioned research would quickly reveal that linguistic categories are rarely incorporated into the analysis. In general, scant attention is paid to the phonology, grammar, and semantics of utterances and the relationships between these linguistic levels. Client-therapist conversations are often restricted to being the means by which the analyst may discover *more important* psychotherapeutic processes. In some cases, the details of spoken interaction serve mainly as a stepping stone to cre-ating psychological categories (e.g., Rennie 1992) and in other cases, to reveal a certain psychotherapeutic process of client development (e.g., Leiman and Stiles 2001; Stiles et al. 2006).

The aims of psychotherapy researchers are certainly different from those of linguists and so it should not come as a big surprise to find that less empha-sis is given to linguistic than to psychological processes. Nonetheless, if lan-guage is argued to be so important in constructions of experience and social relationships, one might expect that more focus be placed on the linguistic and conversational resources that play a part in constructing meanings relevant to the therapeutic process.[1] In order to do that, psychotherapy researchers

---

[1] There are interesting exceptions to this claim. For instance, Freud's (1999a, 1999b) work on dreams and on jokes is illustrative of Freud's keen interest in words and their meanings. In his analysis of jokes, Freud (1999b) identified a variety of techniques in which the structure of words and clauses were modified or transformed with the aim of conveying a novel and humor-ous meaning. Although one could argue that Freud's analysis demonstrated a level

would need to develop a comprehensive model of language or, since models of language already abound in linguistics, to incorporate a model of language that best serves their aims.

Most linguists who adopt a functional as opposed to a formal approach to language, or to use the more general term *discourse analysts* in order to include researchers from anthropology, psychology and sociology with a strong interest in language use, proceed from the premise that language is a central resource through which we construe experience and social relationships as meaningful. Over the years discourse analysts have increasingly made therapy and counseling the target of their investigations. Research has not only focused on specific institutionalized social groups such as couples (Buttny 1993, 1996, 1998; Edwards 1994, 1995; Gale 1991; Kogan and Gale 1997; Muntigl 2004a, 2004b; Muntigl and Hadic Zabala 2008; Muntigl and Horvath 2005), children (Hutchby 2002), families (Aronsson and Cederborg 1994; Grossen 1996), "groups" (Wodak 1981, 1986, 1996), anorexic patients (Labov and Fanshel 1977), Aids patients (Peräkylä 1993, 1995; Peräkylä and Silverman 1991; Silverman 1994, 1997), and persons with psychiatric disorders (Fine 2006), but also on a range of psychotherapy schools, which include psychoanalysis (Billig 1999; Peräkylä 2004; Vehviläinen 2003), narrative therapy (Kogan and Gale 1997; Muntigl 2004a, 2004b), cognitive behavioral therapy (Antaki, Barnes, and Leudar 2005), family systems therapy (Peräkylä 1995) Rogerian client-centered therapy (Weingarten 1990), and experiential therapy (Muntigl 2005).

In general, the majority of discourse-based research on therapy and/or counseling has been informed by either of two diverse approaches to discourse analysis, namely, conversation analysis and systemic functional linguistics.[2] Both approaches are highly sensitive to the interactional details that speakers deploy in co-constructing an orderly, intersubjective world in common.[3] One major difference between these approaches is that conversation analysis constitutes "a *sociological* approach to the study of language and social interaction" (Heritage 2003: 2; italics mine), whereas systemic functional linguistic studies are predicated on *linguistic* analyses of texts, spoken or written, in context. Systemic functional linguistic analyses of spoken texts involve a description of the speakers' use of linguistic resources in construing experience and constructing social relationships. Language, as a meaning making resource consisting of phonology, lexicogrammar, and semantics, is functionally tied to social context in a bi-directional manner; language constructs social context and social context activates a meaning potential by which language choices

---

of sensitivity to linguistic structure and analysis, his ultimate aim was not linguistic but psychological; analyzing jokes can reveal something about the workings of unconscious processes.

[2] Muntigl's work, however, is informed by both approaches (see especially Muntigl 2004a; Muntigl and Ventola in press).

[3] A general overview of conversation analysis can be found in Atkinson and Heritage (1984) and Levinson (1983: chapter 6). Readers wishing to find out more about systemic functional linguistics should consult Halliday (1978, 1994), Halliday and Matthiessen (1999), or Martin (1992).

tend to be realized (for a useful discussion see Halliday 1999). Conversation analysis, on the other hand, is not principally informed by linguistics, and so this type of analysis may, but need not, include linguistic categories. Conversation analysts tend to focus more on the sequential organization of social actions and on how the details of talk can show how speakers are (or are *not*) producing shared understandings.[4]

The aim of this chapter, however, is not to argue for a specific approach to analyzing therapy or counseling, but rather to show that discourse-based research in this field can shed much light on how therapy and counseling, as social activities, are accomplished. Looking at the details of social interaction, whether grounded in linguistics or sociology, can tell us something about how clients and therapists come to shared or divergent understandings of experience and how therapeutic goals are realized in the moment-to-moment unfolding of conversational actions. The bridge between a linguistic/sociological description of interaction and the psychological processes involved in therapy may in all probability still be "under construction". The argument made here is that successful bridge building may best be accomplished by taking the details of talk into consideration, mainly because psychological processes are not independent of language structures. In fact, we may go so far as to say that phenomena such as "consciousness", "identity", "emotions", "psychopathology", and "development" are realized in the so-called micro, mundane, or everyday meaning making resources found in language and other semiotic systems. From this perspective, ignoring language means neglecting a significant area of how human sociality gets accomplished.

In order to topicalize the role of linguistics or language use, I draw my attention to a discursive practice that is centrally constitutive of therapy and counseling. The discursive practice of *diagnostics*, whether it is explicitly or implicitly realized through the use of everyday or technical terms, seems to be a component of most therapeutic activities. Although the term *diagnostics*, as in *making a diagnosis*, is sometimes equated with illness or pathology, I would interpret this term as referring more generally to how problems are socially constructed through language. In this way, diagnostics may involve the discursive construction of problems as a pathology that is internal to the organism, or equally, it may involve the discursive construction of a problem as socially shared.

In the remaining sections of this chapter, I discuss how diagnostic practices in therapy and counseling have been described in the discourse analytic literature. I begin by addressing the issue of how therapy has come to be seen as a social activity that comprises a range of discursive practices or genres, one of which involves diagnostics. Following that is a discussion of the various studies addressing the issue of problem diagnosis, which is then complemented by an illustration of how problem diagnosis can get derailed or off-track. Lastly, I conclude this article by suggesting some future directions that research on diagnostic practices in therapy may take.

---

[4] Comparisons of conversation analysis and systemic functional linguistics can be found in Muntigl (2004a) and Muntigl and Ventola (in press).

2. Therapy as Social Activity: Some Characteristics

How different are counseling and therapy from each other? The difference is given a fairly straightforward interpretation by some researchers. Gaik (1992: 276), for instance, claims that therapeutic practices are non-directive "and thus seek to avoid any prescriptive or directive role—in the interest of motivating the patient into further introspection, self-analysis, and eventual autonomy." Counseling, by contrast, is directive and primarily associated with the social actions of advice giving or providing guidance (Gaik 1992: 276). Silverman (1997: 6), however, argues that many counselors disagree with the attempt to equate counseling with advice giving, or even with the claim that counseling is vastly different from psychotherapy. What is advocated instead is that counseling be seen as comprising different activities, which are not limited to giving advice, but also include, for example, *giving general information* and *client advocacy* (Silverman 1997: 10–11).

Similar definitional problems to those of counseling may occur in the field of therapy or, as it is commonly referred to, psychotherapy.[5] Some of the difficulty with providing therapy with a unitary functional definition may be due to the diverse types of practitioners who claim to be doing therapy. As Garfield and Bergin (1986: 5) have argued, "counseling psychologists, school psychologists, social workers, psychiatric nurses, pastoral counselors, and a number of other professional groups participate in some type of psychotherapy or counseling." Because of this, Garfield and Bergin (1986: 5) go on to conclude that "it is evident that psychotherapy does not constitute a distinctive profession but rather is an activity that is performed by members of many different professions." It is perhaps mainly due to these reasons that Garfield and Bergin (1986: 8) have noted a strong trend towards eclecticism or "the lack of allegiance to any single theoretical system."

Because there is currently no agreement on what constitutes the defining features used to distinguish therapy from counseling or vice versa, I will use "therapy" as a cover term for therapeutic and counseling activities. In the sections to follow, I discuss some important ways in which the therapeutic activity has been conceptualized: the first is that therapy differs in certain respects from everyday talk; the second is that therapy is realized in various interconnected discursive practices or genres.

2.1. Institutional Talk

It has been generally argued that therapy is realized through a range of discursive practices that are institutional in quality. The term *institutional* is meant to serve as a contrast to what may be interpreted as "ordinary" or "everyday" (Drew and Heritage 1992: 21). Drawing from Levinson's (1979) paper on *activity types*, Drew and Heritage proposed that institutional interactions differ from ordinary conversation in three important ways. First, institutional talk

---

[5] Therapeutic practitioners most often refer to their profession as *psychotherapy*, but I will continue using the term *therapy* to include other non-accredited professionals who engage in an institutionalized activity that shares the basic features of psychotherapy.

orients to specialized institutional goals and identities. Second, particular forms of constraints, as for example restrictions on turn taking or topic selection, may be placed on the interaction. Third, institutional talk contains specialized inferential frameworks. For example, a client's expression of certain emotions such as anger or sadness may be given a "theory specific" interpretation by the therapist.

Ferrara (1994: 39) has proposed seven dimensions through which therapy can be differentiated from conversation, many of which index a particular type of modification or constraint that is placed on the interaction. These include *parity, reciprocality, routine recurrence, bounded time, restricted topic, remuneration,* and *regulatory responsibility.* Parity is an important dimension to consider in therapy because, unlike everyday conversation, conversationalists in therapy agree to enter into an unequal relationship. Other differences include non-reciprocal turn-taking patterns, the routine non-spontaneous recurrence of a specific social activity, the temporally bounded nature of the speech event, the restriction in what can be discussed, the exchange of money associated with professional services, and the ability of one conversational participant to regulate how the conversation may unfold.

2.2. Speech Event vs. Genre

Previous linguistic research has also shown that different types of communicative activities get accomplished during therapy (Ferrara 1994; Gaik 1992; Labov and Fanshel 1977; Muntigl 2004, 2006). Depending on the researcher's discourse analytic approach, these so-called communicative activities are given different labels such as *genre* (or *macrogenre*), *activity, social practice, speech event,* and *process.* Taking *genre* as a general rubric for the different theoretical views on communicative activities, Muntigl and Gruber (2005) have argued that genres are associated with specific characteristics. For example, genres have a stabilized yet flexible communicative structure that orients toward a social purpose. In therapy, for example, the communicative structure may be reflected in such activities as "getting background information on clients", "getting clients to present the problem", or "offering solutions to the problem". Further, such activities are often prospective in orientation and therefore purposeful. In this way, getting background information may lead into problem presentation, which may lead into finding ways of getting rid of the problem. Communicative structures in therapy also tend to be associated with specific situational contexts (and are realized in those contexts) and interpersonal roles. For instance, therapists do on average ask more questions than clients, which place the therapist in the dominant role of information seeker (Ferrara 1994: 38).

Two major approaches to therapy as communicative activity will be reviewed below.[6] In Section 2.2.1., therapy is described as a speech event, and in Section 2.2.2. as a macrogenre. Speech event related work on therapy is

---

[6] It should be emphasized, however, that for most of these studies on therapy it is difficult to identify a single core approach to language. In many cases, these studies are transdisciplinary in nature, drawing from a range of different discourse analytic frameworks.

based on the theoretical framework found in Hymes' (1972) ethnography of communication. Within this model, a speech event is defined as "a culturally recognized occurrence that centers around language; the therapy hour is a naturally bounded speech event containing many varieties of language use" (Ferrara 1994: 12). Macrogenre related work, on the other hand, is primarily informed by systemic functional linguistics, which centrally includes Martin's (1992) genre theory. According to Martin (2002: 269), the term *genre* is used for "configurations of meaning that are recurrently phased together to enact social practices." Some examples of everyday genres are narrative, recount, anecdote, service encounter, explanation, and discussion.

2.2.1. THERAPY AS SPEECH EVENT. As Hymes (1972: 56) previously stated, "the term *speech event* will be restricted to activities, or aspects of activities, that are directly governed by rules or norms for the use of speech. An event may consist of a single speech act, but will often comprise several." Speech event characterizations of therapy can be found in the work of Ferrara (1994), Gaik (1992), and Labov and Fanshel (1977). Labov and Fanshel claim that therapy should be characterized as an interview, in which a therapist attempts to extract information from a client. Ferrara (1994: 37), however, argues against this claim because seeking information is not the only, and perhaps not even the primary, activity that constitutes the therapy process. Instead, Ferrara proposes that therapy be subsumed under a larger class of speech event termed *consultation*. According to Ferrara (1994: 37), "consultations occur when one person, A, approaches a specialist, B, to receive assistance in planning future behavior or action, action that can be medical, legal, financial, or other." Different again is Gaik's (1992: 276) conceptualization of therapy as a speech event. Gaik turns his attention primarily to the communicative structure of therapy and the way in which specific language selections provide "contextualization cues" to the conversationalists that they are in a certain activity rather than another. He argues that therapy consists of two activities or modes, which he labels as therapeutic and counseling. The therapeutic mode is non-directive and is oriented to a discovery procedure of what the problem might be, whereas the counseling mode is directive, focusing more on giving advice or finding a solution to the problem.

Although speech event studies have largely focused on the situational contexts in which therapy is done, a significant part of this work, such as Labov and Fanshel's (1977) and Ferrara's (1994) examination of speech act sequences and story telling episodes, has also looked at the way in which language is used to construct these speech events. I would argue, however, that a much more detailed investigation of linguistic practices is needed, particularly if our aim is to learn more about the important role that language serves in the making of a diagnosis. In particular, more attention should be given to the lexicogrammar, and especially to how the therapist's use of grammar influences a client's understanding of "the problem". The macrogenre analysis shown below, which is based on systemic functional linguistic theory, offers an approach to investigating therapeutic practices (and, of course, other institutional or everyday forms of social interaction) that can remedy some of these shortcomings. By using this approach, it can be shown how the therapist's unique choice of linguistic/ grammatical structures has important consequences for the diagnosis of problems and for the subsequent unfolding of therapy.

2.2.2. THERAPY AS MACROGENRE. Macrogenre studies on therapy take communicative structure as a main point of departure. One of the main goals in this type of analysis is to map the therapy process as a system of interconnected genres or macrogenres (Muntigl 2004a, 2004b, 2006). Although many different types of activities are realized during therapy, a macrogenre analysis places its main focus on those activities that centrally involve the discursive negotiation of problems.[7] In other words, the dominant interest lies in identifying the textual unfolding or *logogenesis* of problems and the discursive practices that form a component part of this activity.

Figure 1 illustrates how problem logogenesis in therapy can be modeled in terms of genres. In his examination of the narrative counseling interview, Muntigl (2004a) argued that the overall interview consisted of two main activities, namely *problem construction* and *problem effacement*. Furthermore, these activities or genres are composed of discrete sub-activities or stages, which include *problem identification* and *problem agency* for problem construction as well as *identification of alternative events* and *alternative event/ client agency* for problem effacement. Lastly, the stages involving problem or alternative event identification can be further sub-divided into formulation-reformulation sequences. The genres and stages are sequentially ordered and goal-directed: problems, and subsequently alternative behaviors, are identified so that their causal influences may be explored. This macrogenre representation is modeled in terms of constituency, but see also Muntigl (2006) for non-constituency based representations of narrative counseling.

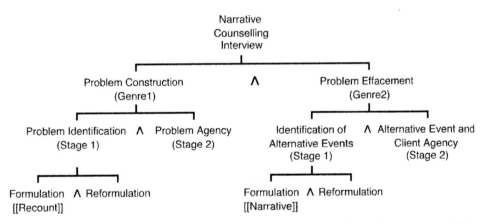

Figure 1.   A constituency representation of the macrogenre and staging structure of the Narrative Counseling Interview (cf. Muntigl 2004a: 119).

---

[7] This "problem-focus" is consistent with the practice of many psychotherapy researchers, who have foregrounded the notion of "problem" in their description of the therapy process. Some examples include *problem formation* and *problem resolution* (Watzlawick, Weakland, and Fisch 1974), *problem-organizing* and *problem-dis-solving* systems (Anderson and Goolishian 1992: 27), and *problem evolution* and *problem dissolution* (Eron and Lund 1993).

An example of problem logogenesis within problem construction, taken from session 3 of couples therapy, is shown in Ex. (1).[8] Wendy (W) recounts her experience of feeling that she is letting down Fred, her spouse, when she does not convey more enthusiasm in situations where they must make joint decisions (see arrowed lines 18–20). Some lines later, the therapist (T) makes a specific referential tie to W's previous formulation by embedding it within a nominal group ("this *letting him down*"; "the history of this idea of *letting him down*"). Through this form of grammatical transformation, T not only draws special attention to W's behavior of "letting him down", he also creates new possibilities for interpreting this behavior. In lines 82–86, W's behavior is placed in a causal relationship in which "this idea of letting him down" is construed as an agent that brings about guilt and fear.

(1)

PROBLEM CONSTRUCTION *"this letting him down"*
<u>Session 3</u>: *Problem Identification*

01	W:	I started
02		but then I I just I've I've lost my uh .hh uh
03		I'm not sure exactly
04		what or how I c'n how I c'n put it dow::n with .hh (0.8)
05		and Fred is tentative in approaching me with anything
06		y'know he's he's got this
07		an he's .hh he's i looked at it fo:r twenty five minutes half hour .hh
08		an he thinks
09		okay this would be really goo:d
10		an then he'll come to me:::
11		an sa:y
12		um uh .hh have yuh thought about
13		what zuh wanna do:: tomorrow or or the next da::y
14		an I will say
15		oh god (.) I can't think that far ahead
16	T:	awright
17		(0.8)
→ 18	W:	a:nd uh then (0.8) I begin to fee:l
→ 19		like I'm letting him down (1.0)
→ 20		cause I'm not enthusiastic about it
21		an I: uh I don't wanna go out anyway (.)
22		I don't wanna (1.0) yeah=
23	T:	=mhm

.
.
.

→ 71	T:	okay su so so you started talking
→ 72		bout um (.) um this letting him down. (.)
73		yeah. now you don't know for sur:e

---

[8] The transcript notation system used for the examples is taken from Atkinson and Heritage (1984: ix-xiv).

```
      74              if you're letting him down? [u::m]
      75     W:       [no]
      76     T:       you're goin on in your head=
      77     W:       =yes
   → 78     T:       u::m what's the history of this idea of letting him down
      79              (2.0) does this go back [a long way]
      80     T:       [it goes ] back quite a long way yeah
      81              (7.5)


                     Session 3: Problem Agency
   → 82     T:       hh does w: this when you when you when you experience
   → 83              this idea that I'm letting him down=
      84     W:       =yeah=
   → 85     T:       =w::: what kinda feelings come with that
   → 86              you mentioned guilt
      87              (1.2)
      88     W:       yes. guilt and uh (1.5) and fear (1.2)
      89              fear that (1.0) he will (1.5) he will do it anyway (1.0) without me
      90              (.) and he'll find some other lady that he likes better than me
```

This first genre of narrative therapy, problem construction, can also be interpreted as a diagnostic genre in which a "problem diagnosis" is made. Problem diagnosis is a 2-step process consisting of 1) grammatically transforming a client's utterance by embedding it within a nominal group, and 2) associating the "embedded" behavior with agency. The evidence for claiming that a problem has been identified by the therapist and client comes from two sources. The first is found in the repeated, consistent grammatical realizations of "letting him down" over the course of therapy. The second relates to the range of additional meanings that are bound up with the use of "letting him down". In order to discursively construct a problem, one must do more than simply *name* it. Additionally, a problem must be given a prospective reading, in the sense that the identification of a problem will implicate further discursive work on the part of the client and therapist. Put differently, problems in narrative therapy have a unique discursive trajectory, in which the naming of a problem leads to the exploration of how the problem is influencing the client's life, especially in terms of what the client thinks and feels. A detailed examination of problem logogenesis in narrative therapy is found in Muntigl (2004a: 179–232).

A genre is identified though unique linguistic patterns, which are jointly produced by the conversationalists. For example, therapist reformulations in problem construction involve the embedding of (part of) the client's formulation within a nominal group. One could say "this letting him down" originated in the client's prior wording of experience, thereby making problem identification a jointly managed activity. But the construction of a problem does not usually signal the end of therapy. If it did, the overall relevance of therapy could certainly be questioned. For the most part, problems are constructed so that they may be gotten rid of and another part of therapy, termed *problem effacement*, is devoted to this "getting rid of" activity. Although I will not discuss problem effacement in this chapter, mainly because the focus here is exclusively on problem diagnosis, readers may consult Muntigl (2004a: 239–240) for a description of this shift in meaning in which W's behavior moves from the "problem-laden" description of "I begin to feel like I'm letting him down" to the alternative description of "no:: I am not going to do that".

In sum, a macrogenre analysis gives insight into how diagnostic genres are produced during therapy and, more generally, how different genres work together to both construct and efface problems. What this brief analysis has shown is that specific genres are associated with unique linguistic structures. By delving more into a speaker's use of grammar, more can be said about what the speaker is "doing" and what activity the speaker is playing a part in co-constructing. This grammatically-informed approach to discourse can also be directed to other, more specific, therapeutic practices. In Section 3, special attention is given to the issue of problem diagnosis, by 1) examining in more linguistic detail the range of discursive practices used to identify problems and 2) suggesting that the *how* of problem diagnosis is related to a specific therapeutic vision.

3. Problem Diagnosis

White and Epston (1990: 6) provide a list of useful analogies that depict how the construction of problems has been viewed in various (social) scientific theoretical frameworks. In the positivistic physical sciences, problems are equated with "damage" or a "breakdown" that needs to be repaired or corrected. Biological models of problems, on the other hand, are associated with pathology, the correct diagnosis of the pathology, and the removal of the pathology. These two theories place problems squarely within the individual, with treatment aimed at repairing that part of the organism that is malfunctioning. Social scientific interpretations of problems differ in significant ways from the physical and biological models outlined above. Here, problems tend to be given an "inter-organism" perspective in which problems need to include but move beyond the individual, to include the individual's social context. White and Epston argue that these social scientific perspectives view problems in terms of a game, a living room drama, a rite of passage, or a behavioral text.

Basically, White and Epston (1990) are suggesting that our overall view of problems will depend on our theoretical background. A therapist who believes in the biological model will most likely attempt to diagnose problems as a certain type of illness. On the opposite side of the spectrum, a narrative therapist will diagnose problems as the social construction of oppressive dominant stories. In this way, the communicative structures and specialized institutional frameworks realized in therapy relate to what Goodwin (1994) has termed a *professional vision*. This means that the therapist's specialized ways of using language correspond to the therapist's "theory" or special way of construing client experience. The therapist's unique ways of diagnosing problems will point to a certain "view" that the therapist brings to bear on how the client's social world is being understood and consequently shaped.

In order to discover how therapists are diagnosing problems, we need to look at the detailed linguistic practices that are used in the making of a diagnosis.

One way of pursuing this aim is to examine how problems are described. Do therapists use a specialized technical terminology in describing problems or are more "everyday" formulations used? Another way of shedding light on the discursive practices of problem diagnosis is to examine the broader context in which problems are identified. For instance, what is the activity within which problem descriptions are realized and what other types of social actions and conversational moves are associated with the actual diagnosis?

3.1. Everyday vs. Technical Descriptions

An examination of the precise way in which problems have been described can divulge much information about the therapist's theory. One useful yardstick that can be used in classifying problem descriptions draws from the distinction made between *commonsense* or *everyday* vs. *technical* taxonomies (Martin 1993; Wignell, Martin, and Eggins 1993). What is a technical term and how can such a term be differentiated from an everyday term? Wignell, Martin, and Eggins (1993: 144–145) suggest the following answer:

> Technicality [. . .] refers to the use of terms or expressions (but mostly nominal group constituents) with a specialized field-specific meaning. For example, the term duck has a different meaning for the cricketer (e.g., out for a duck) as opposed to the bridge player (e.g., to duck a trick), or the haberdasher (e.g., a kind of cloth); and none of these meanings will be equivalent to the commonsense vernacular meaning (a bird with webbed feet and a flat beak).

Technical terms can be expressed as things or nominals in a number of ways. Some examples taken from the field of linguistics will serve to illustrate this point (but see Wignell, Martin, and Eggins 1993: 145–146 for the diverse ways in which technicality is construed in Geography): a technical term may consist of a single noun (e.g., *phonology, morphology, syntax*), a nominal group compound appearing in a Classifier ^ Thing structure (e.g., *Functional Linguistics, Formal Linguistics, Applied Linguistics*), or a nominalization (e.g., *clefting, dislocation, raising*). Technical terms tend to be field-specific, which means that the terms are meaningfully bound to specific institutions and are given a precise interpretation within those institutions. The work of Ravotas and Berkenkotter (1998) provides us with some interesting examples from therapy. The therapist that they examined produced a variety of diagnoses involving technical terms such as *post-traumatic stress disorder, major depression,* and *mixed personality disorder.* These terms not only constitute the typical Classifier ^ Thing nominal structure of technicality, they also draw from a psychiatric register contained within the Diagnostic and Statistical Manual of Mental Disorders IV (Ravotas and Berkenkotter 1998: 212). This means that the meaning of these terms is entrenched within a psychological taxonomy that cannot be confused with everyday interpretations of these terms. For example, the compound *major depression* is associated with illness and not with a vernacular understanding of "being depressed". Furthermore, the term *major* does not simply describe depression (you cannot, for instance, upgrade this term by saying "very major"), but classifies it as a distinct type of depression with specific implications regarding treatment. Ravotas and Berkenkotter are also careful to point out that these technical terms are not directly derived from what clients have said. The client never specifically mentioned that she had a "traumatic stress disorder". Instead, client utterances such as "nauseated by turpentine" are interpreted as a symptom of "intense physical and psychological stress to a memory cue" relating directly to post-traumatic stress disorder (Ravotas and Berkenkotter 1998: 226).

If technicality is associated with field-specific taxonomies, commonsense terms must then be associated with the everyday organization of meaning or knowledge. What this means is that commonsense terms relate to everyday experience rather than the specialized inferential frameworks and goal-directed meanings associated with "institutional" experience. A nice illustration of the difference between technical and commonsense taxonomies is given in Martin (1993: 205–206). Whereas a commonsense taxonomy of infectious diseases would place chickenpox under the general category of *childhood diseases*, a medical taxonomy would classify chickenpox as a *viral disease* of the type *herpes zoster*.

An example of an "everyday" problem was shown in Ex. (1). The term "letting him down" was not derived from an institutional source such as a manual of psychological illnesses. The problem, instead, was derived from the client's articulation of everyday experience in which she expressed a difficulty in refusing to comply with her husband's requests. We also saw that in the process of making a diagnosis, although the therapist grammatically transformed what the client had said, a close connection was maintained with the client's own words. This type of transformation initiated by the therapist is commonly referred to as a discursive practice of abstraction, in which a grammatical unit becomes embedded within another unit, or even becomes nominalized (for a discussion see Martin 1993). What also differentiates these "problem" terms from technical terms is that, unlike technical terms, problem formulations do not remain consistent, but vary in their expression (see Martin 1991: 317 for a discussion of non-technical terms used in history texts). This variability of expression for two different problems, *letting him down* and *being reserved*, is recorded in Table 1 (expressions appear in actual order of occurrence, so that "this letting him down" appears before "the history of this idea of letting him down", etc.). For example, *letting him down* is expressed as a non-finite or finite clause (the nonfinite variety is much more common) and also appears with a different complement (letting *others*

Table 1. A list of the different expressions for the problems "letting him down" and "being reserved"

"Letting him down"	"Being reserved"
—this letting him down	—reserved
—the history of this idea of letting him down	—this idea about about being reserved
—this idea that I'm letting him down	—reserveness
—under the influence of letting others do:w::n	—reservation

do:w:n). Even more variability was found for "being reserved", since it began as an adjective, then became an embedded clause, and finally ended up as (two different!) nominalizations (reserveness, reservation).

An examination of the nominal group structure of these expressions reveals further diversity (see Table 2). If the problem is embedded within a nominal group, it is most commonly realized as the Qualifier of the Thing or head noun. The verb of the embedded clause tends to be realized as a non-finite, present participle construction (e.g., lett*ing*, be*ing*). In its non-finite form, the problem lacks a subject. The therapeutic relevance of these non-finite constructions is that the client (or the client's spouse) no longer becomes directly associated with having that behavior (compare "this letting him down" with "this *you*'re letting him down"). This is in line with what White and Epston (1990) have dubbed *externalizing the problem*. The aim of this externalization is to stop clients from producing what White (2001) terms *negative identify conclusions*, in which the client believes that a behavior such as "letting him down" is an inherent part of the client's identity (Discussions of externalizing practices in narrative therapy are found in Muntigl 2004a: 181, 194; 2004b). The present participle realization of problems may also have additional therapeutic relevance. The form "*letting* him down" is realized in the imperfective (or *realis*) which signals ongoing, habitual behavior (see Halliday 1994: 278). Because the behavior is not a one-time occurrence, the therapist may make the inference that the client's habitually (negatively-laden) construal of experience will be nourishing grist for the therapeutic mill.

A further feature of everyday problems is also the variety of meanings, in this case clause-internally, with which the problem is associated. For instance, "letting him down" qualifies a variety of nouns such as "history", "idea", and "influence" (see Table 2). There are many meanings *packed* within these nominal groups and if we were to unpack them, we may come up with a series of expanded meanings such as 1) the idea of letting him down has a history; 2) letting him down is the product of a certain type of thinking or idea; and 3) thinking that you are always letting others down may influence your life (negatively!).

To sum up, I argued that a *technical* problem diagnosis construes the client's talk as a "symptom" that relates to a type of illness/disorder. *Everyday* problem diagnosis, on the other hand, construes the client's talk as everyday behavior. Diagnosis, however, involves more than wording a problem in a technical or commonsense manner. As Martin (1991) has pointed out, practices of technicality and/or abstraction also involve a certain kind of reasoning or interpretation. It is to these practices that we turn in the next section.

Table 2. The nominal group structure of "letting him down"

Deictic	Thing	Qualifier
This	letting him down	
The	history	of this idea of letting him down
This	idea	that I'm letting him down
The	influence	of letting others do:w::n

3.2. Relating and Interpreting Client Experience

Another important aspect of problem diagnosis involves the therapist's interpretation of the client's talk. This activity of interpreting has most commonly
been examined with respect to therapist formulations or reformulations. The
term *formulation* draws primarily from conversation analytic work and refers
to "the provision of candidate readings for the sense established in preceding
stretches of talk" (Heritage and Watson 1979: 141). These candidate readings
generally do the work of providing the gist or an upshot of what a previous
speaker had said (for examinations of formulations in therapy see Antaki et al.
2005; Davis 1986; Hak and de Boer 1996). The term *reformulating*, by contrast,
often draws from linguistics to include a wider range of rhetorical conjunctive
relations such as clarifying, generalizing, particularizing, exemplifying and
adjusting (see Muntigl 2007).

The interest in (re)formulating, however, goes beyond its conjunctive meaning. By reformulating, therapists tend also to create relevant links between
the client's different modes of experience. This specific focus on how therapists
go about interpreting the client's talk has recently been given due attention
in research on psychoanalysis (Perakyla 2004; Vehvilainen 2003). According
to Perakyla (2004: 297), "the analyst often builds up sequences that enable
him or her to re-explicate the patient's experience in ways that create a match
between its different domains, thus making the potential linkages possible."
This practice of making links is, in all likelihood, a general practice of therapy
and not a specific psychoanalytic practice. For if we return to problem construction in narrative therapy, we also find similar linking practices at work.
The therapist's reformulation of W's talk in Ex. (2) demonstrates how such
linkages are linguistically constructed. Following a series of negative apprais-
als directed at F, W's husband, T does two things that are highly relevant for
diagnosing a problem. First, as has already been shown to be typical for narrative therapy, he re-construes the client's prior formulation ("he likes to lecture? (1.2) on any: any subject . . .") as a nominal group ("this lecturing style").
Second, he relates the lecturing behaviour to W's experience through what in
systemic functional linguistics is called a *relational* clause. To put it a different
way, W's experience is linked to (*is represented by*) F's lecturing style.

your experience Wendy Sue	is	of uh living with a man who has a lecturing style
"x"	*relational verb* "is represented by"	"y"

(2)

    06   W: Fred is a: uh
    07   he likes to lecture? (1.2) on any: any subject
    08   that he feels even mildly uh uh y'know animated abou::t
    09   he likes to lecture
    10   and and go on and on and on and on about it .hh

.
.
.

→ 26   T: your experience Wendy Sue .hh is of uh living with a man
→ 27   who has a lecturing style
   28   W: yes

Additional "causal" links are made later on in the transcript, when T construes lecturing style as an agent. In this way, the lecturing style is made to be causally associated with W's feeling like a child (line 04), W's feeling ignorant (line 06) and W's feeling that she cannot grasp it quickly (line 07).

(3)
   01   T: what are y- impact or effect .hh does this lecturing style that you
   02   experience from Fred
   03   what does what impact does that have on you .hh as a person
→ 04   W: .hh oh well I it makes me feel like uh a child? .hh
→ 05   to a certain degree .hh it makes me feel
→ 06   like I'm (1.0) I'm ignorant
→ 07   that I can't grasp it quickly .hh umm

This section has shown that problem diagnosis may consist of a number of interpretative activities. In narrative therapy, problem diagnosis includes naming an everyday problem and making links between the problem and different domains of the client's experience, with a special emphasis on how the problem may be negatively influencing the client. These diagnostic practices do more than allow clients and therapists to put a label to the problem. The therapist's interpretations especially, since they make links to the client's different domains of experience, build up a complex network of problem-related meanings. This not only demonstrates the far-reaching influence that the problem has on the client's life, it also provides a forceful argument for continuing on with further therapeutic work.

3.3. Off-Track Diagnostic Practices: Resisting the Incitement to Talk

The examples presented so far have illustrated "successful" goal-oriented diagnostic practices at work. By "successful" I mean that problems undergo a specific genesis in which a problem is identified (i.e., named), followed by a series of interpretive practices that link problems to different domains of client experience. As can be expected, there are instances where, for some reason or other, problems do not unfold in the manner that is typical for the specific therapeutic vision being deployed. In these situations, we may speak of a diagnostic practice becoming "off-track" or slightly de-railed from the expectations constitutive of the therapeutic approach.

Counseling, diagnostics, and therapy 447

   In his work on child counseling, Hutchby (2002) identified one such off-track practice. Hutchby noted that, especially during the discussion of 'delicate' topics involving the relationship between a 6 year-old child and his parents,

the child would resist the incitement to talk by denying knowledge of the counselor's question. In these situations, children would utter explicit "don't knows",
often produced with marked stress and with minimal or no pause following the
counselor's prior turn. Furthermore, these denials of knowledge functioned as
a relatively successful attempt to actively close down the counselor's line of
questioning.

　　Denials of knowledge were observed to have a somewhat different conversational organization in couples therapy (Muntigl and Hadic Zabala 2008).
Consider Ex. (4), which contains an instance of "I don't know" (D=Dave;
L=Lisa; T=Female therapist). First, the denial of knowledge is surrounded by
"reluctance markers" such as pauses, prefaces (*usually I just-*) and accounts
(*nothing r↑eally↓ (0.5) I just feel that way↑*), which make it quite clear that an
"answer" is not immediately forthcoming. Second, the lengthy pause following
D's denial of knowledge implicates that D's "answer" is oriented to as expandable; that is, because T withholds from self-selecting a turn, T provides D with
an extra opportunity to say more. Third, the denial of knowledge is ultimately
followed by what Muntigl and Hadic Zabala term a *general expansion elicitor*
(*you just feel that way and↑*) in which T makes explicit to D that she wishes him
to continue talking. This example is a clear case in which problem diagnosis
gets side-lined; T's attempt at constructing a link between D's feeling like a
bad guy and subsequent behavior that is caused by this feeling does not receive
an uptake. But unlike the child counseling example, D is not attempting to
explicitly stop T from pursuing a response. As a result, problem diagnosis gets
stuck in limbo, with T endeavoring to elicit a response and D resisting, however subtly, the incitement to answer.

(4) 23-MR13 Session 4
```
    787   T:   and so when you:↓ (1.0) when you start to feel like the ba:d guy:↓
    788        (3.0)
    789        what do you do?
    790        (3.0) ((D directs gaze closer to L, tugs at hair with left hand))
    791   D:   usually I just- (1.5) ((slight shoulder shrug))
    792        I don't know
    793        nothing r↑eally↓ (0.5) ((partially covers mouth with left hand))
    794        I just feel that way↑
    795        (4.5) ((T maintains gaze at D))
→   796   T:   you just feel that way and↑ (1.0) ((D shifts gaze closer to T))
```

4. Conclusion

One of the main aims of this chapter has been to highlight the achievements
of linguistic-oriented approaches to therapy. It was shown that a detailed linguistic investigation of therapeutic talk can help us to understand how therapeutic practices are accomplished. In a general sense, we could say that one of
the therapist's main tasks is to provide a certain type of order and meaning to
the client's life. This order and meaning is, of course, related to the diagnostic
sense making practices of the therapeutic institution from which the therapist

is drawing. It was shown that one way of creating order is to re-construe client behavior as a technical or abstract term. This practice does not only transform meaning by placing the behavior within a different grammatical structure; it is also transformative in the sense that the new term will now be interpreted with respect to new institutional (or everyday) taxonomies and inferential frameworks. Another way of creating specific forms of social order is to make interpretative links between the client's different domains of experience. We saw in narrative therapy that this consisted of making representational and causal links between the problem and client behavior. Finally, diagnostic practices can become derailed, especially in situations where the client resists the incitement to answer by expressing uncertainty or by denying knowledge. Recent work by Muntigl and Hadic Zabala (2008) has explored how therapists attempt to get the interaction "back on track" by prompting the client to say more.

Our understanding of the discursive activity of problem diagnosis is most likely still in its infancy. What we now need to do is examine the diagnostic sense making practices from other therapeutic approaches and from practitioners stemming from different professions. Research that I am currently conducting with Adam Horvath from Simon Fraser University seeks to address some of these issues. This research draws from a total of 246 audio- and videotaped couples therapy sessions, involving 6 therapists and 41 couples.[9] One of the major aims of this study is to gain a better understanding of how therapy sessions are realized by a series of linguistic genres, how different therapeutic approaches may be differentiated in terms of these specific linguistic patterns and how different linguistic developments generate the particular changes the clients may experience in therapy. Such a focus should give us much more insight into the manifold ways in which problems are discursively bound up with human experience. It should also begin to shed more light on why certain diagnostic practices achieve their desired result within the interaction, while other practices do not.

Another important next step for discourse analysts, especially if their aim is to achieve a deeper understanding of therapeutic processes and the role that language plays in realizing these processes, is to begin a dialogue with psychotherapists about the relevance of language in psychotherapy. Some pioneers in this area are Charles Antaki from Loughborough University and Ivan Leudar from Manchester University. Since 2004, they have played an integral part in organizing an annual conference called "conversation Analysis of psychotherapy", which brings together conversation analysts, ethnomethodologists, and psychotherapy practitioners. The topics of this conference include all aspects of therapeutic interaction, and psychotherapists are encouraged to attend and articulate their own views of therapists' practices. I should think, however, that a psychotherapy forum that casts the net even wider to include other discourse analysts, such as systemic functional linguists, would provoke even more fruitful discussions. Perhaps we should be taking Halliday's advice, which suggests that researchers adopt a "problem-oriented" approach to social

[9] This research is supported by a Social Sciences and Humanities Research Council of Canada Standard Research Grant (No. 410–2004–1816).

interaction, rather than a "discipline-oriented" one. This would make it easier for others to join in the dialogue. It would also help to make the enterprise of psychotherapy research a truly transdisciplinary one.

References

Anderson, Harlene and Harold Goolishian. 1992. The client is the expert: A not-knowing approach to therapy. In: Sheila McNamee and Kenneth Gergen (eds.), *Therapy as Social Construction*, 25–39. London: Sage.

Angus, Lynne and John McLeod (eds.). 2004. *The Handbook of Narrative and Psychotherapy: Practice, Theory and Research.* London: Sage.

Antaki, Charles, Rebecca Barnes and Ivan Leudar. 2005. Diagnostic formulations in psychotherapy. *Discourse Studies* 7(6): 627–647.

Aronsson, Karin and Ann-Christian Cederberg. 1994. Conarration and voice in family therapy: voicing, devoicing and orchestration. *Text* 14(3): 345–370.

Atkinson, J. Maxwell and John Heritage (eds.). 1984. *Structures of Social Action: Studies in Conversation Analysis.* Cambridge: Cambridge University Press.

Billig, Michael. 1999. *Freudian Repression: Conversation Creating the Unconscious.* Cambridge: Cambridge University Press.

Buttny, Richard. 1993. *Social Accountability in Communication.* London: Sage.

Buttny, Richard. 1996. Clients' and therapists' joint construction of the clients' problem. *Research on Language and Social Interaction* 29(2): 125–153.

Buttny, Richard. 1998. Putting prior talk into context: reported speech and the reporting context. *Research on Language and Social Interaction* 31(1): 45–58.

Davis, Kathy. 1986. The process of problem (re)formulation in psychotherapy. *Sociology of Health and Illness* 8: 44–74.

Drew, Paul and John Heritage (eds.). 1992. *Talk at Work. Interaction in Institutional Settings.* Cambridge: Cambridge University Press.

Edwards, Derek. 1994. Script formulations. A study of event descriptions in conversation. *Journal of Language and Social Psychology* 13: 211–247.

Edwards, Derek. 1995. Two to tango. Script formulations, dispositions, and rhetorical symmetry in relationship troubles talk. *Research on Language and Social Interaction* 28(4): 319–350.

Eron, Joseph and Thomas Lund. 1993. How problems evolve and dissolve. Integrating narrative and strategic concepts. *Family Process* 32: 291–309.

Ferrara, Kathleen. 1994. *Therapeutic Ways With Words.* Oxford: Oxford University Press.

Fine, Jonathan. 2006. *Language in Psychiatry. A Handbook of Clinical Practice.* London: Equinox.

Freud, Sigmund. 1999a. *Die Traumdeutung [The Interpretation of Dreams].* Frankfurt a.M.: Fischer Taschenbuch Verlag. First published Wien: Deuticke [1900].

Freud, Sigmund. 1999b. *Der Witz und seine Beziehung zum Unbewußten [The Joke and its Relation to the Unconscious].* Frankfurt a.M.: Fischer Taschenbuch Verlag. First published Wien: Deuticke [1905].

Gaik, Frank. 1992. Radio talk-show therapy and the pragmatics of possible worlds. In: Alessandro Duranti and Charles Goodwin (eds.), *Rethinking Context. Language as an Interactive Phenomenon*, 271–289. Cambridge: Cambridge University Press.

Gale, Jerry. 1991. *Conversation Analysis of Therapeutic Discourse. The Pursuit of a Therapeutic Agenda.* Norwood, NJ: Ablex.

Garfield, Sol and Allen Bergin. 1986. Introduction and historical overview. In: Sol Garfield and Allen Bergin (eds.), *Handbook of Psychotherapy and Behavior Change*, 3rd edition, 3–22. New York: Wiley.

Goodwin, Charles. 1994. Professional vision. *American Anthropologist* 96(3): 606–633.

Grossen, Michele. 1996. Counseling and gatekeeping. Definitions of the problem and situation in a first therapeutic interview. *Text* 16(2): 161–198.

Hak, Tony and Fijgje de Boer. 1996. Formulations in first encounters. *Journal of Pragmatics* 25: 83–99.

Halliday, Michael A.K. 1978. *Language as a Social Semiotic*. London. Edward Arnold.
Halliday, Michael A.K. 1994. *An Introduction to Functional Grammar*, 2nd edition. London: Edward Arnold.
Halliday, Michael A.K. 1999. The notion of "context" in language education. In: Mohsen Ghadessy (ed.), *Text and Context in Functional Linguistics*, 1–24. Amsterdam: Benjamins.
Halliday, Michael A.K. and Christian M.I.M. Matthiessen. 1999. *Construing Experience through Meaning. A Language-based Approach to Cognition*. London: Cassell.
Heritage, John. 2003. Presenting Emanuel A. Schegloff. In: Carlo Prevignano and Paul Thibault (eds.), *Discussing Conversation Analysis. The Work of Emanuel Schegloff*, 1–10. Amsterdam: Benjamins.
Heritage, John and Rodney Watson. 1979. Formulations as conversational objects. In: George Psathas (ed.), *Everyday Language. Studies in Ethnomethodology*, 123–162. New York: Wiley.
Hutchby, Ian. 2002. Resisting the incitement to talk in child counseling. Aspects of the utterance 'I don't know'. *Discourse Studies* 4(2): 147–168.
Hymes, Dell. 1972. Modes of the interaction of language and social life. In: John Gumperz and Dell Hymes (eds.), *Directions in Sociolinguistics. The Ethnography of Communication*, 35–71. Philadelphia: University of Pennsylvania Press.
Kogan, Steven and Jerry Gale. 1997. Decentering therapy. Textual analysis of a narrative therapy session. *Family Process* 36: 101–126.
Labov, William and David Fanshel. 1977. *Therapeutic Discourse. Psychotherapy as Conversation*. New York: Academic Press.
Leiman, Mikael and William Stiles. 2001. Dialogic sequence analysis and the zone of proximal development as conceptual enhancements to the assimilation model. The case of Jan revisited. *Psychotherapy Research* 11(4): 311–330.
Levinson, Stephen. 1983. *Pragmatics*. Cambridge: Cambridge University Press.
Levinson, Stephen. 1992. Activity types and language. In: Paul Drew and John Heritage (eds.), *Talk at Work. Interaction in Institutional Settings*, 66–100. Cambridge: Cambridge University Press. First published in *Pragmatics* 3 (Microfiche) [1979].
McLeod, John. 1997. *Narrative and Psychotherapy*. London: Sage.
McNamee, Sheila and Kenneth Gergen. 1992. *Therapy as Social Construction*. London: Sage.
Martin, James R. 1991. Nominalisation in science and humanities: Distilling knowledge and scaffolding text. In: Eija Ventola (ed.), *Recent Systemic and other Functional Views on Language*, 307–338. Pittsburgh: University of Pittsburgh Press.
Martin, James R. 1992. *English Text*. Amsterdam: John Benjamins.
Martin, James R. 1993. Technicality and abstraction: Language for the creation of specialized texts. In: Michael A.K. Halliday and James R. Martin (eds.),*Writing Science: Literacy and Discursive Power*, 203–220. Pittsburgh: University of Pittsburgh Press.
Martin, James R. 2002. A universe of meaning—How many practices? In: Ann Johns (ed.), *Genre in the Classroom. Multiple Perspectives*, 269–278. Mawah, NJ.: Lawrence Erlbaum.
Meares, Russell. 2004. The conversational model: an outline. *American Journal of Psychotherapy* 58(1): 51–66.
Muntigl, Peter. 2004a. *Narrative Counselling. Social and Linguistic Processes of Change*. (Discourse Approaches to Politics, Society and Culture 11.) Amsterdam/Philadelphia: Benjamins.
Muntigl, Peter. 2004b. Ontogenesis in narrative therapy. A linguistic-semiotic examination of client change. *Family Process* 43(1): 105–124.
Muntigl, Peter. 2005. "So it's sort of like . . .": Linguistic strategies that 'open up' a client's construal of experience. Paper read at the 36th *Annual Meeting for the Society for Psychotherapy Research Conference*, Montreal, Canada.
Muntigl, Peter. 2006. Macrogenre. A multiperspectival and multifunctional approach to social interaction. *Linguistics and the Human Sciences* 2(2): 233–256
Muntigl, Peter. 2007. Reformulations. Transforming client meanings in psychotherapy. In: Wolfram Bublitz and Axel Hubler (eds.), *Metapragmatics in Use*, 235–262. Amsterdam: Benjamins.
Muntigl, Peter and Helmut Gruber. 2005. Introduction: approaches to genre. *Folia Linguistica* XXXIX/1–2: 1–18.
Muntigl, Peter and Loreley Hadic Zabala. 2008. Expandable responses: How clients get prompted to say more during psychotherapy. *Research on Language and Social Interaction* 41(2).

Muntigl, Peter and Adam Horvath. 2005. Language, psychotherapy and client change: An inter-disciplinary perspective. In: Paul Chilton and Ruth Wodak (eds.), *A New Agenda in (Critical) Discourse Analysis*, 213–239. Amsterdam: Benjamins.

Muntigl, Peter and Eija Ventola. In press. Grammar, genre and interaction. In: Carlo Prevignano and Paul Thibault (eds.), *Interaction Analysis and Language. Discussing the State-of-the-art.* Amsterdam: Benjamins.

Perakyla, Anssi. 1993. Invoking a hostile world. Discussing the patients' future in AIDS counseling. *Text* 13(2): 291–316.

Perakyla, Anssi. 1995. *Aids Counseling. Institutional Interaction and Clinical Practice.* Cambridge: Cambridge University Press.

Perakyla, Anssi. 2004. Making links in psychoanalytic interpretations. A conversation analytic perspective. *Psychotherapy Research* 14(3): 289–307.

Perakyla, Anssi and David Silverman. 1991. Owning experience. Describing the experience of other persons. *Text* 11(3): 441–480

Ravotas, Doris and Carol Berkenkotter. 1998. Voices in the text. The uses of reported speech in a psychotherapist's notes and initial assessments. *Text* 18(2): 211–239.

Rennie, David. 1992. Qualitative analysis of the client's experience of psychotherapy. In: Shake Toukmanian and David Rennie (eds.), *Psychotherapy Process Research. Paradigmatic and Narrative Approaches*, 211–233. London: Sage.

Silverman, David. 1994. Describing sexual activities in HIV counseling. The cooperative management of the moral order. *Text* 14(3): 427–453.

Silverman, David. 1997. *Discourses of Counseling.* London: Sage.

Stiles, William. 1986. Levels of intended meaning of utterances. *British Journal of Clinical Psychology* 25: 213–222.

Stiles, William, Mikael Leiman, David Shapiro, Gillian Hardy, Michael Barkham, Niels Detert and Susan Llewelyn. 2006. What does the first exchange tell? Dialogical sequence analysis and assimilation in very brief therapy. *Psychotherapy Research* 16(4): 408–421.

Vehvilainen, Sanna. 2003. Preparing and delivering interpretations in psychoanalytic interaction. *Text* 23(4): 573–606.

Watzlawick, Paul, John Weakland and Richard Fisch. 1974. *Change. Principles of Problem Formation and Problem Resolution.* New York: Norton.

Weingarten, Rudiger. 1990. Reformulierungen in der Gesprachspsychotherapie. In: Konrad Ehlich, Armin Koerfer, Angelika Redder und Rudiger Weingarten (eds.), *Medizinische und therapeutische Kommunikation: Diskursanalytische Untersuchungen*, 228–240. Opladen: Westdeutscher Verlag.

White, Michael. 2001. Narrative practice and the unpacking of identity conclusions. *Gecko: a journal of deconstruction and narrative practice* 1: 1–17.

White, Michael and David Epston. 1990. *Narrative Means to Therapeutic Ends.* New York: Norton.

Wignell, Peter, James R. Martin and Suzanne Eggins. 1993. The discourse of geography. Ordering and explaining the experiential world. In: Michael A.K. Halliday and James R. Martin (eds.), *Writing Science. Literacy and Discursive Power*, 136–165. Pittsburgh: University of Pittsburgh Press.

Wodak, Ruth. 1981. How do I put my problem? Problem presentation in therapy and interview. *Text* 1(2): 191–213.

Wodak, Ruth. 1986. *Language Behavior in Therapy Groups.* Los Angeles: University of California Press.

Wodak, Ruth. 1996. *Disorders of Discourse.* London: Longman.

10

Youth, Discourse, and Interpersonal Management

Jannis Androutsopoulos and Alexandra Georgakopoulou

1. Introduction

This chapter provides an overview of sociolinguistic and discourse-analytic studies of interpersonal management in youth communication. Although we will make use of the terms *adolescents* or *teenagers* in the research reviewed in this chapter, our own preference is for *youth*. The use of the term *adolescence* has come under recent criticism (cf. Bucholtz 2002; Wyn and White 1997) for two main reasons. Based on biological criteria, this term misleadingly suggests a homogeneous socio-cultural experience, which hardly corresponds to the real-life diversity of young people. Moreover, its rigid chronological boundaries ignore the increasingly fuzzy borders between life phases, as well as how social actors experience these borders. Adolescence is defined from the perspective of adults and adulthood as a transitional period marked by lack of autonomy and competence, judged against the normative benchmark of adulthood, and often associated with deviance from adult norms (cf. Bucholtz 2002).

As an alternative, the concept of youth displays some conceptual difficulties too, depending as it does on age borders and social institutions such as schooling and the job market, but it nonetheless offers a more flexible starting point for discourse-based research. Static conceptualizations of youth as a fixed-boundary period and as a transitional, developmental phase are being replaced by relational approaches, which foreground the relation of youth to adult, and child, categories. Youth is then determined "in relation to that which is interpreted as respectively childish or adult" (Fornäs 1995: 3). Such a relational concept of youth is well placed to integrate the fuzziness of youth, extended post-adolescence, and 'emerging adulthood' (Arnett 2006). Likewise, studies of youth culture have progressively shifted focus from class-based youth subcultures in Western societies to the diversity of youth-cultural expressions worldwide, and from deviation and resistance to life-style choices in a variety of ethnic groups and local communities (Shelton and Valentine 1998). Moving a step further, Bucholtz advances an approach that treats youth cultures not in relation to adult and child categories, but as social practices in their own right. Seen this way, the notion of youth emphasizes the here and now of experience, or put differently, the fact that "youth are cultural actors whose experiences are best understood from their own point of view" (Bucholtz 2002: 533).

Such a culturally focused notion of *youth* forms the backdrop for our examination of linguistic forms and discursive practices which have been found to typify the cultures of youth peer groups within sociolinguistics, ethnography, and conversation analysis. We structure our discussion around the discursive processes of aligning and converging on the one hand, setting boundaries and misaligning on the other hand. We depart from recent, practice-based studies, which locate language choices in specific sites and activities that the young people are engaged in (Section 2.). We then specifically look into language choices that are routinely mobilized in each case, that is, as part of interpersonal relationships of alignment (Section 3.) and misalignment (Section 4.). In both cases, we stress the importance of the peer-group either in leisurely or in institutional settings as a focal site for the discursive affirmation of relations of intimacy and solidarity, but also of conflict and hierarchy. We conclude by highlighting the importance of new types of interpersonal communication and community formation via digital media amongst young people (Section 5.).

2. Discourse Sites and Activities in Youth Communication

Earlier sociolinguistic research on adolescence focused on tiny linguistic items (mostly phonological variables), which were in turn mapped in a relatively straightforward way onto the social identity aspect under study (be it age, gender, or social class). From Labov's (1972) seminal study of sociolinguistic variation onwards, it had been acknowledged that the level of formality would shape the choice of language variants. There was also an attempt to collect data in situations that seemed typical of the participants' lives in addition or juxtaposition to those obtained from standard sociolinguistic interviews. It is notable that Labov (1972) himself also had data from the Inner City "hood" and Cheshire (1982) from the playground. However, the site as the social space in which communication occurred was seen more as an independent variable rather than as constitutive of and mutually feeding with the actual communication. This has recently changed within the variationist ethnographic paradigm of which Eckert's study (2000) is a good example. Using ethnographic methods, which included extensive fieldwork, Eckert closely attended to the local understandings and cultures of the female High School students she investigated and linked those with language choices.

However, the emphasis on variables at the micro-linguistic level (e.g., phonological, lexical) has gone hand in hand with a relative neglect of the role of suprasentential units, e.g., episodes, extended sequences, types of text, in the shaping of communication. Attention to such units is normally to be found in more discourse analytic or interactional paradigms. These recognize the importance of the type of sequence and type of activity for actual language choices as well as the fact that such choices are collaboratively produced between speaker and audience. The approaches here are too divergent to be made sense of in a homogenizing way. The concept of genre alone has been defined variously in various paradigms, and our aim here is not to rehearse the debate over what constitutes a genre, a discourse type, etc. (see papers in Gruber and Muntigl 2005). Nonetheless, it is important to note that recently there has been a shift from predominantly text-based analyses to practice-based analyses, as illustrated, e.g., in Androutsopoulos and Georgakopoulou (2003a). In practice-based analyses of youth communication, there is a focus on the socially and culturally recognized events in relatively stable (or typified) settings dedicated to specific communicative purposes and eliciting relatively routine ways of speaking; also, on the participants' roles and relations and their conventionalized expectations about what is to be done in those settings. The analysis then looks at language choices as being integrally connected with such genres (in a broad sense) or activity types. Put differently, activity types are seen as providing "sites of lived experience in which locally motivated linguistic choices can be creatively related to extra-situational social categories and meanings" (Androutsopoulos and Georgakopoulou 2003b: 7).

3. Aligning—Converging—Colluding

There is widely held recognition within socially minded linguistics that language varieties and repertoires play a vital role in the (re-)affirmation of a sense of belonging and of interpersonal relationships of intimacy and solidarity. In the case of research on youth, the exploration of this view has been closely linked with the assumption that socialization within the peer-group and leisure activities associated with it are of paramount importance in the particular life stage. As already suggested, within social sciences (particularly social psychology and anthropology), underlying this specificity of social and cultural practices is an emphasis on adolescence as a distinctive, biologically delimited, and transitional phase that inevitably presents certain differences and all too often conflictual relations with adulthood and adult authority (see Section 4. below). The assumption then is that adolescents tend to fashion their distinctiveness through formation and participation in close-knit groups of close friends.

Within earlier research on sociolinguistics, as we have suggested, this age-linked distinctiveness was explored in terms of linguistic variation: that is, through a focus on the frequency of certain variants in the speech of adolescents that set them apart from "adults". Phonological variants, particularly non-standard ones, were the ones that were mostly put under scrutiny in this respect. Again, there is an underlying assumption here that the speech of adolescents will somehow mirror their propensity for defying anything that is regulated, proper, and standardized, on the one hand, and for (re-)creating peer-group bonds through language convergence on the other hand. Cheshire's (1982) classic study of teenagers in Reading, England, is a case in point. In contrast to previous studies of sociolinguistic variation, Cheshire recognized the importance of social networks in the use of linguistic variants and clearly distinguished the participants she studied between core, secondary, and peripheral members in groups. In this sense, language variation was not only linked with an age-specific feature of socialization (i.e., the peer-group) but also with differentiated participation roles within the peer-group. In her study, language convergence correlated with the degree of integration into the group. On another level, gender proved to shape language use, which provided evidence for the by now widely held idea that it is impossible to talk about adolescence as an undifferentiated whole. In particular, adolescent boys were found to employ more non-standard forms, a finding which Cheshire linked with the covert prestige involved in this use in terms of a specific model of masculinity (based on machismo, sounding, and acting "rough") and of local allegiances. More recent studies by Cheshire and colleagues (e.g. Cheshire, Kerswill, and Williams 1999) have explored the role of adolescents in dialect leveling. The focus has been again on the use of non-standard variants by adolescents but with a comparative regional (three towns in England) and social class focus (working class vs. middle class).

Since the 1980s, sociolinguistic variation studies have become increasingly more contextualized and fine-tuned, and it is no accident that scholars nowadays talk about the current phase of inquiry as the "fourth wave" of variationist sociolinguistic research. It is also worth noting that many of these studies have employed data from "adolescents" (in the biological sense) whilst being interested in documenting how language variation shapes and is shaped by other identity categories, e.g., gender, ethnicity, social class. In this respect, adolescence has remained as a somewhat "hidden" or "unspoken" of category that is taken for granted (see Androutsopoulos and Georgakopoulou 2003b: 6).

The methodological ways in which peer-groups are being researched have also become more situated with an increasing emphasis on ethnographic studies that allow the researcher to develop a good sense of their subjects' emic understandings and local practices. In fact, language itself is increasingly seen as interwoven with social practices and the relationships between the two were documented. In Bucholtz's study (1999a) of high-school female students in California, two communities of practice were identified: the "nerds" and the "popular girls". The participants were recorded in and out of school and a contextually sensitive analysis showed that each of the groups was not solely defined in terms of language choice and repertoires but also in terms of attitudes to and participation in academic life, dating practices, and a host of semiotic choices, including dress code, etc. The language use emblematic of each group was also located in different levels, not just the phonological one, but also lexis, including creative and playful uses of language. Finally, the language ideologies of each group were found to differ, that is, their local theories of how language connects with social life and what is evaluated as good or bad language. This study is a good example of the gradual move within studies of language variation towards an understanding of how we construct identities through language that is based on dynamic and situated views of identities.

At the same time, it has to be noted that studies that may be called postvariationist or variationist ethnographic still work with quantifying language use in order to explore its relationships with social variables. There seems to be a tension then in the relevant literature between quantitative studies that involve a rather large number of participants and data, and qualitative, contextually sensitive studies that focus on how language is shaped within small peer-groups. The former employ phonological variation as their main point of entry inasmuch as they recognize that other language choices, e.g. discourse markers, are inherently multi-functional and thus less amenable to neat categorizing and quantifying.

Micro-analytic studies of specific discourse phenomena on the other hand have found it difficult to yield comparative findings and generalizations. That said, it is notable that the semiotic phenomena that have been proposed by numerous studies as markers or indicators of peer-group alignment and membership belonging form a relatively closed list (e.g., Andersen 1997; Corsaro and Eder 1990; Eble 1996; Eder 1993; Erman 2001; Ito and Tagliamonte 2003; Kallmeyer and Keim 2003; Kataoka 2003; Norrby and Wirdenäs 2003; Stenström 2003). The list includes:

- playful language, e.g., language puns, play with words, coinage of new terms and more generally creative uses of language, jokes-telling
- teasing
- nicknames
- more or less innovative and unexpected or incongruous (in the given cotext) mixings of language registers (e.g. formal—informal) and styles, mainly to humorous effects
- increased and innovative use of certain discourse markers (e.g. *like*), interjections (e.g., *sort of, you know, I mean*), extenders (e.g. *and stuff like that*), invariant tags (*right?, innit?, yeah?*), addressee-oriented tags (e.g. *you know what I mean?*). It must be noted here that there is a lack of consensus as to what is labeled as what in the literature, and some of the terms above are employed with overlapping reference.
- increased use of "intensifiers" (e.g., *so, just, really* followed by a qualifier) and more generally of expressive and affectionate elements, including manipulations of the graphemic code in cases of written language (see Section 5.)
- insulting or obscene terms (e.g., *bitch, fuck, shit*) that are frequently recast as terms of endearment and in-group bonding.

Specific generic forms have also been flagged up as being closely associated with intimate relationships. For instance, collaborative narration (e.g. Eder 1998) that involves various signals of audience participation, ranging from verbal and nonverbal back-channeling to ratification and enhancement of certain story parts (e.g. the climax); moreover, overlaps in turn-taking and various ways of "mirroring" or "echoing" the interlocutors' previous turn in order to stress agreement with the point made. In similar vein, it has been shown that linguistic choices that highlight in-group bonding and membership belonging (e.g. positive politeness strategies) are frequently mobilized in peer-group communication, and that there is a tendency for implicitness and heavy reliance on shared assumptions (e.g. Deppermann and Schmidt 2003; Schmidt 2004; Spreckels 2006). These are frequently alluded to more or less cryptically in order to reaffirm intimacy and sharedness through invoking the familiar, and to rejoice in the recognition of this sharedness. Media references, i.e., references to shared media experiences (e.g., songs, TV series), but also to shared stories from the interactional history of a group are hallmarks of an allusive style that can only be unpacked by the members of a close-knit group (see Georgakopoulou 2003b, 2007; Spreckels 2006; Shankar 2004). Such reaffirmations and repetitive uses of an in-group style of dense referencing may seem to the outsiders as communication about "nothing" inasmuch as it occurs in leisurely settings that involve young people "hanging out". The liminal aspects of such communication as suspensions of the norms of everyday engagement have been duly noted (Rampton 1995).

Nonetheless, it is also important to add a word of caution about the fact that what may be significant, serious, reportable, ordinary, or extra-ordinary is relative to contexts and participants. Code-switching phenomena are a case in point: studies of secondary school students in urban multi-ethnic environments have shown that not only is switching to a variety that is perceived as "ours" associated with affiliative acts, but also that speakers can perform alignments by crossing to a variety that is demonstrably not "theirs" (Rampton 1995). Such takings on of "other" voices have been found to complicate issues of membership authenticity and to level ethnically inflected divisions in favor of local cultures that base their participation on factors other than traditional lines of ethnic or social class belonging. These "new ethnicities as sites of cultural crossing, thresholds that young people move across as they carry on with their cultural business" (Bucholtz 2002: 538) have been closely associated with the context of late modernity in urban multi-ethnic setting and have often formed part of a celebratory discourse that recognizes the agency, creativity, and power of social actors to transcend established boundaries. That said, it is also recognized that the valency of such phenomena is contextually bound (cf. Dirim and Auer 2004). As we will see in Section 4., several of the very language choices that in certain contexts have been found to serve to highlight intimacy and convergence can also serve to accentuate boundaries and act disaffiliatively in other contexts.

4. Boundary Marking—Conflicting—Excluding

We now move on to studies of processes of demarcation and conflict in youth conversational interaction. Young speakers may set themselves apart from a variety or relevant others in discourse, and a broad distinction between intra- and intergenerational boundary setting has been proposed (Deppermann and Schmidt 2003; Schmidt 2004). On the *intra*-generational side, boundaries are drawn to peer-group members or to other youth groups; in the *inter*-generational dimension, to family and relatives, (unknown) adults or persons of institutional authority such as youth workers or schoolteachers. For instance, the teenage male group studied by Deppermann and Schmidt (2001a, 2001b, 2003) delimited itself from: other male youth groups perceived as having "deviant" lifestyles (e.g., gays, students); girls (categorized by appearance and moral criteria); adult figures of authority (such as teachers and youth workers); persons with some kind of authority in the local society; family members; and public personalities (e.g. celebrities).

In particular, rather than being characterized by an egalitarian ethos, youth peer-groups have been found to be shaped by hierarchies built and maintained through verbal interaction. Learning how to establish one's position in the group hierarchy is a major aspect of peer-group socialization; conversely, processes of status negotiation are important episodes in the social life of peer-groups. In this context, what has mainly attracted the attention of researchers is ritual conflict more than less unmitigated, on-the-record conflict talk. Ritual conflict is defined as playful, non-serious verbal dispute that is not aimed at conflict resolution (cf. Stenström, Andersen, and Hasund 2002; Grimshaw 1990). Ritual conflict has elements of performance, being carried out in front of a knowing and judging audience; it is instantiated in different formats/ genres, such as ritual insults, verbal duelling, or dissing; it typically is a multipart activity, including sequential rules (such as initiation, audience reaction, reply, reaction to reply, etc.) and conditions for acceptable propositional content; it is competitive, resulting in "winners" and "losers", without however ending in socially disruptive conflict.

A well known instance of ritual conflict is ritual insult, introduced in the linguistics literature by Labov's classic study on the "sounds" and "dozens" of African American male teenagers (Labov 1972), which are well-elaborated sequences of ritual insults with strict formal and semantic regulations. In similar practices of verbal duelling among Turkish boys (Dundes, Leach, and Özkok 1972; Tertilt 1996) the focus has been more on the symbolic sexual domination and humiliation of the opponent, which has to be asserted and countered in rhyming. Similar genres of ritualized verbal competition are common in other non-Western European languages and cultures, including the Mediterranean, Near East, Latin America, Africa, and Arabic countries. However, global population flows and popular media prompt an even wider spread, thus leading to localized, hybrid practices of ritual conflict among migrant offspring (Tertilt 1996) or even among youths from the majority group, as in the case of German youth appropriating "dissing" from the African-American hip-hop culture (Deppermann and Schmidt 2001b). Although ritual insult and verbal duelling are widely regarded as a specifically male adolescent practice, Stenström et al. (2002: chapter 8) identify a type of ritual conflict among working-class female speakers in London. Their "tough girls' talk" is not primarily competitive in nature, but it nonetheless resembles ritual insults in that it contributes to the development of self-defence strategies and verbal skills. Their playful disputes and staged fights also serve as a means to negotiate appropriate behavior for girls. That said, the line between playful and serious, non-mitigated conflict may be thin, and the choice between the two will often depend on social and contextual parameters such as age, social milieu, and the sort of territorial face-threat involved (cf. Cindark and Keim 2002).

Processes of hierarchy building and competitiveness within the peer-group have also been documented in Goodwin's (1990, 2006) study of African-American working class pre-adolescent groups of girls. Goodwin has specifically focused on a range of interactional activities such as assessment sequences, verbal duelling, stories as devices for sustaining and constructing the group's social and political organisation, as well as managing processes of inclusion and exclusion. Her study has been instrumental in debunking myths about boys' groups being competitive and girls' groups exhibiting a cooperative ethos (see also Branner 2003; Spreckels 2006).

An important type of resource for indexing and negotiating dissent in youth discourse is linguistic divergence on different levels of linguistic description. A first area is socially marked vocabulary, including *jargon, argot,* and *anti-language* (Halliday 1978). Such lexis is often taken to indicate by itself, i.e., through its formation patterns (as Halliday's notion of anti-language suggests; cf. also Kießling and Mous 2006), a delimitation of its speakers from "normal" social values. However, concrete interactional analyses of *how* such forms are deployed in interaction are rare. In two studies examining the use of slang in interactions between adolescents and adults, namely mother/daughter interactions (Augenstein 1998) and conversations between young people and adult field-workers (Schwitalla and Streeck 1989)—the youngsters' use of slang leads to misunderstandings which are subsequently repaired by the youngsters by offering equivalent non-slang lexis. In the case of fieldworker communication, however, the non-slang lexis offered by the young speakers shifted semantically from soft drugs to alcohol, and in this way "translated" a concept from the world of the local youth sub-culture into a concept seen as comparable for the world of adults. Such translation, and its celebration by young participants, sets clear boundaries between young insiders and adult outsiders and offers a nice illustration of the double function of argot/slang lexis as both a sign of belonging and a means of boundary-setting for the outsiders.

Code switching and style shifting are basic linguistic devices of signaling divergence (Giles, Coupland, and Coupland 1991), and studies of their use amongst youth people tend to concentrate on multiethnic or migrant peer groups, involving contrasts between mainstream colloquial varieties of the dominant language and minority (migrant) languages or ethnic styles of speech. For example, research on Turkish/German code switching and code mixing among young "ghetto" females (Keim 2007a, 2007b; Kallmeyer and Keim 2003; Keim and Cindark 2003) reported that negotiating the language of interaction is a fairly regular mechanism for indexing consent or dissent. In particular, when a mixed code is established as the base language of interaction, code switching at turn-taking points is a conventional device for emphasizing a clash of opinions between interlocutors.

Another focal concern in the literature are interactions in which peer-group members jointly produce boundaries to (absent) third parties, such as adult figures of authority or other young people with differing lifestyle orientations. Such episodes are common in the unstructured situations of hanging out that are typical of youth groups (see also Section 2. above), and they draw on resources such as social categorization devices, intertextuality, and stylization. Speakers work on their group profile *ex negativo*, i.e., through stylized representations of others. A key feature of such representations is that they tend to be heavily stereotyped, presenting out-group behavior as inadequate or even grotesque. The orientation of much youth group interaction to producing entertainment (Deppermann and Schmidt 2001a, 2003) favors such stereotypical other-styling. In Schwitalla's study, a group of high school students differentiate themselves from working-class youth from the same neighbourhood through the interactive staging of the latter, drawing to that end on a variety of social-symbolic resources, such as nonlexicalized sounds, stereotypical lexis, and pseudo quotations (double voicing). Here, social difference is evoked and performatively reproduced rather than explicitly discussed (Schwitalla 1994). Such stylized representations of the (supposed) voice of the other may be also achieved by style shifting to a (usually nonstandard) variety, or by intertextually exploiting mass-media voices (cf. Deppermann and Schmidt 2003; Deppermann 2007; Georgakopoulou 2005; Spreckels 2006; Bierbach and Birken-Silverman 2007). However, media allusions and quotations can also be used to directly discriminate and exclude peer-group members (cf. Schlobinski, Kohl, and Ludewigt 2003).

As the preceding discussion suggests, processes of linguistic divergence and stylization may resort to language crossing, i.e., the use of linguistic resources that are felt to belong to other social groups (Rampton 1995, 1999). As already discussed (see Section 3.), language crossing may also be a resource in acts of alignment; the type of crossing most relevant to boundary-setting activities is *varidirectional double-voicing* (following Rampton's 1995 adaptation of Bakhtin's terms): here speakers use social voices (other languages, non-standard varieties of the same language, voices lifted from mass-media sources), but clearly dissociate themselves from these voices, indicating that they are putting them on rather than identifying with them. This enables speakers to do and say things they would never say with their own voice, including showing-off, sexist, and racist aggression. Putting on alien social voices is consonant with the ritual, playful conflict we have already discussed as typical of youth interpersonal communication. It frames on-going interaction, including the propositional content of the utterance conveyed through that voice, as entertaining and non-serious, thus enabling the speaker to withdraw and deny responsibility for their statements in case they are interpreted by addressees as offensive (see also Deppermann 2007; Pujolar 2001).

While language crossing always evokes stereotypical associations of the legitimate, "authentic" speakers of the code crossed into, the code's associative potential may vary by referent, interlocutor, or other aspects of interactional context. Thus Rampton (1995) found that London adolescents used Stylized Asian English towards adult interlocutors to disrupt their attempts to impose interactional order or to challenge them by evoking a relationship of dominance between the adult figure of authority and the pupils. But among peers, Stylized Asian English was used to mark certain behaviors as inappropriate, improper, or marginal, alluding thereby to stereotypical lack of competence. In two strikingly similar cases, Eksner (2001) found that stylized Turkish German among Turkish youth in Berlin-Kreuzberg was used as a threatening device in conflict situations with German adults, but in in-group talk, where the default code for conflict talk was Turkish, it rather served to mock incompetence and to regulate group activities. The Turkish-German female teen ghetto group studied by Keim (2002) used stylized learner's German (*Gastarbeiterdeutsch*) towards their mothers, the authentic speakers of that code, to accentuate intergenerational differences and underscore their criticism for their parents' lack of integration. Among peers, the use of stylized learner's German accentuated their distancing from the stereotype of uneducated migrant workers. Towards German adults, however, it ironically affirmed such stereotypes, thereby putting interlocutors' stereotypes to the test. Keim reports how she, as an adult fieldworker, was confronted with *Gastarbeiterdeutsch* in her first attempt to approach the ghetto girls group; this use of a devalued code was seen as subversive, to the extent that it disrupted the fieldworker's engagement by evoking a relation of inequality.

We move on to settings of institutional interaction, especially classroom discourse, which involve young actors in their specific situated identities (Zimmermann 1998) as pupils. Here, the focus is not just on what those situated identities dictate, but how they are taken up, managed, resisted, or undermined by the participants themselves. One strand here encompasses what might be viewed as prototypical cases of classroom rebellion, i.e., verbal behavior that aims at sabotaging the interactional order in (urban) classrooms, e.g. through

- disruption of the initiation-response-evaluation pattern or other expected patterns of institutional discourse
- choice of a dispreferred language or language variety that is tacitly unwelcome or even explicitly banned from classroom discourse, such as a regional dialect, a minority or migrant language, instead of the expected standard language delivery
- engaging in backstage communication, developing own agendas in the fringes of classroom instruction, thus subverting, more or less openly, the focus of attention and directionality of interaction as defined by the official agenda of the classroom.

Such practices are in sharp contrast to the requirements of task-oriented (pedagogical) communication. At the same time they do relationship work for the pupils, as rebellion may enhance one's status among classmates—i.e., as yet another case where affiliation and conflict are two sides of the same coin. And while these practices are probably as old as schooling institutions, the resources for doing so change over time. In contemporary Western societies at least, extracurricular resources from techno-popular culture, such as singing, humming, or engaging with digital technologies are being introduced into the school life (cf. Rampton 2006), and employed in backstage communication or in disrupting expected patterns of classroom discourse. However, negotiations of status and teacher-pupil relationship are at work in orderly classroom discourse as well, for example, with respect to the ascription of and resistance to stigmatizing social categories. In Hawaii secondary schools, for instance (Talmy 2004), speakers of English as a Second Language (ESL) reject stigmatized categories such as "fob" ("fresh off the boat", a colloquial label for recent immigrants), which are imposed on them by their teacher as part of the institutional routine (e.g. in the form of assignments). By challenging such institutional labelling, students subvert the conflation of language, culture, nationality, and identity (Talmy 2004). At the same time however, these students tease and humiliate recently immigrated classmates with poor ESL competence, thus reproducing in classroom discourse the stigmatized category they reject for themselves.

Overall, multi-ethnic settings emerge in much of the recent literature as sites of styling processes. For ethnic minority youth, multilingual switching, double voicing, and styling are resources for negotiating their relationship with their ethnic community as well as for resisting discrimination by members of the majority society (cf. the papers in Lo and Reyes 2004). Also, what emerges as youth-preferential practice across linguistic and cultural boundaries is a tendency for vivid and performative (as opposed to argumentative) ways of negotiating social boundaries.

5. Beyond Face-to-Face: Mediating Interpersonal Communication

The expanding social spread and domestication of digital information and communication technologies (ICT) is transforming the ways in which identities and relationships are constructed and negotiated. While this is of course not restricted to the young, it is well documented that they have been innovative in making connections (Abbott 1998) through information and communication technologies (ICT), and still use these for social interaction more often than other age groups on an international scale (see, e.g., Bryant, Sanders-Jackson, and Smallwood 2006 for the USA; van Eimeren and Frees 2006 for Germany). Depending on their affordances, ICT for interpersonal communication may be divided into different types:

- technologies for interpersonal interaction, termed as "socially interactive technologies" (Bryant, Sanders-Jackson, and Smallwood 2006), including mobile phones, internet telephone, texting, instant messaging
- formats of public multi-party interaction such as chat, web discussion boards, and three-dimensional environments; and
- spaces of self-presentation in which edited content is complemented by interaction formats, as is the case with personal homepages, weblogs, and social networking environments.

All of these, in turn, may host a multitude of genres (e.g., small talk, joking, greeting) and communicative purposes (e.g., flirting, problem solving, recommending, making arrangements).

The last few years have witnessed the emergence of a substantial volume of language-focused research on computer-mediated communication (CMC) and texting, initially framed in descriptive linguistics and genre analysis, and increasingly positioned in discourse analysis and sociolinguistics as well. Even though patterns and regularities of CMC are often analyzed comparatively to face-to-face discourse, there is currently widespread consensus that CMC needs to be addressed not as a deficient substitute for face-to-face discourse, but as a social practice in its own right (cf. Georgakopoulou 2003a; Herring 2001). This applies to the notion of interaction itself: CMC exchanges display some key features of verbal interaction, such as sequentiality and contextual dependency, while others—e.g., multi-channel immediacy, turn-taking mechanisms, responsibilities for opening and closing interaction—may be much less rigid or altogether missing. Rather than viewing the resulting interaction as less than genuine conversation, the aim is to understand how new media alter the conditions for interpersonal communication by affording complex constellation of familiar and novel, medium-specific resources for interpersonal work. Having said that, it must be noted that the fundamental mechanisms of interpersonal management discussed above repeatedly emerge as valid for computer-mediated discourse as well. We find for instance the copy of elements of the previous message or turn to indicate alignment (cf. Section 3. above), the joint construction of virtual worlds in e-chat, the emergence of common repertoires for interpersonal work in the process of virtual community formation, or style-shifting to strategically converge to chat interlocutors (see, e.g., papers in Beißwenger 2001). On the other hand, there is evidence of code switching and style shifting in CMC in order to foreground contextually relevant social identities, to negotiate conflicts, or to accentuate dissent (see, e.g., Androutsopoulos 2006, 2007).

Most linguistic studies of CMC among young people focus on processes of identity construction or self-presentation, while the negotiation of interpersonal relationships has been relatively less attended to. One relevant question has been whether digital technologies are used by the young to sustain established face-to-face social networks, or rather to create new ones. Several studies have stressed the potential of going online to disrupt traditionally defined identities, to enable play with anonymity, to subvert rigid social features and transgress conventional boundaries (notably gender). Chat channels and newsgroups (and more recently virtual environments such as *Second Life*) in particular have been hailed as sites for the formation of virtual relationships and online communities, which transcend traditional geographical boundaries. By contrast, research on the use of mobile telephones, instant messaging, and texting attends to the ways in which these digital media extend interpersonal communication within existing social networks across space and time (Bryant, Sanders-Jackson, and Smallwood 2006; Kasesniemi and Rautiainen 2002; Schmidt and Androutsopoulos 2004; Thurlow 2003). Studies of texting, in particular, report its significance for phatic and expressive communication, the planning and coordination of joint activities, and notably for conflict resolution as well, as texting is sometimes preferred to face-to-face exchange for reconciliation. Note, however, that the prevailing methods of data collection in this area, i.e., questionnaires and samples of text messages detached from context, leave little space for the study of texting-as-interaction (but see Schmidt and Androutsopoulos 2004; Spilioti 2006).

The repertoires for interpersonal communication are both constrained and enriched in settings of digitally mediated discourse. Constraints arise, as resources of face-to-face interaction have to be done without or compensated for, while at the same time additional resources may be afforded by each medium. The best well known instance of that process is smileys/emoticons, which emerged and were rapidly conventionalized as collective response to the channel reduction in text-only interactive written discourse. Not by coincidence, they do phatic and interpersonal, rather than information oriented, work (cf., e.g., Huffaker and Calvert 2005). On the other hand, emoticons are just a sub-case of a wider tendency to explore the shape of written discourse for identity- and relationship-related work. Creative, unconventional uses of spelling and punctuation serve as a partial compensation of familiar channels (mimics, kinesics, prosody) as much as a resource that is inherent to the written mode and may now be explored in environments which are largely free from normative control over the form of written discourse.

The heavy reliance on code-centered choices, a tendency that has been found to be characteristic of CMC (see Georgakopoulou 2003a), ultimately depends on the manipulation of graphemic form to evoke codes and voices. These do contextualization work in defining, reproducing, or revising relationships between interlocutors. All these processes look back to pre-digital traditions both at the level of expressivity and emotion (see, e.g., Kataoka 2003) and at the level of youth-culture affiliations and everyday micro-politics, i.e., acting as a means of "spelling rebellion" (Sebba 2003). Spelling and punctuation present fuzzy borders with multimodality, the joint use of the verbal and visual mode in meaning making. However, multimodality in CMC has mostly been discussed in terms of self-presentation and identity construction (see as early as Chandler and Roberts-Young 1998), and its relevance for interpersonal communication still remains unexplored. One avenue is to examine how multimodal expression might prompt, or provide occasions, for subsequent digital interaction; for example, self-presentation on graphic surfaces consisting of language, image, sound, and background color offers clues to be taken up in direct exchanges via the technologies offered in each case. The connection of multimodality to interpersonal communication is perhaps more obvious in the case of the enormously popular graphic emoticons, and even more so in still largely unexplored three-dimensional environments such as *Second Life*, where the looks of co-players are massively decisive in initiating interaction.

Information and communication technologies offer the option of editing interactive discourse (as in, e.g., chat lines, forum entries, text messages, etc.), and even though such editing must often be quite rapid in order to sustain the flow of mediated interaction, it may be strategically used to manage interpersonal communication. For instance, planning time affords the packaging of more than one response into the same entry; also, the time of response may be used as an index of interpersonal stance: a swift response is conventionally understood as indexing interest or urgency, a delayed response as indexing lack of interest (Jones 2005). Also, editing time may be used to make the message more appealing, by investing in language play and linguistic experiment involving the visual dimension of written discourse (see preceding discussion). But planning time can also be exploited, especially under conditions of anonymity, for its conflict potential, as in the practice of flaming, which may be viewed as a digital equivalent of unmitigated conflict talk. In an early study of flaming, Karlsson (1998) examined a Swedish chat environment in which a newspaper editor interfered in a youth e-chat, seeking to draw the chatters' attention to educational policy matters, to which young chatters reacted with irony. This culminated in direct confrontation expressed as verbal aggression and flaming. Through flaming, participants disrupted the orderly flow of mediated interaction to defend their autonomy, in a manner somewhat equivalent to the disruption of institutional face-to-face discourse. This nicely illustrates the hybrid nature of interactive written discourse as a composite of both old *and* new resources for aligning and boundary setting.

6. Conclusions

Findings such as the above have gone a long way to shed light on the forms that convergence and alignment on the one hand, divergence and boundary marking on the other take within close-knit groups of young people at different semiotic levels. In fact, more recently, the focus has decidedly shifted away from the monopoly of linguistic choices in the formation of peer-group cultures to their synergy with other semiotic choices (e.g., dress-code, hair-style) as markers of group identity (see, e.g., Eckert 2000; Wilson 2003). However, as we have shown, what remains unclear in studies such as the ones discussed above is exactly how specific to adolescent peer-group micro-cultures is language use of that kind as opposed to being closely associated with relationships of closeness and intimacy across the age span (cf. Kotsinas 1994; Karlsson 1998; Norrby and Wirdenäs 2003). At the same time, it has to be noted that generalizing and forming one-to-one relationships between language use and social identities (in this case, age) has not been the stated aim of this line of inquiry. Instead, the aim has been to draw attention to and document the varying ways in which language use is shaped by and invokes social identities (in interaction with one another) in a multitude of sites.

The other factor that makes drawing generalizations hard is the multi-functionality of linguistic signs, as already mentioned. This means that the same language choice may perform certain social actions in one context and others in another; more locally, the same choice may be used and taken up differently in the same interaction or stretch of discourse, as we saw in the example of code-switching phenomena and more specifically language crossing (Sections 3. and 4.). By the same token, findings about solidarity as a prevalent ethos in peer-group communication should by no means be equated with a picture of social harmony or equally with a suggestion that social class, ethnicity, and other potentially dividing factors no longer work as structuring forces in young people's interactions (see Rampton 2006). Instead, existing studies should form the basis for further nuanced explorations of young people's communication in a multitude of sites.

Finally, a note of caveat is in order regarding the restrictions of available research literature. The aspect of age has not been sufficiently brought to the fore in sociolinguistics and studies of young speakers have often emphasized other social identities, in particular gender. Moreover, there is an unavoidable cultural and linguistic bias since most of the literature in the field deals with Western societies, while comparative studies tend to be missing (cf. Bucholtz 2002). In the light of this, there is an apparent need for further studies in as many cultural settings as possible that will broaden the scope of the inquiry into youth communication.

References

Abbott, Chris. 1998. Making connections: Young people and the internet. In: Julian Sefton-Green (ed.), *Digital Diversions: Youth Culture in the Age of Multimedia*, 84–105. London: University College London Press.

Andersen, Gisle. 1997. "They gave us these yeah, and they like wanna see like how we talk and all that." The use of *like* and other pragmatic markers in London teenage speech. In:

Ulla-Britt Kotsinas, Anna-Brita Stenström and Anna-Malin Karlsson (eds.), *Ungdomsspråk i Norden*, 82–95. (Meddelanden från institutionen för nordiska språk, MINS 43.) Stockholm: Institutionen för nordiska språk, Stockholms universitet.

Androutsopoulos, Jannis. 2006. Multilingualism, diaspora, and the internet: Codes and identities on German-based diaspora websites. *Journal of Sociolinguistics* 10(4): 429–450.

Androutsopoulos, Jannis. 2007. Style online: Doing hip-hop on the German-speaking Web. In: Peter Auer (ed.), *Style and Social Identities*, 279–317. Berlin/New York: de Gruyter.

Androutsopoulos, Jannis and Alexandra Georgakopoulou (eds.). 2003a. *Discourse Constructions of Youth Identities*. Amsterdam/Philadelphia: John Benjamins.

Androutsopoulos, Jannis and Alexandra Georgakopoulou. 2003b. Introduction: *Discourse Constructions of Youth Identities*. In: Jannis Androutsopoulos and Alexandra Georgakopoulou (eds.), *Discourse Constructions of Youth Identities* 1–25. Amsterdam/Philadelphia: John Benjamins.

Arnett, Jeffrey Jensen. 2006. *Emerging Adulthood. The Winding Road from the Late Teens through the Twenties*. Oxford/New York: Oxford University Press.

Augenstein, Susanne. 1998. *Funktionen von Jugendsprache*. Tübingen: Niemeyer. Beißwenger, Michael (ed.). 2001. *Chat-Kommunikation*. Stuttgart: Ibidem.

Bierbach, Christiane and Gabriele Birken-Silverman. 2007. Names and identities, or: How to be a hip young Italian migrant in Germany. In: Peter Auer (ed.), *Style and Social Identities*, 121–154. Berlin/ New York: de Gruyter.

Branner, Rebecca. 2003. *Scherzkommunikation unter Mädchen. Eine ethnographisch-gesprächsanalytische Untersuchung*. Frankfurt/Main: Lang.

Bryant, J. Alison, Ashley Sanders-Jackson and Amber M.K. Smallwood. 2006. IMing, text messaging, and adolescent social networks. *Journal of Computer-Mediated Communication* 11(2), http://jcmc.indiana.edu/vol11/ issue2/bryant.html (last access: November 17, 2007).

Bucholtz, Mary. 1999a. "Why be normal?": Language and identity practices in a group of nerd girls. *Language in Society* 28: 203–223.

Bucholtz, Mary. 1999b. Bad examples. Transgression and progress in language and gender studies. In: Mary Bucholtz, Laurel A. Sutton and A.C. Liang (eds.), *Reinventing Identities: The Gendered Self in Discourse*, 3–24. New York/Oxford: Oxford University Press.

Bucholtz, Mary. 2002. Youth and cultural practice. *Annual Review of Anthropology* 31: 525–552. Bucholtz, Mary and Kira Hall. 2004. Language and identity. In: Alessandro Duranti (ed.), *A companion to linguistic anthropology*, 369–394. Oxford: Blackwell.

Chandler, Daniel and Dilwyn Roberts-Young. 1998. *The Construction of Identity in the Personal Homepages of Adolescents*. http://www.aber.ac.uk/media/Documents/short/strasbourg.html (last access: October 28, 2007).

Cheshire, Jenny. 1982. *Variation in an English Dialect*. Cambridge: Cambridge University Press.

Cheshire, Jenny, Paul Kerswill, Ann Gillett and Ann Williams. 1999. *The Role of Adolescents in Dialect Levelling*. Final report to the Economic and Social Research Council. http://www.ling.lancs.ac.uk/staff/kerswill/ pkpubs/LEVELFIN99.pdf (last access: December 4, 2007).

Cindark, Ibrahim and Inken Keim. 2002. Der Umgang mit dem negativen Face in zwei jugendlichen MigrantInnengruppen. In: Dieter Hartung and Alissa Shethar (eds.), *Kulturen und ihre Sprachen. Ihre Wahrnehmung anders Sprechender und ihr Selbstverständnis*, 57–86. Berlin: Trafo.

Corsaro, William A. and Donna Eder. 1990. Children's peer cultures. *Annual Review of Sociology* 16: 197–220.

Deppermann, Arnulf. 2007. Playing with the voice of the other: Stylized Kanaksprak in conversations among German adolescents. In: Peter Auer (ed.), *Style and social identities*, 325–360. Berlin/New York: de Gruyter.

Deppermann, Arnulf and Axel Schmidt. 2001a. Hauptsache Spaß. Zur Eigenart der Unterhaltungskultur Jugendlicher. *Der Deutschunterricht* 6: 27–37. Deppermann, Arnulf and Axel Schmidt. 2001b. Dissen. *Osnabrücker Beiträge zur Sprachtheorie* (OBST) 62: 79–98.

Deppermann, Arnulf and Axel Schmidt. 2003. Vom Nutzen des Fremden für das Eigene. Interaktive Praktiken der sozialen Abgrenzung in einer jugendlichen peer-group. In: Hans Merkens and Jürgen Zinnecker (eds.), *Jahrbuch Jugendforschung* 3, 25–56. Opladen: Leske + Budrich.

Dirim, Inci and Peter Auer. 2004. *Türkisch sprechen nicht nur die Türken. Über die Unschärfebeziehung zwischen Sprache und Ethnie in Deutschland*. Berlin/New York: de Gruyter.

Dundes, Alan, Jerry W. Leach and Bora Özkok. 1972. The strategy of Turkish boys' verbal dueling rhymes. In: John J. Gumperz and Dell Hymes (eds.), *Directions in Sociolinguistics: The Ethnography of Communication*, 130–160. New York/Chicago: Holt, Rinewort and Winston.

Eble, Connie. 1996. *Slang and Sociability: In-group Language among College Students*. Chapel Hill, NC: The University of North Carolina Press.

Eckert, Penelope. 2000. *Linguistic Variation as Social Practice*. Malden, MA: Blackwell.

Eckert, Penelope. 2002. Demystifying sexuality and desire. In: Kathry Campbell-Kibler, Robert J. Podesva, Sarah J. Roberts and Andrew Wong (eds.), *Language and Sexuality: Contesting Meaning in Theory and Practice*, 99–110. Stanford, CA: Center for the Study of Language of Information Publications.

Eckert, Penelope and John R. Rickford (eds.). 2001. *Style and Sociolinguistic Variation*. Cambridge/New York: Cambridge University Press.

Eckert, Penelope and Sally McConnell-Ginet. 1999. New generalizations and explanations in language and gender research. *Language in Society* 28: 185–201.

Eder, Donna. 1993. "Go get ya a French!": Romantic and sexual teasing among adolescent girls. In: Deborah Tannen (ed.), *Gender and Conversational Interaction*, 17–31. Oxford: Oxford University Press.

Eder, Donna. 1998. Developing adolescent peer culture through collaborative narration. In: Susan M. Hoyle and Carolyn Temple Adger (eds.), *Kids Talk. Strategic Language Use in Later Childhood*, 82–94. Oxford/New York: Oxford University Press.

Eksner, Julia. 2001. Ghetto ideologies, youth identities and stylized Turkish German youth in Berlin-Kreuzberg. MA Thesis, Department of Anthropology, FU Berlin.

Erman, Britt. 2001. Pragmatic markers revisited with a focus on 'you know' in adult and adolescent talk. *Journal of Pragmatics* 33: 1337–1359. Fornäs, Johan. 1995. Youth, culture and modernity. In: Johan Fornäs and Göran Bolin (eds.), *Youth Culture in Late Modernity*, 1–11. London: Sage.

Georgakopoulou, Alexandra. 2003a. Computer-mediated communication. In: Jef Verschueren and Jan-Ola Östman (eds.), *Handbook of Pragmatics* (2001 Installment), 1–20. Amsterdam/Philadelphia: Benjamins.

Georgakopoulou, Alexandra. 2003b. Looking back when looking ahead: Adolescents' identity management in narrative practices. In: Jannis Androutsopoulos and Alexandra Georgakopoulou (eds.), *Discourse Constructions of Youth Identities*, 75–91. Amsterdam/Philadelphia: Benjamins.

Georgakopoulou, Alexandra. 2005. Styling men and masculinities: Interactional and identity aspects at work. *Language in Society* 34: 163–184.

Georgakopoulou, Alexandra. 2007. *Small Stories, Interaction and Identities*. Amsterdam/Philadelphia: John Benjamins. Giles, Howard, Justine Coupland and Nikolas Coupland (eds.). 1991. *Contexts of Accommodation*. Cambridge: Cambridge University Press. Goodwin, Marjorie H. 1990. *He-said-she-said: Talk as Social Organization among Black Children*. Bloomington: Indiana University Press.

Goodwin, Marjorie H. 2006. *The Hidden Life of Girls. Games of Stance, Status and Exclusion*. Oxford: Blackwell Publishing.

Grimshaw, Allen D. 1990. Research on conflict talk: Antecedents, resources, findings, directions. In: Allen D. Grimshaw (ed.), *Conflict Talk. Sociolinguistic Investigations of Arguments in Conversations*, 281–324. Cambridge: Cambridge University Press.

Gruber, Helmut and Peter Muntigl (eds.). 2005. *Approaches to Genre*. Berlin: de Gruyter (Special issue of *Folia Linguistica*, XXXIX/1–2).

Halliday, Michael A.K. 1978. *Language as Social Semiotic: The Social Interpretation of Language and Meaning*. London: Arnold.

Hanks, William F. 1996. *Language and communicative practices*. Colorado/Oxford: Westview.

Herring, Susan C. 2001. Computer-mediated discourse. In: Deborah Schiffrin, Deborah Tannen and Heidi E. Hamilton (eds.), *The Handbook of Discourse Analysis*, 612–634. Malden: Blackwell.

Hill, Jane. 1999. Styling locally, styling globally: What does it mean? *Journal of Sociolinguistics* 3: 542–556.

Huffaker, David A. and Sandra L. Calvert. 2005. Gender, identity, and language use in teenage blogs. *Journal of Computer-Mediated Communication* 10(2), http://jcmc.indiana.edu/vol10/issue2/huffaker.html (last access: October 28, 2007).

Ito, Rika and Sali Tagliamonte. 2003. *Well* weird, *right* dodgy, *very* strange, *really* cool: Layering and recycling in English intensifiers. *Language in Society* 32: 257–279.

Jones, Rodney. 2005. Sites of engagement as sites of attention: Time, space and culture in electronic discourse. In: Sigrid Norris and Rodney Jones (eds.), *Discourse in Action: Introducing Mediated Discourse Analysis*, 141–154. London: Routledge.

Kallmeyer, Werner and Inken Keim. 2003. Linguistic variation and the construction of social identity in a German-Turkish setting. In: Jannis Androutsopoulos and Alexandra Georgakopoulou (eds.), *Discourse Constructions of Youth Identities*, 29–46. Amsterdam/ Philadelphia: Benjamins.

Karlsson, Anna-Malin. 1998. 'Genre' instead of 'variety'? Suggestions for a different understanding of young (and middle aged) verbal interaction. In: Jannis Androutsopoulos and Arno Scholz (eds.), *Jugendsprache—youth language—langue des jeunes*, 259–280. Frankfurt/ Main: Peter Lang.

Kasesniemi, Eija-Liisa and Pirjo Rautiainen. 2002. Mobile culture of children and teenagers in Finland. In: James E. Katz and Mark A. Aakhus (eds), *Perpetual Contact: Mobile Communication, Private Talk, Public Performance*, 170–192, Cambridge: Cambridge University Press.

Kataoka, Kuniyoshi. 2003. Emotion and youth identities in personal letter writing: An analysis of pictorial signs and unconventional punctuation. In: Jannis Androutsopoulos and Alexandra Georgakopoulou (eds.), *Discourse Constructions of Youth Identities*, 121–150. Amsterdam/Philadelphia: John Benjamins.

Keim, Inken. 2002. Bedeutungskonstitution und Sprachvariation. Funktionen des Gastarbeiterdeutsch in Gesprächen jugendlicher Migrantinnen. In: Arnulf Deppermann and Thomas Spranz-Fogasy (eds.), *be-deuten. Wie Bedeutung im Gespräch entsteht*. Tübingen: Stauffenburg.

Keim, Inken. 2004. Kommunikative Praktiken in türkischstämmigen Kinder- und Jugendgruppen in Mannheim. *Deutsche Sprache* 3/04: 198–226. Keim, Inken. 2007a. *Die "türkischen Powergirls". Lebenswelt und kommunikativer Stil einer Migrantinnengruppe in Mannheim*. Tübingen: Narr.

Keim, Inken. 2007b. Socio-cultural identity, communicative style, and their change over time: A case study of a group of German-Turkish girls in Mannheim/Germany. In: Peter Auer (ed.), *Style and Social Identities*, 155–186. Berlin/New York: de Gruyter.

Keim, Inken und Ibrahim Cindark. 2003. Deutsch-türkischer Mischcode in einer Migrantinnengruppe: Form von "Jugendsprache" oder soziolektales Charakteristikum? In: Eva Neuland (ed.), *Jugendsprachen—Spiegel der Zeit*, 377–393. Frankfurt/Main: Peter Lang.

Kießling, Roland and Maarten Mous. 2006. "Vous nous avez donné le français, main nous sommes pas obliges de l'utiliser comme vous le voulez". Youth languages in Africa. In: Christa Dürscheid and Jürgen Spitzmüller (eds.), *Perspektiven der Jugendsprachfor-schung/Trends and Developments in Youth Language Research*, 385–402. Frankfurt/Main: Lang.

Korobov, Neill and Michael Bamberg. 2004. Positioning a 'mature' self in interactive practices: How adolescent males negotiate 'physical attraction' in group talk. *British Journal of Developmental Psychology* 22: 471–492.

Kotsinas, Ulla-Britt. 1994. *Ungdomsspråk*. Uppsala: Hallgren & Fallgreen. Labov, William. 1972. *Language in the Inner City: Studies in the Black English Vernacular*, Philadelphia: University of Pennsylvania Press.

Lo, Adrienne and Angela Reyes (eds.). 2004. *Relationality. Pragmatics* 14(2/3). Special Issue on *Discursive Constructions of Asian Pacific American identities*.

McRobbie, Angela. 2006. The new sexual contract: Young women's identities today. Public Lecture for the Identities Lecture Series, 1st February, 2006. http://www.identities. org.uk. (last access: Nobember 18, 2007).

Neumann-Braun, Klaus, Arnulf Deppermann and Axel Schmidt. 2002. Identitätswettbewerbe und unernste Konflikte: Interaktionspraktiken in Peer-Groups. In: Hans Merkens and Jürgen Zinnecker (eds.), *Jahrbuch Jugendforschung 2*, 241–264. Opladen: Leske + Budrich.

Norrby Catrin and Karolina Wirdenäs. 2003. Swedish youth discourse: On performing relevant selves in interaction. In: Jannis Androutsopoulos and Alexandra Georgakopoulou (eds.), *Discourse Constructions of Youth Identities*, 247–278. Amsterdam/Philadelphia: John Benjamins.

Pujolar, Joan. 2001. *Gender, Heteroglossia and Power. A Sociolinguistic Study of Youth Culture*. Berlin/New York: Mouton de Gruyter.

Rampton, Ben. 1995. *Crossing. Language and Ethnicity among Adolescents*. London: Longman.

Rampton, Ben (ed.). 1999. Styling the other. Special Issue, *Journal of Sociolinguistics* 3: 421–427.

Rampton, Ben. 2006. *Language in Late Modernity. Interaction in an Urban School*. Cambridge: Cambridge University Press.

Schlobinski, Peter, Gaby Kohl and Irmgard Ludewigt. 1993. *Jugendsprache. Fiktion und Wirklichkeit*. Opladen: Westdeutscher Verlag.

Schmidt Axel. 2004. *Doing peer-group—Die interaktive Konstitution jugendlicher Gruppenpraxis*. Frankfurt/Main: Peter Lang.

Schmidt Axel. 2005. Oberaffengeil ist peinlich! Von der Jugendsprache zur *Peergroup*-Kommunikation. In: Klaus Neumann-Braun und Birgit Richard (eds), *Cool-hunters. Jugendkulturen zwischen Medien und Markt*, 83–100. Frankfurt/ Main: Suhrkamp.

Schmidt, Gurly and Jannis Androutsopoulos. 2004. "löbbe döch". Beziehungskommunikation mit SMS. *Gesprächsforschung—Online-Zeitschrift zur verbalen Interaktion* 5: 51–76. www.gespraechsforschung-ozs.de/heft2004/heft2004 (last access: October 15, 2007).

Schwitalla, Johannes. 1994. Die Vergegenwärtigung einer Gegenwelt. Sprachliche Formen der sozialen Abgrenzung einer Jugendlichengruppe in Vogelstang. In: Werner Kallmeyer (ed.), *Kommunikation in der Stadt, Band 1*. 467–509. Berlin/ New York: de Gruyter.

Schwitalla, Johannes and Juergen Streeck. 1989. Subversive Interaktionen: Sprachliche Verfahren der sozialen Abgrenzung in einer Jugendlichengruppe. In: Volker Hinnenkamp and Margret Selting (eds.), *Stil und Stilisierung*, 229–252. Tübingen: Niemeyer.

Scollon, Ron and Susanne Wong Scollon. 2004. *Nexus Analysis: Discourse and the Emerging Internet*. London/New York: Routledge.

Sebba, Mark. 2003. Spelling rebellion. In: Jannis Androutsopoulos and Alexandra Georgakopoulou (eds.), *Discourse Constructions of Youth Identities*, 151–172. Amsterdam/Philadelphia: John Benjamins.

Shankar, Shalina. 2004. Reel to real: Desi teens' linguistic engagement with Bollywood. *Pragmatics* 14(2/3): 317–335. Shelton, Tracey and Gill Valentine. 1998. *Cool Places. Geographies of Youth Cultures*. London/New York: Routledge.

Shuman, Amy. 1986. *Storytelling Rights. The Uses of Oral and Written Texts by Urban Adolescents*. Cambridge: Cambridge University Press.

Spilioti, Thiresia. 2006. Text messages and social interaction: Genres, norms and sociability in Greek SMS. Unpublished PhD Thesis, King's College London.

Spreckels, Janet. 2006. "Britneys, Fritten, Gangschta und wir": Identitätskonstitution in einer Mädchengruppe. Eine ethnographisch-gesprächsanalytische Untersuchung. Frankfurt/ Main: Lang.

Stenström, Anna-Brita. 2003. 'It's not that I really care, about him personally you know': The construction of gender identity in London teenage talk. In: Jannis Androutsopoulos and Alexandra Georgakopoulou (eds.), *Discourse Constructions of Youth Identities*, 93–117. Amsterdam/ Philadelphia: John Benjamins.

Stenström, Anna-Brita, Gisle Andersen and Ingrid Kristine Hasund. 2002. *Trends in Teenage Talk. Corpus Compilation, Analysis and Findings*. Amsterdam/Philadelphia: John Benjamins. Talmy, Steven. 2004. Forever fob: The cultural production of ESL in a high school. *Pragmatics* 14(2/3): 149–172.

Tertilt, Hermann. 1996. *Turkish Power Boys. Ethnographie einer Jugendbande*. Frankfurt/Main: Suhrkamp.

Thurlow, Crispin. 2003. Generation Txt? The sociolinguistics of young people's text messaging. *Discourse Analysis Online* 1. http://extra.shu.ac.uk/daol/ (last access: October 28, 2007).

Van Eimeren, Birgit and Beate Frees. 2006. ARD/ZDF-Online-Studie 2006. *Media Perspektiven* 8: 402–415.

Wilson, Anita. 2003. 'Nike Traiuners, My One True Love—Without You I Am Nothing': Youth, identity and the language of trainers for young men in prison. In: Jannis Androutspoulos and Alexandra Georgakopoulou (eds.), *Discourse Constructions of Youth Identities*, 173–196. Amsterdam/Philadelphia: John Benjamins.

Wyn, Johanna and Rob White. 1997. *Rethinking Youth*, London: Sage. Zimmerman, Don. 1998. Identity, context and interaction. In: Charles Antaki and Sue Widdicombe (eds.), *Identities in talk*, 87–120. London: Sage.

11

Language and Discourse
Skills of Elderly People

Anna-Maija Korpijaakko-Huuhka and Anu Klippi

1. Introduction

The number of elderly people will increase significantly in the near future throughout the world. In the European Union, the proportion of people over 65 years is predicted to rise up to 25 % of the total population by 2030, and by 2050 the figure is estimated to be almost 30 % (Nieminen 2005). The most rapidly growing age group is people of at least 80 years of age; in the United Kingdom their proportion is expected to reach 5.7 % by 2020 (Butler, Oberlink, and Schechter 1998). In the United States, the proportion of population over 85 years is expected to increase to 5 % by 2050 (Administration on Aging 1998).

Aging should be seen as a "natural process, part of the developmental lifespan" (Maxim and Bryan 1994: 2). Aging as such, however, is the main factor predisposing to conditions, such as cerebral vascular accidents and dementing diseases (Cutler and Mattson 2006), which affect linguistic ability and interpersonal communication. Thus, much research on language and aging clearly belongs to what Coupland, Coupland and Giles (1991: 8–13) call a deficit paradigm, i.e., studies focusing on the decrement and decline of linguistic and communicative abilities in elderly people. It is, however, important to understand how language processing and communicative skills may change in old age, especially when it concerns differentiating typical age-related features (see Section 3) from deviant features, such as those found in aphasic disorders or dementia (see Section 4). It is equally important to find ways for elderly people to maintain and enhance their active communicator role and autonomy in various life situations. Participation in relationships, self-expression, and autonomy are core elements of quality of life. For older people's quality of life, communication skills, and opportunities to interact with other people are fundamental (Worral and Hickson 2003). In addition, it is necessary to remember that many of the communication partners of old people are themselves aged, which multiplies the challenges of maintaining active life and of compensating for possible age-related changes in interpersonal communication.

As the authors of this chapter have close connections with health-care and also long experience as speech-language therapists, the overall theoretical orientation of this chapter is based on the new biopsychosocial model of the

World Heath Organization (2001), the *International Classification of Functioning, Disability and Health* (ICF) (see Section 2).

2. The International Classification of Functioning, Disability and Health (ICF)

The ICF model is used here to cover the many-faceted research on language, discourse, and aging. Thus, different approaches within neurophysiology, psycholinguistics, and sociolinguistics are subordinated to the general frame of the ICF. According to the ICF, a person's health condition—in this context, his or her age (see Worral and Hickson 2003, 20–25)—can be described from various perspectives that interact with each other. The two basic aspects of any health condition are called the level of *body structures and functions* and the level of *activity and participation*. A third and equally important angle included in the ICF model is that of *environmental and personal factors* which may either enhance or inhibit body functions or activities and participation of the individual in question. On the whole, the ICF model focuses on functioning instead of disorders or deficits, and the same philosophy is adopted in this chapter, too.

To help the reader to follow the reasoning in the following sections, a short presentation of relevant items in the ICF model is provided. In the context of this chapter, the brain and other organs participating in speech and language production and comprehension are of interest. Deviations and diseases in these *body structures* affect various functions which are prerequisites for linguistic interaction. *Sensory and motor functions*, such as auditive acuity and articulatory accuracy, respectively, are necessary premises for oral-verbal communication. Language processes, such as lexical access, linguistic memory functions, and discourse processing, are included in the body's *psychological functions*. All the functions or processes can be described in terms of resources or losses. Resources include preserved hearing ability or appropriate linguistic memory. *Disability* or *disorder* refer to the loss of functions when a person has problems in sensory, motor, or linguistic-cognitive functions.

A person's ability to accomplish various communicative tasks and to participate in various discourses in life-situations belongs to the level of *activity and participation* in the ICF model. Expressing one's thoughts and conversing with other people, as well as participating in business and leisure activities, are essential contributors to psychosocial well-being and quality of life. When old people for any reason lose their skill or opportunity to act communicatively or to take part in life-situations, we talk about activation limitation or participation restriction.

The most important *environmental factors* which affect old people's communicative activities and participation are their communication partners' skills, social attitudes towards their roles and competencies, and the availability of services for elderly people. Thus, in each section of this chapter, we have—according to the ICF philosophy—taken into account contextual factors that may affect linguistic processes and discourse skills. At various points, after describing the possible age-related changes in linguistic processes and discourse activities, we have tried to suggest some ways to modify the environment in order to help elderly people to maintain their communicative autonomy. Accordingly, we will also discuss some new interventions that seem promising in enhancing the life-participation of elderly people with communicative problems and their significant others.

3. Language Processing and Discourse in Healthy Aging

Getting older means inevitable physiological changes that may affect one's linguistic and bodily functioning. In the absence of clear neurological or other pathologies, i.e., diseases or traumata, these changes are considered to be part of *healthy aging* (*successful aging, active aging,* or *aging well,* cf. Worrall and Hickson 2003: 30). The structural and biochemical changes in the aging nervous system are many (for a review, cf. Nicholas et al. 1998), and these contribute to age-related deteriorations in motor, sensory, and cognitive functions. As a result, language and discourse skills may be affected, for example, by impaired hearing, limited working memory capacity, and lowered speed of information processing typical in elderly populations (Wignfield 2000). It is thus suggested that language changes in relation to healthy aging should be considered linguistic manifestations of changes in sensory, motor and higher-level cognitive abilities rather than linguistic deteriorations as such (also Nicholas et al. 1998). In Section 3.1., these changes will be discussed in relation to processes of language comprehension and production. Section 3.2. then concentrates on discourse and social interaction, while Section 3.3. focuses on *individual* paths of linguistic-cognitive aging.

3.1. Language Comprehension and Production

Changes in language-related processes are minor before the 70th or even the 80th birthday, and comprehension seems to be more susceptible to age-related deteriorations than production (Nicholas et al. 1998). Old people themselves have also been shown to be aware of these changes as they complain, for example, about hearing impairment, memory problems, and difficulties in finding words (Worral and Hickson 2003). They also report having difficulty in speaking clearly and understanding other people's speech.

In healthy aging, sensory-motor and histological changes affecting the speech system may result in a decline of articulatory accuracy and speech rate (Benjamin 1997). These do not, however, affect the general intelligibility of utterances, nor do the typical age-related changes in voice quality (e.g., raised or lowered pitch, reduced loudness, hoarseness; cf. Worral and Hickson 2003: 9). If there are problems in understanding the message of an older individual because of the quality of his or her motor speech performance and voice quality, environmental variables should be adjusted to match the communicative demands. These variables include evaluating and—if necessary—optimizing the denture, lowering the volume of surrounding noise, and ensuring direct eye-contact between the interlocutors to enhance the multimodal interpretation of the linguistic content.

Healthy elderly people without major hearing impairment have been shown to comprehend natural, redundant speech in good listening conditions as well as younger people (Obler et al. 1985). However, the proportion of hearing impairments affecting speech perception and comprehension clearly increases with age. Wingfield (2000) summarizes large-scale studies conducted in the United States estimating that the proportion of hearing impairments that are severe enough to affect speech comprehension amongst the younger old (aged under 75 years) is 24–30 %, while it may be as high as almost 50 % in the group of older old (75 years or more).

Difficulty in hearing high-frequency sounds properly is probably one of the best known signs of sensory decline in elderly people. This age-related hearing impairment, *presbyacusis*, may be crucial for the comprehension of messages in natural situations, as it affects auditory acuity and, thus, the discrimination and recognition of certain high-frequency and low-energy phonemes, specifically plosives and sibilants (Wingfield 2000). It is especially hard for people with presbyacusis to follow other speakers in noisy circumstances. Thus, acoustic disturbances should be reduced to ensure optimal communication environment for the hearing-impaired old person (Gordon-Salant and Fitzgibbons 1997). The most important means to improve the speech perception of a person with presbyacusis, however, is the use of personal hearing aids and also of induction loops in public service surroundings, churches, etc. (for details, cf. Garstecki and Erler 1998). In addition, the compensation of impaired hearing by visual speech perception, that is lip-reading, often takes place unconsciously during the deterioration of hearing. Some elderly people, however, and also their communicative partners, may need special instruction that facilitates speech perception and comprehension. In this connection, especially the age-related deterioration of eyesight should be remembered, and eyesight should be corrected with glasses when necessary.

Fortunately, old people with impaired hearing do not lose their ability to make use of contextual cues and their accumulated linguistic knowledge when interpreting each other's expressions, at least, if other age-related cognitive deteriorations are not severe and affect the top-down processing (for details, cf. Wingfield 2000). It is also worth noting that hearing impairments do not affect writing and reading abilities, and these modes of expressing one's thoughts may also serve as alternative or augmentative means of communication for people with impaired hearing and their communication partners.

In addition to diminished auditory acuity, speech comprehension may be affected by lowered working memory capacity, i.e., difficulty in retaining, monitoring and manipulating recently received (auditory) information within a limited time-frame, and difficulties in processing rapidly proceeding, natural speech (Wingfield 2000). Older individuals have been shown to have more difficulties in comprehending long and syntactically complex sentences than younger people, especially when the complex sentences convey implausible information (Davis and Ball 1989). However, such findings may, as Maxim and Bryan (1994: 40) point out, be related to the experimental tasks used. Thus, comprehension problems may not be evident in familiar everyday contexts, where old people typically perform complex tasks efficiently on the basis of their accumulated experience and knowledge (Park and Hall Gutchess 2000).

Although impaired working memory capacity is a common explanation for comprehension deficits in the elderly, it cannot fully explain the difficulties of some elderly people in comprehending on-line speech. It is known that the speed of processing linguistic information slows down with aging, and this also contributes to speech comprehension problems (for a review, cf. Wingfield, 2000). This is especially evident in word-recall tasks: Both young and old people perform worse the faster the speech input rate, but with increasing speech rates older people show more decline in recall accuracy than younger people. It is also evident that both young and old people become cognitively overloaded when receiving too much information too rapidly. When input speeds are increased, older individuals show a steeper decline than do younger ones in recalling semantic information (propositions). Wingfield (2000: 192) further states that the older adults' comprehension of spoken messages can be facilitated by offering them more processing time; the interlocutors are instructed to lower their speech rate, especially by increasing pausing time between clauses or sentences. However, this should not result in patronizing elderly talk, for example with simplified grammar or vocabulary and exaggerated intonation patterns, i.e., "an ageist form of communication [. . .] based on stereotypical views of older people" (Worral and Hickson 2003: 35; see also Coupland, Coupland, and Giles 1991).

In addition to possible deterioration of speech comprehension, old people often complain about lexical retrieval failures, especially problems remembering proper names of persons and places, and words in response to definitions. While some researchers (Nicholas et al. 1998) report changes in picture naming based on both cross-sectional and longitudinal studies, others (Cruice, Worral, and Hickson 2000) claim that in longitudinal studies, no significant changes in word retrieval are observed. However, the decline in accessing words seems to start as early as before the 50th birthday, but it is only in their 70s to 80s that people seem to have more serious problems with word-finding (Connor et al. 2004; Nicholas et al. 1998; Zec et al. 2005). In connected speech elicited in picture description tasks, age has no effect on the number of content units (i.e., lexicalizations), but compared to younger people the older old convey information with reduced efficiency; what they say takes longer (LeDorze and Bédard 1998; MacKenzie 2000b). The reduced efficiency is assumed to result from slower access to words and disfluencies in terms of repetitions of same words, or commenting on one's word-finding difficulty (LeDorze and Bédard 1998). Lexical knowledge (vocabulary) does not show age-related decline (Park 2000)—it may even expand as new concepts emerge in everyday discourse situations (Maxim and Bryan 1994: 34). Thus, the picture of older people's lexical ability is controversial, and no coherent model is available that explains why elderly people experience word-finding problems (for a discussion, cf. Nicholas et al. 1998).

3.2. Discourse and Social Interaction

The connection of linguistic and (other) cognitive processes—especially memory functions—is of special importance when the discourse skills of elderly people are considered. In a study of discourse comprehension of middle-aged and young elderly people, Guimaraes dos Santos and Nespoulous (1993) had different texts with varying schematic structures—descriptive, argumentative, and narrative—read to the subjects. On group level, the subjects recalled the narrative text best, and the descriptive text poorest; the typical schematic structure of a narrative most obviously enhanced the subjects' ability to recall the content of the story. The older sub-group, however, performed worse than the younger one in terms of the amount of content recalled. This and other studies (e.g., Ulatowska et al. 1998) suggest that older people comprehend and remember the most salient and essential information in stories but leave out minor details that do not affect the overall coherence of the story. The sparcity of content is evident in tasks where older subjects should remember the explicit content of a story, i.e., in tasks that place heavy demands on working memory capacity, and especially if the information cannot be recovered from real world knowledge (Ulatowska et al. 1998). Results from reading comprehension studies (for a review, cf. Kahn and Cordon 1993) also point to the role of prior knowledge in discourse processing; older people seem to differ from younger ones only in tasks where the information processed is not familiar to them.

The ability of elderly people to produce coherent texts in spite of gaps in propositional content has been claimed to depend on their maintained and even highly developed macro-level integrative processes. That is, it rests on strategies, such as information reduction, generalization, and interpretation, which compensate for their memory problems with detailed information (Ulatowska et al. 1998). In a longitudinal study, Ulatowska et al. (1998) followed 16 healthy home-dwelling people aged 80–95 years for approximately three years (range 1.5–5 years). They used various discourse tasks (retelling, constructing summaries, extracting gists and morals, explaining the meaning of proverbs) to evaluate macro-level processing, and on the group-level they found no significant decrease in applying the three strategies in any of the tasks. On the contrary, the interpretation of familiar proverbs seemed to improve during follow-up.

Moreover, Ulatowska et al. (1998) found that the participants continued using complex syntax and high-level vocabulary; these skills are actually necessary for the processes of reduction and generalization. The result is in accordance with Labov and Auger's (1993) findings from two longitudinal studies, the Montreal corpus and the South Philadephia study, where 176 subjects were interviewed at 13–17 year intervals. By the latter interview, the subjects were in their 60s–80s. The interviews covered various topics, such as neighbors, television, and the mother tongue. In these studies, the overall measures of complexity (complex T-units and left-branching T-units) were influenced by the proportion of narratives in the interview. This was expected, as narratives are known to produce lower syntactic complexity than expository texts. No statistically significant age effect was detected, or if there was a trend, it was in the direction of greater complexity in the latter interviews.

These findings are clearly contradictory to what Kemper, Thompson, and Marquis (2001) report about the reduction of syntactic complexity in the old age based on statistical models. They followed a group of 30 healthy individuals over a span of 8–15 years. The participants were 65–75 years of age at the beginning of the follow-up, and showed the steepest decline in syntactic complexity between ages 74 and 78. In an earlier study, Kemper et al. (1990) observed that the oldest age group (80 years or more) produced the most complex stories (personal experiences and fantasy tales) which included multiple episodes, embedded episodes, and evaluative codas. The oldest group, however, produced these stories with decreased syntactical complexity compared to the younger adults (60 years of age). In spite of reduced syntactic complexity, a group of 10 listeners evaluated the stories of the oldest participants somewhat higher than the stories of younger individuals. The authors discussed the possible effect of decreased working memory capacity on the older adults' story-telling skills, i.e., whether it is too much for an old person to recount complex story content and complex syntactic structures simultaneously. They concluded, however, that the oldest people, during their long life, may have learned the style of producing interesting, appealing, and hierarchically complex stories with simple clauses (see also Kemper and Kemtes 2000).

In story generation tasks, the density of informational content has been reported to diminish as people grow old (Juncos-Rabadán, Pereiro, and Soledad Rodrigues 2005). Juncos-Rabadán, Pereiro, and Soledad Rodrigues (2005) asked their subjects (aged 40–91 years) to produce stories with the help of three sets of six-framed cartoons. The reduction of relevant ("faithful") content was accompanied by reduced cohesive reference (see also Stover and Haynes 1989; Ulatowska and Chapman 1991). In addition, compared to younger people the older adults produced more details not explicit in the picture frames (irrelevant information) and demonstrated greater verbosity. Verbosity, however, is not unanimously considered typical of elderly persons' behavior, but in many cases a symptom of some degenerative process that disrupts the inhibitory function of the frontal lobes (for a review, see Kemper and Kemtes 2000).

The style of conversational interaction has also been observed to alter with advancing age (MacKenzie 2000b). When talking with the researcher about the weather, employment, day-to-day activities, etc., the oldest participants (75–88 years of age) in Mackenzie's (2000b) study showed a tendency towards verbosity, failure to adhere to the topic, poor turn-taking, and unclear reference. By contrast, in conversations with their peers, elderly people (aged 78–90 years) have shown preserved topic maintenance skills (Stover and Haynes 1989). In addition, it should be noted that group-level results disregard individual performance, as many participants in Mackenzie's (2000b) study had excellent conversational skills: approximately 50 % of the participants over 75 years-ofage achieved maximum scores for referencing and topic maintenance, and about 40 % had maximum scores for turn-taking and *non*-verbosity.

Thus, the picture drawn from group-level results seems to strengthen the stereotypical conception of old people being excessively talkative and often getting off-track in conversation. More data providing evidence against the concept of elderly people just talking about the same old things over and over again come from Stuart (2000). Stuart looked at 28 participants' natural conversations during noon lunch hours in a senior citizens' center. In addition, he conducted natural field observations of the participants and interviewed their significant others as well as professionals meeting elderly people in their work (priests, insurance officers, medical doctors, etc.). Stuart found out that most of the participants did indeed repeat the same core stories over the following days. Most interestingly, however, they typically expanded the core story with new or elaborated information. In many cases, they connected the stories not only to past experiences but to the present time, as when comparing the way of life "then and now". In addition to individual monologues, group stories emerged when other visitors participated in constructing the story: these stories were often based on an acknowledgement of common knowledge, like the interlocutors having experienced something similar. Thus, in these conversations between elderly people, narration seems to serve the transmission of various values and cultural maintenance.

3.3. Individual Paths of Linguistic-Cognitive Aging

Although some rough age-related trends are found in linguistic-cognitive functions, as described in Sections 3.1 and 3.2, elderly people do not represent a homogeneous group. Different paths of aging can be found in neurologically healthy individuals, and both intra-individual (Hertzog, Dixon, and Hultsch 1992) and inter-individual (Ylikoski et al. 1999) variation in test performance has been shown to increase with normal cognitive aging. In a sample of 120 healthy, home-dwelling people aged 55–85 years, Ylikoski et al. (1999) found three main groups using neuropsychological tests: 1) a group of average aging, 2) those with above-average level of performance (successful aging), and 3) individuals at risk of cognitive decline. Those at risk were clearly the oldest (75 years and above) of the whole sample. However, in this oldest age group, individuals with high level education, high general intelligence, and active life participation showed successful aging, and those with very good linguistic skills belonged to the group of averagely aging persons.

The connection between age and level of education seems especially important when linguistic-cognitive skills are evaluated or predicted. In language comprehension tasks, the combination of young age (below 60 years) and high education (university level) results in best achievement, while neurologically healthy older elderly people, aged 75 years or more, who have left school at the age of 14 or 15, may even perform similarly to persons manifesting clear pathologies, such as aphasia (Mackenzie 2000a). In language production, those with minimum education produce shorter and less complete picture descriptions than those with longer education, but conversational interaction seems not to be affected by level of education (Mackenzie 2000b). Gender does not have an effect on discourse comprehension tasks (Mackenzie 2000a) or on production tasks, although Mackenzie (2000b) found that in a group of 189 neurologically healthy people women had a tendency to produce longer and more interpretive content descriptions than men.

Thus, it can be concluded that a healthy, elderly individual can be expected to perform well even in demanding discourse contexts if he or she has a high level of education and has spent an active life that has enhanced the development and maintenance of intellectual processes, language use included. In addition, the age-related changes, when apparent, can be compensated by learnt, top-down strategies and by communication partners who adjust their speech style or act as external cognitive aids (Dixon 2000: 37). Moreover, communication may be enhanced by making the environment suitable for the elderly person's communication needs.

4. Language and Communication Disorders in the Elderly

Aging does not, however, always proceed successfully. The main causes of disorders in speech, language, and interaction in the elderly are brain illnesses, such as cerebral vascular accidents (brain infarct or cerebral hemorrhage) leading to stroke and degenerative processes of the brain resulting in dementia. Thus, old people may be facing communication problems suddenly and usually unexpectedly or progressively over a longer period of time.

In Sections 4.1. and 4.2., two conditions mainly responsible for elderly people's problems in communication and interaction are discussed, namely aphasia and dementia. Language deficits in aphasia and dementia are partly similar, but the nature of communication problems is different. In aphasia, the main problems are seen in the level of microprocessing, i.e., in lexical and syntactic processes, whereas in dementia—especially, Alzheimer's type dementia—the problems are connected with disordered macroprocesses, such as problems with the coherence of discourse, or pragmatic deviations (Glosser and Deser 1990). Different forms of aphasia and dementia affect a fairly large group of older people, who thus need specific services to support their living in the most appropriate surroundings.

4.1. Language and Communication in Aphasia

Aphasia is an acquired linguistic-cognitive disorder in adulthood, and is typically a result of a stroke. It has been estimated that each year in the United Kingdom, approximately 20,000 new cases of aphasia are diagnosed (Parr et al. 1997), and about 100,000 new cases in the United States (Damasio 1992). As the risk to cerebrovascular diseases, such as stroke, increases significantly with age, the number of people with aphasia is expected to increase as the population lives to become older than before. Currently, aphasia is present in 21–38 % of patients suffering from acute stroke (Berthier 2005).

Aphasia is typically a multimodal disorder and affects both the comprehension and production of spoken and written messages. Chapey (1986: 6–7) defines aphasia as an acquired impairment in language and the cognitive processes underlying language caused by organic damage to the brain. It is characterized by a reduction and dysfunction of language content or meaning, language form or structure, and language use or function and the cognitive processes underlying language, such as memory and thought.

Aphasia as such, however, does not affect general intelligence. In addition, aphasia takes different forms, that is, it manifests as different syndromes, it varies in severity, and the symptoms may change over time. Aphasic disturbances are seen in phonology, syntax, semantics, and pragmatics, but the individual syndromes vary widely. The most common feature in all forms of aphasia is difficulty in finding words. The main distinction is made between non-fluent and fluent forms of aphasia (Damasio 1998). The non-fluent aphasia syndromes are further classified into *Broca's aphasia, transcortical motor aphasia,* and *global aphasia.* A typical form of non-fluent aphasia is Broca's aphasia with slow and laborious speech production. Grammatical structures are simple, and a speaker may mainly use single-word utterances in conversation (e.g., Klippi 1996). It has been claimed that morpho-syntactical disorder (agrammatism) is a common but not universal feature of Broca's aphasia (Goodglass 1993). Helasvuo, Klippi, and Laakso (2001) point out that word searching and repetitive attempts to repair errors of speech make the sentence structures distorted. Speech comprehension in people with non-fluent aphasia is regarded as relatively good compared to speech production although the understanding of complex linguistic structures is often impaired.

A common type of aphasia is *anomic aphasia,* one of the fluent aphasia syndromes (Goodglass 1993). It is considered a relatively mild disorder characterized by word-finding difficulties. In discourse, a person with anomic aphasia typically produces long pauses and false starts, uses pronouns for proper nouns, and reiterates successfully accessed words. In more severe cases of anomia, the person has serious difficulties in accessing the target words, and the production of semantic substitutions and use of indefinite terms (*thing, some, something, anything*) are frequent. A severe form of fluent aphasia is called *Wernicke's aphasia.* Language comprehension problems are a fundamental part of this syndrome, but in general the speech flows fluently, and the prosody is preserved. A speaker with Wernicke's aphasia typically produces lexical and phonological substitutions, and even neologistic word forms which make it very difficult for the communication partner to understand the content of the utterances. In addition, specific nouns are often substituted with indefinite terms. However, the grammatical structures are well preserved. One of the clinical symptoms of Wernicke's aphasia is the "pressure of speech output" as people with Wernicke's aphasia sometimes speak excessively rapidly and seemingly without awareness of their speech errors (Goodglass 1993).

Several studies have reported that people with Broca's aphasia are significantly younger than people with global aphasia and Wernicke's aphasia (e.g., Kertesz and Sheppard 1981). Many explanations have been offered for this finding, but no consensus has so far been reached in this issue (Nicholas et al. 1998). Nevertheless, it seems that, as a group, people with Wernicke's aphasia are some 10 years older than people with Broca's aphasia. Thus, a severe language comprehension problem combined with old age and low educational level may hinder old people with aphasia from maintaining communicative initiative and predispose them to social isolation.

The discourse problems of people with aphasia are traditionally thought to result from disorders in microprocessing (lexical and syntactic problems) rather than macroprocessing (problems in text production, pragmatic skills, or cognitive processes in general; e.g., Glosser and Deser 1990). This paradigmatic notion, however, has been challenged in recent years, and the role of aphasic difficulties in using the linguistic resources to construct coherent discourse has been the focus of research more frequently than before (e.g., Armstrong 2005; Ulatowska and Streit Ollnes 2000). The difficulty that people with aphasia have in lexicalizing their ideas is manifest in increased number of hesitations, revisions, circumlocutions, paraphasic errors (substitutions), and ambiguous pronouns in comparison with non-aphasic control subjects. This formulation difficulty can be considered the main reason for the disrupted coherence of the various types of discourse (Chapman, Peterson Highley, and Thompson 1998). The frequent word-finding problems in aphasia directly affect the syntactic structures and cohesion of a text (Glosser and Deser 1990). When the speaker is unable to access the targeted words, the clauses may remain incomplete (Bird and Franklin 1996), and relevant information may be missing from the intended message (Christiansen 1995). If the speaker also starts a complicated repair sequence or a new word search, the clause structures will break down (Helasvuo, Klippi, and Laakso 2001), as will the thematic continuity of the text (Korpijaakko-Huuhka 2008). Word-finding problems also result in lexical ambiguity and loosen the lexical cohesion of the text (Glosser 1993; Glosser and Deser 1990). In addition, the impreciseness of pronominal reference found in the discourse of people with aphasia (Armstrong 1991; Gleason et al. 1980; Ulatowska et al. 1983) affects the grammatical cohesion of the text.

In spite of the obvious problems described above, Korpijaakko-Huuhka (2008) claims that people with aphasia have not totally lost their text production skills. In a story-generation task, a group of 15 people with aphasia seemed to be well aware of the narrative genre and struggled to complete the story. Although their texts did not always turn out well-formed stories, fragments of narrative structures or individual coherent episodes could be found in what they produced. Typically, however, the listener needs all the contextual cues available to understand the message of the aphasic speaker. It is also likely that people with aphasia rely on their partner's ability to interpret their utterances with the aid of contextual information. For example, the use of exophoric pronominal reference as a compensatory strategy if the speaker is unable to access the targeted nouns seems more frequent the more severe the aphasic disorder is. In the most severe cases, the partner's help and prompting serve as a resource for the speakers with aphasia, and support them in completing the task and saving face in a difficult situation. Finally, Korpijaakko-Huuhka (2008) concludes that the role of aphasic language in text production is fundamental. If the listener is unable to understand what the speaker is talking about and how the events described are related to each other and to the discourse context, no coherent text emerges.

Moreover, studies in conversation analysis have produced a new, more detailed understanding of the everyday talk-in-interaction with people with aphasia (cf., e.g., Damico, Oelschlaeger, and Simmons-Mackie 1999; Goodwin 2003). First, the study of word-finding problems and problems in producing coherent conversational turns has revealed the nature of repair work in aphasic conversation. Aphasic word searches have similar features to those found in normal conversation (e.g., Laakso 1997; Laakso and Klippi 1999; Oelschlaeger 1999), and most often the person with aphasia tries first to self-repair the problem (Laakso 1997). If the word search is unsuccessful, collaboration is established by shifting the orientation to a co-participant (e.g., a speech language therapist, a spouse, or a family member), and these collaborative repair sequences are often long and complex (Klippi 1996; Laakso 1997; Laakso and Klippi 1999). Second, the study of embodiment has shown that persons with aphasia often use gestures, facial expressions, and head positions in spoken interaction to convey meanings and to elaborate their expressions (e.g., Klippi 1996; Klippi and Ahopalo 2008). Finally, the analysis of pragmatic competence and social life (e.g., Goodwin 2003) has focused on the study of resources in talk-in-interaction, not only on the troubles and restrictions.

4.2. Communication in Dementia

Another common clinical syndrome in the elderly is dementia, with severe decline in several cognitive functions. Dementia is characterized by the breakdown of intellectual and communicative functioning, as well as personality change (American Psychiatric Association 1994). Kempler (1995) has estimated that in dementing diseases, communication disorders are present in 88–95% of cases. In the early stages of dementia, the communication impairment is mild, but as the disease progresses, deficits in linguistic communication become more pronounced. In addition, it is important to understand that, depending on the type of dementia, communication disorders vary (Bayles 1986), and that not all aspects of linguistic communication or intellectual functioning are affected to the same degree.

The most common etiology of dementia is Alzheimer's disease, which progressively affects multiple cognitive functions, such as memory, language skills, praxis, visuospatial perception, and executive functions. It causes remarkable restrictions of social and occupational competence among elderly people (American Psychiatric Association 1994). The prominent feature throughout the course of the disease is memory impairment. Memory processes can be divided into explicit and implicit memory. Explicit memory is further subdivided into episodic and semantic memory. The most typical early feature of Alzheimer's disease is the decrement of episodic memory, which leads to the loss of memory of recent events and experiences (Salmon, Heindel, and Butters 1997).

The general picture of language and communication in people with Alzheimer's type dementia shows impaired semantic and pragmatic skills, whereas phonology and syntax are relatively well preserved. Difficulties in finding words (Kempler 1995), impaired performance, and circumlocutory responses in verbal fluency tasks (Pekkala 2004) are common. The problems are particularly obvious in discourse tasks (Ulatowska and Chapman 1995) and in spontaneous conversational speech (Bucks et al. 2000). In addition, comprehension impairments are already discernible in the early and middle stages of dementia (Kempler 1995). To sum up, the communication problems of people with Alzheimer's disease are typically seen in two areas of language: lexicon (word knowledge) and pragmatics.

The second most common type of dementia is vascular dementia, caused by multiple cerebral infarctions in both cortical and subcortical parts of the brain. It is estimated that 15–20 % of all dementia cases are of the vascular type (Molloy and Lubinski 1995). People with vascular dementia form a much less homogeneous group than those with Alzheimer's disease, and the cognitive and linguistic profile of each person depends on the volume and location of the brain lesions. Unlike in Alzheimer's disease, clear aphasic disorders may be found in vascular dementia, and the language deficit of a person with vascular dementia may even be restored (Molloy and Lubinski 1995). In addition to Alzheimer's disease and vascular dementia, there are several other types of dementia, and the reader is recommended to seek a more detailed overview, for example, in Lubinski (1995).

Although the linguistic impairments in Alzheimer's disease are not regarded as aphasia proper, persons with Alzheimer's disease may display language deficits similar to those of people with aphasia (see Section 4.1.). However, the communication breakdown in dementia differs from aphasic problems: Language and communication problems apparently result from a more general cognitive deficit and they manifest in conversation, for example, as unexpected and sudden topic changes not seen in conversations of people with aphasia.

While aphasia is of sudden onset and will slowly be restored (within a certain upper limit), the symptoms of dementia get progressively worse. For example, Hamilton's (1994) study interestingly shows how the language used by a person with Alzheimer's disease (Elsie) changed over time. In the earlier stages of Elsie's illness, the changes were minor; she was capable of making extensive use of her linguistic means as she could request, express wishes, elicit information, express concern for others, provide excuses for her unexpected behavior, and refuse or accept offers. In the later stages, Elsie did no longer initiate an exchange verbally, but only responded to the researchers' utterances, for instance by agreeing with them by using *mhm*, or requesting repetition by uttering *mhm?*, and expressing pleasure with *mmm*.

4.3. Social Consequences of Brain Damage

As the overviews in Sections 4.1. and 4.2. show, a fairly comprehensive picture of speech and language disorders in people with aphasia and dementia has emerged, based on large numbers of clinical studies. However, very few studies deal with everyday communication and interaction in elderly people with aphasia or dementia. One of the few is a recent study by Davidson, Worral, and Hick-son (2003) which identified the communication activities of older people with aphasia. Based on naturalistic observations, everyday communication with healthy older people and older people with chronic aphasia were compared. From the coded communicative activities, conversation was the most frequently occurring discourse in both groups. As expected, compared to healthy older people, older people with aphasia had significantly fewer activities making telephone calls, in reading, and in writing. These findings were interpreted as evidence of the negative impact of aphasia on both leisure and business activities. People with aphasia were observed to have fewer communication partners and more restricted social contexts for interacting than non-aphasic people.

Further, according to Davidson, Worral, and Hickson (2003), topics common to all participants were related to food and beverages, friends, neighbors and family, health issues, and regular weekly activities. Common topics for the healthy older people—but infrequent for the people with aphasia—were books, news and current affairs, local politics, travel, computers, expressing opinions about social issues, and conversing about other cultures and languages. For the people with aphasia, restricted opportunities for conversations involving reflection, storytelling, discussion of opinions and ideas were found, and the range of conversation topics in general was found to be small. Thus, the results of the study clearly demonstrate that communication for older people means not merely the transfer of information, but also, and possibly more importantly, a means of social affiliation, and that people with aphasia obviously are at risk of social isolation.

A study by Linell and Korolija (1995) analyzed the division of interactive labor in family conversations involving aphasic participants (multiparty conversations). Their results reveal that people with aphasia experienced particular difficulties in getting their voices heard in conversation. The discussions were typically asymmetrical, and the people with aphasia were relegated to secondary roles. They could seldom develop the episodes and remain in the interactive focus throughout the episodes. In many cases, the people with aphasia were not active as speakers but provided listener support items when others spoke. Another interesting phenomenon was found in Lindsay and Wilkinson's (1999) study where they compared conversations between a person with aphasia and a speech-language therapist or the spouse. These dyadic conversations revealed different interactive patterns. The speech-language therapists worked to minimize the interactive consequences of aphasic problems in conversation, whereas the spouses contributed by exposing and prolonging the repairs. The researchers suggested that "being a spouse" allows certain behaviors that are not so evident in other types of interactions.

The psychosocial effects of aphasia have been divided by Byng, Pound, and Parr (2000) into three main categories: 1) effects on lifestyle (e.g., employment, education, leisure), 2) effects on the person (e.g., psychological effects, identity, self-esteem), and 3) effects on others in the immediate social context (e.g., identity, relationships, changes of roles). Thus, the maintenance of social relationships is of the utmost importance for people with aphasia after stroke, as well as for people suffering from degenerative diseases. Maintaining social relationships and receiving informational support predict better health-related quality of life for people with chronic aphasia (Hilary and Northcott 2006). However, people with aphasia typically feel more or less isolated from their previous contexts, and this isolation from social networks takes place soon after the stroke (Parr et al. 1997).

4.4. Enhancing Activities and Participation

As the knowledge and understanding of the linguistic-cognitive functions and discourse skills of elderly persons has grown in recent years, new approaches to the preservation, activation, and restoration of the speech and language functions of old people have also been developed. The rehabilitation of aphasia has long roots (for reviews, cf. Chapey 1986; Howard and Hatfield 1987), whereas communicative interventions for people with dementia are only gradually emerging (e.g., Lubinski and Orange 2000).

Speech-language therapy is considered the mainstay of the treatment of aphasia, and, over the past decade, speech and language therapists have been increasingly influenced by the biopsychosocial model of functioning and health (World Health Organization 2001) and the social model of disability (e.g.,

Duchan and Byng 2005). Accordingly, the understanding of the social role of language in various contexts has increased. This understanding has led to the development of communication-focused therapy, sometimes referred to as *functional therapy* or *pragmatic therapy*. The main purpose of such therapy is to facilitate and enhance optimal interaction using all the verbal and non-verbal resources available (Lesser and Perkins 1999: 14). As the focus in this section is on elderly people with communication disorders, only approaches specifically intended to enhance their communicative activities and participation in social life will be mentioned.

The treatment of people with aphasia in group-settings is an established therapeutic approach. Group treatment has several advantages over individual treatment (Elman 1999). For example, it fosters pragmatic skills, including improved turn-taking and communicative initiative, and increases the variety of communicative functions. Group environments are seen to provide an opportunity for a wider array of communicative partners and natural tasks, thereby enhancing participation in various discourses at home and in community environments. Group treatment may directly and indirectly improve a person's psychosocial functioning by providing a supportive environment for communication. In addition, group treatments are regarded as a cost-effective way of providing treatment compared to individualized speech-language therapy.

Recently, new interventions have been developed to alleviate aphasic communication problems. One of the approaches is called *conversational partner training programmes* in aphasia (Turner and Whitworth 2006), and they directly aim to capitalize on the potential of partners to facilitate maximally effective communication through their own conversational behavior. These methods (e.g., Hopper; Holland, and Rewega 2002; Kagan 1998; Lock, Wilkinson, and Bryan 2001) are designed to increase communicative access for the person with aphasia, the core idea being to provide a model for the communication partners (family members, friends, and volunteers) of how to interact with people with aphasia and to increase their life participation. These methods also have potential for application to dementias. Promising results have been achieved, for instance, through a cognitive-linguistic intervention program for patients with mild-to-moderate Alzheimer's disease (Mahendra and Arkin 2003).

5. Concluding Remarks

In this chapter, we applied the new biopsychosocial model of the WHO, the International Classification of Functioning, Disability and Health (ICF), as a general framework for discussing language and discourse skills in the elderly. We introduced some possible causes of age-related changes in language and discourse, but—according to the model—we have focused on the functional impacts of such changes rather than on the causes as such. In addition, we followed the ICF model also in that the impact of the environment on a person's functioning has been taken into account in relation to both healthy aging and pathological conditions.

Growing old causes inevitable physiological and cognitive changes for everyone. These changes may affect one's linguistic and bodily functioning, and thereby one's quality of life. The quality of elderly people's lives seems to suffer more from restricted opportunities to interact and communicate with other people than from deteriorations found in experimental tasks. Moreover, in familiar, everyday contexts healthy old people typically perform complex tasks efficiently, relying on their accumulated experience and knowledge. In discourse, age-related changes, such as difficulty in recalling details, may be compensated by the intact cognitive strategies and environmental support. Moreover, some linguistic skills have been shown to develop throughout the whole life span. For example, the adoption of new concepts and corresponding words, as well as the use of elaborate narrative style, are possible if not typical developmental trends as people grow older.

Our positive conception is, thus, that changes in the course of aging are not necessarily only declines, and old people should be considered competent communicators with active and satisfying lives. This conception, however, is radically changed when aging is accompanied by sudden or progressive diseases affecting language and discourse skills. The linguistic-cognitive deficits in aphasia or dementia restrict life-participation and constitute a major risk factor for the social isolation of elderly people. To avoid the negative social consequences of aphasia and dementia, specific rehabilitative interventions are needed. In addition, more attention should be paid to the physical and social environments of elderly people. Lubinski (1995: 258–271) emphasizes that the environment should provide opportunities for individual control, personalization, choice, and interpersonal communication. The role of communication partners forming the social environment in enhancing and maintaining the communicative competencies of old people with aphasia or dementia is fundamental, and their role is also essential for those without any communication disorders.

Within the philosophical framework of the social model of disability (Duchan and Byng 2005), people with disabilities are considered experts on their own conditions. This insight has raised the question about the possibilities for people with communication disorders also to be involved in decisions about the course of therapy and how it is implemented. One solution is that service providers present the available choices and opportunities, which are then discussed with the client to create a solid basis for the intervention. The voices of people with communication disorders should be heard more often in research, too. Their expectations and experiences are valuable, but they will be reached only when the traditional instruments of data collection are modified to meet the needs of people with communication disorders. This reasoning shows that, in the future, we clearly need to further extend the research of language, discourse and aging to everyday contexts to gain ecologically valid results, which will help us to enhance our understanding of both group-level and individual changes in healthy aging.

References

Administration on Aging. 1998. *A profile of Older Americans: 1998.* Online document: http://www.aoa. dhhs.gov (Last access: 02. 09. 2007).
American Psychiatric Association. 1994. *Diagnostic and Statistical Manual of Mental Disorders.* 4th edition. Washington, DC: American Psychiatric Association.

Armstrong, Elizabeth. 2005. Language disorder: A functional linguistic perspective. *Clinical Linguistics & Phonetics* 19(3): 137–153.

Bayles, Katherine A. 1986. Management of neurogenic communication disorders associated with dementia. In: Roberta Chapey (ed.), *Language Intervention Strategies in Adult Aphasia*, 462–473. Baltimore: Williams & Wilkins.

Benjamin, Barbaranne J. 1997. Speech production of normally aging adults. *Seminars in Speech and Language* 18: 135–141.

Berthier, Maecelo L. 2005. Poststroke aphasia: Epidemiology, pathophysiology and treatment. *Drugs Aging* 22: 163–182.

Bird, Helen and Sue Franklin. 1996. Cinderella revisited: A comparison of fluent and non-fluent aphasic speech. *Journal of Neurolinguistics* 9: 187–206.

Bond Chapman, Sandra, Amy Peterson Highley and Jennifer L. Thompson. 1998. Discourse in fluent aphasia and Alzheimer's disease: Linguistic and cognitive considerations. In: Michel Paradis (ed.), *Pragmatics in Neurogenic Communication Disorders*, 55–78. Oxford: Elsevier Science.

Bucks, Romola S., S. Singh, J.M. Cuerden and Gordon K. Wilcock. 2000. Analysis of spontaneous, conversational speech in dementia of Alzheimer type: Evaluation of an objective technique for analysing lexical performance. *Aphasiology* 14: 71–91.

Butler Robert H., Mia Oberlink and Mal Schechter. 1998. The elderly in society: An international perspective. In: Raymond Tallis, Howard Fillit and J.C. Brocklehurst (eds.), *Brocklehurst's Textbook of Geriatric Medicine and Gerontology*, 1445–1460. Edinburgh: Churchill Livingstone.

Byng, Sally, Carol Pound and Susan Parr. 2000. Living with aphasia: A framework for therapy interventions. In: Ilias Papathanassiou (ed.), *Acquired Neurogenic Communication Disorders: A clinical perspective*, 47–75. London: Whurr.

Chapey, Roberta. 1986. An introduction to language intervention strategies in adult aphasia. In: Roberta Chapey (ed.), *Language Intervention Strategies in Adult Aphasia*, 2–11. Baltimore: Williams & Wilkins.

Chapman, Sandra Bond, Amy Peterson Highley and Jennifer L. Thompson. 1998. Discourse in fluent aphasia and Alzheimer's disease: Linguistic and cognitive considerations. In: Michel Paradis (ed.), *Pragmatics in Neurogenic Communication Disorders*, 55–78. Oxford: Elsevier Science.

Christiansen, Julie Ann. 1995. Coherence violations and propositional usage in the narratives of fluent aphasics. *Brain and Language* 51: 291–317.

Connor, Lisa T., Avron Spiro, Lorraine K. Obler and Martin L Albert. 2004. Change in object naming ability during adulthood. *Journal of Gerontology: Psychological Sciences* 59B: 203–209.

Coupland, Nikolas, Justine Coupland and Howard Giles. 1991. *Language, Society and the Elderly: Discourse, Identity and Aging*. Oxford/ Cambridge: Blackwell.

Cruice, Madeline N., Linda E. Worral and Louise M.H. Hickson. 2000. Boston Naming Test results for healthy older Australians: A longitudinal and cross-sectional study. *Aphasiology* 14: 143–155.

Cutler, Roy G. and Mark P Mattson. 2006. Introduction: The adversities of aging. *Ageing Research Reviews* 5: 221–238.

Damico, Jack, Mary L. Oelschlaeger and Nina Simmons-Mackie. 1999. Qualitative methods in aphasia research: Conversation analysis. *Aphasiology* 13: 667–679.

Damasio, Antonio. 1992. Aphasia. *New England Journal of Medicine* 326: 531–539. Damasio, Antonio. 1998. Signs of aphasia. In: Martha Taylor Sarno (ed.), *Acquired Aphasia*, 25–42. 3rd edition. San Diego: Academic Press.

Davidson, Bronwyn, Linda Worrall and Louise Hickson. 2003. Identifying the communicative activities of older people with aphasia: Evidence from naturalistic observation. *Aphasiology* 17: 243–264.

Davis, G. Albyn and Hillary E. Ball. 1989. Effects of age on comprehension of complex sentences in adulthood. *Journal of Speech and Hearing Research* 32: 143–150.

Dixon, Roger A. 2000. Concepts and mechanisms of gains in cognitive aging. In: Denise C. Park and Norbert Schwarz (eds.), *Cognitive Aging: A Primer*, 23–41. Philadelphia: Psychology Press.

Duchan, Judith Felson and Sally Byng. 2005. Social model philosophies and principles: Their applications to therapies for aphasia. *Aphasiology* 19, 906–922.

Elman, Roberta J. 1999. Introduction to group treatment of neurogenic communication disorders. In: Roberta Elman (ed.), *Group treatment of neurogenic communication disorders*, 4–7. Boston: Butterworth & Heinemann.

Garstecki, Dean C. and Susan F. Erler. 1998. Hearing loss, control, and demographic factors influencing hearing aid use among older adults. *Journal of Speech, Language, and Hearing Research* 41: 527–537.

Gleason, Jean Berko, Harold Goodglass, Lorraine Obler, Eugene Green, Mary R. Hyde and Sandra Weintraub. 1980. Narrative strategies of aphasic and normal-speaking subjects. *Journal of Speech and Hearing Research* 23: 370–382.

Glosser, Guila. 1993. Discourse production patterns in neurologically impaired and aged populations. In: Hiram H. Brownell and Yves Joanette (eds.), *Narrative Discourse in Neurologically Impaired and Normal Aging*, 191–212. San Diego: Singular.

Glosser, Guila and Toni Deser. 1990. Patterns of discourse production among neurological patients with fluent language disorders. *Brain and Language* 40: 67–88.

Goodglass, Harold. 1993. *Understanding Aphasia*. San Diego: Academic Press.

Goodwin, Charles. 2003. Introduction. In: Charles Goodwin (ed.), *Conversation and Brain Damage*, 3–20. Oxford: Oxford University Press.

Gordon-Salant, Sandra and Peter J. Fitzgibbons. 1997. Selected cognitive factors and speech recognition performance among young and elderly listeners. *Journal of Speech, Language, and Hearing Research* 40: 423–431.

Guimaraes dos Santos, Claudio L.N. and Jean-Luc Nespoulous. 1993. Narrative discourse processing in normal aging: A neuropsychological and comparative study. In: Hiram H. Brownell and Yves Joanette (eds.), *Narrative Discourse in Neurologically Impaired and Normal Aging*, 135–147. San Diego: Singular.

Hamilton, Heidi. 1994. *Conversations with an Alzheimer's patient*. Cambridge, Cambridge University Press.

Helasvuo, Marja-Liisa, Anu Klippi and Minna Laakso. 2001. Grammatical structuring in Brocas's and Wernicke's aphasia in Finnish. *Journal of Neurolinguistics* 14: 231–254.

Hertzog, Christopher, Roger A. Dixon and David F. Hultsch. 1992. Intraindividual change in text recall of the elderly. *Brain and Language* 42: 248–269.

Hilari, Katherine and Sarah Northcott. 2006. Social support in people with chronic aphasia. *Aphasiology* 20: 17–36.

Hopper, Tammy, Audrey Holland and Molly Rewega. 2002. Conversational coaching: Treatment outcomes and future directions. *Aphasiology* 16: 745–761.

Howard, David and Francis Hatfield. 1987. *Aphasia Therapy: Historical and Contemporary Issues*. Hove/Hillsdale: Lawrence Erlbaum.

Juncos-Rabadán, Onésimo, Arturo X. Pereiro and Maria Soledad Rodriguez. 2005. Narrative speech in aging: Quantity, information content and cohesion. *Brain and Language* 95: 423–434.

Kahn, Helen J. and Danielle Gordon. 1993. Qualitative differences in working memory and discourse comprehension in normal aging. In: Hiram H. Brownell and Yves Joanette (eds.), *Narrative Discourse in Neurologically Impaired and Normal Aging*, 103–114. San Diego: Singular.

Kagan, Aura. 1998. Supported conversation for adults with aphasia: Methods and resources for training conversation partners. *Aphasiology* 12: 816–830.

Kemper, Susan and Karen Kemtes. 2000. Aging and message production and comprehension. In: Denise C. Park and Norbert Schwarz (eds.), *Cognitive Aging: A Primer*, 197–213. Philadelphia: Psychology Press.

Kemper, Susan, Shannon Rash, Donna Kynette and Suzanne Norman. 1990. Telling stories: The structure of adults' narratives. *European Journal of Cognitive Psychology* 2: 205–228.

Kemper, Susan, Marilyn Thompson and Janet Marquis. 2001. Longitudinal changes in language production: Effects of aging and dementia on grammatical complexity and propositional content. *Psychology and Aging* 16: 600–614.

Kempler, Daniel. 1995. Language changes in dementia of the Alzheimer type. In: Rosemary Lubinski (ed.), *Dementia and Communication*, 98–114. San Diego: Singular.

Kertesz, Andrew and Ann Sheppard. 1981. The epidemiology of aphasia and cognitive impairment in stroke: Age, sex, aphasia type and laterality differences. *Brain* 104: 117–128.

Klippi, Anu. 1996. *Conversation as an Achievement in Aphasics*. (Studia Fennica: Linguistica 6.) Helsinki: Suomalaisen Kirjallisuuden Seura.

Klippi, Anu and Liisa Ahopalo. 2008. The interplay between verbal and nonverbal behaviors in aphasic word search in conversation. In: Anu Klippi and Kaisa Launonen (eds.), *Communication Disorders in Finnish and in Finland*, 148–176. (Communication Disorders Across Languages.) London: Multilingual Matters.

Korpijaakko-Huuhka, Anna-Maija. 2008. Text production of Finnish speakers with aphasia. In: A. Klippi and K. Launonen (eds.), *Communication Disorders in Finnish and in Finland*, 99–126. (Communication Disorders Across Languages.) London: Multilingual Matters.

Laakso, Minna. 1997. *Self-initiated Repair by Fluent Aphasic Speakers in Conversation*. Helsinki: Suomalaisen Kirjallisuuden Seura.

Laakso, Minna and Anu Klippi. 1999. A closer look at the 'hint and guess' sequences in aphasic conversation. *Aphasiology* 13: 345–363.

Labov, William and Julie Auger. 1993. The effect of normal aging on discourse: A sociolinguistic approach. In: Hiram H. Brownell and Yves Joanette (eds.), *Narrative Discourse in Neurologically Impaired and Normal Aging Adults*, 115–134. San Diego: Singular.

Le Dorze, Guylaine and Christine Bédard. 1998. Effects of age and education on the lexico-semantic content of connected speech in adults. *Journal of Communication Disorders* 31: 53–71.

Lesser, Ruth and Lisa Perkins. 1999. *Cognitive Neuropsychology and Conversation Analysis in Aphasia*. Gateshead: Whurr.

Linell Per and Natasha Korolija. 1995. On the division of communicative labour within episodes in aphasic discourse. *International Journal of Psycholinguistics* 11: 143–165.

Lindsay, Jayne and Ray Wilkinson. 1999. Repair sequences in aphasic talk: A comparison of aphasic-speech and language therapist and aphasic-spouse conversations. *Aphasiology* 13: 305–325.

Lock, Sarah, Ray Wilkinson and Karen Bryan. 2001. *Supporting Partners of People with Aphasia in Relationships and Conversation (SPPARC): Resource Pack*. Bicester: Speechmark Publishing.

Lubinski, Rosemary B. (ed.). 1995. *Dementia and Communication*. San Diego: Singular.

Lubinski, Rosemary B. 1995. Environmental considerations for elderly patients. In: Rosemary B. Lubinski (ed.), *Dementia and Communication*, 257–278. San Diego: Singular.

Lubinski, Rosemary B. and Joseph B. Orange. 2000. A framework for the assessment and treatment of functional communication in dementia. In: Linda E. Worral and Carol M. Frattali (eds.), *Neurogenic Communication Disorders: A Functional Approach*, 220–246. New York: Thieme.

Mahendra, Nidhi and Sharon M. Arkin. 2003. Move it or lose it: Benefits of exercise for residents with dementia. *Activities Directors' Quarterly for Alzheimer's and Other Dementin Patients*, 4(4): 11–22.

Maxin, Jane and Karen Bryan. 1994. *Language of the Elderly: A Clinical Perspective*. London: Whurr. Mackenzie, Catherine. 2000a. The relevance of education and age in the assessment of discourse comprehension. *Clinical Linguistics & Phonetics* 14: 151–161.

Mackenzie, Catherine. 2000b. Adult spoken discourse: The influences of age and education. *International Journal of Communication Disorders* 35: 269–285.

Molloy, D.William and Rosemary B. Lubinski. 1995. Dementia: Impact and clinical perspectives. In: Rosemary B. Lubinski (ed.), *Dementia and Communication*, 2–21. San Diego: Singular.

Nicholas, Marjorie, Lisa Tabor Connor, Loraine K. Obler and Martin L. Albert. 1998. Aging, language, and language disorders. In: Martha Taylor Sarno (ed.), *Acquired Aphasia*, 413–449. San Diego: Academic Press.

Nieminen, Mauri. 2005. *Eurooppa eläköityy eri tahtiin* [Europe retires at various paces]. Online document: http://www.stat.fi/tup/tietotrendit/tt-01–05-nieminen.html (Last access: 02. 09. 2007).

Obler, Loraine K., Marjorie Nicholas, Martin L. Albert and Steven Woodward. 1985. On comprehension across the adult lifespan. *Cortex* 21: 273–280.

Oelschlaeger, Mary L. 1999. Participation of a conversation partner in the word searches of a person with aphasia. *American Journal of Speech-Language Pathology* 8: 62–71.

Park, Denise C. 2000. The basic mechanisms accounting for age-related decline in cognitive function. In: Denise C. Park and Norbert Schwarz (eds.), *Cognitive Aging: A Primer*, 3–21. Philadelphia: Psychology Press.

Park, Denise C. and Angela Hall Gutchess. 2000. Cognitive aging and every day life. In: Denise C. Park and Norbert Schwarz (eds.), *Cognitive Aging: A Primer*, 217–232. Philadelphia: Psychology Press.

Parr, Susie, Sally Byng, Sue Gilpin and Chris Ireland. 1997. *Talking about Aphasia*. Buckingham: Open University Press.

Pekkala, Seija. 2004. Semantic fluency in mild and moderate Alzheimer's disease. University of Helsinki. Publications of the Department of Phonetics 47.

Salmon, David, William C. Heindel and Nelson Butters. 1997. Patterns of cognitive impairment in Alzheimer's disease and other dementing disorders. In: Rosemary B. Lubinski (ed.), *Dementia and Communication*, 37–46. San Diego: Singular.

Stover, Susan E. and William O. Haynes. 1989. Topic manipulation and cohesive adequacy in conversations of normal adults between the ages of 30 and 90. *Clinical Linguistics and Phonetics* 3: 356–380.

Stuart, Sheela. 2000. Understanding the storytelling of older adults for AAC system designs. *Augmentative and Alternative Communication* 16: 1–12.

Turner, Sonja and Anne Whitworth. 2006. Conversational partner training programmes in aphasia: A review of key themes and participants' roles. *Aphasiology* 20: 483–510.

Ulatowska, Hanna K. and Sandra Bond Chapman. 1995. Discourse studies. In: Rosemary B. Lubinski (ed.), *Dementia and Communication*, 115–132. San Diego: Singular.

Ulatowska, Hanna K., Sandra Bond Chapman, Amy Petterson Higley and Jacqueline Prince. 1998. Discourse in healthy old-elderly adults: A longitudinal study. *Aphasiology* 12: 619–633.

Ulatowska, Hanna K., Renee Freedman-Stern, Alice Weiss Doyel, Sara Macaluso-Haynes and Alvin J. North. 1983. Production of narrative discourse in aphasia. *Brain and Language* 19: 317–334.

Ulatowska, Hanna K. and Gloria Streit Ollnes. 2000. Discourse revisited: Contributions of lexico-syntactic devices. *Brain and Language* 71: 249–251.

Wignfield, Arthur. 2000. Speech perception and the comprehension of spoken language in adult aging. In: Denise C. Park and Norbert Schwarz (eds.), *Cognitive Aging: A Primer*, 175–195. Philadelphia: Psychology Press.

World Health Organisation. 2001. *International Classification of Functioning, Disability and Health*. Geneva: World Health Organisation.

Worral, Linda E. and Louise M. Hickson. 2003. *Communication Disability in Aging: From Prevention to Intervention*. Clifton Park, NY: Delmar Learning.

Ylikoski, Raija, Ari Ylikoski, Pertti Keskivaara, Reijo Tilvis, Raimo Sulkava and Timo Erkinjuntti. 1999. Heterogeneity of cognitive profiles in aging: Successful aging, normal aging, and individuals at risk for cognitive decline. *European Journal of Neurology* 6: 645–652.

Zec, Ronald F., Stephen J. Markwell, Nicole R. Burkett and Deb L. Larsen. 2005. A longitudinal study of confrontation naming in the "normal" elderly. *Journal of the International Neuropsychological Society* 11: 716–726.

12

Nonverbal Communicative Competence

Nancy M. Puccinelli

Imagine you are at a party and you can't help but notice that the guest you have just been introduced to seems quite distraught. As you are left alone to continue the conversation, you wonder if you should acknowledge his dour mood by taking on a sympathetic tone or even asking after his well-being. It may be that he has just had a disagreement and he would invite the opportunity to recount the illogical argument of his colleague or perhaps he has recently lost his mother and this evening represents his first effort to venture out and have a good time. Clearly, being able to identify whether or not he will appreciate having his mood acknowledged is critical to the success of this interaction.

As social beings, we frequently find ourselves in situations in which we must be attuned to our own expressions as well as receptive to cues from others. Learning to navigate the complexities of social interaction is challenging, yet critical, to communicative competence. It has been suggested that communicative competence can take two forms: Effectiveness and appropriateness. Effectiveness takes an actor-based perspective as it valorizes empowerment and action (Parks 1994). It has been argued that control over one's own behavior and that of another is key to effective communication. In contrast, appropriateness takes a more observer-based perspective as it valorizes social harmony (Parks 1994). In considering how one can communicate to satisfy one's needs and desires, nonverbal behavior is a key component. Nonverbal behavior's paramount role stems from evidence that the majority of information, especially sensitive information, is communicated nonverbally. This chapter will examine how nonverbal encoding and decoding work separately and in concert to aid individuals in successful communication.

1. Power of Nonverbal Behavior in Interpersonal Exchange

Research suggests that nonverbal behavior, such as facial expressions and body movement, communicates more information about what one is thinking or feeling than words. Even conservative estimates of the role of nonverbal behavior suggest that 60 % of what is communicated is done so nonverbally (Burgoon 1994). When nonverbal and verbal cues conflict, nonverbal cues are more likely to be believed. Thus, nonverbal behavior appears to provide unique insights into an individual's thoughts and feelings that are not otherwise accessible (Bonoma and Felder 1977). Research that has examined interactions in which access to nonverbal cues is eliminated, such as over email, finds that people prefer media channels in which nonverbal cues are available (Westmyer, DiCioccio, and Rubin 1998). In addition, they find people with whom they communicate in these channels warmer and more personal. Moreover, when verbal content is unclear, people seem to rely almost exclusively on nonverbal cues. Research looking at the effect of courtroom judges' expectations on jury decisions finds that these expectations can be communicated nonverbally. Specifically, when the instructions for the jury are complex judges' expectations have a greater effect on jury decisions than when the jury receives simplified instructions (Halverson et al. 1997). It seems nonverbal behavior also communicates a great deal about one's competence. Research that had observers evaluate photographs of salespeople were able to predict the most successful salesperson (Walker and Raghunathan 2004). Further, it seems these effects are independent of physical attractiveness. Research finds that nonverbal behavior is a better predictor of how someone will be evaluated than physical attractiveness (Ambady and Rosenthal 1993). Further, in a medical context, doctors' nonverbal cues predict patient compliance better than a doctor's verbal cues (Milmoe, Rosenthal, Blane, Chafetz, and Wolf 1967).

The goal of this chapter is to better understand how communicative competence may be enhanced through an understanding of the role of nonverbal behavior in communication. To this end, the first section will consider what is meant by nonverbal behavior and the behaviors that appear to be the most fruitful for examination. Second, encoding, or the expression of nonverbal behavior, and decoding, or the interpretation of nonverbal behavior, will be considered. Within each of these domains, research that bears on the effectiveness or appropriateness of the communication will be discussed. Finally, the impact of encoding and decoding in concert will be examined in applied contexts.

2. Meaning of Nonverbal Behaviors

Because of the importance of nonverbal behavior to interpersonal perception, considerable research has sought to understand the meaning of different behaviors. Early research in this area focused on what is now termed "molecular" cues, or discrete actions that are easily coded (e.g., number of smiles, frequency of eye contact, Ambady and Rosenthal 1993; Grahe and Bernieri 2002). Within research on molecular cues, several broad categories of behavior represent the greatest focus of attention (Knapp and Hall 2002): gestures, posture, touching behavior, facial expressions, eye behavior, and vocal behavior (e.g., tone of voice, pauses, and rhythm). While static cues such as age and clothing are also thought to play a role in nonverbal communication (Hulbert and Capon 1972), the lion's share of the research has focused on dynamic cues that are produced during the interaction.

Considering dynamic cues in more detail, several lines of research have identified the signatures for the expression of certain attributes in an interaction. Research suggests, for example, that empathy can be communicated through leaning forward, closer proximity, more eye contact, more open-ness of arms and body, more direct body orientation, and less eye movement (Hall, Harrigan, and Rosenthal 1995). Dominance seems to be communicated through less smiling, more touching, more frequent initiation of speech, lower likelihood of breaking a mutual glance, more violation of social norms, a more raised head, lowered or frowning brows, and more relaxed, expansive posture (Knapp and Hall 2002). Further, the meaning of nonverbal cues such as these appears to persist across cultures (Elfenbein and Ambady 2002a, 2003).

These prescriptions for communicating specific attributes must be con-sidered with caution, however, as many of the cues that we associate with spe-cific attributes can be spurious. For example, liars appear to exhibit fewer stereotypical cues for lying (such as gaze aversion and fidgeting), compared to non-liars (Mann, Vrij, and Bull 2004). Similarly, cues one may emit to signal confidence may also be misleading as the correlation between the confidence in a statement and its accuracy is zero (Brown 1986). Thus, even non-liars could mislead us with their courage of conviction. Moreover, contextual cues, such as the position of the actor and what the actor is doing can influence judgement of the actor independent of the actor's behavior (Puccinelli et al. 2007).

More recently there has been a shift toward a focus on more "molar" (hol-istic) judgments of behavior that examine a perceiver's overall impression of an individual based on the individual's nonverbal behavior. For example, rather than asking an observer to count the number of times the actor smiled, the observer might indicate her overall impression of how friendly the actor seemed on a nine-point scale. Researchers find that molar judgments are more accurate and are used more frequently (Ambady and Rosenthal 1993; Grahe and Bernieri 2002). In sum, nonverbal cues can reveal a great deal about what people are thinking and feeling that is both encoded and can be decoded in an interaction.

3. Encoding: The Expression of Nonverbal Behavior

To enable a deeper treatment of nonverbal behavior, we will first consider the process of encoding, or an actor's expression of nonverbal behavior. Examin-ation of encoding tendency is a fairly recent development. In 1980, Howard Friedman developed the Affective Communication Test (ACT) to measure individual differences in one's likelihood to be nonverbally expressive. So, for example, an actor who is more likely to tap their foot when they hear music is would score higher on the affective communication test.

Several factors influence one's encoding and expression of nonverbal beha-vior. While in some cases this behavior appears conscious and goal-directed, in other cases it seems quite unintended. On the conscious side, it seems that actors can signal greater conviction in a speech using nonverbal cues (e.g., fre-quent eye contact and low self-touching, Hart and Morry 1996). There also seem to be telling signs that one is seeking to initiate a relationship with a partner. This research finds that the nonverbal cues expressed by unattached men and women during an interaction with an attractive other differ (Simpson, Gang-estad, and Biek 1993). More interestingly, they find that the nonverbal behavior of unattached individuals in this interaction differ markedly from those of attached individuals. Thus, given that they are interacting with an attractive partner, one can infer that the difference in behavior between attached versus unattached actors represent cues to initiate a relationship. Finally, research finds that singular expressions, such as anger, are more accurately recognized than compound expressions, such as anger and encouragement. If one's goal is to communicate anger, for example, they are more likely to be understood than if the same angry expression is mixed with a conflicting signal such as an encouraging smile (La-Plante and Ambady 2000). Thus, it seems nonverbal behavior gives people the power to demonstrate conviction, signal the desire to initiate a relationship, or simply communicate how they are feeling.

Less conscious seem to be the effects of personality, gender, culture, and situational context on an actor's expressiveness and encoded behavior. In terms of personality, more sociable, higher self-esteem, and less shy people are more effective at encoding nonverbal cues of agreeableness (Ambady, Hallahan, and Rosenthal 1995). In terms of gender, it seems women will exhibit more positive behavior than their male counterparts (Rafaeli 1989). Culturally, it seems that actors from different cultures exhibit culture-specific cues that enable others to detect their cultural origin. This research had observers look at photographs of Japanese nationals and Japanese Americans and found observers were able to accurately distinguish between the two groups (Marsh, Elfenbein, and Ambady 2003). Japanese Americans may avoid culture specific signals in order to fit in more effectively in the US; however, a Japanese national may seek to retain these cues to maintain inclusion in an in-group. Similarly, for extroverts, expressing nonverbal behavior that signals their agreeableness may facilitate the social connections they need. Extending beyond culture, the immediate environment can also influence encoding. In a study that looked at 11,717 salesperson-customer interactions, the researchers found that salespeople exhibit more positive expressions when wearing a uniform, there are not customers waiting in line, the salesperson is working alone, or the salesperson is serving a male customer (Rafaeli 1989). While these differences in encoding may not be entirely conscious, they may still fill important needs for the actor. In a retail setting, employees may feel a need to be consistent with the professional air of a uniform or be more responsive to male clients who historically have had higher status. Overall, there appear to be a number of factors that affect the nonverbal behavior that one encodes and while not goal directed, may serve important functions for the individual.

The notion that not all behavior is emitted consciously is supported by previous research. It has been suggested that a leakage hierarchy exists such that certain behaviors are more controlled and thus intentional while others are less controlled and unintentional. In particular, researchers find that while facial expression and verbal content are highly controlled by the individual and thus less revealing (overt cues), body movements and tone of voice are less controlled and thus may be highly revealing (covert cues; see Figure 1).

Evidence finds that while we can control behavior responsible for both overt and covert cues, we typically attend only to regulation of behavior associated with overt cues. Behavior associated with covert cues is then left to be dictated by habit (e.g. tapping your foot when you are nervous, Ekman and Friesen

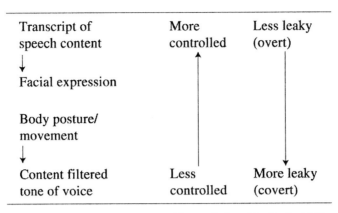

Figure 1.   Leakage Hierarchy (Rosenthal and DePaulo 1979a, 1979b)

1969). However, that which one intends to express does not always match what one is truly thinking or feeling. For example, while you might intend to express a desire to help a colleague who has stopped by your office, you secretly wish they would leave as your anxiety builds with a fast approaching deadline. The colleague skilled at reading covert cues may detect your anxiety and be offended you feel he has disturbed you (Puccinelli et al. 2004). Thus, it seems that behavior such as body movements and tone of voice can serve as covert cues to an actor's thoughts and feelings and be responsible for what has been termed the "unintentional display effect" (Bonoma and Felder 1977). That is, the actor may reveal their thoughts or feelings inadvertently. When an actor's true thoughts and feelings are in conflict with those that the actor intends to communicate, the less controlled, leaky nonverbal behavior may reveal more valid information about how an individual truly feels than more controlled behavior (Ekman and Friesen 1969). That is, the less controlled, leaky nonverbal behavior may be more diagnostic especially in situations in which social desirability or other factors may be constraining the more controlled behavior. As a result, an observer trying to judge if an actor is lying is more likely to detect the liar during a telephone call (through access to cues from their tone of voice) and least likely from a written statement. An interesting study that tested this found that when research assistants assigned to helping a subject actually did not want to help, their covert cues dissuaded some subjects from asking for help (DePaulo and Fisher 1981). Specifically, subjects skilled at decoding covert cues were less likely to ask for help than were subjects with lesser decoding ability. Thus, subjects able to decode the research assistant's covert cues were able to detect the lack of desire to help and so did not seek help. Similarly, individuals who hold a negative appraisal of an interaction partner will display behavior that is critical of the partner nonverbally but not verbally, which in turn appeared to lead to lower self-esteem in the criticized partner (Swann, Stein-Seroussi, and McNulty 1992). The critical partner acts in accordance with social norms that discourage overt criticism but do not suppress their dislike of the partner through more covert cues. As one might expect, this phenomenon has a number of implications for communicative competence. For example, we can imagine a situation in which someone seeks to manage the impression they give to others. If we consider the example at the opening of the chapter of the distraught party guest, we might consider the extent to which he intends to express this negative emotion. It may be that he is smiling in hopes of convincing everyone of his jovial mood, and it is only through his body movements and tone of voice that you discern his true sad state.

4. Encoding Competence

Given that behavior may be both intentional and unintentional, the challenge of encoding competence becomes quite formidable. Competent encoding may take the form of enabling actors to achieve their objectives and/or smooth the social interactions. In an effort to understand how encoding competence might be enhanced, it is instructive to consider examples in which actors appear to achieve specific goals through their nonverbal encoding.

The first challenge is assessing encoding ability. While the ACT discussed before measures expressivity, it does not speak to the efficacy of actors or the ability of actors to be accurately interpreted, which would seem necessary for communicative competence. That is, while an individual may self-report that they are expressive; people around them may not be able to recognize the meaning of their expressions. Therefore, while actors may believe they smile a lot when they are happy, the ACT does not enable us to assess the degree to which observers are able to detect the actor's mood of happiness, but rather just the actor's subjective assessment of the actor's likelihood of emitting the behavior.

However, other research has found ways in which encoding skill may be reliably measured. It finds that competent encoders can signal task competence and social skill. Certain nonverbal behavior can communicate competence in a task and enable the actor to be more influential, e.g., well-moderated tone of voice and rapid speech (Driskell, Olmstead, and Salas 1993). Moreover, signaling task competence appears to be more effective for increasing one's status in a group than displaying dominance cues (e.g., loud, tense voice, and knitted brows). Interestingly, the circumstances that lead one to enact nonverbal behavior that signals competence are different for men and women. While women emit cues that signal competence when speaking with a superior, men are more likely to signal competence when speaking with a peer (Steckler and Rosenthal 1985). Finally, good encoders appear to be able to signal their social skill non-verbally through the gestures they use and the time they spend talking (Gifford, Ng, and Wilkinson 1985).

There is also evidence that encoding ability has real-world benefits. It seems good encoders can lead interviewers to hire them in spite of a weak resume (Kinicki, Lockwood, Hom, and Griffeth 1990) and poor verbal quality of responses to interviewer questions (Rasmussen 1984). Specifically, candidates that were more expressive (i.e., held more eye contact, smiled more, and gestured more) were judged more positively (Rasmussen 1984). Further, once hired, good encoders appear to be able to command better treatment from supervisors (Naquin and Paulson 2003) and serve clients better (Ambady, Koo,

Rosenthal, and Winograd 2002) through their nonverbal behavior. Naquin and his colleagues find that more assertive employees are able to get fairer treatment from a superior. Similarly, Ambady and her colleagues (2000) find that therapists who smile, nod, and frown less seem to help patients improve their physical and cognitive functioning, whereas therapists who engage in negative behavior cause a decline in patient functioning.

Much of the work summarized above would seem to represent examples of nonverbal behavior that were both effective and appropriate. That is, the behavior that enables people to achieve their objectives would do so because the behavior was also appropriate to the setting. One piece of research, however, looked at encoding behavior strictly enacted to be appropriate and smooth the interaction. Work on politeness theory (Brown and Levinson 1987) has examined ways in which speech is often altered so as to couch a communication, such as a request, to attenuate the impact of the communication on the listener—in essence to be more appropriate and allow a smoother interaction in spite of the request. For example, instead of saying, "Pass the salt," one might instead say, "Could I please trouble you to pass the salt?" More recently, it has been found that such politeness strategies are also implemented nonverbally (Ambady et al. 1996). The researchers examined other-orientation (e.g., the degree to which the person was attentive), affiliation (e.g., the degree to which the person was open), and circumspection (e.g., the degree to which the person was indirect). They found that while used somewhat differently within each cultural group, each of these politeness strategies was used by both American's and Korean's as politeness strategies to smooth interactions.

Before leaving the topic of encoding competence, it is also worthwhile to note the concept of emotional labor (Hochschild 1983). While the focus of this chapter is on ability, that is the ability to effectively and appropriately encode nonverbal behavior to achieve one's goals, it must also be recognized that such skillful encoding excises a cost for the actor. Specifically, the effort that is often necessary to express positive affect that is effective and appropriate in a given situation may be exerting for the actor. Early work in this area considers the example of flight attendants and the tremendous challenge of expressing positive affect in the face of a long flight, disgruntled passengers, and sleep deprivation. Not surprisingly, emotional labor has been linked to job satisfaction, emotional exhaustion, and well-being (Glomb, Kammeyer-Mueller, and Rotundo 2004). Moreover, it seems that employees from cultures in which emotion regulation is less common (e.g., the US) may face even more significant challenges than those coming from a culture characterized by more emotion regulation (e.g., France, Grandey, Fisk, and Steiner 2005). Thus, as we consider ways in which communicative competence may be enhanced through more effective and appropriate encoding, we must consider both personal limits as well as those that may derive from socialization.

5. Decoding Competence: Interpreting the Behavior of Others

Relative to encoding, considerably more research has looked at decoding competence or ability to accurately interpret the behavior of others. Some of the earliest work in this area developed a measure, the Profile of Non-verbal Sensitivity (PONS), to assess an individual's accuracy in interpreting nonverbal cues. Further, it seems that different cues (covert vs. overt) not only communicate different information, but different people appear to be skilled at reading each, as measured by subtests of the PONS. Someone can be accurate at reading overt cues, covert cues, neither, or both (Rosenthal, Hall, DiMatteo, Rogers, and Archer 1979). More recently, a measure using still photographs and expressions of positive and negative emotions has been developed to measure an observer's ability to detect positive and negative emotion expressed either overtly or covertly (Nowicki and Duke 1994). It should be noted that at the base of each of these measures is the intentional enactment of a specific emotion or situation. The accuracy of the observer is determined by the degree of correspondence between the enacted emotion or situation and the observer's interpretation.

There are also many instances in which we would like to have observers interpret the behavior of actors in a real-world setting. For evaluating real interactions, many researchers use judgment studies in which short video clips of an actor's behavior are recorded and shown to naïve observers. To assess observer accuracy, observers' ratings are correlated with one of a number of other sources of converging evidence. For example, for assessing accuracy in judging personality characteristics, converging evidence may take the form of a self-report by the actor, agreement with people who know the actor or consensus with a larger group of observers. Judgment studies have been found to be very reliable and an accurate means for assessing emotion or personality from nonverbal behavior. Further, while we might expect that observers would need to observe a great deal of nonverbal behavior to make an accurate judgment; this does not appear to be the case. Research finds that observers can make remarkably accurate judgments from a thin slice of behavior in the form of a 30-second clip (Ambady and Rosenthal 1993). Thus, measures for assessing competence in decoding ability are quite well-developed and may represent a useful starting point for assessing one's communicative competence.

As with encoding ability, there are a number of moderators of decoding ability that include personality of the observer, sex of the observer, characteristics of the actor, and the setting judgment (Hall and Andrzejewki 2007). In terms of personality, people who score high on self-monitoring seem to be better decoders. Surprisingly, those who are better decoders are not more extraverted and may even be less sociable (Ambady, Bernieri, and Richeson 2000; Ambady et al. 1995). Yet among children, higher sociometric status is predicted by better decoding ability (Edwards, Manstead, and MacDonald 1984). That is, more popular children appear to be characterized by better decoding ability. In terms of sex of the observer, the finding that women are better at decoding is well-documented (Ambady et al. 1995; Rosenthal et al. 1979). In terms of characteristics of the actor, research finds that observers are able to more accurately interpret nonverbal behavior of someone from their same ethnic group compared to that of someone in a different ethnic group (Elfenbein and Ambady 2002a). Finally, in terms of occupational setting, it seems that better teachers, clinicians and law enforcement officers are better at accurately decoding nonverbal behavior (Mann et al. 2004; Rosenthal et al. 1979). Police officers reporting considerable experience interviewing suspects were more likely to detect a liar. Further, you might expect an experienced police officer to have awareness of this skill based on his experience yet, it turns out that such decoding skill is difficult to judge in one's own self and is best judged by a supervisor or spouse (Rosenthal et al. 1979). Finally, the task the actor is engaged in as well as the position of the actor relative to the observer impacts accurate perception (Puccinelli et al. 2004). Many of the explanations for these results have centered around skill development that has emerged through socialization to serve specific communication objectives. For example, it may be important to discern subtle cues to one's affect in someone else in your ethnic group to achieve in-group acceptance. In the case of occupational advantages, this may be explained by self-selection that is fostered by experience.

Given the utility of accurate decodings, research has naturally looked at methods for improving decoding ability. Unfortunately, efforts at training to improve decoding skill have met with dismal results (Ambady and Gray 2002; Bernieri, Gillis, Davis, and Grahe 1996; Gillis, Bernieri, and Wooten 1995; Grahe and Bernieri 2002). Perhaps this is why law enforcement personnel, such as FBI and CIA agents, are not more skilled than college students (Ekman and O'Sullivan 1991). Further, it seems thinking too long about one's interpretation of nonverbal behavior may actually impair an observer's accuracy. In research looking at the effect of mood on accuracy, Ambady and Gray (2002) find that sad observers are less accurate than neutral observers. They propose and find support for a deliberative information-processing explanation. Specifically, it seems sad subjects engage in more deliberative processing of nonverbal behavior and this over-analysis not only takes longer but is also less accurate (Ambady and Gray 2002).There also appear to be some contextual factors that influence decoding and decoding ability. For example, research finds that decoders under stress may be more likely to base their judgment on their first impression (Srinivas and Motowidlo 1987). Raters made to do a stressful exercise showed less dispersion in evaluations of a videotaped target compared to raters made to do a non-stressful exercise. Given that first impressions are typically more accurate, this may represent a strategy for improving accuracy. Thus, consistent with Ambady and Gray (2002), a more heuristic processing style that relies on first impressions, appears more accurate.

As one might expect, the general implications of decoding ability are quite positive. Decoding skill is associated with a number of aspects of workplace performance such as IQ and interpersonal skill as well as the ability to diagnose patients effectively (Halberstadt and Hall 1980; Hall and Andrzejewki 2007; Harrigan and Rosenthal 1986). People who are more interpersonally sensitive are perceived as more effective leaders, have more satisfied subordinates, and are evaluated as more successful (Elfenbein and Ambady 2002b; Riggio, Riggio, Salinas, and Cole 2003). Further, research suggests that decoding ability plays a key role in rapport development between a service provider and client (Hall et al. 1995). Perhaps this decoding ability enables service providers to adapt their behavior in response to the client's behavior more effectively (Spiro and Weitz 1990). Research looking at adaptive selling suggests that service agents who self-report adapting their behavior to customers are more effective sales agents, as indicated by a generally positive relationship between adaptive selling and sales performance (Park and Holloway 2003).

However, as suggested earlier, different aspects of behavior may reveal different types of information, some of it unintentional. Research suggests that there are at least some instances when decoding ability may be disadvantageous. For example, research finds that one's sexual orientation can be discerned from nonverbal cues (Ambady, Hallahan, and Conner 1999) and yet we can imagine contexts in which an actor may wish to conceal this information and respond negatively to explicit recognition of this attribute. The ability to accurately decode less controllable covert cues (e.g., body movement) opposed to more controllable nonverbal overt cues (e.g., facial expressions) has been termed by researchers "eavesdropping" ability (Rosenthal and DePaulo 1979a). As the label would suggest, this is a somewhat invasive practice on the part of the observer that can have negative ramifications. Research finds that people skilled at eavesdropping, or decoding of covert cues to what one is thinking or feeling, report experiencing more difficulty in social relationships (e.g. are less popular and seen to have less social understanding, Rosenthal and DePaulo 1979a). More recently, this finding was replicated in an organizational setting. Employees skilled at eavesdropping on negative emotions were evaluated more negatively by both supervisors and peers (Elfenbein and Ambady 2002b; Tickle-Degnen and Puccinelli 1999). Further, this effect appears to be exacerbated by the predisposition of the actor to experience negative emotions. Research finds that when eavesdroppers are paired with someone prone to experience negative affect, both the actor and the observer experience a more negative interaction (Puccinelli and Tickle-Degnen 2004). On the flipside, it seems people may appreciate having covert positive emotions detected. Employees skilled at eavesdropping on positive emotions were evaluated more positively by supervisors and peers. Thus, it seems while we might be eager to share our secret joy from a recent success, we prefer to conceal our disappointment with a recent failure.

Evidence also suggests that the effect of eavesdropping may be moderated by occupational setting. Eavesdropping clinicians were rated higher by supervisors in a pediatric rehabilitation setting, lower in a psychiatric rehabilitation setting, and the same in a physical rehabilitation setting relative to clinicians less skilled at detecting covert cues (Tickle-Degnen 1998). This research suggests that in the pediatric setting, where the young patients may be less able to communicate using speech and controllable overt cues, less controlled covert cues may provide important clues for diagnosis and treatment. However, in a psychiatric context, where patients work to adapt to everyday life, it may be important to respect a patient's self-presentation goals and respond only to the controlled overt cues. Thus, it may be important to consider the situational context of the actor before responding to specific nonverbal cues of the actor. If we consider our example of the distraught guest, we might try to discern if the negative affective state is being expressed through his face, which may signal a desire to have the negative mood recognized, or through his body movements, which may be unintentional, making it unwise to comment on it.

6. Nonverbal Communication Competence in the Real World

In applying work on encoding and decoding to the real world, it seems important to consider skills in these areas in concert. In reality, there are myriad
behaviors and reactions to behaviors that can take place during a single
interaction that affect the subjective experience of the actors and the interaction's outcomes. While specific nonverbal behaviors in a negotiation, for
example, can signal dominance, deference, and equality (Soldow and Thomas
1984), it seems impossible to conceive of a given negotiation strictly in terms
of specific behaviors. Further, the exchange of nonverbal cues in a negotiation
appear critical to establishing trust and rapport as well as reaching an optimal outcome (Drolet and Morris 2000; Naquin and Paulson 2003). On a project
team, nonverbal exchange is a key predictor of whether that team member is
seen as contributing to the project. In teams that interfaced electronically,
actual contribution predicted perception of a group member's contribution;
while in face-to-face interactions, liking predicted perception of a group member's contribution (Weisband and Atwater 1999). In a retail context, it seems
customers engage in tell tale cues signaling their objectives in a sales or service encounter (Kirmani and Campbell 2004). Customers may be "goal seek-
ers" and attempt to use the salesperson to help them achieve their goals or
they may be "persuasion sentries" and seek to avoid marketing persuasion at
all costs. It would seem critical for salespeople in these settings to be attuned
to these cues when serving customers.

Nonverbal behavior also has a significant impact on the dynamics of
interpersonal exchange. Several streams of research find that the behavior
of one actor in an interaction affects the behavior of their interaction partner.
Interestingly, the nature of this effect seems to depend on the type of behavior
encoded by the actor. Sometimes an actor's behavior can lead to a Pygmalion
effect whereby their partner will conform to the expectations of the actor while
at other times it will take the form of emotional contagion whereby the affective state of an actor is spread to the partner.

Evidence of a Pygmalion effect is well-documented. Robert Rosenthal's
early work in this area found that if teachers were told a student was an
"early bloomer" the student performed better (Rosenthal 1991; Rosenthal and
Jacobson 1992). Further investigation found that the teacher would give off
subtle nonverbal cues of encouragement that would lead the student to do
better. This effect has been replicated across age groups and in a wide range
of educational and business contexts. There is also evidence to suggest that
this effect may be stronger under certain circumstances. Research finds a
stronger effect among men, when the leader and subordinate are in a military environment and if the expectations for the subordinate had been especially low (Dvir, Eden, and Banjo 1995; McNatt 2000). The effect of sex may
be explained in part by a difference in the response of men versus women to
feedback. This research finds that while men are more productive and satisfied when they received negative feedback in a positive tone of voice; women
were more productive and satisfied when they received feedback that was
positive in a negative tone of voice (LaPlante and Ambady 2000). Thus, as we
think about the Pygmalion effect with respect to communicative competence

we might consider the typical objectives of a teacher or a squadron leader. To the extent that they hope that their students and subordinates will perform well, expectations for this may lead their nonverbal behavior to make this a self-fulfilling prophecy.

A second way in which nonverbal behavior affects the dynamics of interaction is through emotional contagion. Elaine Hatfield (1994) was among the first to document that the affective state of one individual can be communicated to an interaction partner in such a way that the partner actually experiences the same affective state. Emotional contagion has been observed in the work place, retail settings and even among members of professional sports teams. Research finds that the mood of supervisors not only affects the mood of their employees but also influences employee coordination and employee effort exerted to achieve organizational goals (Sy, Côté, and Saavedra 2005). In a retail context the mood of sales staff appears to extend to customers and not only makes customers feel better but increases the time the customer spends in the store, the customers willingness to return, and the customer's tendency toward positive word of mouth (Tsai and Huang 2002). Finally, it seems certain individuals may be more susceptible to emotional contagion than others. For example, in the case of the professional sports team, older, more committed players appear more likely to catch the mood of their teammates (Totterdell 2000). Linking emotional contagion to communicative competence, we might be able to imagine a situation in which it would be effective to bring others to your mood state to more clearly appreciate your point of view. Along similar lines, emotional contagion may form the critical foundation for rapport building that enables smoother interactions. So while it may not seem appropriate to inflict your mood on another, your inclination to catch the mood of an interaction partner could be advantageous.

Thus it seems nonverbal communicative competence is best conceived of as a dynamic process of encoding and decoding that sits within the larger scheme of dialogue and natural interaction. While focusing specifically on the communication of emotion, researchers have begun discussing a new intelligence, that of emotional intelligence. First introduced by Peter Salovey (Salovey, Hsee, and Mayer 1993) and popularized by Daniel Goleman (1995), emotional intelligence (EI) encompasses the entire spectrum from the encoding of emotion, and restraint in encoding when necessary, to the sensitive decoding of behavior in others. It has been established that EI is distinct from other personality measures and may predict life satisfaction and job performance (Law, Wong, and Song 2004). Further, it has been argued that emotional intelligence may be as critical as technical knowledge to the success of a firm.

In summary, nonverbal behavior clearly plays a critical role in being a competent communicator. How effectively people encode their needs and signal their strongest attributes has a significant impact on their ability to achieve their goals. Similarly, the ability to accurately decode and appropriately respond to the cues of others is also key to this process. Focusing on these specific skill sets are a good starting point for understanding their role in the more complex exchange that is social interaction and the processes, such as the Pygmalion effect and emotional contagion that occur there.

References

Ambady, N., F. J. Bernieri., and J. A. Richeson. 2000. Toward a histology of social behavior: Judgmental accuracy from thin slices of the behavioral stream. *Advances in Experimental Social Psychology 32:* 201–207.

Ambady, N. and H. M. Gray. 2002. On being sad and mistaken: Mood effects on the accuracy of thin-slice judgments. *Journal of Personality and Social Psychology 83*(4): 947–961.

Ambady, N., M. Hallahan, and B. Conner. 1999. Accuracy of judgments of sexual orientation from thin slices of behavior. *Journal of Personality and Social Psychology 77*(3): 538–547.

Ambady, N., M. Hallahan, and R. Rosenthal. 1995. On judging and being judged accurately in zero-acquaintance situations. *Journal of Personality and Social Psychology 69*(3): 1–12.

Ambady, N., J. Koo, F. Lee and R. Rosenthal. 1996. More than words: Linguistic and nonlinguistic politeness in two cultures. *Journal of Personality and Social Psychology 70*(5): 996–1011.

Ambady, N., J. Koo, R. Rosenthal, and C. H. Winograd. 2002. Physical therapists' nonverbal communication predicts geriatric patients' health outcomes. *Psychology and Aging 17*(3): 443–452.

Ambady, N. and R. Rosenthal. 1993. Half a minute: Predicting teacher evaluations from thin slices of nonverbal behavior and physical attractiveness. *Journal of Personality and Social Psychology 64*(3): 431–441.

Bernieri, F. J., J. S. Gillis, J. M. Davis, and J. E. Grahe. 1996. Dyad rapport and the accuracy of its judgment across situations: A lens model analysis. *Journal of Personality and Social Psychology 71*(1): 110–129.

Bonoma, T. V. and L. C. Felder. 1977. Nonverbal communication in marketing: Toward a communicational analysis. *Journal of Marketing Research 14*(May): 169–180.

Brown, P. and S. C. Levinson. 1987. *Politeness. Some Universals in Language usage.* New York NY: Cambridge University Press.

Brown, R. 1986. *Social Psychology* (2 ed.). New York: The Free Press.

Burgoon, J. K. 1994. Nonverbal signals. In:: M. L. Knapp (ed.), *Handbook of Interpersonal Communication,* 229–285 (2nd ed.). Thousand Oaks: Sage.

DePaulo, B. M. and J. D. Fisher. 1981. Too tuned-out to take: The role of nonverbal sensitivity in help-seeking. *Personality and Social Psychology Bulletin 7*(2): 201–205.

Driskell, J., E., B. Olmstead, and E. Salas. 1993. Task cues, dominance cues, and influence in task groups. *Journal of Applied Psychology 78*(1): 51–60.

Drolet, A. L. and M. W. Morris. 2000. Rapport in conflict resolution: Accounting for how face-to-face contact fosters mutual cooperation in mixed-motive conflicts. *Journal of experimental social psychology 36*(1): 26–50.

Dvir, T., D. Eden, and M. L. Banjo. 1995. Self-fulfilling prophecy and gender: Can women be pygmalion and galatea? *Journal of Applied Psychology 80*(2): 253–270.

Edwards, R., A. S. R. Manstead, and C. J. MacDonald. 1984. The relationship between children's sociometric status and ability to recognize facial expressions of emotion. *European Journal of Social Psychology 14*(2): 235–238.

Ekman, P. and W. V. Friesen. 1969. Nonverbal leakage and clues to deception. *Psychiatry 32*(1): 88–106.

Ekman, P. and M. O'Sullivan. 1991. Who can catch a liar? *American Psychologist 46*(9): 913–920.

Elfenbein, H. A. N. and Ambady. 2002a. On the universality and cultural specificity of emotion recognition : A metaanalysis. *Psychological Bulletin 128*(2): 203–235.

Elfenbein, H. A. and N. Ambady. 2002b. Predicting workplace outcomes from the ability to eavesdrop on feelings. *Journal of Applied Psychology 87*(5): 963–971.

Elfenbein, H. A. and N. Ambady. 2003. When familiarity breeds accuracy: Cultural exposure and facial emotion recognition. *Journal of Personality and Social Psychology 85*(2): 276–290.

Gifford, R., C. F. Ng, and M. Wilkinson. 1985. Nonverbal cues in the employment interview: Links betweeen applicant qualities and interviewer judgements. *Journal of Applied Psychology 70*(4): 729–736.

Gillis, J. S., F. J. Bernieri, and E. Wooten. 1995. The effects of stimulus medium and feedback on the judgment of rapport. *Organizational Behavior and Human Decision Processes 63*(1): 33–45.

Glomb, T. M., J. D. Kammeyer-Mueller, and M. Rotundo. 2004. Emotional labor demands and compensating wage differentials. *Journal of Applied Psychology* 89(4): 700–714.

Goleman, D. C. 1995. *Emotional Intelligence.* NY: Bantam Books.

Grahe, J. E. and F. J. Bernieri. 2002. Self-awareness of judgment policies of rapport. *Personality and Social Psychology Bulletin* 28(10): 1407–1418.

Grandey, A. A., G. M. Fisk, and D. D. Steiner. 2005. Must "service with a smile" be stressful? The moderating role of personal control for American and French employees. *Journal of Applied Psychology* 90(5): 893–904.

Halberstadt, A. G. and J. A. Hall. 1980. Who's getting the message? Children's nonverbal skill and their evaluation by teachers. *Developmental Psychology* 16(6): 564–573.

Hall, J. A. and S. A. Andrzejewki. 2007. Psychosocial correlates of interpersonal sensitivity: A meta-analysis. Unpublished manuscript.

Hall, J. A., J. A. Harrigan, and R. Rosenthal. 1995. Nonverbal behavior in clinician-patient interaction. *Applied and Preventive Psychology* 4(1): 21–37.

Halverson, A. M., M. Hallahan, A. J. Hart and R. Rosenthal. 1997. Reducing the biasing effects of jedges' nonverbal behavior with simplified jury instruction. *Journal of Applied Psychology* 82(4): 590–598.

Harrigan, J. A. and R. Rosenthal. 1986. Nonverbal aspects of empathy and rapport in physician-patient interaction. In: P. D. Blanck, R. Buck and R. Rosenthal (eds.), *Nonverbal Communication in the Clinical Context,* 37–73. London: The Pennsylvania State University.

Hart, A. J. and M. M. Morry. 1996. Nonverbal behavior, race, and attitude attributions *Journal of Experimental Social Psychology* 32(2): 165–179.

Hatfield, E. 1994. Mechanisms of emotional contagion. II. Emotional experience and facial, vocal, and postural feedback. In: E. Hatfield, J. Cacioppo and R. L. Rapson (eds.), *Emotional contagion* 48–78.

Hochschild, A. 1983. *The Managed Heart: The Commercialization of Human Feeling.* Berkeley, CA: University of California Press.

Hulbert, J. and N. Capon. 1972. Interpersonal communication in marketing: An overview. *Journal of Marketing Research IX:* 27–34.

Kinicki, A. J., C. A. Lockwood, P. W. Hom, and R. W. Griffeth. 1990. Interviewer predictions of applicant qualifications and interviewer validity: Aggregate and individual analyses. *Journal of Applied Psychology* 75(5): 477–486.

Kirmani, A. and M. C. Campbell. 2004. Goal seeker and persuasion sentry: How consumer targets respond to interpersonal marketing persuasion. *Journal of Consumer Research* 31(3): 573–582.

Knapp, M. L. and J. A. Hall. 2002. *Nonverbal Communication in Human Interaction* (5th ed.). London: Thomas Learning, Inc.

LaPlante, D. and N. Ambady. 2000. Multiple messages: Facial recognition advantage for compound expressions. *Journal of Nonverbal Behavior* 24(3): 211–224.

Law, K. S., C.-S. Wong, and L. J. Song. 2004. The construct and criterion validity of emotional intelligence and its potential utility for management studies. *Journal of Applied Psychology* 89(3): 483–496.

Mann, S., A. Vrij, and R. Bull. 2004. Detecting true lies: Police officers' ability to detect suspects' lies. *Journal of Applied Psychology* 89(1): 137–149.

Marsh, A. A., J. A. Elfenbein, and N. Ambady. 2003. Nonverbal "accents": Cultural differences in facial expressions of emotion. *Psychological Science* 14(4): 373–376.

McNatt, D. B. 2000. Ancient pygmalion joins contemporary management: A meta-analysis of the result. *Journal of Applied Psychology* 85(2): 314–322.

Milmoe, S., R. Rosenthal, H. T. Blane, M. E. Chafetz, and I. Wolf. 1967. The doctor's voice postdictor of successful referral of alcoholic patients. *Journal of Abnormal Psychology* 72(1): 78–84.

Naquin, C. E. and G. D. Paulson. 2003. Online bargaining and interpersonal trust. *Journal of Applied Psychology* 88(1): 113–120.

Nowicki, S. and M. P. Duke. 1994. Individual differences in the nonverbal communication of affect: The diagnostic analysis of nonverbal accuracy scale. *Journal of Nonverbal Behavior* 18(1).

Park, J.-E. and B. B. Holloway. 2003. Adaptive selling behavior revisited: An empirical examination of learning orientation, sales performance, and job satisfaction. *Journal of Personal Selling and Sales Management* 23(3): 239–251.

Parks, M. R. 1994. Communicative competence and interpersonal control. In: M. L. Knapp (ed.), *Handbook of Interpersonal Communication,* 589–618 (2nd ed.). Thousand Oaks: Sage.

Puccinelli, N. M. 2006. Putting your best face forward: The impact of customer mood on salesperson evaluation. *Journal of Consumer Psychology* 16(2): 156–162.

Puccinelli, N. M. and L. Tickle-Degnen. 2004. Knowing too much about others: Moderators of the relationship between eavesdropping and rapport in social interaction. *Journal of Nonverbal Behavior* 28(4): 223–243.

Puccinelli, N. M., L. Tickle-Degnen and R. Rosenthal. 2003. Effect of dyadic context on judgements of rapport. Dyad task and partner presence. *Journal of Nonverbal Behavior* 47(4).

Puccinelli, N. M., L. Tickle-Degnen and R. Rosenthal. 2004. Effect of target position and target task on judge sensitivity to felt rapport. *Journal of nonverbal Behavior* 28(3), 211–220.

Rafaeli, A. 1989. When clerks meet customers: A test of variables related to emotional expressions on the job. *Journal of Applied Psychology* 74(3): 385–393.

Rasmussen, K. G. 1984. Nonverbal behavior, verbal behavior, resume credentials, and selection interview outcomes. *Journal of Applied Psychology* 69(4): 551–556.

Riggio, R. E., H. R. Riggio, C. Salinas, and E. J. Cole. 2003. The role of social and emotional communication skills in leader emergence and effectiveness. *Group Dymnamics: Theory, Research, and Practice* 7(2): 83–103.

Rosenthal, R. 1991. Teacher expectancy effects: A brief update 25 years after the pygmalion experiment. *Journal of Research in Education* 1(1): 3–12.

Rosenthal, R. and B. M. DePaulo. 1979a. Sex differences in accommodation in nonverbal communication. In: R. Rosenthal (ed.), *Skill in Nonverbal Communication: Individual Differences,* 68–103. Cambridge, MA: Oelgeschlager, Gunn and Hain.

Rosenthal, R. and B. M. DePaulo. 1979b. Sex differences in eavesdropping on nonverbal cues. *Journal of Personality and Social Psychology* 37(2): 273–285.

Rosenthal, R., J. A. Hall, M. R. DiMatteo, P. L. Rogers, and D. Archer. 1979. *Sensitivity to Nonverbal Communication: The Pons Test.* Baltimore: Johns Hopkins University.

Rosenthal, R. and L. Jacobson. 1992. *Pygmalion in the Classroom* (2 ed.). New York: Irvington Publishers, Inc.

Salovey, P., C. K. Hsee, and J. D. Mayer. 1993. Emotional intelligence and the self-regulation of affect. In: D. M. Wegner and J. W. Pennebaker (eds.), *Handbook of Mental Control. Century Psychology Series,* 258–277. Englewood Cliffs, NJ: Prentice-Hall.

Simpson, J. A., S. W. Gangestad, and M. Biek. 1993. Personality and nonverbal social behavior: An ethological perspective of relationship initiation. *Journal of Experimental Social Psychology* 29(5): 434–461.

Soldow, G. F. and G. P. Thomas. 1984. Relational communication: Form versus content in the sales interaction. *Journal of Marketing* 48(1): 84–93.

Spiro, R. L. and B. A. Weitz. 1990. Adaptive selling: Conceptualization, measurement, and nomological validity. *Journal of Marketing Research* 27(1): 61–69.

Srinivas, S. and S. J. Motowidlo. 1987. Effects of raters' stress on the dispersion and favorability of performance ratings. *Journal of Applied Psychology* 72(2): 247–251.

Steckler, N. A. and R. Rosenthal. 1985. Sex differences in nonverbal and verbal communication with bosses, peers and subordineates. *Journal of Applied Psychology* 70(1): 157–163.

Swann, W. B., A. Stein-Seroussi, and S. E. McNulty. 1992. Outcasts in a white-lie society: The enigmatic worlds of people with negative self-conceptions. *Journal of Personality and Social Psychology* 62(4): 618–624.

Sy, T., S. Côté, and R. Saavedra. 2005. The contagious leader : Impact of the leader's mood on the mood of group members, group affective tone, and group processes. *Journal of Applied Psychology* 90(2): 295–305.

Tickle-Degnen, L. 1998. Working well with others: The prediction of students' clinical performance. *The American Journal of Occupational Therapy* 52(2): 133–141.

Tickle-Degnen, L. and N. M. Puccinelli. 1999. The nonverbal expression of negative emotions: Peer and supervisor responses to occupational therapy students' emothonal attributes. *The Occupational Therapy Journal of Research* 19(1): 18–39.

Totterdell, P. 2000. Catching moods and hitting runs: Mood linkage and subjective performance in professional sport teams. *Journal of Applied Psychology* 85(6): 848–859.

Tsai, W.-C. and Y.-M. Huang. 2002. Mechanisms linking employee affective delivery and customer behavioral intentions. *Journal of Applied Psychology* 87(5): 1001–1008.

Walker, R. E. and R. Raghunathan. 2004. Nonverbal cues-based first impressions: What can static images of salespersons tell us about their success at selling? In: M. F. Luce and B.

Kahn (eds.), *Advances in Consumer Research,* 198–199. (Vol. 31). Austin, TX: Association of Consumer Research.

Weisband, S. and L. Atwater. 1999. Evaluating self and others in electronic and face-to-face groups. *Journal of Applied Psychology 84*(4): 632–639.

Westmyer, S. A., R. L. DiCioccio, and R. B. Rubin. 1998. Appropriateness and effectiveness of communication channels. *Journal of Communication 48*(3): 27–48.

13

Media Competence

Daniel Perrin and Maureen Ehrensberger-Dow

Children call their grandparents to thank them for new clothes, teenagers send each other photos of themselves with their mobile phones, and brides-to-be email their mothers' website addresses for them to preview wedding dresses: every generation has its preferred tools for conveying information. Media such as the telephone (Hutchby 1991) and the internet (Crystal 2001) encourage, facilitate, impede, or hinder certain types of communication and language use: primarily verbal or primarily non-verbal, spoken or written, spontaneous or planned, face-to-face or apart, personal or business, informal or formal, public or private, as senders, receivers, or in alternating roles. How people communicate depends very much on the medium that they choose to bridge the gap across space and time. Within the range of what is technically possible, people can use a medium more or less skillfully, appropriately, or purposefully.

This chapter examines such media competence—specifically, in terms of language use. It defines and links the terms "media" and "competence" (section 1); infers from sample discussions the specific language competence involved in medially-transmitted communication (section 2); explains the methodology of research into media competence with examples of journalistic processing of discussions and producing media texts (section 3); presents an overview of research into appropriate and successful language use in mediallytransmitted public communication (section 4); and identifies current gaps in the general area of research into media competence (section 5).

1. Media and Competence—Basic Concepts

In communication, a medium can be anything that contributes to someone being able to convey something to someone else—even the air that carries the sound waves of speech. Here it seems sensible, however, to define the term more narrowly and understand media as technical equipment for communication or, even more precisely, as technical equipment for the production, storage, reproduction, and transmission of signs. This definition of media would still encompass all technical communication aids including, for instance, a post card, a corporate intranet, or an auditorium's sound system. With such a broad use of the term, any deeper understanding of a particular area of language application is difficult—since technical media are part of every form of communication except non-amplified speech and signing.

A more focused definition refers primarily to journalistic media: the technical means used to produce and publish communication for the public under economic conditions. Journalistic media characterize an autonomous, socially relevant area of language application. The concept of journalistic media is specified communicatively, socio-politically, and economically. "Publish" means to distribute outside of the production context to a wide circle of recipients personally unknown to the sender; "communication for the public" contributes to establishing a general public in societies whose relationships extend past direct contacts such as within a village; and "economic conditions" signify the pressure and the opportunity to create value in a technical process based on the division of labor.

Nevertheless, the borders between public and private communication are becoming blurred because of media convergence. This phenomenon results from the technical developments from digitization and networking that allow texts from several sign systems to be conveyed with a single technical device for various sensory channels. Media have developed interdependently and fused together in the form of computers, the universal communication device. A net-worked computer can process anything digital: for example, all visual and auditory signs. It can tap into libraries and radio programs or act as a typewriter, game console, and telephone. It can be both receiver and sender in the internet, with push and pull offers. As a push-medium, it sends offers of communication to an individual or any number of addressees anywhere in the world-wide web, instantly. As a pull-medium, it has offers of communication stored in the network so that people with official permission or other interested parties can access them according to personal preference.

The former strict separation between personal and journalistic media has thus disappeared, so personal and public communication have also become more closely meshed. For example, someone who reads, hears, or sees an interesting news item on the computer can make a comment on it and forward both to a friend with the computer; previously, an alternate communication channel would have had to be used. Nonetheless, people communicate differently with familiar and selected recipients than with unfamiliar and incalculable masses. The analytical distinction between personal and public communication thus continues to be justified despite media convergence—particularly concerning the inter-relationships between language, media, and competence. Personal and public communication conveyed through media differ in one important respect, namely in terms of the relation of senders to recipients. For this reason, they draw on fundamentally different competences of media specific language use.

Competence here is understood as the individually-determined, socially-influenced, and socially-formative cognitive capacity to solve specific problems in an effective and appropriate way within the framework of specific expectations. Media-specific language competence refers to the capacity to use language in a socially appropriate way and apply it successfully to meet one's own communication objectives (and those of other relevant concerned parties) in interpersonal, organizational, and public settings. People with a sufficient degree of media competence work incrementally at five levels: a) appropriately assessing themselves, their communication partners, situations, and tasks, b) weighing their own views against how they presume others view things, c) planning and carrying out offers of communication, d) sensibly monitoring the actions of other participants, and e) drawing conclusions that feed into continual planning. Personal and public communication conveyed through media differ primarily in d) and e). The following section explores these in more detail.

2. Types of Media Competence

Appropriate and successful language use in communication conveyed through media presupposes three types of competence: a) underlying self, social, and subject competences that play a role in every instance of communication; b) topic-specific subject competence; and c) event-related competence, determined by the social event in which communication takes place. Social events are complex, temporally and spatially determined and limited patterns of behavior that certain groups use to solve certain problems and that mark certain forms of communication: complex patterns of language used to solve communication problems (Keppler 1994; Luckmann 1986), such as a family discussion at the dinner table or a business call. The precise form of communication is highly dependent on the use of media and signs and the corresponding competences for media-specific language use.

How social events, communication forms, media use, and ultimately competences for media-specific language use interact is demonstrated in the following examples of discussions in private and professional life (2.1). A more in-depth example, a CEO doing a television interview, illustrates the interaction between basic competences and form-specific competence (2.2). Finally, a shift in perspective to the journalistic production of a television interview highlights typical possibilities and conflicts inherent in social events in terms of competent media-specific language use (2.3).

2.1. Media Competence in Everyday Situations

A consultation on the phone, a business call, a discussion between parents and children as they watch television, a flirt while watching a movie in a theater, an e-mail message to a friend, an entry in a blog—these are all examples of communication forms. Each of these discussion types involve typical participants who solve typical problems with typical media and language resources and thereby employ certain competences. As is explained in more detail below, participants can a) carry out real-time discussions through a medium, such as in a consultation on the phone or a business call; b) talk face-to-face but be stimulated by previous or simultaneous use of media, as an audience; and c) initiate or respond to discussions by sending or leaving messages through media with potentially unrestricted access.

a. In a consultation on the phone, listening is of primary importance for the advice giver: not just for the verbal message, but also to understand the prosodic and paralinguistic signs and signals such as pauses and intonation, voice and breath quality. Added to this are the abilities to empathize, to treat the other person's comments respectfully, to indicate this paraverbally and verbally, and of course in general the ability to communicate with others about problems and possible solutions using nothing but spoken language. By contrast, business calls across cultural boundaries require experience with culture-specific discourse conventions in addition to listening skills, quick decisions, and assertiveness through spoken language. Common to all telephone discussions is that usually one of the participants triggers the contact, that both or all of the participants organize the course of the discussion together by resorting to standard patterns and formulations, such as for the beginning and end of the discussion, and that participants have to limit themselves to auditory input (Luke and Pavlidou 2002).

b. Anyone who watches television with their children is familiar with another media-influenced form of communication: audience talk while viewing. Such discussions contribute significantly to cognitive and emotional development and to understanding media content (Klemm 2000). The adults follow the video action, interpret children's comments, verbally respond briefly but helpfully to individual children's emotional and cognitive difficulties, if possible during pauses, and mediate any quarrels. A flirt during a movie, also a type of audience talk, requires the ability to ascertain the approachability of the partner, to stimulate the latter with physical proximity without overly disturbing the social surroundings, to follow the story on the screen, and to make such pithy, pointed comments related to the shared experience that it can be assumed the partner feels attracted and involved. The shared feature of all audience talk is multitasking: following the medially-conveyed experience, including the comments and concerns of the social surroundings, and contributing purposefully to the discussion at hand.

c. Transcending the problems of both space and time, computer-mediated communication such as email, newsgroups, and weblogs allow people to initiate or respond to discussions instantaneously. Since these are disembodied forms of communication, however, they do not demand instantaneous reception or provide immediate feedback. Although email can be quite speech-like, often making use of typeface features, punctuation, and devices like so-called emoticons to compensate for a lack of paralinguistic cues (Baron 2000), it differs in the extent of its potential for distribution to an unintended, unknown audience. A technical problem with a provider's server or an accidental click of a button can be all it takes for a message to be sent to the wrong person or people. Contributors to open weblogs, by contrast, intend their messages to be read by the public: Schlobinski and Siever (2005) estimate that by January 2005 there were about 8 million "bloggers" and that 30 % (50 million) of all US internet users may visit weblogs. Despite its speed and apparent transience, all forms of computer-mediated communication are characterized by their potential for distribution and permanence, thanks to ever-increasing storage capacity, access, and logging of texts in interconnected computer networks.

In addition to the capacity to access and use media tools, media competence involves various types of competence that allow people to simultaneously process different types of input at various levels, understand the limitations and potential of specific types of media, and communicate appropriately for the particular task at hand. The following sections deal with how basic competences and media-specific language competence interact.

2.2. Media Competence in Media Situations

". . . ah, um, our wor- . . . work- . . . um . . . valued employees . . . " Anyone who talks like this to the television camera in the morning runs the risk of experiencing the same discomfort that evening while watching the interview on TV, knowing it might be seen by hundreds of thousands of viewers including customers, colleagues, and supervisors who could refer to it later. A media appearance, whether for print or on-line media, for radio or television, represents a threefold burden for media laypersons (Perrin 2006a). First, people often appear in the media acting as representatives of an organization, a particular group, or a subject area, although the expectations of their employers, professional colleagues, and interest groups can diverge wildly from their own. Role conflicts are inevitable. Second, any work with media professionals is heavily influenced by the industrial production routines of the media enterprise. There is always a rush. And third, through the microphone and camera, people are exposed indirectly and put on full display to a diffuse, dispersed public that receive only an excerpt of the whole appearance in the media item, can hardly ask questions, but probably still form an opinion within a few seconds. The social event of the media interview takes place in the center of this triangle of communication task, production routines, and public opinion making.

Media-specific language use is based on various types of basic competence: on self-competence, for instance, in handling personal values and emotions and on social competence in dealing with other people's perceptions, roles, groups, and social processes. A CEO being interviewed, for example, employs various competences before and during the social event of a television interview, in order to:

- perceive, reflect on, and expand on personal values, abilities, and skills (What impression do I want to make? Can I handle a cross-examination by communication pros? Can I spontaneously convey complex ideas? How can I become more courageous, more quick-witted?)
- handle emotions and symptoms of stress, anxiety, or stage fright (How can I make positive use of my tension? How can I stay calm and focused when someone is trying to rush me? What can I do if my hands start shaking? How can I sleep well before the media appearance?)
- perceive the other people's behavior and assess how others perceive one's own behavior (What effect does my enthusiastic shop-talk have on the

television producers? How can I recognize that? Do I notice when I speak too quickly and my voice rises?)

- handle groups and group dynamics (How should I play the part of an expert in a round-table discussion or podium? How can I recognize whether and how hierarchies are forming? How do I deal with assigned hierarchical levels and how can I change group constellations?)
- perceive and help organize large-scale individual and social processes (How do I set topics? How do I structure relationships? How, for whom, and according to which measure do I increase my value? How do I get into and out of crises?)
- negotiate roles (Who assigns which role to whom? How does the discussion partner, the interviewer, do this before, during, and after the discussion? How can I recognize the attempt to assign roles? How do I develop my own role?)

Above and beyond these basic types of competence, such a CEO will also employ competences for media-specific language use that he might need only for discussions, or only for television interviews or live television interviews, or even only for controversial, conflict-laden live television interviews—different types of competence precisely for certain types of media-influenced communication forms. Before and during an interview the CEO would employ such competences in order to:

- assess the framework of discourse (Who publicly sets which topics at present, and who defends which positions? Where does my discussion partner, the journalist, the editors or producers, and/or the audience probably stand in this discourse framework—and where do I stand?)
- respond appropriately to an encounter and help organize the framework (Will a discussion take place? Do I take part myself or does someone else from my side? When, how, and where should an interview take place, if I have a part in these decisions?)
- be prepared for the announced topic and other possible topics and for the expected form of topic management by the journalist (What are the facts about the designated topic and other current topics that the journalist could tie into my role? How should I respond? What should I not respond to? What arguments should I use?)
- construct a suitable model of the discussion partner and other possible addressees and continually adapt it while monitoring the discussion (What does the journalist or the discussion partner want to achieve with their contribution? Which institution, organization, position, or interest group do they represent? What reaction can they trigger in the various addressees of the media item?)
- listen attentively, respond to questions, keep own objectives in view, and make an appropriate impression on the various addressees (What is the interviewer saying, and what does the interviewer mean by it? How does the journalist want to include my statement after the discussion? What do the interviewer's questions and behavior say about the planned media item?)

After the interview, the journalist might produce a media item that provides a frame for parts of the discussion. In another variant of the television interview, the discussion is transmitted live, in real-time, and incorporated into a program of public communication. Here, too, the audience does not simply see the discussion itself but rather a well-designed reconstruction of the discussion: with light and camera angles, sound levels, picture inserts, moderator input, and overall program context all carefully planned. Even a live interview is journalistically structured well beyond the guidance of the discussion by the interviewer. All of this represents the work that goes into a television interview from the perspective of the journalists, the producers, the media enterprise, and the whole system of public, medially-transmitted communication. People with certain roles are at work here, media professionals who also employ their competences for media-specific language use. They rely on them continually to overcome typical conflicts.

2.3. Media Competence in Media Production

Anyone working in journalistic mass media production is subject to conflicting expectations with respect to their role. In the interest of the media enterprise, journalists should achieve high impact at low cost but in the public interest still address socially relevant topics in a nuanced way. Or they have to be ready to respond to the unexpected every day while working within rigid production structures. Such conflicting demands lead to problems in balancing the elements of journalistic text production outlined in (a) to (f) below, all of which assume corresponding competences (Perrin 2004).

a) *Limiting the topic.* Which topic and which aspect of a topic should I choose, and how much detail should I go into?

In an item about a new airport terminal, journalists pick up on the loudest voices in the current discussion about the airport and focus on the high costs in economically tight times. They could also have developed the topic further and included other positions in their report, which might have presented the new terminal as an anti-cyclical long-term investment, for example. This would have prolonged the media production and incurred more expense, though, which would have led to a conflict with (f).

b) *Finding sources.* How seriously do I look into a situation with respect to reliable sources, and how should I reproduce them?

In the item about the airport terminal, a building site manager comments extensively about the complexity of the construction details, giving the impression of unreasonable structural expenditures. The journalists could have had the site manager or other protagonists indicate where and how costs would be saved over the long-term with the buildings under discussion. However, this would have deprived the item of a gripping hypothesis: conflict with (c).

c) *Establishing and formulating own position.* Which perspective should I assume; what is my hypothesis on the topic?

An item on reductions in social benefit payments for single parents includes an excerpt of an interview that makes it clear that the official responsible does not know the price of diapers, milk, or bread. The journalist frames the excerpt with the criticism that anyone making decisions about cuts in social benefits should know what the cost of living is. The journalist could have assumed a more neutral position, but this would have taken the advocacy sting out of the item: conflict with (e).

d) *Guiding the role play.* How much space do I give to the facts of the matter I have researched, to the sources I have asked, and to myself, and how do I link things together?

In the item on social benefits, the journalist supports her interpretation of the matter with an interview excerpt. The portrayed official indicates that he has little idea about how expensive life is for the people whose benefit levels he has to decide upon. The journalist could have kept the interview more open, with fewer leading questions, or reproduced other excerpts from it, but this would have weakened her position: conflict with (c).

e) *Establishing relevance for the audience.* What previous knowledge of which audience do I want to tie into; which expectations do I want to fulfill; and what effect do I want to achieve?

In an item on the hostage release from a Moscow concert hall, for example, the media professionals have a suitable expert explain the physical difficulties the Moscow authorities had to deal with when they flooded the hall with stun gas. The media producers could also have presented this explanation to their lay audience with didactic means such as animated graphics. However, this would have been beyond the scope of a short item in a news broadcast: conflict with (f).

f) *Holding to space and time restrictions.* How do I treat my topic adequately with the resources at hand, in the prescribed space, and in the prescribed time?

In the item on the Moscow hostage release, the media professionals decide to be satisfied with a rather ponderous statement from an expert who is not in top form. There is no time to rehearse because the camera team has another assignment. Perhaps the expert could have been prompted for a better formulation, but this would have detracted from the authenticity of the source's comment: conflict with (b).

This close-up zoom from selected discussions (2.1.), to a television interview (2.2.), and from there to conflicts for media professionals (2.3.) has demonstrated that whereas basic competences also allow appropriate and successful action in many areas other than media and language use, the specific types of competence are oriented to certain topics, roles, media, and communication forms in social events. Media competence encompasses general, topic-specific, and event-specific abilities that together make it possible to solve tasks appropriately and effectively with medially-transmitted communication. These abilities are cognitively determined in the individuals concerned, thus a part of people's retrievable and usable knowledge about themselves, others, and the world. The abilities are socially influenced and influential, developing as individuals deal with themselves, others, and the world and having repercussions on their surroundings.

Researching media competence, accordingly, means relating observed cognitive and social practices to measures of their appropriateness and effectiveness (Deppermann 2004).

3. Researching Media Competence in Newsrooms

Which media-specific language use is appropriate for a task and its social surrounding and leads to success in that context depends, on the one hand, on the use of language itself and, on the other, on what is considered appropriate and successful. Competence is thus a term related to norms. Empirical research on competences does not assume such norms as given but rather establishes evidence of them with the norm providers in the area of study. For an investigation of media competence in journalistic settings, possible norm providers include the public, professional organizations, media houses, and production teams. Such communities—and their individual participants—can set language norms either explicitly such as with editorial guidelines or implicitly by tacit modeling and reproduction in everyday behavior. For example, since no-one speaks loudly in an open-plan office, the norm holds that people do not speak loudly in an open-plan office. Practices and norms thus interact with each other (for a basic review, see Giddens 1984; for an example with journalistic offices, see Wyss 2004).

Both the practices and the norms have to be determined when media-specific language competences are being investigated using standards of empirical research. Media linguistics is a branch of applied linguistics that concerns itself with the area of journalistic text production, using four approaches (Perrin and Ehrensberger 2007) to investigate the language products themselves (3.1.) as well as language use as a cognitive (3.2.), social (3.3.), or cognitive-social activity (3.4.). One method from each of the four approaches is outlined below and illustrated with an empirical research project that works primarily with this method.

3.1. Investigating Language Products With Version Analysis

Version analysis is a linguistic approach for obtaining and analyzing data that tracks language features in intertextual chains. Version analysis indicates how language functions and structures change when statements are incorporated into media items and successively revised at several processing levels such as those of correspondents, news agencies, editors, and producers, or when media report several times successively on the same topic. One example of the usefulness of version analysis is to track how the significance or meaning of a quote can change after it is taken out of its interview context and incorporated into a new text on its own. Text and discourse analyses of individual media items and their precursors in the production flow form the basis for comparing various versions of texts.

In another application of version analysis, Dor (2003) relied on it as the key method in his study of newspaper headlines. He examined the features that characterize headlines considered successful by editorial staff, using the case of the popular Israel newspaper Ma'ariv. From email correspondence between copy editors and the senior editor in chief, Dor reconstructed the development of 134 headlines that appeared between 1996 and 1998. He analyzed the semantic and pragmatic differences between headlines that were rejected and those that were accepted. Using empirically derived criteria, Dor (2003: 716) illustrated that the "art of headline production" was a case of optimizing relevance for the reader.

A relevance optimized headline is easy for the reader to understand because it is kept short, clear, unambiguous, and highly readable; in addition, it triggers expectations in the reader because it makes the topic sound new and interesting. Part of the optimization is that the headline contains newsworthy names and concepts, refers to established facts, and does not rely on unknown presuppositions. According to Dor's results, optimizing the relevance of headlines in this sense is also part of the media-specific language competence of people working at a newspaper's news-desk.

What version analysis cannot do, however, is provide information about whether journalists make conscious decisions when recontextualizing excerpts; whether some practices are typical for certain media with certain target readerships and audiences; and whether practices and associated problems in the production and editorial process are discussed and negotiated or not. To investigate these sorts of questions, methodical access to cognitive practices is required.

3.2. Investigating Cognitive Practices With Progression Analysis

Progression analysis is a multi-method linguistic approach for obtaining and analyzing data that addresses the text production process directly as a cognitively-based activity and indirectly as a socially-based activity. For example, what exactly does a journalist do and why does he do it when he removes a comment from a source text and incorporates into his own text? With progression analysis, data about such a writing process can be obtained at three levels and related to each other: before writing begins the work situation is established with interviews and participant observation; during the actual writing all movements are measured with computer-supported recordings; and after the writing process, the repertoire of writing strategies is inferred through event-specific retrospective verbal protocols.

Progression analysis was the key method used in a case study of media text construction by Sleurs, Jacobs, and van Waes (2003). They examined how Dutch corporate press releases and the quotes they contain are constructed. As part of a larger investigation, they recorded in detail how a 26-year-old writer in a PR agency produced a single press release for a corporate client and what explanations he offered for his actions. The data support the hypothesis that PR writes use pseudo-quotes and preformulations of text so that media journalists can take over as much as possible directly from the press release. In order to avoid alienating media journalists, the writer in the case study also takes care that the quotes do not sound too much like advertising or promotion. For this reason, he formulates quotes to sound more neutral—or he attributes quotes to a more credible or neutral source, such as a customer of his client's company or an analyst. In addition, the writer attempts to place his client's company in a positive light; he thus tries to meet the expectations of people in the media at the same time as those of his clients. Overall, Sleurs et al. conclude that the structure and function of quotes in press releases are more complex than previous research has indicated. Writing journalistically acceptable and attractive quotes proves to be a good working strategy for the writer in the case study and in general might be part of media-specific language competence in PR.

"Might be" . . . in fact, progression analysis deals with practices of the individual language users under study. If the question of interest, however, is how a whole discourse community such as the news staff of a media enterprise produce texts, then progression analysis has to be combined with methods that allow more direct inferences to be made about social practices—about what normally happens in a particular setting.

3.3. Investigating Social Practices With Variation Analysis

Variation analysis is a linguistic approach for obtaining and analyzing data that indicates the special features of the language of certain discourse communities. For example, what do news staff from one newsroom do with the individual comments of an interviewed person compared to what they usually do with such comments and to what another newsroom usually does in such situations? Upon investigation, it becomes apparent that the language in such a situation differs from the language of the same participants in other situations or from the language of other language users. Critical discourse analysis (CDA), a variant of variation analysis, also seeks markers of ideologies that are expressed in the language of a community—markers like hidden political judgments or social stereotypes (Fairclough 1995).

Variation analysis was the key method for Choi (2002) in a study of how language is used in the media to pursue ideological objectives. The corpus consisted of Washington Post and China Daily articles about the collision between an American and a Chinese aircraft above the South China Sea that occurred on April 1, 2001. Choi examined the choice of lexis, syntactic and semantic structures, focal points, and the use of indirect quotations. The choice of lexis seemed significant: the China Daily described the American plane as a spy aircraft, implying illegal activity, whereas the Washington Post referred to it as a surveillance plane, implying legitimate monitoring. Furthermore, the verb form that China Daily used ("bumped into") implied agency on the part of the American plane whereas the Washington Post's choice stressed the accidental nature of the incident ("collided with"). Linguistic resources are adapted to suit the conflicting interests of the political forces that dominate where the articles are produced. According to Choi's findings, therefore, the use of linguistic resources to supply recipients with politically opportune frameworks for interpretation is part of media-specific language competence.

Although variation analysis gains breadth compared with an approach like progression analysis, it suffers from a lack of depth. Variation analysis cannot determine why and at whose request the members of a newsroom frame an event with linguistic choices that conform politically and whether this happens consciously or not—despite many CDA studies inferring language users' thoughts directly from linguistic choices. Some depth of analysis could be regained with an approach that considered not only the text products like variation analysis, and not only the strategies and ideas of individual text producers like progression analysis, but rather the institutionalized discussions and discourse about language use of a whole newsroom. One such approach, metadiscourse analysis, is explained in the next section.

3.4. Investigating Cognitive-Social Practices With Metadiscourse Analysis

Metadiscourse analysis is a linguistic approach for obtaining and analyzing data to determine the socially and individually anchored (language) awareness within discourse communities. Metadiscourse analysis investigates communication through communication and language. For example, at their regular staff meetings how does a newsroom team discuss the ideas they share about acceptable ways of dealing with interview excerpts? Which language practices do they approve of and which do they reject? What source of norms is referred to? Analyzing metadiscourse reveals how rules about language use in a discourse community are consciously negotiated and applied. Linguistic techniques for analyzing verbal communication form the basis for metadiscourse analysis.

Metadiscourse analysis was the key method for Häusermann (2007) in his study of original soundbites and their interpretation. He was interested in the practical possibilities of editing soundbites appropriately for radio scripts, of reflecting on how to incorporate them, and of putting them in a suitable context for interpretation. He analyzed not only the language use, but also the meta-communication of the media staff when things did not work according to plan. This meta-communication allows inferences to be made about the language awareness of the people under study. The analysis tracks the production phases of original soundbites: recording, editing, and then incorporating them. For the recording phase, Häusermann found that journalists and sources usually work together: journalists are able to obtain media-appropriate statements by guiding their informants and re-recording if attempts are less than successful at first. In doing so, though, they influence and distort the soundbite. In the phase when the soundbite is incorporated into a script, the relationship between the journalist and the informant can change. For example, the journalist might act as a cooperative partner during the recording but then put the jointly produced soundbite into a critical context, thereby purposefully recontextualizing differently. Recognizing, questioning, indicating, or avoiding such practices is, according to Häusermann, part of the media-specific language competence of media professionals. According to him, recognizing and questioning these practices is also part of the competence of all media users.

Cognitive and social language practices can be systematically determined with the four approaches outlined above with their linguistic and linguistically-based interdisciplinary methods. The findings allow theoretically and empirically supported conclusions to be drawn about what participants actually do with language in medially-transmitted communication—and what they want to do and should do. In turn, these findings lay a foundation to describe types of media-specific language competence—in the sense of Hymes' (1972) framework of different types of communicative competence. These range from the actual competences of individual language users (e.g. Sleurs et al. 2003) and competences strived for by institutions (e.g. Dor 2003; Choi 2002) to potential competences that would be possible with the help of advice and training (e.g. Dor 2003; Häusermann 2007) and ideal competences that are justified as desirable from a general theoretical perspective (e.g. Häusermann 2007). Such knowledge about media-specific language competence is outlined in the next section, using journalistic text production as an example.

4. Research Questions and Findings

This section provides a systematic overview of specific research questions and findings in the area of appropriate and successful media-specific language competence in the context of journalist text production. The research is first categorized in terms of variously complex settings for language use (4.1.), then language functions (4.2.), and finally linguistic structures (4.3.). Each subsection addresses issues that can be dealt with insightfully from that particular perspective—mostly theory-driven issues but also practice-driven questions of appropriate and successful language use in journalism, such as interview strategies for questioning and answering.

4.1. The Perspective of Setting

The next four subsections outline four approaches to media language that differ according to the setting of the language use: a) interpersonal, b) inter-situational, c) intertextual, and d) intersemiotic. The description of these settings becomes more complex from one level to the next, and each level builds incrementally on the previous one.

a) *Interpersonal setting.* Communicative language use is interpersonal in that it is directed to other people. The beginnings of journalistic communication are also discussions, although the participants are aiming beyond their immediate communication situation, and are oriented not only to their discussion partner but also to the media audience. The theoretical question of interest for linguistics at this interface of interpersonal setting and media competence is how interview participants can address their contributions appropriately for different target audiences. Natural, easily accessible data for such investigations are available in media interviews, where microphones, cameras, and recordings belong to the field of activity itself and are not artificial intrusions by researchers. From the point of view of practice, the question arises as to how media interviews manage to address all of the relevant target audiences at the same time. Media linguistics can employ tools from discourse linguistics to identify and consider the language competence that interviewers and interviewees use to establish a relationship with multiple target audiences— for example, the use of loaded questions.

A loaded question is a complex contribution to a discussion that consists of a claim or observation plus a question designed to elicit an answer that also indicates acceptance of the claim or question. In this area, Bucher (2000) as well as Clayman and Heritage (2002) examine the relationship between questions and claims in loaded questions. Clayman (1993) identifies strategies that politicians use to react to loaded questions by reformulating the questions into a form that they find acceptable whereas Harris (1991) finds that politicians use strategies such as changing the topic after a loaded question, forgetting the question, or frankly refusing to give an answer. Ekström (2001) discusses the process of editing loaded questions out of interview recordings for television news, and Roth (2005) highlights the practice by interviewers before elections to spring surprise questions on candidates in order to make them appear ignorant.

b) *Inter-situational setting.* Even things that seem fleeting and spontaneous in journalistic media are inter-situational and done deliberately: with calculable effort and expenditure, for a pre-determined time frame or space, with the simplest possible access for an unknown audience far away from the production situation. Texts for media items are therefore usually produced in written form even if they are later presented in spoken form. The theoretical question of interest for linguistics at this interface of inter-situational setting and media competence is how writers produce their texts, whether alone or sharing authorship. This can be easily determined at journalistic workstations: writing processes here are predictably short and integrated into computer systems, which simplifies following the text development step-by-step. From the point of view of practice, the question arises as to how journalistic contributions can be produced under economical production conditions, with multiple authors, and in a media- and task-specific interplay of spoken and written modes. Media linguistics can employ tools from writing research to identify and consider the corresponding language competence—for example the writing strategies of experienced media professionals.

A writing strategy is an established, conscious, and thus articulable idea of how decisions are to be made during writing in order that there is a greater probability that the writing process or text product takes on the intended form and fulfills the intended function. Examples of research into writing strategies include studies by Wolf and Thomason (1986) and Laakaniemi (1987) on strategy-oriented approaches of writing coaches in newsrooms; by Androutsopoulos (2000) on writing strategies of writers of fanzines; by Dor (2003) on writing strategies and news headlines; by Perrin (2001; Perrin and Ehrensberger 2006) on the differences between experienced and inexperienced journalists; by Perrin (2004; 2006b) on expanding repertoires of journalistic writing strategies in consulting projects; by Ruhmann and Perrin (2002) on typical journalist conflicts of interest during writing; and by Sleurs et al. (2003) on a PR writer's writing strategies for dealing with quotes.

c) *Intertextual setting.* Journalistic text production transmits societal discourse, thus basically draws on discussions and fixed offers of communication. This recourse to intertextuality occurs in journalistic communication through several steps according to its own domain-specific rules about dealing with sources. The theoretical question of interest for linguistics at this interface of intertextual setting and media competence is how societal discourse functions; that is, how discourse communities communicate about certain topics over time and space and pick up on previous contributions to those topics. Items in journalistic media support such discourse and also record it for analysis at a later date. From the point of view of practice, the question arises as to how discourse can be conveyed from sources to audience in a journalistically appropriate and economically acceptable way. Media linguistics can employ tools from text linguistics to identify and consider the corresponding language competence with which media professionals create, simulate, and blur intertextuality—for example by clustering items or intensifying them with quotes.

Clustering is a term to describe the linguistic activity of preparing a media contribution as a non-linear compilation of intertextually linked texts within a perceptual field. Intensifying is used to describe a linguistic activity whereby utterances are (re-)constructed to lead to a main claim having public appeal. A quote is a unit in a media item that is represented as a faithful replication of a source's utterance. An example of research into clustering is Bucher's (1996) study, which shows it to be a text design strategy in daily newspapers, with a text cluster arising from several individual items such as reports and comments or from an individual item that is comprised of sub-sections, boxes, tables, etc. clustered together. Lugrin (2001) also investigates text clusters in terms of differences between them in a prestige and a tabloid newspaper. Burger (2001) considers quotes in television news broadcasts; Marinos (2001) examines the authenticity of reported speech in newspaper reports; Ekström (2001) describes how the same utterances from politicians can be subject to completely different journalistic intentions in various television news items; and Häusermann (2007) and Sleurs et al. (2003) discuss quotes in PR texts that are invented and formulated in such a way that they intensify a journalistic focus.

d) *Intersemiotic setting.* The symbolic system of language, whether spoken or written, is always intersemiotically integrated in media items: language never occurs as language alone. The various forms of journalistic media permit and demand their own links between language and other symbolic systems. This has repercussions for the use of language. The theoretical question of interest for linguistics at this interface of intersemiotic setting and media competence is how language interacts with other symbolic systems. The technology of each medium allows its own interaction of symbolic systems and the dramaturgy demands it: print with its script and still pictures; television with moving pictures; and radio with the background noise of the reported events. From the point of view of practice, the question arises as to how signs from several systems can be coordinated with each other. Media linguistics can employ tools from semiotics to identify and consider the corresponding language competence with which media items can be illustrated, scripted, sound-tracked, and linked—for example the gap between spoken text and pictures, the text/image divide.

The text/image divide refers to the divergence between the meaning of verbal utterances and simultaneously perceptible images in media items. Some examples of relevant research include Jucker (2003) on media convergence that lets print, radio, and TV items appear to be special cases of hypermedia; Quinn (2005) on the general problems of multimedia reporting; Ballstaedt (2002) on text-image design; and Huth (1985) and Oomen (1985) on functions of images in television news. Renner (2001) discusses the metaphor of "shears" to describe the text/image divide. He differentiates among strong and weak confirmation, contradiction, and lack of reference between text and image, and recognizes them to be functional in various ways for the four genres of documentary film, reportage, explanatory film, and essay. The metaphor of a zipper in place of shears is offered by Holly (2005) as an alternate view of the relationship between text and image.

4.2. The Perspective of Function

This section outlines four approaches to media language that differ according to the function of language: a) referential, b) cognitive, c) interactive, and d) social-constitutive. The description of these settings becomes more complex from one level to the next, and each level builds incrementally on the previous one.

a) *Referential function.* Language usually refers to things outside itself: it relates to non-verbal phenomena and labels things in the world. Every form of communication makes use of this labeling, the primary function of language. However, as the term suggests, journalistic news is concerned with conveying new information. It has to be able to refer quickly to things that have not been labeled previously. The theoretical question of interest for linguistics at this interface of referential function and media competence is what linguistic utterances mean in everyday life. Linguistic inquiry focuses on the meaning of words and complex linguistic units, on logical connections of meaning, on hierarchies of meaning, and on themes. In journalistic media, it discovers that attempts to make meaning public are ongoing, rapid, and routine. From the point of view of practice, the question arises as to how it is possible to regularly report about current events and often about unfamiliar things with well-known signs and symbols. Media linguistics can employ tools from semantics to identify and consider the corresponding language competence with which media professionals quickly and routinely link what is familiar to what is new—for example with metaphors.

Metaphors transpose the meaning of a sign from a familiar field to a new field that is then perceived as similar. Research into the use of metaphors in the media can be found in Settekorn (2001) on metaphor transfers between journalism and advertising as well as between sports and economic reporting;

Burger (2004) on metaphors in intertextual journalist text production; Zinken (2003) on the connection between metaphors and ideology in the Polish press at the collapse of communism; Kobozeva (2005) on metaphors in the Russian press; Koller (2004a; 2004b) on metaphors in media items about women in management positions; Dirks (2005) on metaphors in press commentaries about peace demonstrations; Stenvall (2003) on the use of metaphors by international news agencies in reporting about terrorism; Peck MacDonald (2005) on metaphors in journalist reports about hormone therapies; Johnson and Suhr (2003), Johnson, Culpeper, and Suhr (2003), and Toolan (2003) on metaphors in media items that have political correctness as a main or secondary theme.

b) *Cognitive function.* The use of language requires and generates cognitive processes: by speaking or writing, people express thoughts in the form of language and then by understanding language, thoughts are triggered. In journalistic communication, though, language production is disconnected from language comprehension. The media professionals cannot directly track what the chosen linguistic devices trigger in their audience. The theoretical question of interest for linguistics at this interface of cognitive language function and media competence is how language is processed in the mind, how a language user's previous knowledge contributes to understanding texts, and how this knowledge can be activated. Journalistic communication, with its practically unknown addressees, has to build on basic assumptions of general prior knowledge. From the point of view of practice, the question arises as to how news journalism can report in an illuminating and attractive way. Media linguistics can employ tools from psycholinguistics to identify and consider the corresponding language competence with which media professionals strive for such features of quality—like framing, establishing coherence, and comprehensibility.

Framing refers to the representation or interpretation of an extract of reality in terms of cognitively and socially anchored patterns of interpretation. Coherence is the capacity of an understood text to connect together through additional thoughts it triggers. Comprehensibility is determined by all of the features of a text that are suitable for influencing how addressees understand that text. Some examples of research into framing are studies by Fang (2001) on framing politically sensitive events in Chinese newspapers and by Lind and Salo (2002) on framing feminism in American radio news. On the subject of coherence, Dorenbeck (1997) examines a newsmagazine's "strategy" of leaving coherence gaps open at critical points for the audience to fill as they like; Eggs (1996) discusses multi-stranded, associative argumentation in newspaper commentaries; and Perrin (1999) identifies coherence problems in patching together agency news reports. Finally, comprehensibility has been considered by Lutz and Wodak (1987) in their comparisons of various versions of the same news; by Hardt-Mautner (1992) with radio news; by McAdams (1993) in terms of the readability of newspaper texts; and by Bucher (2005) for journalism in general.

c) *Interactive function.* Cognitive change favors interactive change: when knowledge changes, behavior can change. Communication aims for such effects. People do things with language so that something happens; they communicate purposefully. Participants in a communication situation can pursue the same objectives—or complementary or exclusory objectives. The theoretical question of interest for linguistics at this interface of pragmatic language function and media competence is how verbal and non-verbal activities interact, what intentions language users have, and how meaning is negotiated in communication. In journalistic communication the intended actions and conflicts of various actors overlap systematically: those of the media professionals, the sources, the target audience, and the broader public. From the point of view of practice, the question arises as to how to make an offer of communication available to the public and at the same time sell it. Media linguistics can employ tools from pragmatics to identify and consider the corresponding language competence with which media professionals choose and dramaturgically prepare their topics—for example storytelling.

Storytelling consists of designing an offer of communication as a story, with typical text roles, scenes, action, and perspectives. There are many examples of research into journalistic storytelling: Tuchman (1976) discusses news journalism as telling stories, similar to Schudson (1982), Bennett, Gresset, and Haltom (1985), Redd (1991), Pietilä (1992), Püschel (1992), Kunelius (1994), Jaworski and Connell (1995), Hickethier (1997), Ekström (2000), and Ungerer (2000). Le (2004) examines journalistic self-positioning and the dramaturgical function of text actors in editorials; Hartley (1982), Fiske (1987) and Roth (2002) investigate the dramaturgical representation of interviewees in radio; Koller (2004a) that of business women in media items; Spranz-Fogasy (2003) of managers; Ekström (2001) of politicians; Burger (1996) of the lay public; and Kleinberger (2004) of the lay public and experts. Luginbühl (2004) focuses on authenticity in television news, similarly to Coupland (2001) with a television news review; Jacobs (1996) on storytelling and crises; and Jaworski, Fitzgerald, and Morris (2003) on storytelling when reporting about future events.

d) *Social-constitutive function.* Finally, communication has a social-constitutive function: people can establish common ideas and discourse communities with language and, conversely, the chosen language indicates which discourse community people belong to. Journalistic communication translates between the languages of communities, such as between the languages of text actors and addressees. By doing so it overcomes social differences—and at the same time consolidates them. The theoretical question of interest for linguistics at this interface of social language function and media competence is how communities differ in their languages and language variants and how language use changes—also under the influence of journalistic media. From the point of view of practice, the question arises as to how to reliably reach different addressees with linguistic means while at the same time defining a unique profile in the market and committing audience, sources, and advertising clients over the long-term. Media linguistics can employ tools from sociolinguistics to identify and consider the corresponding language competence with which media professionals commit their target groups—so-called audience design.

Audience design refers to tailoring a media item for certain target groups: a) adjusting to the expectations, prior knowledge, and receptiveness of addressees; b) using a different style from other offers in the market; and

c) contributing to the commitment of users. Research into audience design in journalist media has been carried out by Bell (1984; 2001), who examines the conflict between adaptation to the norms of the market and an independent profile in the market; by Selting (1983), who discusses a radio moderator's practice of purposefully using different linguistic styles for different tasks and with different discussion partners—using high register in discussions with experts and the proximity of dialect in discussions with persons affected by an issue; by Schwitalla (1993), who views the changes of journalistic genres as a consequence of audience design; by Roeh (1982), who considers the repercussions of audience design on the content of journalistic news; and by Schudson (1982) and Cameron (1996), who explore the political background of audience design.

4.3. The Perspective of Structure

The following subsections outline four approaches to media language that differ according to the structure of the verbal utterances: a) sound, b) word, c) sentence, and d) text. The description of these structures become more complex from one level to the next, and each level builds incrementally on the previous one.

a) *Sound structure.* Language connects the smallest possible units that distinguish meaning: sounds, letters, characters, and elements of signs that people can produce and convey and that they can perceive as systematically different. Journalistic communication has to limit itself to technically transmitted signs—at present to visible and audible signs. The theoretical question of interest for linguistics at this interface of sound structure and media competence is how auditory features of language contribute to comprehension. Individual sound segments and their articulation are of interest, as is prosody, the supra-segmental sound of language. In the spoken language of journalistic media, articulation and prosody are intended to be as widely accepted as possible. From the point of view of practice, the question arises as to how to structure the auditory component of media items, including the sound of spoken language. Media linguistics can employ tools from phonetics and phonology to identify and consider the corresponding language competence with which media professionals speak effectively—for example prosodic phrasing.

Prosodic phrasing is the linguistic phenomenon of a speaker using prosodic means to emphasize the semantic and pragmatic structure of an utterance. Prosodic means include broad patterns such as intonation curves as well as emphasis with loudness, pitch, or duration. For example, Bell (1982; 1991) discusses the differences in the spoken English of newscasts in six New Zealand radio stations that target audiences from various social levels by choosing appropriate linguistic means. Schubert and Sendlmeier (2005) examine the sound features of newscast language that is positively judged by test audiences in listening trials, finding that one of the key features is the division of the news text into sensible sections with the aid of breaks. Bergner and Lenhart (2005) ascertain similarities in prosodic arrangement between radio news of a public and private station, allowing producer-independent generalizations to be made about genre-specific patterns. The point of a "prescriptive notation" for radio news is explored by Marx (2005): written advice about prosody should make it simpler to say news texts as comprehensibly as possible, so that the semantic and pragmatic structure and thereby the meaning and understood more easily.

b) *Word structure.* Language combines meaningfully distinctive units into meaningful units: linguistic symbols that stand for specific details in the world. The details, their perception by the language user, and communication requirements change over time, so language users create new words, some of which establish themselves in the language community. The theoretical question of interest for linguistics at this interface of word structure and media competence is how new words form, spread, change, and disappear. Journalistic media are especially interesting in this context for three reasons: they constantly create new words to meet their own needs, they spread language to many other users, and their media products allow methodologically simple access to the language output. From the point of view of practice, the question arises as to which types of words suit media tasks. Media linguistics can employ tools from morphology to identify and consider the linguistic devices with which media professionals are recognized in public discourse, talk about new things concisely in a way that is easily remembered, and relieve communication of the duress of creativity—for example by using idioms, on the one hand, or coinages, on the other.

An idiom consists of a group of words in a specific order that has a set meaning as a whole. For example, the idiom "give something the green light" means something different from the sum of the meanings of the individual words. Thus, idioms do not operate according to the composition principle. By contrast, a spontaneous coinage or neologism is a word that is made up or applied spontaneously in a concrete situation and relies on users being able to deduce its particular meaning from its components or the context. Some examples of relevant research include Burger (1999) on idioms in the press and Burger (2004) on idioms in intertextual chains of journalistic text production. Sawitzki (2001) examines neologisms in German newsmagazines, and Holly (2002) does so in columns written by a well-known German author, Elke Heidenreich, for the German woman's magazine "Brigitte". Peck MacDonald (2005) considers word choice and sentence structure in sensationalist popular science articles; and Jesensek (1998) discusses the function of coinages as catchwords in political press commentaries.

c) *Sentence structure.* Language, whether spoken or written, is represented linearly, one symbol after the other. In terms of meaning, the symbols form cross-connections, networks, and hierarchies. Symbols for actors and actions combine into propositional units that are linearly represented as sentences. Journalistic communication verbalizes the propositions densely and in portions as appropriate to the product templates and target group models. The theoretical question of interest for linguistics at this interface of sentence level and media competence is what sentences are—how they are linked internally and with each other. The use of sentence structures change over time, but even at any particular point in time the possible patterns are used differently with various intentions and for various tasks. In journalistic language use this can be easily traced. From the point of view of practice, the question arises as to how sentences and chains of sentences can be formed so that addressees can quickly understand the key message. Media linguistics can employ tools from syntax to identify and consider the language competence with which media professionals create sentence structures specific to the task at hand— for example, condensing and portioning information.

Condensing information is the linguistic process of conveying as much information as possible with the fewest possible signs. Portioning information refers to dividing linguistic utterances into units that are easy to process cognitively. An example of research into sentence structure in journalism is Jucker's (1992) study that shows that the sentence structures in British daily newspapers are more similar within a section of the paper than between different sections or editorial offices. Biber (2003) identifies the presence of condensed nominal phrases in newspapers; Mardh (1980) discusses "headlinese", the structural characteristics of headlines on the title pages of English newspapers; Kniffka (1980) examines headlines and formulations of leads in American dailies; Bell (1991) considers the omission of the definite article in certain types of apposition; and Perrin (2005) describes which strategies journalists use to condense their source's utterances. The functions of the beginnings of sentences in German news articles are examined by Schröder (2001), and Cotter (2003) considers the function of the connectors "and" and "but" in the newspaper language of the 20th century. Specifically addressing the technique of portioning, Häusermann (2005) explains that the technique helps in the editing of illogical or confusingly structured complex sentences. After editing, sentences convey information step-bystep with clear links.

d) *Text structure.* Ultimately, linguistic complexes form meaningful units: texts that deal with a certain topic and embody certain intended actions. For recurring topics and intentions in recurring communication situations, text patterns or genres develop. Journalistic communication makes use of such patterns and constantly breaks out of them as it strives for market share and media evolve. The theoretical question of interest for linguistics at this interface of text level and media competence is what makes a text a text and which patterns develop from this in language use, even in the rapid, industrial pace of journalistic media. From the point of view of practice, the question arises as to how to make text processing simpler by using text patterns while still appearing autonomous. Media linguistics can employ tools from text linguistics to identify and consider the language competence with which media professionals use and break away from familiar patterns—the strategic variation of text patterns such as genres.

A text genre is a socially determined pattern for texts in a particular setting and with a certain function and/or structure. Genre change is the continuous evolution of a genre as it used over a longer period of time. Text pattern variation is the purposeful adaptation and development of text patterns in the sense of audience design. Some examples of research in this area include Adam's (2001) analysis of journalistic genres; Ljung's (2000) examination of the repertoire of genres in English-language quality newspapers; Grosse's (2001) study of the development of genres in journalism; Östman and Simon-Vandenbergen's (2004) investigation into text genre mixing and change; Bell's (2003) discussion of genre change in informative journalism; Ungerer's (2000) arguments about new media changing newspaper reporting; Van Dijk's (1988a) overview of the various text structures of 250 newspaper reports from 100 countries on the same event; studies by Lorda (2001) and Moirand (2001) about journalistic texts that do not fit into any of the usual genres of today; and Kropf's (1999) criticism of the so-called pyramid model of journalistic news and his proposal of a new "docking" model for radio news that can be completely understood upon first hearing.

From setting through to function and structure, this section has opened up a system of language use and competence and filled it for one particular area of the media, that of journalistic text production. It has shown that structural features of language (4.3) depend on the functions of that language (4.2) in certain settings (4.1). A quote from an interview becomes a headline condensed in the practices of the organizationally, institutionally, and socially linked participants, whereby the practices are influenced by structures such as norms and resources but also have a reverse effect on them. For example, the norm that competent interviewers of a particular television station do not preformulate answers for ineloquent interviewees might only hold until an interviewer otherwise considered competent and exemplary does so with conviction.

This is a very broad view of things. For practical reasons, the individual empirical approaches can seldom take a broad enough view to be able to vividly yet firmly grasp the complex construct "media competence". At this point, the issue of blank spots or current gaps in research in this area needs to be addressed.

5. Current Gaps in Research Into Media Competence

Media competence clearly involves being able to access and make appropriate use of various types of individual, institutional, and media-specific language competence as the setting demands. As yet, few studies have managed to investigate media competence in all its complexity. An example of an investigation that attempts to address various types of language competence in a complex setting is Perrin, Schanne, and Wyss's (2005) research project on language policy, norms, and practices in the Swiss national radio and television broadcasting company. The project is part of a national research program on language competence and diversity in Switzerland, a country of about 7 million people and four national languages. The public broadcaster, in a monopoly position, has the mandate that its programs contribute to an understanding of, integration of, and communication between the country's linguistic and cultural communities. The outcomes of the project are consultations, coaching, and training of the media professionals working in the company—all measures to improve their media-specific language competence. Beforehand, it is necessary to determine how the Swiss national broadcasting company does, should, and could deal with language. This is done in the four research modules outlined below.

- Module A traces the development of the explicit and implicit external language policy expectations of the Swiss broadcaster, using document analysis and thematic interviews. Consistencies and contradictions become discernible in the demands on the overall institution, its enterprise units, and its programs.
- Module B reconstructs actions and reactions, interpretations and reasons of the broadcaster's management and those of their leading media outlets, using document analysis and thematic interviews. Organizational-hierarchical internal rules and resources for language use in programs and broadcasts become identifiable.
- Module C investigates text production practice for the most important information broadcasts in German and French with process and product analysis. The institutional, organizational, and individually motivated strategies and practices of media professionals as well as traces of their actions become recognizable in the language of the programs.
- Module D uses discourse analysis to investigate the quality control follow-up communication in the editorial offices of the leading news programs in German and French: Tagesschau and téléjournal. The language awareness that the Swiss company's language professionals and trainers bring to broadcasting becomes evident in such communication.

The practical complexities of research into media competence become particularly apparent in certain settings. When media competence refers to the capacity to use language appropriately and successfully in medially-transmitted communication, then this competence is not just part of an individual—but part of a socially integrated individual. In order to reconstruct the repertoire of competences at someone's disposal or that someone could or should have available, then research must investigate the practices of the individuals under study in complex, social settings—for sufficiently long and in enough depth. A field of applied linguistics that understands itself to be "dealing with practical problems of language and communication that can be identified, analyzed or solved" (AILA 2006) cannot avoid expanding its previous boundaries in order to tackle practical, relevant questions about media-specific language competence.

The preceding sections provide examples of the type of research that is being done in the area of media competence. Despite much systematic study of media-specific language use in variously complex settings (interpersonal, inter-situational, intertextual, inter-semiotic), of functions of media-specific language (referential, cognitive, interactive, socially-constitutive), and of media-specific language structures (sound, word, sentence, text), some serious gaps remain.

The first main gap primarily concerns the "competence" in media competence. In order to more easily handle an integrative, competence-oriented project such as that in the public broadcasting company described above, applied linguistics needs more solid, (inter-)disciplinary knowledge about the interconnections between language and other semiotic systems; language products and processing; production and reception processes; cognitive-individual and social practices; public and personal communication; scientific, systematic knowledge and practical, experiential knowledge; knowledge creation and transfer; as well as quantitative and qualitative methods. The mission of applied linguistics to address questions in their practical complexity basically includes all areas of language use and all research areas in the field. The gaps in knowledge are particularly disadvantageous with respect to medially-transmitted communication, though, because it is so important in daily life and business, in private and public, and will quickly become even more important.

A second gap concerns the "media" in media competence and is based directly on the pace of development of media technology. Digitization, networking, and media convergence are quickly opening up new technical possibilities for medially-transmitted communication. The subject of interest is developing far faster than research can track it. Street television, for example, where "peripheral groups juggle power relations and subvert the conventions of television" (Renzi 2005) by broadcasting their own ideas of television via the internet, can concern avant-garde media makers and users for years before the topic also appears in linguistic research. Counter-examples do exist, such as Crystal's (2001) treatment of language and the internet, which was written and distributed quite early on, and the internet site www.mediensprache.net that presents research news about language use in the (new) media. As early as August 2006, for instance, there was already a link to an on-line publication with contributions about the language of Chinese, German, English, Italian, Polish, Portuguese, Russian, Swedish, and Spanish weblogs (Schlobinski and Siever 2005)—although nothing yet on the topics of podcasting or talking over the internet using VoIP (Voice over Internet Protocol).

As Van Dijk (1988b: 23) observed about two decades ago: "The field [of mass media discourse analysis] is only 20 years young, with most of its substantial work having been done in the last decade. For many levels and dimensions of analysis, we still lack the theoretical instruments. Thus, we still know little about the precise structures and processes of media discourse." For media practitioners, those words must seem rather guarded. Journalists who prepare new topics for publication every day or sales staff who have to understand and explain the navigation logic of new models of mobile phones every week (with media competence in terms of practical, on-the-job experience with media) should be able to expect a couple of good ideas from a field that has been considering the topic for a number of years now. On the other hand, recognizing complex interconnections (media competence as a theoretical construct for understanding and communicating appropriately with media) requires a certain degree of distance.

A few years after the first, enthusiastic studies about the language of email messages appeared, Dürscheid (2005: 94), for example, determined that there were only a small number of linguistic features typical of email communication and that they usually occur only if the sender uses the reply and quote functions of the email program. Even what until now has been considered typical about the telephone can be called into question, since it may soon dissolve in general media convergence. Many mobile communication devices and laptop computers have built-in cameras and programs that allow people to "phone" via the internet and with pictures. Children may soon be chatting to their grandparents face-to-face despite being in different geographical locations, and brides-to-be may be able to model their wedding dresses live from distant cities to get their mothers' opinion. Media technology comes and goes, just like the telegraph, the fax machine, and the DOS computer with its dial-up analog modem. For the concept of media competence, the key issue is one's position on the scale between personal and public communication.

References

Adam, J.-M. 2001. Genres de la presse écrite et analyse de discours. *SEMEN* 13: 7–14.

AILA. 2006. What is AILA. Retrieved 2.09.06, from http://www.aila.info/about/index.htm

Androutsopoulos, J. 2000. Non-standard spellings in media texts: The case of German fanzines. *Journal of Sociolinguistics* 4(4): 514–533.

Ballstaedt, S.-P. 2002. Schreibstrategien zum Medienwechsel. Text-Bild-Design. In: D. Perrin, I. Boettscher, O. Kruse, and A. Wrobel (eds.), *Schreiben. Von intuitiven zu professionellen Schreibstrategien*, 139–150. Wiesbaden: Westdeutscher Verlag.

Baron, N. S. 2000. *Alphabet to Email. How Written English Evolved and Where It's Heading.* London/New York: Routledge.

Bell, A. 1982. Radio: The style of news language. *Journal of Communication* 32(1): 150–164.

Bell, A. 1984. Language style as audience design. *Language in Society* 13(2): 145–204.

Bell, A. 1991. *The Language of News Media.* Oxford: Blackwell.

Bell, A. 2001. Back in style. reworking audience design. In: P. Eckert and J. R. Rickford (eds.), *Style and sociolinguistic variation*, 139–169. Cambridge: Cambridge University Press.

Bell, A. 2003. A century of news discourse. *International Journal of English Studies* 3: 189–208.

Bennett, B. L., L. A. Gresset, and W. Haltom. 1985. Repairing the news. A case study of the news paradigm. *Journal of Communication* 35(2): 50–68.

Bergner, U. and H. Lenhart. 2005. Analyse von Hörfunknachrichten am Beispiel zweier Sender. Eine sprechwissenschaftlich- empirische Studie. In: N. Gutenberg (ed.), *Schreiben und Sprechen von Hörfunknachrichten. Zwischenergebnisse sprechwissenschaftlicher Forschung*, 41–119. Frankfurt am Main: Lang.

Biber, D. 2003. Compressed noun-phrase structures in newspaper discourse. In: J. Aitchison and D. M. Lewis (eds.), *New media language*, 169–181. London: Routledge.

Bucher, H.-J. 1996. Textdesign—Zaubermittel der Verständlichkeit? Die Tageszeitung auf dem Weg zum interaktiven Medium. In: E. W. B. Hess-Lüttich, W. Holly, and U. Püschel (eds.), *Textstrukturen im Medienwandel*, 31–59. Frankfurt am Main: Lang.

Bucher, H.-J. 2000. Geladene Fragen. Zur Dialogdynamik in politischen Fernsehinterviews. Retrieved 16.12.04, from http://www.medienwissenschaft.de/forschung/ geladene_fragen/ start.html

Bucher, H.-J. 2005. Verständlichkeit. In: H. J. Kleinsteuber, B. Pörksen, and S. Weischenberg (eds.), *Handbuch Journalismus und Medien,* 464–470. Konstanz: UVK.

Burger, H. 1996. Laien im Fernsehen. Was sie leisten—wie sie sprechen—wie man mit ihnen spricht. In: B. U. Biere and R. Hoberg (eds.), *Mündlichkeit und Schriftlichkeit im Fernsehen*, 41–80. Tübingen: Narr.

Burger, H. 1999. Phraseologie in der Presse. In: N. Bravo Fernandez, I. Behr, and C. Rozier, (eds.), *Phraseme und typisierte Rede*, 77–89. Tübingen: Stauffenburg.

Burger, H. 2001. Das Zitat in den Fernsehnachrichten. In: D. Möhn, D. Roß, and M. Tjarks- Sobhani (eds.), *Mediensprache und Medienlinguistik. Festschrift für Jörg Hennig*, 45–62. Frankfurt am Main: Lang.

Burger, H. 2004. Phraseologie (und Metaphorik) in intertextuellen Prozessen der Massenmedien. In: Christine Palm Meister (ed.), *EUROPHRAS 2000. Internationale Tagung zur Phraseologie vom 15.–18. Juni. 2000. in Aske/Schweden*, 5–13. Tübingen: Stauffenburg.

Cameron, D. 1996. Style policy and style politics: A neglected aspect of the language of the news. *Media, Culture and Society* 18: 315–533.

Choi, D. 2002. *A Critical Discourse Analysis on Different Representations of the Same Event in the Media*. Essen: LAUD Linguistic Agency.

Clayman, S. E. 1993. Reformulating the question. A device for answering/not answering questions in interviews and press conferences. *Text* 13: 159–188.

Clayman, S. E. and J. Heritage. 2002. *The News Interview. Journalists and Public Figures on the Air*. Cambridge: Cambridge University Press.

Cotter, C. 2003. Prescription and practice. Motivations behind change in news discourse. *Journal of Historical Pragmatics* 4(1): 45–74.

Coupland, N. 2001. Stylization, authenticity, and TV news review. *Discourse Studies* III(4): 413–442.

Crystal, D. 2001. *Language and the Internet*. Cambridge: Cambridge University Press.

Deppermann, A. 2004. "Gesprächskompetenz"—Probleme und Herausforderungen eines möglichen Begriffs. In: M. Becker-Mrotzek and G. Brünner (eds.), *Analyse und Vermittlung von Gesprächskompetenz*, 7–14. Frankfurt am Main: Verlag für Gesprächsforschung.

Dirks, U. 2005. Pressekommentare zur größten Friedensdemonstration vor dem Irakkrieg (2003) aus transkultureller Perspektive—Eine Dokumentarische Gattungsanalyse. In: C. Fraas and M. Klemm (eds.), *Mediendiskurse—Bausteine gesellschaftlichen Wissens*, 286–308. Frankfurt: Lang.

Dor, D. 2003. On newspaper headlines as relevance optimizers. *Journal of Pragmatics* 35: 695–721.

Dorenbeck, N. 1997. Zweifelhafte Wegweiser. Pragmatische Charakteristika und kommunikative Strategie der SPIEGEL-Story. *Sprache und Literatur* 80: 83–95.

Dürscheid, C. 2005. E-Mail—verändert sie das Schreiben? In: T. Siever, P. Schlobinski, and J. Runkehl (eds.), *Websprache.net. Sprache und Kommunikation im Internet*, 85–97. Berlin: de Gruyter.

Eggs, E. 1996. Formen des Argumentierens in Zeitungskommentaren—Manipulation durch mehrsträngig-assoziatives Argumentieren? In: E. W. B. Hess-Lüttich, W. Holly, and U. Püschel (eds.), *Textstrukturen im Medienwandel*, 179–209. Frankfurt am Main: Lang.

Ekström, M. 2000. Information, storytelling and attractions: TV journalism in three modes of communication. *Media, Culture and Society* 22(4): 465–492.

Ekström, M. 2001. Politicians interviewed on television news. *Discourse and Society* 12(5): 563–584.

Fairclough, N. 1995. *Media Discourse*. London: Arnold.

Fang, Y.-J. 2001. Reporting the same events? A critical analysis of Chinese print news media texts. *Discourse and Society* 12(5): 585–613.

Fiske, J. 1987. *Television Culture. Popular Pleasures and Politics*. London: Methuen.

Giddens, A. 1984. *The Constitution of Society*. Cambridge: Polity Press.

Grosse, E.-U. 2001. Evolution et typologie des genres journalistiques. Essai d'une vue d'ensemble. *SEMEN* 13: 15–36.

Hardt-Mautner, G. 1992. *Making Sense of the News. Eine kontrastiv-soziolinguistische Studie zur Verständlichkeit von Hörfunknachrichten*. Frankfurt am Main: Lang.

Harris, S. 1991. Evasive action. How politicians respond to questions in political interviews. In: P. Scannell (ed.), *Broadcast Talk*, 76–99. London: Sage.

Hartley, J. 1982. *Understanding News. Studies in Communication*. London: Methuen.

Häusermann, J. 2005. *Journalistisches Texten. Sprachliche Grundlagen für professionelles Informieren (2 ed.)*. Konstanz: UVK.

Häusermann, J. 2007. Zugespieltes Material. Der O-Ton und seine Interpretation. In: Harun Maye, Cornelius Reiber, and Nikolaus Wegmann (eds.), *Original / Ton. Zur Mediengeschichte des O-Tons*. Konstanz: UVK.

Hickethier, K. 1997. Das Erzählen der Welt in den Fernsehnachrichten. Überlegungen zu einer Narrationstheorie der Nachricht. *Rundfunk und Fernsehen* 45(1): 5–18.

Holly, W. 2002. "Klare und normale Sprache" als sozialer Stil. Zu Elke Heidenreichs 'Brigitte'-Kolumnen. In: I. Keim and W. Schütte (eds.), *Soziale Welten und kommunikative Stile*, 363–378. Tübingen: Niemeyer.

Holly, W. 2005. Zum Zusammenspiel von Sprache und Bildern im audiovisuellen Verstehen. In: D. Busse, T. Niehr, and M. Wengeler (eds.), *Brisante Semantik. Neuere Konzepte und Forschungsergebnisse einer kulturwissenschaftlichen Linguistik*, 353–373. Tübingen: Niemeyer.

Hutchby, I. 1991. *Conversation and Technology: From the Telephone to the Internet.* Oxford: Polity.

Huth, L. 1985. Bilder als Elemente kommunikativen Handelns in den Fernsehnachrichten. *Zeitschrift für Semiotik* 7(3): 203–234.

Hymes, D. 1972. On communicative competence. In: J. B. Pride and J. Holmes (eds.), *Sociolinguistics*, 269–293. Harmondsworth: Penguin.

Jacobs, R. N. 1996. Producing the news, producing the crisis. Narrativity, television and news work. *Media, Culture and Society* 18: 373–397.

Jaworski, A. and I. Connell. 1995. Telling journalistic stories. *Zeszyty Prasoznawcze* 36(1–2): 49–73.

Jaworski, A., R. Fitzgerald, and D. Morris. 2003. Certainty and speculation in news reporting of the future: the execution of Timothy McVeigh. *Discourse Studies* 5(1): 33–49.

Jesensek, V. 1998. Zur Leistung der okkasionellen Lexik im politischen Pressekommentar. In: B. Kettemann, M. Stegu, and H. Stöckl (eds.), *Mediendiskurse. verbal- Workshop Graz 1996*, 133–140. Frankfurt am Main: Lang.

Johnson, S., J. Culpeper, and S. Suhr. 2003. From "politically correct councillor" to "Blairite nonsense": disourses of "political correctness" in three British newspapers. *Discourse and Society* 14(1): 29–47.

Johnson, S. and S. Suhr. 2003. From "political correctness" to "politische Korrektheit": discourses of "PC" in the German newspaper Die Welt. *Discourse and Society* 14(1): 49–68.

Jucker, A. H. 1992. *Social Stylistics. Syntactic Variation in British Newspapers.* Berlin/New York: de Gruyter.

Jucker, A. H. 2003. Mass media communication at the beginning of the twenty-first century. *Journal of Historical Pragmatics* 4(1): 129–148.

Keppler, A. 1994. *Tischgespräche. Über Formen kommunikativer Vergemeinschaftung am Beispiel der Konversation in Familien.* Frankfurt am Main: Suhrkamp.

Kleinberger, U. 2004. Mediale Einbettung von Textsorten und Texten. Am Beispiel von Laien und Experten in der Wirtschaftsberichterstattung am Fernsehen und im Internet. *Medienwissenschaft Schweiz* 2: 109–115.

Klemm, M. 2000. *Zuschauerkommunikation. Formen und Funktionen der alltäglichen kommunikativen Fernsehaneignung.* Frankfurt am Main: Lang.

Kniffka, H. 1980. *Soziolinguistik und empirische Textanalyse. Schlagzeilen und Leadformulierungen In: amerikanschen Tageszeitungen.* Tübingen: Niemeyer.

Kobozeva, I. M. 2005. Identification of metaphors in the political discourse of mass media: a pragmatic approach. In: W. Kallmeyer and M. N. Volodina (eds.), *Perspektiven auf Mediensprache und Medienkommunikation*, 145–158. Mannheim: Institut für Deutsche Sprache.

Koller, V. 2004a. Businesswomen and war metaphors: "Possessive, jealous and pugnacious"? *Journal of Sociolinguistics* 4(1): 3–22.

Koller, V. 2004b. *Metaphor and Gender in Business Media Discourse.* Basingstoke: Palgrave Macmillan.

Kropf, T. 1999. Von den Schwierigkeiten mit dem klassischen Nachrichten-Aufbau—oder: Ein "Andock-Modell" als Alternative zum "Pyramiden-Modell". *Publizistik* 44(2): 200–216.

Kunelius, R. 1994. Order and interpretation: A narrative perspective on journalistic discourse. *European Journal of Communication* 9: 249–270.

Laakaniemi, R. 1987. An analysis of writing coach programs on American daily newspapers. *Journalism Quarterly* 2–3(64): 567–575.

Le, E. 2004. Active participation within written argumentation: metadiscourse and editorialist's authority. *Journal of Pragmatics* 36(4): 601–629.

Lind, R. A. and C. Salo. 2002. The framing of feminists and feminism in news and public affairs programs in U.S. electronic media. *Journal of Communication* 52(1): 211– 228.

Ljung, M. 2000. Newspaper genres and newspaper English. In: F. Ungerer (ed.), *English Media Texts—Past and Present*, 131–149. Amsterdam: Benjamins.

Lorda, U. C. 2001. Les articles dits d'information: la relation de déclarations politiques. *SEMEN* 13: 119–134.

Luckmann, T. 1986. Grundformen der gesellschaftlichen Vermittlung des Wissens: Kommunikative Gattungen. In: F. Neidhardt, R. M. Lepsius, and J. Weiß (eds.), *Kultur und Gesellschaft*, 191–211. Opladen: Westdeutscher Verlag.

Luginbühl, M. 2004. Staged authenticity in TV news. An analysis of Swiss TV news from. 1957. until today. *Studies in Communication Sciences* 4(1): 129–146.

Lugrin, G. 2001. Le mélange des genres dans l'hyperstructure. *SEMEN* 13: 65–96.

Luke, K. K. and T.-S. Pavlidou (eds.). 2002. *Telephone Calls: Unity and Diversity in Conversational Structure across Languages and Cultures*. Amsterdam: Benjamins.

Lutz, B. and R. Wodak. 1987. *Information für Informierte. Linguistische Studien zu Verständlichkeit und Verstehen von Hörfunknachrichten*. Wien: Verlag der Österreichischen Akademie der Wissenschaften.

Mardh, I. 1980. *Headlinese. On the Grammar of English Front Page Headlines*. Lund: CWK Gleerup.

Marinos, A. 2001. *"So habe ich das nicht gesagt!" Die Authentizität der Redewiedergabe im nachrichtlichen Zeitungstext*. Berlin: Logos.

Marx, U. 2005. Entwicklung und Begründung einer präskriptiven Notation von Hörfunknachrichten und Vergleich mit empirisch deskriptiver Analyse. In: Norbert Gutenberg (ed.), *Schreiben und Sprechen von Hörfunknachrichten. Zwischenergebnisse sprechwissenschaftlicher Forschung*, 121–193. Frankfurt am Main: Lang.

McAdams, K. C. 1993. Readability reconsidered. A study of reader reactions to fog indexes. *Newspaper Research Journal* 1: 50–59.

Moirand, S. 2001. Du traitement différent de l'intertexte selon les genres convoqués dans les évènements scientifiques à caractère politique. *SEMEN* 13: 97–118.

Oomen, U. 1985. Bildfunktionen und Kommunikationsstrategien in Fernsehnachrichten. In: G. Bentele and E. W. B. Hess-Lüttich (eds.), *Zeichengebrauch in Massenmedien. Zum Verhältnis von sprachlicher Information in Hörfunk, Film und Fernsehen*, 155–191. Tübingen: Niemeyer.

Östman, J.-O. and A.-M. Simon-Vandenbergen. 2004. Media discourse—extensions, mixes, and hybrids (special issue), introduction. *Text* 24(3): 303–306.

Peck MacDonald, S. 2005. The language of journalism in treatments of hormone replacement news. *Written Communication* 22: 275–297.

Perrin, D. 1999. Woher die Textbrüche kommen. Der Einfluß des Schreibprozesses auf die Sprache im Gebrauchstext. *Zeitschrift für Deutsche Sprache* 2: 134–155.

Perrin, D. 2001. *Wie Journalisten schreiben. Ergebnisse angewandter Schreibprozessforschung*. Konstanz: UVK.

Perrin, D. 2004. Journalistisches Schreiben—Coaching aus medienlinguistischer Perspektive. In: K. Knapp, G. Antos, M. Becker-Mrotzek, A. Deppermann, S. Göpferich, J. Grabowski, M. Klemm, and C. Villiger (eds.), *Angewandte Linguistik. Ein Lehrbuch*, 255–275. Tübingen: Francke.

Perrin, D. 2005. "Den Leuten die Sachen verdichten"—Kreativ schreiben unter Druck. In: K. Ermert and O. Kutzmutz (eds.), *Wie aufs Blatt kommt, was im Kopf steckt. Beiträge zum Kreativen Schreiben*, 34–54. Wolfenbüttel: Bundesakademie für kulturelle Bildung.

Perrin, D. 2006a. Coaching im Umgang mit Medien. In: Eric Lippmann (ed.), *Coaching*, 201–214. Heidelberg: Springer.

Perrin, D. 2006b. Verstanden werden. Vom doppelten Interesse an theoriebasierter, praxisgerichteter Textberatung. In: H. Blühdorn, E. Breindl, and U. Hermann Waßner (eds.), *Text—Verstehen. Grammatik und darüber hinaus*, 332–350. Berlin: de Gruyter.

Perrin, D. and M. Ehrensberger. 2007. Progression analysis: Tracing journalistic language awareness. In: M. Burger (ed.), *L' analyse linguistique des discours des médias : théories, méthodes en enjeux. Entre sciences du langage et sciences de la communication et des médias*. Québec: Nota Bene.

Perrin, D. and M. Ehrensberger-Dow. 2006. Journalists' language awareness: Inferences from writing, *Revista Alicantina de Estudios Ingleses* 19: 319–343.

Perrin, D., M. Schanne, and V. Wyss. 2005. *SRG SSR idée suisse—Sprachpolitik, Sprachnorm und Sprachpraxis am Beispiel der SRG SSR* (Forschungsgesuch an den Schweizerischen Nationalfonds zur Förderung der wissenschaftlichen Forschung, Programm NFP 56). Winterthur: Institut für Angewandte Medienwissenschaft.

Pietilä, V. 1992. Beyond the news story: News as discoursive composition. *European Journal of Communication* 7: 37–67.

Püschel, U. 1992. "guten abend und die welt hält den atem an." Berichte nach Skripts in den Fernsehnachrichten über den 19. August. 1991. in Moskau. In: Joachim Dyck (ed.), *Rhetorik. Ein internationales Jahrbuch. Band 11: Rhetorik und Politik*, 67–84. Tübingen: Niemeyer.

Quinn, S. 2005. *Convergent Journalism. The Fundamentals of Multimedia Reporting*. Frankfurt am Main: Lang.

Redd, T. M. 1991. The voice of time. The style of narration in a newsmagazine. *Written Communication* 2(8): 240–258.

Renner, K. N. 2001. Die Text-Bild-Schere. Zur Explikation eines anscheinend eindeutigen Begriffs. *Studies in Communication Sciences* 1(2): 23–44.

Renzi, A. 2005. Power, hegemony and the language of tactical street television. In: Book of abstracts for the international conference *Language in the Media: Representations, identities, ideologies*, 12th–14th September 2005, University of Leeds.

Roeh, I. 1982. *The Rhetoric of News in the Israel Radio. Some Implications of Language and Style for Newstelling*. Bochum: Brockmeyer.

Roth, A. L. 2002. Social epistemology in broadcast news interviews. *Language in Society* 31: 355–381.

Roth, A. L. 2005. "Pop Quizzes" on the campaign trail. *The Harvard International Journal of Press/Politics* 10(2): 28–46.

Ruhmann, G. and D. Perrin. 2002. Schreibstrategien in Balance. Was Wissenschaftler von Journalistinnen lernen können. In: D. Perrin, I. Boettcher, O. Kruse, and A. Wrobel (eds.), *Schreiben. Von intuitiven zu professionellen Schreibstrategien*, 129–138. Wiesbaden: Westdeutscher Verlag.

Sawitzki, I. 2001. Zu okkasionellen Wortbildungen in der Pressesprache. Dargestellt an Substantiven in den Magazinen Focus, Spiegel und Stern. In: Jörg Meier and Arne Ziegler (eds.), *Deutsche Sprache in Europa. Geschichte und Gegenwart. Festschrift für Ilpo Tapani Piirainen zum 60. Geburtstag*, 385–400. Wien: Edition Praesens.

Schlobinski, P. and T. Siever. 2005. Sprachliche und textuelle Merkmale in Weblogs. Ein internationales Projekt. *Networx* 46. Retrieved August 11, 2006, from http://www.mediensprache.net/ networx/networx-46.pdf

Schröder, T. 2001. Im Vorfeld. Beobachtungen zur Satzstruktur in Zeitungsnachrichten. In: U. Breuer and J. Korhonen (eds.), *Mediensprache—Medienkritik*, 129–144. Frankfurt am Main: Lang.

Schubert, A. and W. Sendlmeier. 2005. Was kennzeichnet gute Nachrichtensprache im Hörfunk? Eine perzeptive und akustische Analyse von Stimme und Sprechweise. In: Walter Sendlmeier (ed.), *Sprechwirkung—Sprechstile in Funk und Fernsehen*, 13–70. Berlin: Logos.

Schudson, M. 1982. The politics of narrative form: The emergence of news conventions in print and television. *Deadalus* 4: 97–112.

Schwitalla, J. 1993. Textsortenwandel in den Medien nach. 1945. in der Bundesrepublik Deutschland. Ein Überblick. In: B. U. Biere and H. Henne (eds.), *Sprache in den Medien nach 1945*, 1–29. Tübingen: Niemeyer.

Selting, M. 1983. Institutionelle Kommunikation. Stilwechsel als Mittel strategischer Interaktion. *Linguistische Berichte* 86: 29–48.

Settekorn, W. 2001. Tor des Monats—Tor zur Welt. Zum Metapherngebrauch in Massenmedien. In: D. Möhn, D. Roß, and M. Tjarks-Sobhani (eds.), *Mediensprache und Medienlinguistik. Festschrift für Jörg Hennig*, 93–110. Frankfurt am Main: Lang.

Sleurs, K., G. Jacobs, and L. Van Waes. 2003. Constructing press releases, constructing quotations: A case study. *Journal of Sociolinguistics* 7(2): 135–275.

Spranz-Fogasy, T. 2003. Kommunikationsstilistische Eigenschaften gesellschaftlicher Führungskräfte im Spiegel der Presse. In: S. Habscheid and U. Fix (eds.), *Gruppenstile. Zur sprachlichen Inszenierung sozialer Zugehörigkeit*, 171–187. Frankfurt am Main: Lang.

Stenvall, M. 2003. An actor or an undefined threat? The role of "terrorist" in the discourse of international news agencies. *Journal of Language and Politics* 2(2): 361–404.

Toolan, M. 2003. Le politiquement correct dans le monde français. *Discourse and Society* 14(1): 69–86.

Tuchman, G. 1976. What is news? Telling stories. *Journal of Communication* 26(6): 93–97.

Ungerer, F. 2000. News stories and news events: A changing relationship. In: F. Ungerer (ed.), *English media texts—past and present*, 177–195. Amsterdam: Benjamins.

Van Dijk, T. A. 1988a. *News Analysis. Case Studies of International and National News in the Press*. Hillsdale/London: Erlbaum.

Van Dijk, T. A. 1988b. *News as Discourse*. Hillsdale/London: Erlbaum.

Wolf, R. and T. Thomason. 1986. Writing coaches. Their strategies for improving writing. *Newspaper Research Journal* 3(7): 43–59.

Wyss, V. 2004. Journalismus als duale Struktur: Grundlagen einer strukturationstheoretischen Journalismustheorie. In: M. Löffelholz (ed.), *Theorien des Journalismus. Ein diskursives Handbuch (2. überarb. Aufl)*, 305–320. Opladen: Westdeutscher

Verlag. Zinken, J. 2003. Ideologic al imagination: intertextual and correlational metaphors in political discourse. *Discourse and Society* 14(4): 507–523.

Index

About the Editor

David Matsumoto, PhD, is an internationally acclaimed author and psychologist. He received his BA from the University of Michigan in 1981 with high honors in psychology and Japanese. He subsequently earned his MA (1983) and PhD (1986) in psychology from the University of California at Berkeley. He is currently professor of psychology and director of the Culture and Emotion Research Laboratory at San Francisco State University, where he has been since 1989. He has studied culture, emotion, social interaction, and communication for 25 years. His books include well-known titles such as *Culture and Psychology* and the *Cambridge Dictionary of Psychology*. He is the recipient of many awards and honors in the field of psychology, including being named a G. Stanley Hall lecturer by the American Psychological Association. He is the series editor for Cambridge University Press's series on *Culture and Psychology*. He is also editor for the *Journal of Cross-Cultural Psychology* and the Culture and Diversity section of *Social and Personality Psychology Compass*.